Bonhoeffer's
Theology

Classical and
Revolutionary

Bonhoeffer's Theology

Classical and Revolutionary

James W. Woelfel

 NASHVILLE • Abingdon Press • NEW YORK

BONHOEFFER'S THEOLOGY

Copyright © 1970 by Abingdon Press

ISBN 0-687-03640-2
Library of Congress Catalog Card Number: 77-97571

Scripture quotations are from the Revised Standard Version of the Bible, copyrighted 1946 and 1952 by the Division of Christian Education, National Council of Churches, and are used by permission.
Quotations from the following works are reprinted by permission of Harper & Row, publishers: *Christ for Us in the Theology of Dietrich Bonhoeffer*, by John A. Phillips. Copyright © 1967 by John A. Phillips. *Act and Being*, by Dietrich Bonhoeffer. Copyright © 1956 by Christian Kaiser Verlag. Copyright © 1961 by William Collins Sons & Co., London and Harper & Row, Publishers, Inc., New York. *Life Together*, by Dietrich Bonhoeffer. Copyright © 1954 by Harper & Row, Publishers, Incorporated. *No Rusty Swords*, by Dietrich Bonhoeffer. Copyright © 1947 by Christian Kaiser Verlag. Copyright © 1965 by William Collins Sons & Co., London, and Harper & Row, Publishers Inc., New York. *Christ the Center*, by Dietrich Bonhoeffer. Copyright © 1960 by Christian Kaiser Verlag, in *Gesammelte Schriften*, Vol. 3. Copyright © 1966 in the English translation by William Collins Sons & Co., London, and Harper & Row, Publishers, Inc., New York. *The Communion of Saints*, by Dietrich Bonhoeffer. Copyright © 1960 by Christian Kaiser Verlag. Copyright © 1963 in the English translation by William Collins Sons & Co., London, and Harper & Row, Publishers, Inc., New York.
Quotations from the following works are reprinted by permission of Fortress Press: *Bonhoeffer in a World Come of Age*, edited by Peter Vorkink, II. Copyright © 1968 by Fortress Press. *Preface to Bonhoeffer*, edited by John D. Godsey. Copyright © 1965 by Fortress Press. *World Come of Age*, edited by Ronald Gregor Smith. Copyright © 1967 by Fortress Press; copyright © 1961 by Mrs. Priscilla Collins, used by permission.
Quotations from the following works are reprinted by permission of The Westminster Press: *The Theology of Dietrich Bonhoeffer*, by John D. Godsey. Published by The Westminster Press, Philadelphia. Copyright © W. L. Jenkins 1960. Used by permission. *Luther: Lectures on Romans*, Newly Translated and Edited by Wilhelm Pauck, D. Theol. Volume XV in The Library of Christian Classics. Published simultaneously in the United States of America and in Great Britain by The Westminster Press, Philadelphia, and the SCM Press, Ltd., London. Copyright © 1961 W. L. Jenkins. Used by permission. *Truth as Encounter*, by Emil Brunner. A New Edition, Much Enlarged, of *The Divine-Human Encounter*. Copyright © 1943 by The Westminster Press and 1964 by W. L. Jenkins. Used by permission.
Quotations from *Proverbs and Ecclesiastes: Introduction and Commentary*, by Edgar Jones, copyright © 1961 by SCM Press, Ltd., are used by permission.
Quotations from *Church Dogmatics*, by Karl Barth, published in 1936 and 1956 by T. & T. Clark, Edinburgh, are used by permission of the publishers.
Quotations from *The World View of Physics*, by Carl F. von Weizsäcker, published in 1952 by Routledge & Kegan Paul, London, are used by permission of The University of Chicago Press, including Canadian rights as per telephone conversation by the author with Mrs. Connie Walker on September 15, 1969.
Quotations from the following works are reprinted by permission of The Macmillan Company: *The Cost of Discipleship*, by Dietrich Bonhoeffer. Copyright © 1960 by The Macmillan Co. *Ethics*, by Dietrich Bonhoeffer. 4th printing 1961. Copyright © 1955 by The Macmillan Co. *Letters and Papers from Prison*, by Dietrich Bonhoeffer. Revised ed. 1967. Copyright © 1953 by The Macmillan Co.
The author's article, "Bonhoeffer's Portrait of the Religionless Christian," first appeared in *Encounter*, Vol. 28, No. 4, Autumn 1967, and is reprinted, with adaptations, by permission of *Encounter*.

SET UP, PRINTED, AND BOUND BY THE
PARTHENON PRESS, AT NASHVILLE,
TENNESSEE, UNITED STATES OF AMERICA

To My Teachers

Philip Nolan
Clayton Feaver
William Wolf
Owen Thomas
Edgar Dickie

through whose instruction and example I discovered
the intellectual riches of human civilization and Christian faith and the meaning of Christian humanism

Contents

Preface

A nervous plane flight from Boston to New Orleans early in December of 1961 may be said to have marked the beginning of this book. Suspended "between heaven and earth," where one's thoughts tend to become "other-worldly" in more than one sense, I opened a just-purchased paperback edition of a collection of letters and literary fragments written in prison by a martyred German theologian whose name seemed to be on everyone's lips. I found there not only the rich humanity of a man who was a cultured, liberally educated, life-loving product of Western civilization at its best; just as excitedly, I came across fragments of a vision of a reinterpreted Christianity for the secular world in which we live—a "religionless Christianity" for a world "come of age." The more I read, the less I was able to decide whether my agitation resulted from the "other-worldliness" of the air journey or from the robust "this-worldliness" of the Christianity about which I was reading.

The book, of course, was *Letters and Papers from Prison;* the man was Dietrich Bonhoeffer. That same paperback edition is now torn and heavily underlined from many rereadings. My knowledge of the full scope of Bonhoeffer's thought has increased considerably (and, I hope, accurately) during the past nine years. Yet to this day, after repeated and detailed examinations of virtually every word, every nuance of phrase in *Letters and Papers,* I never fail to read it again as something fresh, to discover something new in it which I had not seen before, and to be profoundly moved by the poignancy of this warmly human and vigorously Christian man living almost daily with death.

Amid the dispersion of energies which mark a final year in theological seminary, I managed to find time to read one or two more of Dietrich Bonhoeffer's works. A Fulbright Scholarship for a year's study at the University of St. Andrews in Scotland gave me the opportunity to give his thought my undivided attention. In the autumn of 1962 I began research designed to trace the background in Bonhoeffer's own thought of the elements which went to make up the "religionless Christianity" project of the prison writings. The more deeply I probed into his thought as a whole, the more I came to admire both the man and what he had to say. A two-year interruption of my work on Bonhoeffer's theology was followed by another year in which I was able to continue and to bring the research to a completion. The results were embodied in a dissertation which was accepted by the University of St. Andrews for the doctorate in November of 1966. The present book is a considerably revised version of that dissertation.

"One more book about Bonhoeffer" is no longer likely to be received with excited anticipation. In a remarkably short period of time the life and thought of the young theologian have been rather thoroughly mined. We now have five excellent comprehensive studies of Bonhoeffer: John Godsey's early contribution, *The Theology of Dietrich Bonhoeffer,* and the massive Marxist thesis of East German theologian Hanfried Müller, *Von der Kirche zur Welt,* were available at the time I was researching Bonhoeffer. The other three significant general works have been written (or at least published) since then: John A. Phillips' scholarly analysis, *Christ for Us in the Theology of Dietrich Bonhoeffer;* the eminently readable Roman Catholic foray into Bonhoeffer interpretation, William Kuhns's *In Pursuit of Dietrich Bonhoeffer;* and, of course, the definitive biography *Dietrich Bonhoeffer* by the man who knew him best, his close friend and editor Eberhard Bethge.

Add to the above the profusion of articles, essays, and collections thereof, dealing with specific topics in Bonhoeffer's life and thought, and a formidable mosaic of "Bonhoefferana" shapes up for the serious inquirer. Among the collections of occasional pieces, special mention should be made of *The Place of Bonhoeffer,* edited by Martin Marty; the multi-volume *Die Mündige Welt; World Come of Age,* edited by Ronald Gregor Smith; *I Knew Dietrich Bonhoeffer,* edited by Smith and Wolf-Dieter Zimmermann; the *Two Studies in the Theology of*

Bonhoeffer by Jürgen Moltmann and Jürgen Weissbach; and *Bonhoeffer in a World Come of Age,* edited by Peter Vorkink.

Why, then, another general study of Bonhoeffer's theology? I would plead, first of all, simply that there is a profound sense in which we in the Christian and especially in the theological community need to "work through" Bonhoeffer and all the disturbing things he has bequeathed to us—even at the risk of literary overkill. His phenomenal influence on the many facets of the theological exploration of the secular over the past fifteen years and for the foreseeable future drives us again and again back to the seminal texts for fresh insight. Peregrine and fragmentary as those texts are, the task and the insights are potentially inexhaustible.

Secondly, I would classify the present work as a series of interconnected essays on main topics in Bonhoeffer's thought rather than as an exhaustive, full-scale study. The works by Godsey, Phillips, Kuhns, and Bethge have excellently and thoroughly explored the development of Bonhoeffer's thought through his life. This is at the same time the most obvious and certainly one of the most illuminating ways of presenting Bonhoeffer. It has already been said many times that Bonhoeffer was a theologian whose thinking was intimately and reciprocally related to the dramatic events of his life, and the observation needs no arguing.

I wish to make no claim, then, to the thoroughness and completeness of the comprehensive studies I have mentioned. I have chosen rather to examine Bonhoeffer's theology in terms of what I consider to be some of its major elements. Each topic is explored as a unit, as it develops from Bonhoeffer's early writings to *Letters and Papers.* Perhaps an advantage of this approach is that of enabling us to view the origins, development, and fruition of a particular idea in a unitary and sustained fashion. Such a perspective may also further highlight what I consider to be a central feature of Bonhoeffer's thought, its underlying dialectical unity from beginning to end. Thus, for example, the relationship among the various "periods" in Bonhoeffer's understanding of the church—one of the most disputed aspects of his theology—is hopefully clarified and shown to be variations on a basic dialectical theme rather than fundamental shifts in ecclesiology.

I have chosen what I believe to be the major elements in Bonhoeffer's theological development; but under no circumstances would I presume to have picked every one of "the" elements which might be highlighted. As John Phillips rightly points out in *Christ for Us in the Theology of Dietrich Bonhoeffer*: "In Bonhoeffer study, organization itself cannot escape being interpretation." * I believe that a great deal of light can be shed on the totality of Bonhoeffer's outlook in terms of the headings under which I have examined his thought; but it would be foolhardy for me to imagine that my selection of themes is the only one possible or fruitful, that other emphases are not legitimate, or that I have not omitted anything of importance. The very nature of a thematic or topical approach to Bonhoeffer entails a rigorous kind of selectivity which simply omits or touches lightly what it believes to be peripheral or irrelevant to the topic at hand. For example, my study of Bonhoeffer includes details about his life only where these are immediately germane to the element of his thought being discussed. As a result, a book like mine should not be consulted for a biography of Bonhoeffer. Each of the comprehensive studies mentioned above does this already in an admirable manner, above all Bethge's massive and detailed treatment, which is surely in its own way the "last word" on Bonhoeffer's life. What I have tried to do is simply to illuminate Bonhoeffer through some of his leading ideas and their development —nothing more, and, I trust, nothing less.

A third reason for offering a study such as the present one to the theological public is that I think I may genuinely have something to add to the Bonhoeffer discussion. Much that I have to say in the pages that follow will not be new to the serious student of Bonhoeffer. But here and there I believe that I may have emphasized important elements of his thought which I have not found similarly emphasized elsewhere. In other places I may have looked at now-familiar material in a fresh and hopefully suggestive way. There are furthermore a number of problems in Bonhoeffer's thought about which scholars disagree: both issues concerning the interpretation of his theology as a whole, and specific matters related to various aspects or phases of his ideas. I have written the present volume of essays from a definite standpoint on these problems, as a contribution to the ongoing discussion and clarification of Bonhoeffer's thought.

Throughout the researching and writing of this study I have

* (New York: Harper & Row, 1967), p. 21.

deliberately and cheerfully engaged in a "willing suspension of disbelief." For some time now it has been my firm conviction that there is simply no other way to a real grasp of someone else's thought than to set aside temporarily one's presuppositions and doubts and questions insofar as possible, and simply to immerse oneself in the other's viewpoint. This approach has manifested itself throughout the present work in the enthusiastic and wholly positive treatment of Bonhoeffer. There is too much trigger-happy criticism in the world of scholarship. To me the profoundest criticisms of a thinker can come only after we have for a time "seen the world through his eyes." My own study of Bonhoeffer, whatever its flaws, has attempted to be just such an empathic seeing; I have desired to keep myself as much as possible absorbed in the object of my research without regard for a number of possible considerations and implications.

I cannot stand where Bonhoeffer stood theologically. The long period I have spent with his writings has produced for me fundamental questions about virtually every aspect of his thought, questions too numerous and far-reaching even to mention adequately in brief compass. Much work of a critical nature on Bonhoeffer has already been done and a great deal more will undoubtedly and rightly appear. I have sought in this study to confine myself to what I have indicated as the essential first stage in understanding and criticism: the "willing suspension of disbelief" in order to understand Bonhoeffer's thought as fully and sympathetically as possible.

I wish to acknowledge with grateful thanks the help of Professor Edgar P. Dickie, of the University of St. Andrews, who supervised my doctoral research on Bonhoeffer. A gracious representative, along with the Baillie brothers, of that admirable twentieth-century Scottish theological blend of classical and liberal insights and a person whom I number with the saints, Professor Dickie gently but insistently kept the "revolutionary ideas" after which I was panting in proper historical and theological perspective. I would like also to remember with appreciation the late Professor Ronald Gregor Smith of the University of Glasgow, who examined the original dissertation and offered generous appreciation and helpful criticisms and suggestions. Through the good offices of Professor Smith some translations of material in Bonhoeffer's *Letters and Papers from Prison* which I made in the course of my research and used in the dissertation came to the attention of Mr. John

15

S. Bowden, editor of SCM Press. I wish to express my gratitude for his gracious invitation to submit my translations for incorporation into the new revised translation of *Letters and Papers,* which was then in preparation. Through his efforts I was privileged to make a small contribution to a much-improved English edition of a book very close to my heart. My thanks go also to numerous colleagues from graduate school days who "suffered this fool gladly," letting me bounce ideas off them and responding with constructive insights. My wife Judy, who has more than enough to do anyway, kindly typed the final draft of the manuscript, earning her husband's undying appreciation.

Lawrence, Kansas

J. W. W.

Abbreviations Used in This Work

AB   *Act and Being,* trans. by Bernard Noble with an Introduction by Ernst Wolf from the German *Akt und Sein* (Munich: Kaiser Verlag, 1956). New York: Harper & Row, 1962; London: William Collins Sons & Company, 1961.

CC   *Christ the Center,* trans. by John Bowden with an Introduction by Edwin H. Robertson from the German *Christologie* (in *Gesammelte Schriften III,* pp. 166-242), New York: Harper & Row, 1966. British ed. entitled *Christology,* London: Collins, 1966.

CD   *The Cost of Discipleship,* trans. by Reginald H. Fuller with memoir by G. Leibholz from the German *Nachfolge* (Munich: Kaiser Verlag, 1955), sec. ed., unabridged and revised, New York: Macmillan, 1963; London: SCM Press, 1959.

CS   *The Communion of Saints,* trans. by Ronald Gregor Smith and others from the German *Sanctorum Communio* (Munich: Kaiser Verlag, 1960). New York: Harper & Row, 1964. British ed. entitled *Sanctorum Communio,* London: Collins, 1963.

E   *Ethics,* ed. by Eberhard Bethge, trans. by Neville Horton Smith from the German *Ethik* (Munich: Kaiser Verlag, 1949). New York: Macmillan, and London: Collins, 1955.

GS   *Gesammelte Schriften,* ed. by Eberhard Bethge, four vols. Munich: Kaiser Verlag, 1958-1961.

LPP   *Letters and Papers from Prison,* ed. by Eberhard Bethge, trans. by Reginald H. Fuller, rev. by Frank Clarke and others from the German *Widerstand und Ergebung* (12th ed., Munich: Kaiser Verlag, 1964). New York: Macmillan, and London: SCM Press, 1967.

LT   *Life Together,* trans. with an Introduction by John W. Doberstein from the German *Gemeinsames Leben* (Munich: Kaiser Verlag, 1955), New York: Harper & Row, and London: SCM Press, 1954.

NRS   *No Rusty Swords: Letters, Lectures and Notes 1928-1936 from the Collected Works of Dietrich Bonhoeffer Volume I,* trans. by Edwin H. Robertson and John Bowden from the German *Gesammelte Schriften,* New York: Harper & Row, and London: Collins, 1965.

WF   *The Way to Freedom: Letters, Lectures and Notes 1935-1939 from the Collected Works of Dietrich Bonhoeffer Volume II,* trans. by Edwin H. Robertson and John Bowden from the German *Gesammelte Schriften,* New York: Harper & Row, 1967; London: Collins, 1966.

Chapter One

Liberal Culture and Secularity

After an initial year at the University of Tübingen, Dietrich Bonhoeffer matriculated in 1924 at the University of Berlin. Berlin was undoubtedly the center of liberal German culture. Nowhere was this more in evidence than in the theological faculty of its university. The Berlin faculty included among its distinguished members Adolf Harnack, Adolf Deissmann, and Hans Lietzmann—all representatives of the German liberal theology which flowered in the nineteenth and early twentieth centuries. The thought of Ernst Troeltsch, the relentless pursuer of the full logic of liberalism who died just before Bonhoeffer came to Berlin, continued to make a great impact on the students.

Bonhoeffer's formal theological education took place largely within this liberal milieu. At Berlin the young scholar imbibed theological and secular humanism at its best. In the "Christianity without religion" project of the mature Bonhoeffer this early liberal influence reappeared in a profound appreciation of and respect for secularity, a concern for history reflected in the historical and cultural analysis of a world "come of age," a singularly this-worldly christology, and a passion for truth and integrity. Although Bonhoeffer soon became associated with the Barthian revolt against theological liberalism, he never really neglected the influence of his Berlin mentors.[1]

During the Berlin period Bonhoeffer acquired some mastery of sociology through reading the works of Troeltsch, Max Weber, and Ferdinand Tönnies. His dissertation for the degree of licentiate of theology at Berlin, *The Communion of Saints,* was a theological examination of the church as a sociological entity.[2] Sociological categories influenced Bonhoeffer's understanding of revelation as a concrete occurrence within the ambiguities of historical institutions. The "non-religious" interpretation of revelation in the writings from prison has as part of its framework this early interest in and knowledge of sociology as a key to comprehending revelation in contemporary thought forms.

Intellectual Honesty

The lasting influence of Adolf Harnack upon his young Berlin neighbor and university student Bonhoeffer was his passion for truth and his intellectual integrity. In the memorial address which Bonhoeffer delivered on behalf of Harnack's students on the occasion of his death, the young theologian paid this tribute to him: "It became clear to us through him that truth is born only of freedom. We saw in him the champion of the free expression of a truth once recognized, who formed his free judgment afresh time and time again." [3] In his essay "Bonhoeffer's *Christologie* of 1933," Jaroslav Pelikan rightly observes that "Bonhoeffer's eulogy for Harnack and his other statements about the master make it clear that Bonhoeffer could not join the company of those whose quest for certainty has caused them to suppose that they have outgrown Adolf Harnack." [4]

The passion for truth and intellectual honesty which Bonhoeffer learned from Harnack appears again and again in his writings. All of Bonhoeffer's writings, discussing wide-ranging topics such as church and state, war and peace, history and philosophy, as well as purely theological and exegetical themes, display a painstakingly careful concern to clarify precisely the issues involved and to offer concrete solutions based on explicit premises.

A statement on the Age of Reason from Bonhoeffer's last years might well have been written by Harnack himself:

Intellectual honesty in all things, including questions of belief, was the great achievement of emancipated reason and it has ever since been one of the indispensable moral requirements of western man. Contempt for the age of rationalism is a suspicious sign of failure to feel the need for truth-fulness. If intellectual honesty is not the last word that is to be said about things, and if intellectual clarity is often achieved at the expense of insight into reality, this can still never again exempt us from the inner obligation to make clean and honest use of reason.[5]

In his final vision of a "religionless Christianity" for a world "come of age" Bonhoeffer displayed a radical and soul-searching intellectual honesty from which many would shrink.

The Man of Liberal Education

Bonhoeffer was deeply attached to the whole German liberal tradi-tion in life and letters. The prison writings bear eloquent testimony to his appreciation of "liberal culture." He states that his real ambition while in prison has been "to become thoroughly familiar with the nineteenth century in Germany." [6] *Letters and Papers* is full of ref-erences to Bonhoeffer's reading, and it is largely in nineteenth-century German authors such as Gotthelf, Stifter, Immermann, Fontane, and Keller.[7] He laments contemporary neglect and lack of appreciation for the nineteenth century. He tends to describe this neglect in filial terms, as the ungratefulness of a son or grandson toward his forebears. "There are so few people now," he says, "who want to have any inti-mate spiritual association with the eighteenth and nineteenth cen-turies. . . . Who bothers at all now about the work and achievements of our grandfathers, and how much of what they knew have we al-ready forgotten?" [8] As part of the neo-orthodox revolt against nine-teenth-century liberalism, Bonhoeffer was nevertheless one who could never in any sense despise the liberal heritage out of which he and his Neo-Reformation colleagues had come. This abiding appreciation of liberal theology was a major factor in the kinds of questions which Bonhoeffer raised in his "religionless Christianity" project: such ques-tions as the meaning of modern history, the rights of the secular, and the urgent need to translate the gospel into contemporary language and action.

Disintegration of life in Germany caused Bonhoeffer to gaze nostal-gically at the serene wholeness of scholarship in the nineteenth century.[9] Bonhoeffer goes on, however, to affirm his faith that even the fragments contribute integrally to the whole and are taken up by God into his purpose. The martyred theologian's own writings are poignantly fragmented, the result of a combination of factors including the very bent of his thought, his active participation in the stormy events of the 1930's and '40's, and his untimely death. At the same time, these theological fragments which are his legacy have been seen by the postwar church to have been taken up by God into his purpose of Christian renewal in the twentieth century.

A deep and familial sense of indebtedness to the liberal education and culture which represented Germany at its finest permeates Bonhoeffer's outlook. It is true to say, I think, that a sensitive appreciation of one's own past is so important to Bonhoeffer that he would very probably include it under the commandment, "Honor thy father and thy mother." Germany's liberal culture infused the life of the country with whatever dimension of quality and nobility it possessed. Bonhoeffer was in the best sense of the word an "aristocrat." One of his most urgent pleas on behalf of the modern world was against the false egalitarianism of modern life which believes that democracy means uniformity, mediocrity, and a general leveling out of distinctions. He deplored what he considered to be the cheapening and vulgarization of life which resulted from modern notions of "mass culture." Great leadership, which Bonhoeffer knew would be so sorely needed in all countries after the war, could not arise out of such superficial roots, but only out of a sense of quality and life which comes from awareness of the liberal past which is Europe's highest achievement.[10]

Very significantly, Bonhoeffer considered the liberally educated person, the "man of culture," to be the secular counterpart of the mature Christian, and definitely saw them as allies in the modern world. Classical liberal education is not only the expansion of the mind but also the training and discipline for coping maturely with life, just as Christianity is intended to be. Furthermore, like the mature Christian, the "liberal" man approaches life with wholeness: "The Christian and the 'cultured' man . . . cannot split up his life or dismember it, and the common denominator must be sought both in thought and in a personal and integrated attitude to life." [11] One of Bonhoeffer's favorite themes in describing the mature or "religionless" Christian was this quality of wholeness, which he characterized with the musical metaphor of "polyphony." [12]

Bonhoeffer was deeply impressed, during the war years, by the way in which men who represented the German liberal tradition at its best sought refuge and comradeship among those who suffered in the name of Christ. Nazism was the supreme trial of both the Christianity and the liberal heritage of Europe. Liberal culture, estranged from its Christian roots and thoroughly secularized, ironically found sanctuary in the uncompromisingly dogmatic Christianity of the Confessing Church— *yet without surrendering its secularity or its suspicion of "religion" and the church.* Bonhoeffer considered this alliance to have profound implications for a proper understanding of the meaning of Christianity in a world "come of age." He interpreted the common cause between these "good men without God"—the secular forces who epitomized the humane ideals of the *Aufklärung*—not in terms of a "return to religion," but as a manifestation of the power of the name of Jesus Christ himself to draw to himself as their true source all manifestations of goodness, truth, and justice. The man of liberal education was for Bonhoeffer the paradigm of man "come of age," and thus the brother of the "religionless" Christian.

It was because Bonhoeffer was himself so profoundly a man imbued with liberal European culture that he could appreciate the intimate kinship between mature Christianity and mature liberality. His interests ranged widely beyond theology proper, as almost every page of *Letters and Papers from Prison* attests. He discoursed knowledgeably about art, and (like his mentor Barth) loved music with a passion second only to his love of God. He began writing a novel while in prison, and we are fortunate in having five poems which he wrote during his confinement included among the prison writings. Bonhoeffer's urban, educated middle-class upbringing and his broad education at the center of German liberal culture, Berlin, laid the foundations of a Christian understanding of the world which was large, integrated, and affirmative. Bonhoeffer loved the world passionately, in part because he had seen and experienced the heights and breadths to which the human spirit, as the work of God, could attain.

Liberality *versus* Liberalism

An essay by Alec R. Vidler entitled "Christianity, Liberalism, and Liberality" [13] provides us with a terminological distinction which is very useful in assessing the influence of liberal thought and culture on Bonhoeffer. Vidler distinguishes between *liberalism,* the religious and political movement which flourished in the nineteenth and early twentieth centuries, and *liberality*. The word "liberal," he says, as the adjectival form of "liberality,"

denotes not a creed or a set of philosophical assumptions or any 'ism, but a frame of mind, a quality of character, which it is easier no doubt to discern than to define. A liberal-minded man is free from narrow prejudice, generous in his judgment of others, open-minded, especially to the reception of new ideas and proposals for reform. Liberal is the opposite not of conservative, but of fanatical or bigoted or intransigent. It points to the *esprit large* and away from the *idee fixe*. ... The liberal frame of mind does not appear to be more common among the adherents of Liberalism, or other 'isms that are ostensibly progressive, than among the adherents of systems that are professedly conservative.[14]

Such a definition of "liberal" fits Bonhoeffer precisely. He came very early in his theological career to espouse the "new conservatism" or "neo-orthodoxy" of Barth. Therefore he rejected the liberalism of his Berlin teachers. But he never rejected—indeed, he affirmed with his whole being—the *liberality* of the great liberals like Harnack. Bonhoeffer championed what most interpreters would regard as conservative hypotheses and conclusions in the areas of biblical exegesis and dogmatic theology. Yet through it all runs Bonhoeffer's *esprit large,* his open-mindedness, his affirmative modernity; and it is precisely this liberality of outlook which gives all his writings a freshness, an originality, and a contemporaneity which are poles apart from "orthodoxy" in the hackneyed sense.

What seems to be the radical theological liberalism of Bonhoeffer's "non-religious" interpretation of Christianity is in fact a radical theological *liberality* for the sake of a world "come of age." Classical and Neo-Reformation themes and language stand side by side with what looks on the surface like an almost purely humanistic interpretation of the gospel in the *Letters and Papers from Prison*. What we have here is not confused juxtaposition, but rather a theological dialectic which is struggling for expression—a dialectic whose roots are to be found in Bonhoeffer's fruitful synthesis of classical theology and true liberality throughout his theological career.

An important statement from the prison writings incisively illuminates Bonhoeffer's own appreciation of the liberal theological tradition and his incorporation of the affirmative liberality of its encounter with the world into his own project for a "non-religious" interpretation of Christianity. Discussing the urgent need for the church to get back into the "open air" of intellectual discussion with the world after its introspective retrenchment during the *Kirchenkampf* and the war years, he says: "I feel obliged to tackle these questions as one who, although a 'modern' theologian, is still aware of the debt that he owes to liberal theology." [15] In another place he observes that it was liberal theology which posed the central question of modern theological interpretation: "Christ and the world that has come of age." While it was the "weakness" of liberalism "that it conceded to the world the right to determine Christ's place in the world," it was its strength "that it did not try to put the clock back, and that it genuinely accepted the battle (Troeltsch), even though this ended with its defeat." [16] The major Neo-Reformation attempts to reconstruct theology along new lines, Bonhoeffer goes on to say, have rightly reasserted the centrality of the biblical Christ, but they have failed to come to grips with the problem which the liberals faced squarely: the problem of interpreting the Christ intelligibly to a mature secular world. In the "religionless" project Bonhoeffer set himself the task of doing justice to both poles of the problem, Christ and the world, and thus of fulfilling and correcting the one-sided approaches of both liberalism and neo-orthodoxy. "Only in that way," he says, ". . . will liberal theology be overcome . . . and at the same time its question be genuinely taken up and answered." [17]

Of course, some of the truly great Neo-Reformation theologians have been men who transcended the liberalism of the older liberals for the sake of a truer interpretation of the gospel, but who have never lost their liberality, their open-mindedness and contemporaneousness. Foremost in this regard, along with Bonhoeffer, are Reinhold Niebuhr, Rudolf Bultmann, and Paul Tillich.[18]

Barth, too, was at bottom a man of genuine liberality (*esprit large* is a particularly apt characterization of this theological titan). Young scholars who went to Basel to study with or listen to Barth have almost unanimously testified to his intellectual humility and openness, his constant criticism of his own position and appreciation of other viewpoints. Yet Barth was always plagued, first of all, by the thunder of his early theology and the scholastic tendencies of his dogmatic work; and secondly, by the inability of many of his followers to hold together a vigorous orthodoxy and a liberality of outlook as Barth himself did in his own person. Some "Barthians" have interpreted his dogmatic work with narrowness of spirit and an uncharitable dogmatism which were not fundamentally characteristic of Barth himself.[19] Perhaps Barth's greatest rebuke to such "Barthians" was his brilliant ability to enter sympathetically and accurately into the liberal philosophical and theological thought of the nineteenth and early twentieth centuries.[20] Barth understood the great liberals with compassion and involvement, whereas "Barthians" have tended to reject impatiently and scornfully the whole liberal tradition.

Jaroslav Pelikan's remark, quoted earlier, that "Bonhoeffer could not join the company of those whose quest for certainty has caused them to suppose that they have outgrown Adolf Harnack," raises an important issue. Clearly Bonhoeffer stands in what we might call the "Barthian succession." Yet he is in no way a "Barthian" in the above sense, but an original and independent theologian who out of liberality of spirit and deep concern for intellectual honesty did what Barth repeatedly urged his disciples to do: He took up where Barth left off and even corrected him sharply at certain points, rather than slavishly repeating the master and creating a new Protestant scholasticism based this time on the writings of Barth rather than those of Luther and Calvin. By facing the contemporary world with more honesty and daring than Barth himself, Bonhoeffer opened up exciting possibilities in Barth's method. I suggest that it was Bonhoeffer's fearless liberality which enabled him to create what we might aptly describe as a second Barthian revolution. If present trends in continental theology, which is reexamining the whole liberal tradition with new insight, are slowly proving able to carry on where Barth as well as Bultmann left off, it is in at least some part due to the revolutionary "Barthian liberality" of Bonhoeffer.[21]

Bonhoeffer's *Menschlichkeit*
Martin Luther and Karl Barth are often coupled together as two great Protestant Christians possessed alike of a rare *Menschlichkeit*—what Professor T. F. Torrance translates as "rich humanity." [22] Their writings ring with the sheer love of things human and the joy and humor which follow from such a love. In them the heights of Christian affirmation overflow into devotion to and delight in the myriad facets of the world which is reconciled to God in Christ. There is a healthy

worldliness about Luther and Barth which springs from a fusion of native *joie de vivre* and the Christian gospel.

To these two must be added the name of Dietrich Bonhoeffer, whose chief mentors, significantly, were Luther and Barth. Both in his writings and in the writings of his commentators we are introduced to a man who by temperament was a lover of people and of earthly joys. Bonhoeffer's liberal German education broadened and sensitized his natural delight in the riches of human culture. Furthermore, at an early age *Lebensphilosophie* exercised a powerful attraction for him, especially the works of the passionately earth-loving Nietzsche. His lifelong quest for utter concreteness in the things of God was the theological manifestation of his zeal that the Christian gospel be a message for flesh-and-blood men on this earth.

Former students of Bonhoeffer from his years as director of an unusual seminary of the Confessing Church at Finkenwalde, like Eberhard Bethge and Paul F. W. Busing, recall with special emphasis and appreciation his great *Menschlichkeit*.[23] Bonhoeffer could savor and cherish an after-dinner cigar, a Bach fugue, a "pagan" author, or the simple joys of conviviality as readily as the peculiarly "religious" experiences of life in the Christian church. He was a deadly foe of pietism, which he regarded as an introspective blanket which threatened to suffocate "the clean and true air of the Word." [24] The atmosphere of the community at Finkenwalde, of which the book *Life Together* is a partial description, "was neither ascetic nor pietistic, but one of real joy and freedom under the Word of God." [25] In this Bonhoeffer stood squarely with the Reformers and against the religiosity of much post-Reformation piety.

For Bonhoeffer, as for Luther and Barth, this affirmation of humanity and of the earth was inextricably bound up with an understanding of the gospel. Nowhere does Bonhoeffer's *Menschlichkeit* and its relation to his theology come out more clearly and positively than in the *Letters and Papers from Prison*. It is precisely the "religionless" Bonhoeffer who displays a deeper and more expansive love of man and the world than ever before.

The prison writings abound with "rich humanity" and with a vision of Christian theology in which the Incarnation is the basis of true humanism. Bonhoeffer's accounts of his relations with fellow prisoners and with his warders, of the place of earthly joy in the Christian life, of

27

the "polyphony" of life, of his desire to have his "animal existence" awakened in the profoundest sense, of the importance of personal relationships simply in themselves—all these themes testify to his intense *Menschlichkeit,* his robust *joie de vivre.*

Theologically Bonhoeffer's "rich humanity" was manifest in his positive evaluation of a world "come of age," in his apprehension of faith as the integrator of life, in his incessant pursuing of the question of the meaning of Christ to a mature world, in his conception of transcendence as "the beyond in the midst of life," in his christology of Jesus "the man for others," in his understanding of the Christian not as "a *homo religiosus,* but simply a man," and in his love and concern for the "good pagan." He drove home the point negatively by his bitter attack on Christian apologetics, "existentialism," and "psychoanalysis" [26] for what he believed to be their conscious or unconscious degradation of man; and by an unchanging warfare on religiosity as a pretense and an affectation divorced from real life.

One of the most intriguing facets of Bonhoeffer interpretation has been a tendency on the part of some to couple him with Albert Camus, the contemporary French novelist. Such interpreters as Peter Berger and William Hamilton have tended to see Camus as a kind of non-Christian counterpart to Bonhoeffer.[27] For Berger and Hamilton, Camus is the highly articulate representative of the world "come of age." He epitomizes the man to whom Bonhoeffer is addressing a "religionless Christianity." Camus, better than communist man or any other current ideological "believer," represents the "good man without God," the mature "non-religious" man who Bonhoeffer believed is gradually predominating at least in Western society.

Albert Camus combined a profound and radical this-worldliness with an explicit rejection of traditional Christian theodicy. His novels and other writings abound in a quite remarkable affirmation of life and its values totally apart from divine sanction or reprobation. Deeply aware of tragedy, evil, and injustice, Camus could not make sense out of a God who would permit such a world. God, not man, is the guilty one, because God is the great bystander. He is rejected because he is unjust, not because he is improbable. Belief in God has enabled man to justify and perpetuate the existing order of things in the name of a heavenly kingdom; justice and freedom are not possible on earth until God has been abolished.

Since we must reject God and affirm the surd givenness of the world, we must ourselves create whatever good there is to be found in life. Despite the tragic ambiguity of all our actions and experiences, the task of being human is the bold decision to plunge oneself into the midst of life and wrest from it what it can yield of truth, beauty, and goodness. Some of Camus's most exquisitely beautiful and moving passages describe very simple joys and triumphs which persons in all circumstances actually experience in their relation to other persons and to the world. He speaks of natural beauty, of friendship, of courage, as one who has participated sensitively in life as a fully secular man.[28]

Bonhoeffer's *Letters and Papers From Prison* are strikingly reminiscent of the writings of Camus in some respects. They breathe the same air of world affirmation, of *Menschlichkeit*. They acknowledge the right of the world to its own existence. They reveal an intense love for man simply as man. Significantly, Camus, like Bonhoeffer, was deeply influenced by the *Lebensphilosophie* of Friedrich Nietzsche and by existentialism. Both Camus and Bonhoeffer were also part of the resistance movement during World War II, Camus in occupied France and Bonhoeffer in Nazi Germany. Having been born only seven years apart (Bonhoeffer in 1906 and Camus in 1913), they witnessed the same history unfold in Europe. Both men experienced the halcyon joys of prewar life and the abysmal horror of the war. One was a Christian and one an atheist; yet their reactions to life itself were to some extent remarkably similar.

There is little doubt that part of Bonhoeffer's current popularity stems from a recognition that in his life and thought he seems to have been the Christian reply to the healthy-minded secularity of men like Camus. Bonhoeffer showed that the Christian faith is not incompatible with the richest sort of life affirmation; indeed, he believed that the Christian faith *demands* the full affirmation of Camus' world—the world which has "come of age." Bonhoeffer's intense *Menschlichkeit* must be seen as an integral factor—perhaps we may call it the temperamental element—in his quest for a "religionless Christianity."

Secularization and the Redefinition of Nihilism

Etsi deus non daretur

A "world come of age" (*eine mündige Welt*) is Bonhoeffer's expression meaning, in his words, "the world that has become conscious of itself and the laws that govern its own existence." Elsewhere he describes a "come-of-age" world as a world in which the *autonomy of man* is being increasingly realized, a world having begun to achieve *adulthood* or *maturity*. Bonhoeffer traces the beginnings of the world's maturity from about the thirteenth century. Although he does not specify how these first glimmerings of autonomy were manifested, we may fairly safely assume that he has in mind such phenomena as the rise of nominalism in theology and philosophy and the breakdown of feudal society in the religious, social, and economic spheres. This movement of Western history is characterized, Bonhoeffer states, by "the discovery of the laws by which the world lives and deals with itself in science, social and political matters, art, ethics, and religion." [29] The rapid expansion of the frontiers of human knowledge is the keynote of the modern world—the world which has "come of age."

In a letter of July 16, 1944, Bonhoeffer attempts to trace in rough outline what he believes to be the key intellectual development which has led to the idea of an autonomous world. He finds its *theological* beginnings in the deistic Lord Herbert of Cherbury, who believed that reason was the adequate organ of religious knowledge. Ideas of *ethical* autonomy Bonhoeffer traces to Montaigne and Bodin, who substituted moral principles for the revealed ethics of the Decalogue. Machiavelli was the emancipator of *politics* from divine tutelage. Grotius, from a quite different perspective, nevertheless formulated international law as a law of nature, a self-subsisting law which is valid *etsi deus non daretur*—even if God does not exist. *Philosophy* experienced the beginnings of autonomy in Descartes, for whom the world was a self-contained mechanism (deism) ; and in Spinoza, who simply identified God with nature (pantheism). Later philosophers merely developed these tendencies: Kant on the deist side, Fichte and Hegel on the pantheist side. The autonomy of *natural science* began, according to Bonhoeffer, with Nicolas of Cusa and Giordano Bruno. Both men asserted the infinity of space over against the finite cosmos of classical and medieval thought. All these strains have produced the intellectual fabric of a world "come of age." All deal with the behavior patterns of reality as autonomous, as laws which function *etsi deus non daretur*— even if God is not "given." [30]

Bonhoeffer's historical analysis of the modern world as a world which no longer needs to employ "God" as a working hypothesis in its knowledge was immediately influenced by Carl F. von Weizsäcker's book *The World View of Physics*,[31] which he was reading in prison. He remarks in a letter written about a month before the reflections outlined above that Weizsäcker's book has reinforced his growing conviction that it is a fundamental mistake for "religion" to view God as "a stop-gap for the incompleteness of our knowledge." [32]

It is illuminating to look briefly at what Bonhoeffer probably found most provocative in Weizsäcker's book. Weizsäcker discusses the concept of the infinity of space held by Nicolas of Cusa and Giordano Bruno, and says of Bruno's theory: "It is on the world that the glory of infinity now falls—that glory which was unknown to antiquity and, in the Middle Ages, was reserved for God. It is for the sake of this glory that modern man loves and conquers the world." [33] Here is the beginning, in science, of the breakdown of the relation of the world to God and the assertion of the world's autonomy. "Christianity," Weizsäcker goes on to say,

made the infinite and unconditioned the goal of our striving. The secularized man of modern times has continued to strive in this direction, and has simply sought the fulfillment of his urge on another plane. It is therefore the essence of his relation to nature that he transcends the limits and conditions of his existence, which originates in nature. He presses on, to put it in ancient terms, into a realm where there are no gods, or whose gods are strange to us. He thus acquires a knowledge and a power which would have seemed to all earlier times no less improper than impossible.[34]

Weizsäcker, himself a Christian, shows how in the realm of knowledge "God" has become an evershrinking stopgap:

Once the symbolic relation between God and world is broken, a material relation cannot well be salvaged. The step from Kepler to Newton is historically intelligible, that from Newton to Laplace objectively necessary. For Kepler the positive knowledge of science points to God, while for Newton it is just the gaps in this knowledge which leave room for God. But such gaps are usually filled in in further development, and science cannot rest satisfied until they are filled in. Even if the hypotheses of Laplace had been false in some particulars, still every scientist must certainly set himself the goal of making the hypothesis "God" superfluous in his field. God and the faded, half-religious concepts which have often been substituted for him in recent times, always designate, as scientific hypotheses for the explanation of particular facts, only the incomplete points in science, and therefore with the advance of knowledge they find themselves in continuous and dishonourable retreat.[35]

The God who no longer functions as a "working hypothesis" has been relegated to the realm of man's *personal life,* says Weizsäcker:

Modern science has excluded . . . [the question of God] from the circle of its obligatory premises and has banished it to the private sphere. Thus it determined in advance the result at which it has now arrived. At the same time it gradually removed from that level of experience the means of expression which would make it generally intelligible, and has thus made the way to full consciousness more and more difficult for it.[36]

Bonhoeffer believed that "religion," in its aspect as inwardness or individualism, has accepted and tried to capitalize on this retreat of "God" to the purely private sphere of each person's "inner life."

Bonhoeffer concludes his analysis of the "come-of-age" world by stating that "God as a working hypothesis in morals, politics, or science, has been surmounted and abolished; and the same thing has happened in philosophy and religion (Feuerbach!). For the sake of intellectual honesty, that working hypothesis should be dropped, or as far as possible eliminated." [37] Bonhoeffer's appeal to "intellectual honesty" is fundamental to his quest for a "religionless Christianity," and is in part an inheritance from his teacher Harnack and the liberal tradition. The analysis of the modern world as a world which has learned to live without using God as a "working hypothesis" is an important manifestation of Bonhoeffer's own forthright attempts in the prison writings to be intellectually honest. "And we cannot be honest," he concludes, "unless we recognize that we have to live in the world *etsi deus non daretur.*" [38]

From Idolatry to Nihilism

Bonhoeffer believed that the progressive "de-divinization" of the world "has in our time reached an undoubted completion. Man has learnt to deal with himself in all questions of importance without recourse to the 'working hypothesis' called 'God.' " Here is the crux of the matter as far as "religion" is concerned. "Religion," according to Bonhoeffer, employs "God" as a "working hypothesis" by which to explain those mysteries which knowledge has not yet been able to probe. The more man discovers "the laws by which the world lives," the more "God" as a metaphysical hypothesis retreats to the ever-shrinking periphery of existence. In a world "come of age," "everything gets along without 'God'—and, in fact, just as well as before. As in the scientific field, so in human affairs generally, 'God' is being pushed more and more out of life, losing more and more ground." [39] A world "come of age," then, is an increasingly *"religionless"* world, in the terms of Bonhoeffer's analysis of "religion." In his "Outline for a Book," Bonhoeffer speaks of the "religionlessness of man who has come of age [*des mündig gewordenen Menschen*]. 'God' as a working hypothesis, as a stop-gap for our embarrassments, has become superfluous." [40] "Nature," Bonhoeffer says, "was formerly conquered by spiritual means, with us by technical organization of all kinds." [41] The ability of the autonomous man of a world "come of age" to deal with virtually all matters of existence without recourse to "God" as an explanation is the central thesis of Bonhoeffer's conception of a "nonreligious" world.

Traditional Christian apologetics would probably counter this thesis by saying that a world "come of age," far from being a "religionless" world, is simply a world in which new possibilities of *idolatry* exist; and idolatry is by definition a religious phenomenon. "Autonomous man" is nothing but a new (and idolatrous) religion—the religion of the Enlightenment.[42] This seems to accord with the usual interpretation of biblical faith, and it is the view of Karl Barth and of Bonhoeffer in his earlier writings.[43] We have only one statement of Bonhoeffer's in *Letters and Papers* which speaks to this argument, but it is an important one. In a letter of June 27, 1944, he tells his friend Eberhard Bethge of a short commentary he is writing:

I am at present writing an exposition of the first three commandments. I find No. 2 particularly difficult. The usual interpretation of idolatry as "wealth, sensuality, and pride" seems to me quite unbiblical. That is a piece of moralizing. Idols are worshipped, and idolatry implies that people still worship something. But we do not now worship anything, not even idols. *In that respect we are truly nihilists.*[44]

Fortunately, Bonhoeffer's exposition of the "First Table" of the Commandments has been preserved.[45] Here he expands slightly on what he means by nihilism:

For us [i.e., modern men] the world has lost its gods; we no longer worship anything. We have experienced too clearly the frailty and invalidity of all things, of all men, and of ourselves for us still to be able to deify them. We have lost too much confidence in the whole of existence for us still to be capable of having and worshiping gods.

Bonhoeffer goes on to suggest that perhaps nihilism itself is the last idol: "If we still have an idol, perhaps it is nothingness, obliteration, meaninglessness." [46] It is clear from his wholly sympathetic characterization of contemporary "nihilist" man in the prison writings, however, that he does not take seriously this tentative suggestion. The statement reflects an "existentialist" mood which Bonhoeffer rejects vehemently at several points in *Letters and Papers*. Generally speaking, it seems clear that he did not find very helpful the suggestion that "worshiping nothing" was itself idolatry; it was for him much more the end of idolatry.

Nihilism, then, means the end even of *idolatrous* "religion." Bonhoeffer's concept of nihilism is crucial to his analysis of the decay of "religion" in the modern world. What follows is an attempt to elucidate the brief material which Bonhoeffer devotes specifically to the idea of nihilism. First of all, he regards the decay of "religion" in a mature world as a *gradual* process, just as the world's "coming of age" itself is a slow progress toward mature autonomy.[47] Hence we may expect that certain aspects of "religion" remain longer than others even in a world "come of age," as part of its "growing pains." "Religion" as worship or deification lingers on when "religion" as the "God-hypothesis" is gone.[48]

But secondly, in a world "come of age," a world which discovers the *autonomy of man*, this lingering desire to worship or deify is fastened on man himself. The Christian apologist may point out that this is really the oldest, not the newest, form of idolatry. But Bonhoeffer might reply as follows: Until the beginning of the world's maturity, man's self-deification was defined only over against the greater reality of "God" or "the gods," who impinged in a significant way upon man's tenuous existence. That is to say, self-idolatry was defined only by the *negation* of true worship; it constituted *rebellion* against a more fundamental reality, "God" or "the gods." In a secularized world, however, self-worship is defined only in terms of itself, since "God" as a metaphysical hypothesis has outrun worship in falling into decay. In other words, the deification of man becomes a *positive* idolatry and the fundamental reality. Man takes the place of God as the "working hypothesis." The possibilities of worship of the new man might seem to have been limitless, as the eighteenth and nineteenth centuries believed, since man was now freed from the necessity to refer his self-worship to a more fundamental reality. Hence he was liberated also from the fear of forces beyond his control, from metaphysical guilt, and from supernatural judgment.

But it is precisely because man in the final analysis *is* an *idol*—the last idol—that the Enlightenment worship of man ends, not in the kingdom of humanity, but in nihilism. The final, the absolute, idolatry —the idolatry which no longer possesses the "God-hypothesis" to remind it that it *is* idolatry—cannot sustain itself and falls into a state of *nihil:* the worship of nothing at all. Bonhoeffer seems to be saying, if the implications of his brief remarks have been rightly interpreted, that *the fully "religionless" world is nihilistic.* As long as autonomous man still persists in worshiping himself, "religion" is not finally dead, even though the "God-hypothesis" is dead. The true death of "religion" is nihilism: "We have experienced too clearly the frailty and invalidity of all things, of all men, and of ourselves for us still to be able to deify them." Out of his experiences of the life and thought of the twentieth century, Bonhoeffer concludes that the world "come of age" has begun to come to fruition. It is precisely these nihilistic tendencies in our day which he seems to have in mind. A race of men are growing up—some of whom Bonhoeffer meets and knows in his resistance activities and in concentration camps—who can no longer worship even such things as a political ideology, the progress of science, or the future of man; they can no longer "worship" anything. These are the citizens of a fully "religionless" world. Fully to understand the world *etsi deus non daretur* is to worship nothing; it is nihilism.

There is a profound piety, a fervent inner attitude, about the confident humanist who worships the "new man." Although religion-as-metaphysics has died, religion-as-inwardness continues in the humanist deification of man. With the end of modern idolatry, however, nihilist man cannot even share the early humanist's "piety."

Bonhoeffer's theory of a world "come of age," contrary to a persistent misunderstanding, is not progressivistic or naïvely optimistic. In a letter of July 18, 1944, he says, speaking of the Christian task in a world which has reached maturity:

> When we speak of God in a "non-religious" way, we must speak of him in such a way that the godlessness of the world is not in some way concealed, but rather revealed, and thus exposed to an unexpected light. The world that has come of age is more godless, and perhaps for that very reason nearer to God, than the world before its coming of age.[49]

The completion of a world come of age in nihilism is the ultimate godlessness. Self-deification by autonomous man is still a *"religious"* godlessness; with nihilism man no longer has even "godless religion." Perhaps Bonhoeffer is saying that it is when the last shred of "religion" is gone, when there is only man in the world without even his delusions of grandeur as a "religious" comfort, that man is "nearer to God." He remarks in one place that "our coming of age leads us to a true recognition of our situation before God." [50] As long as "religion" exists, it is always potentially a cushion by which man can protect himself against God and against the stark reality of the world's ungodliness. When the new man becomes a nihilist, his godlessness is exposed to him as never before.

But while it is wrong to understand this nihilistic awareness in a progressivistic sense, it is likewise a mistake to interpret it in what Bonhoeffer would call a "psychotherapeutic" or "existentialist" sense. Nihilistic man, according to Bonhoeffer, is not necessarily or even usually "trembling over the abyss," experiencing "ontological nausea" or the "sickness unto death." This singularly positive concept of nihilism is by no means what we would expect in light of its usual connotations. It is a mark of striking originality in Bonhoeffer's thought, particularly in the *Ethics* and in *Letters and Papers,* that he is concerned as much about the "good" man, the ordinary person of decency and strength, as he is about the reprobate who can point vividly to his wretchedness apart from Christ.

In *Ethics* Bonhoeffer has a chapter on "The Church and the World" which includes a section specifically entitled "Christ and Good People." His remarks in this chapter are made with the Germany of the 1930's and early 1940's very much in mind. The dramatic way in which the Nazi nightmare had brought together Christians and "non-religious" men of good will was making a profound impression on Bonhoeffer, and he sought here and in the prison writings to articulate the phenomenon theologically.

Bonhoeffer says that when he speaks of "good people," he is

here taking the concept of good in its widest sense, that is to say, simply as the contrary of vicious, lawless and scandalous, as the opposite of public transgression of the moral law, as good in contrast to the publican and harlot. Good, in this sense, contains an extremely wide range of gradations, extending from the purely external observance of good order to the most intimate self-examination and character-formation and to personal self-sacrifice for the most sublime human values.[51]

He cautions against interpreting goodness in terms of "bourgeois self-satisfaction." He sees it rather as a habitual discipline and decency to which quite ordinary people are capable of attaining, and largely unselfconsciously.

Bonhoeffer criticizes the church for its traditional preoccupation with the wicked to the neglect of the good:

Over and over again the Church, when she has based herself upon Scripture, has given thought to the relationship of Jesus Christ to the wicked and to wickedness. . . . Yet the question of the relationship of the good man to Christ remained remarkably neglected. The good man here was either the Pharisee and hypocrite who needed to be convinced of his wickedness; or else he was the man who had been converted from his wickedness to Christ and who was now enabled by Him to do good works.[52]

The chaos and disruption of the period in which Bonhoeffer is writing, however, have raised decisively the issue of "Christ and good people":

The experience of our own time is that it is the good who find their way back to Christ and that the wicked obstinately remain aloof from Him. Other times could preach that a man must first become a sinner, like the publican and the harlot, before he could know and find Christ, but we in our time must say rather that before a man can know and find Christ he must first become righteous like those who strive and who suffer for the sake of justice, truth and humanity.[53]

But surely, one may ask, we cannot have it both ways, simply on the basis of changing historical circumstances: Which is the authentically

Christian understanding of the matter? Characteristically, Bonhoeffer responds in a profoundly *dialectical* way:

Both of these principles are alike paradoxical and in themselves impossible; but they make the situation clear. Christ belongs both to the wicked and to the good; He belongs to them both only as sinners, that is to say, as men who in their wickedness and in their goodness have fallen away from their origin. He summons them back to the origin so that they shall no longer be good and evil but justified and sanctified sinners. But before we express this ultimate in which evil and good are one before Christ, we must not avoid the question which is set us by our own experience and by our own time, the question of what is meant by saying that the good find Christ, in other words the question of the relationship of Jesus Christ to good people and to goodness.[54]

Two elements of importance in Bonhoeffer's ethics appear in the above passage. One is his theological analysis of fallen man as separated from his origin in God. Separation from God creates the knowledge of good and evil; union with God is "trans-moral," "beyond good and evil" in their relative human sense. Before Christ, therefore, who is the way back to union with God, man is not relatively good or bad but simply a sinner who has fallen away from his origin in God. Thus both the "good man" and the "bad man" stand together in their need of justification and sanctification through Christ.

But what we have in the doctrine of "original sin" is an "ultimate" interpretation of the human situation, and now enters the second element: Bonhoeffer's equal concern for the "penultimate." The fact that before Christ all men are sinners does not obliterate the penultimate but real distinctions between goodness and evil. The church, says Bonhoeffer, has tended to focus exclusively on man's ultimate status before God; as a result it has slipped into the serious error, not only of neglecting penultimate goodness, but also of unconsciously translating ultimate sinfulness into penultimate terms. Hence man's objective universal situation as one fallen away from his divine origin is distorted into a psychologistic insistence that every particular person is at bottom wretched and evil. At this point Bonhoeffer's appreciation of penultimate goodness joins hands with his emphatic denunciation of Christian pastors and their "secularized offshoots" ("existentialists" and "psychotherapists") who feel that they must "drive people to inward despair" before they can "save" them. Penultimately there are genuinely good persons, many of whom are neither Christian nor "religious," and the gospel of the Incarnation embraces them too. A proclamation of the gospel which focuses obsessively on human sin and weakness rather than claiming goodness and strength also as Christ's is a one-sided interpretation which will make little impact on many of earth's noblest sons, especially in a world which has begun to "come of age."

Bonhoeffer interpreted the goodness of the "good pagan" as *fides directa,* unconscious faith, but his life was cut short just as he was beginning to reflect seriously on the matter. In a theological discussion which he and Eberhard Bethge were carrying on by correspondence, Bonhoeffer speaks of "unconscious Christianity," equating it with what an earlier generation called "natural piety." Classical theology would categorize as "natural piety" what Bonhoeffer describes as the strength and goodness of modern "nihilist" man. "Religion," even "natural religion," is no longer an operative category in a world "come of age"; but "unconscious Christianity" is—assuming, as Bonhoeffer does, that Christian faith in its essence is "non-religious." [55]

The *Ethics* contains a few tantalizingly brief remarks which indicate that Bonhoeffer was operating with some notion of *fides directa,* but nothing more. In the chapter on "The Church and the World," he speaks of the rallying of the forces of truth and goodness around the name of Christ during the contemporary struggle in Germany. That, he says, is because Christ is the origin of all truth and goodness, whatever form they take, and in times of crisis they will instinctively, as it were, find their way back to their origin, to Christ. For

He is the centre and strength of the Bible, of the Church, and of theology, but also of humanity, of reason, of justice and of culture. Everything must return to Him; it is only under His protection that it can live. There seems to be *a general unconscious knowledge* which, in the hour of ultimate peril, leads everything which desires not to fall victim to the Antichrist to take refuge with Christ.[56]

In a discussion of love, Bonhoeffer contends that "the biblical concept of love, and it alone, is the foundation, the truth and the reality of love, in the sense that any natural thought about love contains truth and reality only in so far as it participates in this its origin, that is to say, in the love which is God Himself in Jesus Christ." [57] We find an implied recognition here that all manifestations of authentic love participate, however unconsciously, in the objective reality of the love of God revealed in Christ.

It would be illegitimate to attempt to erect a detailed theological exposition out of such fleeting remarks. The concept of *fides directa* or "unconscious Christianity" remains simply as the way in which Bonhoeffer was beginning to interpret the goodness of "non-religious" "good people" at the end of his life. It is a theme which is vital, however, to any attempted development of Bonhoeffer's "non-religious interpretation" project.[58]

When Bonhoeffer speaks of the "nihilist" man, the "good man without God" of the modern secular world, he is talking not only about the Western intelligentsia, who might be expected to be "advanced" and "liberated" in their outlook, but also about the "average person," the ordinary, usually middle-class or working-class citizen. The day-to-day willingness of ordinary people to "take life as it comes" with dignity and modesty and without the comforts or preoccupations of "religion" made a remarkable impression on Bonhoeffer. In the letter of June 8, 1944, he describes the "religionless" "good man" as follows:

The ordinary man, who spends his everyday life at work and with his family, and of course with all kinds of diversions, . . . has neither the time nor the inclination to concern himself with his existential despair, or to regard his perhaps modest share of happiness as a trial, a trouble, or a calamity.[59]

The "religionless," the nihilistic, man, then, is *not* in the majority of instances a morbid, despair-ridden individual swimming in seventy thousand fathoms and looking desperately for a rope to grasp. He is a man whom the Christian meets in strength as often as in weakness. This seemingly untraditional notion is one of the major themes in Bonhoeffer's understanding both of a world "come of age" and of "religionless Christianity." To Bonhoeffer the mature world, even in its utter godlessness, is a world where ordinary persons of genuine dignity and happiness live. It is a world in which, even with their last idol smashed, "nihilistic" men can live sanely and responsibly. Deeply aware of their godlessness as never before, content to master the job at hand, and grateful for whatever modest share of truth and beauty and goodness comes their way, quite ordinary persons are somehow able to "make the best of it." It is these autonomous human beings to whom the church must address a "non-religious" message.

The Failure of Christian Apologetics and Its Secular Counterparts

What has been the church's attitude thus far to a world which has come to maturity? A largely negative one, says Bonhoeffer, who criticizes the church severely on this score. The prevailing attitude of Christian apologetics toward postmedieval history is to regard this "coming of age" as "the great defection from God, from Christ, . . . and the more they claim and play off God and Christ against it, the more the development considers itself to be anti-Christian." The adulthood of the world is bewildering and frightening to the church. What is especially disheartening about it, from the standpoint of Christian apologetics, is that "false developments and failures do not make the world doubt the necessity of the course that it is taking, or of its development; they are accepted with fortitude and detachment as part of the bargain, and even an event like the present war is no exception." [60] This from a Christian in a concentration camp amid the horrors of war who lived daily in the shadow of death! Such a statement reinforces Bonhoeffer's central conviction that the nihilism of a mature world is not, in most instances, a neurotic staring into the void. The courage of the "new man," who would rather understand his world and face the task at hand than enjoy the comforts of "religion," finds great sympathy from Bonhoeffer.

The church's response to this "healthy-minded" nihilism has been a retreat to the "ultimate" questions such as death and guilt.[61] Bonhoeffer, however, asks with a daring which drives his point home, "But what if one day they [i.e., the ultimate questions] no longer exist as such, if they too can be answered 'without God'?" [62] The main thrust of Christian apologetics in a world "come of age," then, has been the attempt to salvage a place for "God" in the steadily shrinking sphere of human ignorance and helplessness. In the earlier stages of the world's "coming of age," the church lashed out in a reactionary way against Copernicanism and Darwinism. Bonhoeffer considers this "apologetics" (actually polemics!) totally misguided. The more recent tendency has been the one described above, wherein the church, to use

41

the terminology of a world which has reached maturity, has claimed for God the few remaining areas of man's childhood.[63] Christian apologetics tries to show the "healthy-minded" nihilist that in his "inner life" he is really sick and wretched. The church's name for the cure is "God," a metaphysical *deus ex machina* which is cranked on stage as the only resolution of human ills.

The church's efforts to intimidate men into belief by impugning their maturity and preying upon the lingering vestiges of their childhood are scathingly denounced by Bonhoeffer.[64] His criticism of the church in an autonomous world is that it is heteronomous—that it attempts to absolutize what was simply a "religious" stage in the history of man rather than pointing him to his true absolute, the fully human (rather than narrowly "religious") reality of Jesus Christ. Christian apologetics asks autonomous man to "return to religion," to submit to a now alien structure of his childhood, instead of acknowledging his "religionless" and God-willed maturity.[65]

The issue Bonhoeffer raises in his "attack upon 'Christendom' " has become a decisive one for the contemporary church. It is a mark of his penetrating insight into and profound appreciation of the modern world (which for Bonhoeffer are thoroughly grounded in biblical and christological presuppositions) that he refuses to regard secularity as a deadly foe to the church. The very notion of a "religionless Christianity" for a world which has "come of age" signifies that Bonhoeffer understands secularity not only as a creative opportunity for the church but also as the defining form of its message.

On numerous occasions in *Letters and Papers* Bonhoeffer criticizes not only Christian pastors and apologists, but also their "secularized offshoots," the "existentialists" and the "psychotherapists," for pruriently feeding on people's "inner lives." He violently rejects the assumption that a man must be driven to the brink of despair and disgust with his life before he can be "saved" by the gospel, by tragic courage, or by analysis. The "modern" parson, the "existentialist," and the "psychotherapist," "demonstrate to secure, contented, and happy mankind that it is really unhappy and desperate and simply unwilling to admit that it is in a predicament about which it knows nothing, and from which only they can rescue it." [66] Bonhoeffer's approach to all questions is theological, and his impassioned attack on Christian apologists and their "secular counterparts" is no exception. He traces this obsession with despair and wretchedness to Christianity's desperate efforts, in the face of an increasingly "non-religious" world, to "clear a space" for God in the world:

The displacement of God from the world, and from the public part of human life, led to the attempt to keep his place secure at least in the sphere of the "personal," the "inner," and the "private." And as every man still has a private sphere somewhere, that is where he was thought to be the most vulnerable.[67]

The theological realm of the sinful recesses of the innermost soul, the psychoanalytical sphere of the libidinal unconscious, and the existentialist portrait of the lonely and hellish insides of estranged modern man—all are preoccupations with the "inner life," as if the one who held the key to this mysterious citadel had the secret mastery, the final mocking word, over the public forces of scientific explanation and the naïveté of people who imagine they are happy. Bonhoeffer castigates the clergy explicitly and scathingly on this score, speaking of "the 'clerical' sniffing-around-after-people's-sins in order to catch them out." [68]

Speaking from the standpoint of personal experience, Bonhoeffer asks on one occasion, "What does one's attitude mean, anyway? . . . I know less than ever about myself, and I am no longer attaching any importance to it. I have had more than enough psychology, and I am less and less inclined to analyse the state of my soul. . . . There is something more at stake than self-knowledge." [69] Throughout his adult life Bonhoeffer had a profound suspicion of subjectivity for its own sake.[70] He believed that the gospel is the objective reality of God revealed in Jesus Christ. In his early criticisms of his personalist-existentialist philosophical mentors,[71] he put forth the theological proposition that the nature and meaning of reality have been disclosed *extra nos,* from outside ourselves, in the biblically attested self-disclosure of God; otherwise, he claimed, we are inescapably locked up in our subjectivity. But to be locked up in subjectivity is to be enslaved to oneself, for man is fallen; his subjectivity is the *cor curvum in se.* The only true liberation is the joyous gospel of judgment, forgiveness, and reconciliation in Christ. Bonhoeffer never deviated from this position, and this objective standing point liberated him from self-preoccupation and for creative thought and action. Hence his suspicion of the modern cult of "introspective analysis," of subjective self-scrutiny, inso-

43

far as it pretends to be the last word of truth and deliverance for man. There is indeed "something more at stake than self-knowledge," in Bonhoeffer's opinion.

It is significant that Bonhoeffer sees the true "nihilist" man of a world "come of age" as the ordinary person who is too healthily absorbed in job, family, interests, etc., to have either the "time" or the "inclination" for introspective self-obsession. One of the two characteristics of "religion," according to Bonhoeffer, is "inwardness." The mature, "non-religious" person of the modern world lacks "inwardness," the "religious" preoccupation with one's "inner self." The "existentialist" and the "psychotherapist" do not reach this person. Whom do they affect? "A small number of intellectuals, of degenerates, of people who regard themselves as the most important thing in the world, and who therefore like to busy themselves with themselves," replies Bonhoeffer.[72]

Bonhoeffer attempts to analyze the preoccupation of clergy, "psychotherapists," and "existentialists" with the "inner life" from both a sociological and theological point of view. Sociologically he calls it part of the "revolt of inferiority," the vulgarizing of life by the prurient assumption that all people are hypocrites, and the corresponding satisfaction in exposing or seeing exposed the wretchedness and sinfulness of one's fellow human beings.[73] With his profound concern for the dignity and freedom of man, which was truly "aristocratic" in pleading for a sense of quality and excellence in human life, Bonhoeffer could only regard all attempts to prey upon man's weaknesses as vulgarity, as the cheapening and degradation of persons. He keenly recognized that this "revolution from below," this exaltation of inferiority, permeates all strata of society. "A basic anti-social attitude of mistrust and suspicion," Bonhoeffer summarizes, "is the revolt of inferiority."

From a theological perspective the revolt of inferiority is characterized by two errors: "First, it is thought that a man can be addressed as a sinner only after his weaknesses and meannesses have been spied out." We have seen in our discussion of the *bonus vir,* the nihilist "good man," that Bonhoeffer distinguishes between man's ultimate, objective situation as a sinner and his penultimate, subjective condition as relatively good or evil. The church has repeatedly made the mistake of speaking of man's ultimate sinfulness in penultimate terms, of psychologizing it. Hence the theological proposition that every individual man is at bottom base, lascivious, and miserable, and that his goodness (unless he is a Christian) is hypocrisy. To this error Bonhoeffer replies, "man is certainly a sinner, but is far from being mean or common on that account. . . . It is not in the least necessary to spy out things; the Bible never does so."

The second theological error is an exclusive preoccupation with the "inner life": "It is thought that a man's essential nature consists of his inmost and most intimate background; that is defined as his 'inner life,' and it is precisely in those secret human places that God is to have his domain!" In answer to this error, Bonhoeffer appeals to the biblical anthropology, which views man as a concrete psycho-physical whole and never divorces "inner" and "outer," "soul" and "body." Man in the whole of his existence is oriented either toward or away from God.[74] The whole of the *Ethics* attempts to develop a genuinely biblical-christological ethics. The writings which comprise the *Ethics* should be consulted for a "fleshing out" of Bonhoeffer's concern for the total person in his concrete existence. He criticizes ethical systems based on "good intentions" or, in formal ethical parlance, on motives:

What right have we to stop short at the immediate motive and to regard this as the ultimate ethical phenomenon, refusing to take into account the fact that a "good" motive may spring from a very dark background of human consciousness and unconsciousness and that a "good attitude" may often be the source of the worst of actions?

In motivational ethics "the question of good is posed in abstract terms and in isolation from reality." "Good" is not some subjective criterion of the "inner life," such as motive, conscience, feeling, reason, or will:

Good is reality itself, reality seen and recognized in God. The question of good embraces man with his motives and purposes, with his fellow-men and with the entire creation around him; it embraces reality as a whole, as it is held in being by God.

Bonhoeffer refers to Genesis 1:31, which says of the entire creation, "Behold, it was very good." Applied specifically to man, good as reality itself

demands the whole, not only the whole of a man's outlook but his whole work, the whole man, together with the fellow-men who are given to him.

... Man is an indivisible whole, not only as an individual in his person and work but also as a member of the community of men and creatures in which he stands.[75]

Bonhoeffer emphasizes man as a *social* being, as an I-Thou reality. This authentically biblical understanding of man naturally found the modern "religious," "existentialist," and "psychotherapeutic" concentration on the "inner man" to be a pernicious abstraction from reality.

Most pernicious of all, however, is the effect of this "interiorization" on the doctrine of God: "It is precisely in those secret human places that God is to have his domain!" The growing autonomy of the world has pushed "God" steadily back to the frontiers of knowledge and existence. The church, aided by the findings of its "secular offshoots," has found its frontier; it has staked out the "inner life" of man as the sphere of divine activity. "God" has shrunk to the dimensions of individual human subjectivity. Bonhoeffer considers this retreat ignominious both to God and to man. It is the last in a series of futile strategies designed to claim the few remaining areas of man's childhood:

I therefore want to start from the premise that God should not be smuggled into some last secret place, but that we should frankly recognize that the world, and people, have come of age, that we should not run man down in his worldliness, but confront him with God at his strongest point, that we should give up all our clerical tricks, and not regard psychotherapy and existentialist philosophy as God's pioneers. The importunity of all these people is far too unaristocratic for the Word of God to ally itself with them.[76]

Bonhoeffer's diatribe against the "revolt of inferiority" also reflects his lifelong insistence on a healthy reserve among persons as an essential manifestation of human dignity and freedom under Christ. The philosophical and theological expression of Bonhoeffer's deep respect for human integrity is his personalism. In a letter of November 27, 1943, he describes the terror of his fellow prisoners during a night bombing raid. He observes that after the raid people "talk quite openly about how frightened they were." Bonhoeffer is rather struck by this frankness: "Fright is surely something to be ashamed of. I have a feeling that it should not be talked about except in the confessional, otherwise it might easily involve a certain amount of exhibitionism. ...."[77] He observes that, while on the one hand there is a "naïve frankness" which is merely "disarming," "there is a cynical, I might almost say ungodly, frankness, the kind that breaks out in heavy drinking and fornication, and gives the impression of chaos. I wonder whether fright is not one of the *pudenda,* which ought to be concealed." Bonhoeffer adds, "I must think about it further." [78]

He did continue to think about the matter of "cynical frankness." In a letter headed "Advent II" (December 5, 1943), he reflects at greater length on the subject:

I have been thinking again over what I wrote to you recently about our own fear. I think that here, under the guise of honesty, something is being passed off as "natural" that is at bottom a symptom of sin; it is really quite analogous to talking openly about sexual matters. After all, "truthfulness" does not mean uncovering everything that exists. God himself made clothes for men [Gen. 3.21]; and that means that *in statu corruptionis* many things in human life ought to remain covered, and that evil, even though it cannot be eradicated, ought at least to be covered. Exposure is cynical, and although the cynic prides himself on his exceptional honesty, or claims to want truth at all costs, he misses the crucial fact that since the fall there must be reticence and secrecy.[79]

It is worth pointing out that here, as everywhere, Bonhoeffer seeks "to think theologically," which for him always means biblically and christologically, and he simply cannot be adequately understood except on this basis. In the "trans-moral" state of original unity with God there would quite automatically be nothing hidden, no secrets. But in a world separated from its original unity a healthy reticence and secrecy about certain things preserves order by preserving human integrity and respecting the limits of life. Bonhoeffer's analysis, in *Creation and Fall* [80] and in the *Ethics,*[81] of a healthy sense of *shame* as a quality preservative of the dignity and boundaries of human existence in a fallen world, is integral to his criticisms of "cynical frankness."

Clearly, Bonhoeffer sees the "revolt of inferiority," the obsessive prying of clergy, "existentialists," and "psychotherapists" into men's private lives, as the chief manifestation of "cynical frankness." He considers such an attitude unbiblical and therefore unchristian: The Bible understands man as a whole (not simply as his "inner life") and as fallen (not as a Rousseauesque creature who has the right to lay bare everything). Furthermore, the "revolt of inferiority" is unworthy of a world which has "come of age," for it preys upon the weaknesses of man's lingering immaturity rather than affirming the strength of his maturity.

In the light of the profound influence of philosophical existentialism on his own theology, Bonhoeffer's violent attack on "existentialists" in the prison letters must be seen as one-sided. Nothing in his previous writings prepares us for this vehement onslaught. We are left to surmise that he must have seen *tendencies* in existentialism, particularly among its popularizers, such as he describes and castigates. It is a fact that existentialism is popularly thought of as a philosophy of obsessive introspection and pervasive despair, and this image has a real (though partial) basis in the gloomy melancholy of Kierkegaard, the exhausting intensity of Dostoyevsky, the preoccupation with death of Heidegger, and the lonely freedom of Sartre. Yet existentialism is at the same time a wholly concrete account of human existence and a radical personalism, two aspects which contributed profoundly to Bonhoeffer's own thought. The "interiorization" of existentialist analysis is by no means the pietistic Christian concentration on the "soul" in detachment from the "body." It is rather an examination of how man as a concrete individual "thrown" into a particular time and place in history understands his existence in the world. Furthermore, there can be little doubt that the explicitly "godless," "non-religious" affirmation of authentic human existence as a life of courage, freedom, dignity, and maturity, which we find in the writings of Heidegger, Sartre, and Bonhoeffer's own "secular counterpart" Albert Camus, is definitely one valid expression of Bonhoeffer's "come-of-age," "nihilist" man.

The same thing must be said of psychotherapy. Popular culture has caricatured it with the lurid image of the psychoanalyst gleefully laying bare one's innermost secrets, especially those of a sexual nature. However unjustly, this irresponsible popularization of certain elements in psychotherapy has its roots in Freudian analysis. Yet Bonhoeffer was doubtless acquainted with responsible psychotherapeutic theory and practice, both in Freud and in his followers. Who among the great psychotherapists was less the sort of person whom Bonhoeffer criticizes than Carl Jung, with his strongly holistic and social view of man and his optimistic analysis of the human situation? [82]

Clearly Bonhoeffer is in fact criticizing *irresponsible, popularized* existentialism and psychotherapy, although his unguarded and uninterpreted remarks suggest a blanket condemnation of the two movements. It must be remembered that Bonhoeffer wrote his severe criticisms of existentialism and psychotherapy in private letters to a friend; naturally he had no idea that they would ever appear in print. Had he been writing for publication, he would almost certainly have qualified his remarks to show the positive aspects of the two movements.

Nevertheless, it is precisely in popularized, often distorted, forms that intellectual movements permeate and shape the outlook and practice of the "common man" during any historical epoch. This penetration of the mental fabric of a generation is often subtle and unconscious, and therefore all the more real and powerful a force in everyday personal and social life. Bonhoeffer quite accurately, if very partially, perceived what "existentialism" and "psychotherapy" have become in the debased form in which they affect the lives of most people. It is the "existentialism" and "psychotherapy" of advertising, magazines, newspapers, popular novels and plays, and radio, television, and the cinema, which bombard the average person and go so far toward molding his outlook on life. It is in this way that "existentialism" and "psychotherapy" participate in a formative way in the "revolt of inferiority," the vulgarization of life, which is a marked feature of twentieth-century Western society. Bonhoeffer is incensed by the part he believes existentialist philosophers and writers and psychotherapists have played in fostering and to some degree capitalizing on this widespread "egalitarianism" of mutual exposure. He is confident, however, that a majority of "ordinary persons" today—the truly "nihilistic" men—possess the strength to ignore the blandishments of this vulgarized "innerness." The "revolt of inferiority" is the final attempt of what might be called "secularized religion" to keep man an adolescent; it is definitely *fin de siècle* and not "come-of-age." As man becomes increasingly mature and hence "non-religious," these appeals to the murky depths of his "inner life," Bonhoeffer thinks, will simply become irrelevant and a matter for impatience.

Bonhoeffer was also keenly concerned about the negative role of "existentialism" and "psychotherapy" in modern culture because he saw the enthusiasm with which too many Christian pastors and apologists have greeted these movements as fundamentally misguided. He was vigorously resisting, in the name both of the gospel and of a world

49

"come of age," the widespread (and still very popular) tendency of the church to rejoice all too hastily over existentialism and psychotherapy as independent corroboration of man's radical sinfulness and wretchedness and therefore as a kind of *praeparatio fidei*. In fastening onto existentialism and psychotherapy (and only their negative aspects at that) as the new "natural theology," Christianity has picked the wrong allies in its apologetical task. The "come-of-age" world will simply leave the church behind, along with its "secularized offshoots," because they refuse to understand the mature world even as well as it understands itself—much less better than it understands itself. Furthermore, and more fundamental still, the church has betrayed its foundation in the biblical testimony to Christ by allying itself so eagerly and completely with existentialism and psychotherapy. Unlike the Scriptures, it has tended to make sin and not Christ the decisive issue; it has psychologized the theological affirmation of original sin; and it has split man into "inner" and "outer" and confined God to the former segment.

Bonhoeffer's analysis of the modern Western world as "come of age" and of the nihilist man who is its microcosm represents the most provocative contribution to the Christian discussion of man in the modern world in the last twenty-five years. What is more, it offers to the secular dialogue on this question a Christian viewpoint which has been hitherto undreamed of by secularists, as the ferment which Bonhoeffer's "non-religious" interpretation has caused even in Marxist countries illustrates.[83] The striking thing about his remarks on the modern world is that in a way he "out-theologized" the theologians and "out-secularized" the secularists. Bonhoeffer meant to examine every issue biblically and theologically. In the *Ethics* and above all in the prison writings he turns the very ammunition of the Christian apologists—Scripture and doctrine—back against them, as he defends the secularity of the world on biblical and christological principles. At the same time, he challenges the right of the "existentialists" and (predominantly Freudian) "psychotherapists" to be the sole spokesmen for secularity. To Bonhoeffer the modern world, despite the horrors of two world wars, is *not* at bottom the alienated, depersonalized Joseph K. of Franz Kafka's *The Trial*. Nihilist man keenly experiences despair, meaninglessness, alienation, and depersonalization; he is gnawed at by guilt, suffering, and the knowledge that he must die. But according to Bonhoeffer he is too "outer-directed," too healthily absorbed in the life of the world around him, to be paralyzed and rendered helpless by these experiences. He regards them as the price we pay for being human, and gets on with the task at hand. Above all, when he experiences the painful limits of his existence, they do not drive him into the arms of "religion" in any form, "traditional" or "secular."

Agreement with Bonhoeffer's call for a "religionless Christianity" depends to a large degree upon acceptance of the validity of his highly positive analysis of the contemporary and future world as a world which has "come of age." Is "religion," i.e., piety and metaphysics, in fact a dying phenomenon? Can "men as they now are" no longer be "religious"? Has the world "learned to solve its problems without recourse to the 'working hypothesis' called 'God'?" Does the earth today live *etsi deus non daretur?* Is the man of the future the healthy-minded nihilist: the man of liberal culture and the ordinary person who "makes the best of it" and lives decently and even nobly without "religious" comfort? These are some of the basic questions to be dealt with in assessing Bonhoeffer's "Christianity without religion" project.

A final word on a world "come of age": While Bonhoeffer does not speak directly of a "religionless" world as part of God's purpose, it is clear that he sees it as such. The very notion of a "mature" world, evolving from infancy through adolescence to adulthood, seems to speak of divine purpose. Further evidence is seen in Bonhoeffer's remark that the "come-of-age" world is "nearer to God than the world before its coming of age." He sums up his attitude toward the place of a "religionless" world in the divine purpose with the following words:

God would have us know that we must live as men who manage our lives without him. The God who is with us is the God who forsakes us (Mark 15:34). *The God who lets us live in the world without the working hypothesis of God is the God before whom we stand continually.* Before God and with God we live without God.[84]

In this striking passage Bonhoeffer affirms vigorously that the world "come of age" is not a purely subjective reality constituted by those for whom, in Nietzsche's phrase, "God is dead." It is above all the work of God himself. The utter secularity of the modern world, its "religionlessness," is itself the result of the activity of the Lord of history, and in no sense "the great defection from God." It is a development which began with God's creation of a world entirely distinct from himself, received its meaning when God came among us simply as a man, and grew up under God into the implications of that meaning with the rise of the autonomy of human existence.

Chapter Two

The Personalist-Existentialist Revolution in Philosophy

Bonhoeffer spent his first year at university (1923-34) in Tübingen. There he was introduced to the personalist-existentialist revolution in philosophy and theology. Personalism,[1] also called dialogical philosophy or the philosophy of I and Thou, was one dimension of the larger movement generally called existentialism, which in its twentieth-century expressions centers in the phenomenological analysis of human existence and in ontologies based on such analysis.

The influence of personalist-existentialist thought on Dietrich Bonhoeffer's theology has not been given the attention it deserves by his interpreters. The philosophical framework of his theology is a personalism which understands reality in terms of the concrete social encounter of I and Thou, of self and neighbor. It is centrally important to an understanding of Bonhoeffer's theology as a whole, and his later theology in particular, to keep in mind the influence of the existentialist philosophical and theological revolution on his thought.

Karl Heim, the leading Christian exponent of dialogical philosophy and the phenomenological analysis of human existence, was one of Bonhoeffer's teachers in Tübingen. In the introductory notes to the English volume of selections from Bonhoeffer's collected miscellaneous writings, Edwin H. Robertson comments that Bonhoeffer listened to Heim "and for a time was influenced. But Heim did not please him, neither as a student, nor in later years." [2] It is true that both theologically and temperamentally Bonhoeffer found himself in disagreement

53

with Heim until the end of his life. Yet such a statement neglects the all-important fact that it was Heim who in large part introduced the young Bonhoeffer to the new world of philosophical and theological existentialism which was opening up. Heim symbolizes Bonhoeffer's lifelong indebtedness to personalism. Equally important, Heim focuses our attention on Bonhoeffer's early and positive involvement in philosophical issues. Although Bonhoeffer, under the influence of Karl Barth, came very soon to an exclusive preoccupation with questions of dogmatics and exegesis, neither he nor Barth himself ever really escaped the existentialist philosophical framework in which the Neo-Reformation theological revolution had begun.

Heim sought, as the subtitle of the first volume of his six-volume *Der Evangelische Glaube und das Denken der Gegenwart* indicates, to construct a "philosophical foundation for a Christian view of life" [3] on the basis of existentialist phenomenological analysis of reality in terms of the dimensions of "I," "Thou," and "It." His work paralleled, and was indebted in varying degrees to, that of such seminal thinkers as the Jewish philosopher Martin Buber, whose *I and Thou*[4] is the charter document of dialogical philosophy; Martin Heidegger, whose *Being and Time*[5] holds a similar place in the area of technical phenomenological ontology; and Eberhard Grisebach, who approached analysis and dialogue from a rigorously ethical, metaphysically skeptical point of view in his book *Gegenwart*.[6]

The Limitations of Philosophical Existentialism

During his early years as a theologian, Bonhoeffer engaged in vigorous dialogue with existentialist philosophy and theology, and in particular with Heim, Heidegger, and Grisebach. The fruits of this philosophical-theological conversation are embodied primarily in *Act and Being*. Bonhoeffer found much in the existentialists which was not only very congenial but downright vital to his own thought as a theologian. Along with most Neo-Reformation theologians, he recognized that personalist-existentialist thought had come remarkably close to the biblical outlook, with its emphases on such themes as the psychophysical concreteness, temporality, and finitude of human existence and the centrality of the I-Thou relationship.[7]

Yet Bonhoeffer was committed to the Barthian understanding of theological science. Theology is determined solely by its object, and that object is the extraordinary self-disclosure of God in Jesus Christ. From the standpoint of theology so conceived, even existentialist analysis and dialogical personalism, when undertaken on their own purely as philosophical enterprises, are trapped in the egocentricity of all philosophy.

For Bonhoeffer the key issue was the relationship between philosophy and theology. He took the position, following Barth, that the revelation of God in Jesus Christ, coming to man as it does wholly from without, necessarily shatters the entire structure of philosophy. Since philosophy never reckons seriously with revelation as an actuality in human existence, its boldest efforts to transcend the individual human ego fail. It succeeds only in erecting the rational ego into the final arbiter of reality and therefore into an idol. When philosophy attempts to define the limits, the boundaries (*Grenzen*), of the ego, it is always the rational ego itself which, more or less arbitrarily, sets those limits. Thus the human knower always remains sovereign and fails to transcend himself. This is true not only of idealism, which absorbs reality into the ego from the outset, but also of realism, which begins by recognizing the independence of the "world" but ends by letting the ego construct the very system which establishes its independence.

Theology, on the other hand, if it is to be true to its object and its method, must insist before philosophy that a wholly different intellectual starting point has been given to us *extra nos*. If the data of revelation are taken with full seriousness, then a basis has been laid for an entirely new approach to the key philosophical questions of epistemology and ontology.

The self-disclosure of God in Jesus Christ, in the thought of Barth and Bonhoeffer, establishes the true epistemological order of things. It is only revelation which lays down the real boundaries of human knowing, both on the I-Thou and the I-It levels. The Thou of God in the concrete person of Jesus Christ is the foundation for an authentic understanding of our knowledge of one another, because it alone insures that neither the I of the self nor the Thou of the neighbor becomes an absolute, as in purely immanental and self-contained attempts to establish the nature and limits of interpersonal knowledge. Likewise it is the disclosure of God the Creator in Christ which is the sole ground of true I-It knowledge. The boundaries between ego and entity vacillate confusedly on a purely philosophical basis, because reason, however chaste its claims before "objective reality," is inevitably and of course quite variously the arbiter of the boundaries. Only in the revelation of the Creator are we solidly guaranteed a "world," and with it a truly finite and unpretentious ego in concrete correlation with it.

Ontologically, revelation shatters all philosophical attempts to establish the nature of "being," of the "really real." With the event of Christ there is seen to be no "being-itself," no *ousia* or *essentia* which all entities, including God, share. There is only the being of God in the person of Jesus,[8] and the wholly derived being of all other entities. Above all, revelation discloses that this being of God is *person*. "Ultimate reality" is person—"I"—and through his word the divine person creates other persons—"Thous"—to share in his life.[9] Hence the true "ontology" is simply the obedient theological witness to the divine-human "personalism" attested in the Holy Scriptures, and not the vain search for independent definitions of "being" which never really escape the human ego.

Heidegger, whose analysis of being in terms of *Dasein* (the uniquely human mode of existence) takes philosophy a considerable distance in the right direction, nevertheless ends up, according to Bonhoeffer, perilously close to idealism: "Being is essentially *Dasein*, but *Dasein* is mind in its historicity."[10] "It is the basic thesis of this ontological metaphysics," Bonhoeffer states, "that *Dasein* in temporality already possesses, at all times, understanding of being, that it is (so to speak) 'open' to itself, and that *Dasein* in this way becomes insight into being."[11] Thus for Bonhoeffer, Heidegger fails to transcend the egocentricity of previous philosophy. Heidegger's version of the locked-up ego is reinforced by his interpretation of being in radically finite terms:

Heidegger's philosophy is a consciously atheistic philosophy of finitude. It relates everything to the self-incapsulation, in *Dasein*, of the finite. . . . In its essence the philosophical concept of finitude is that of incapsulated finitude. Here, then, no room has been left for the idea of revelation, and *with the knowledge in revelation that finiteness is creatureliness, i.e. is open to God, all concepts of being must be formed anew*. It follows that Heidegger's concept of being, despite its powerful expansion of philosophy through discovery of the Existential sphere, cannot be adapted for the purposes of theology.[12]

In his inaugural lecture at the University of Berlin, which formed the basis of *Act and Being*, Bonhoeffer stated his criticism of Heidegger even more explicitly by characterizing his thought in the following way:

Man is made master of the world in that he soars above himself to tragic solitude. Man alone remains, he understands himself from himself, being in the world has no significance for his self-understanding. . . . Precisely because man grasps his existence wholly in this world, he is eventually able to overpower the world.[13]

Bonhoeffer heartily welcomed the philosophical "discovery of the Existential sphere," but he rejected the continued insistence by the existentialists that the basis of ontology is finite self-understanding (*Selbstverständnis*).

Of all the I-Thou existentialist philosophers, Bonhoeffer found Eberhard Grisebach the most congenial because of his two basic presuppositions: (1) man can understand his existence only from outside himself and contingently; and (2) this understanding is ethical, not theoretical.

Grisebach . . . will no longer fix even the limits of man by thought, but declares the concrete "Thou" as the limit of man. Existence is in reality only in encounter with a Thou. Here is a real limit, no longer an imagined one, and therefore one which is no longer involved in reflection, here is the "present" [*die "Gegenwart"*]. Human existence is only in the present.[14]

Bonhoeffer acknowledges that "Grisebach is right, and comes a long way to meet Christian thought, when he says that man can be shown the way to reality only from outside." [15] But although "Grisebach's intentions certainly deserve serious consideration, . . . he is unable to carry them through with his own means." [16] Those means are purely philosophical, and therefore they are encased finally in egocentricity. Even a philosophy which begins, not from man's possibilities but from his limits, ends up by more or less arbitrarily drawing those limits itself. "But that means it is a limitation which man has always already gone beyond in principle, beyond which he must first have stood in order to draw it." [17] Thus Grisebach merely transfers the I's claim to absoluteness to the Thou:

If . . . the I is called into reality by the Thou, if the Thou shows it the way to its existence, this certainly appears to open to Thou and I a possibility of being and understanding themselves in reality, of reciprocally "placing" each other "into truth," without God and revelation. . . . It therefore follows that such a "critical" philosophy is useless as a theological hypothesis, *for the one hypothesis of theology is that revelation is man's only possibility of entering truth.*[18]

Grisebach, like Heidegger, is tried and found theologically wanting. For Bonhoeffer the same criticism applies to the thought of the Neo-Reformation theologian Friedrich Gogarten, who attempted to make Grisebach's insights into a basis for theological interpretation, as Bultmann did with Heidegger. By applying this philosophical *a priori* or "pre-understanding" to theological interpretation, Gogarten fell short of genuine theological reflection as Bonhoeffer conceived it.[19] Again we are led back to the insistence that only a truly *theological* existentialism, an understanding of existence based from beginning to end on revelation, enables thought to transcend its egocentricity.

Bonhoeffer's fundamental criticism of his teacher, Karl Heim, seems to have been that Heim never makes it clear whether he is doing philosophy or theology, nor what the relation is between the two disciplines. In a trenchant review of the first edition of Heim's book *Glaube und Denken* the young Bonhoeffer had this to say of Heim's distinctive contribution to philosophical and theological thought, the concept of dimensionality:

Heim already speaks of God in the framework of the ontology of dimension and to do just this is impossible. *The category of revelation cannot be spoken of apart from revelation in Christ.* . . . The ontological scheme of dimensions as a framework for revelation makes speaking of revelation, of God and of man within this scheme impossible. Because an uncritical ontology underlies the whole of Heim's sketch, an ontology which provides the basis for speaking about man and his relationship to God, what is said about man in revelation must come to grief.[20]

Here we have the persistent Barthian demand that in the light of revelation theology simply cannot begin from an independent philosophical scheme of reality.[21]

Significantly, Heim's rather thoroughgoing revision of *Glaube und Denken* for the third edition was partly in response to criticisms such as Bonhoeffer's. In the Notes at the end of the third edition, where Heim addresses himself to various criticisms of the first two editions, he states the following in the course of his reply to Bonhoeffer's review:

> In order to meet this objection, which arose from the impression conveyed by previous editions, I decided to build my argument in this edition without the help of ontological considerations. I wished to employ all the means at my disposal to encourage the reader to look on the actual facts, not through the spectacles of any philosophy, but with a desire to see, as it were for the first time, the significance of these relationships of "I," "Thou," and "It". . . . I therefore expunged from this edition all phrases which might distract the attention of the readers from the *phenomenological structure* of the "I"-"Thou"-"It" world as it lies open to our eyes. *I make only the modest demand that we should define the meaning of the words which we all constantly employ, and that we have a clear understanding of distinctions which are drawn by all of us.*[22]

Here we have the issue in a nutshell. Heim, like Bonhoeffer, believed that the knowledge of God is wholly the gift of faith in the biblically witnessed revelation. "When we ask about the Creator, we have in so doing passed beyond all the possibilities of human knowledge. The question could never even arise in our mind by our own evocation; it comes by the act of the Creator Himself." [23] Unlike Bonhoeffer, however, Heim believed that it was both possible and urgently desirable to engage in objective analysis of the phenomenological structures of human existence quite apart from revelation and theology. Heim devoted his life to trying to show that a dispassionate existentialist analysis of man and the world was the firmest sort of *praeparatio fidei et theologiae.* He believed that he had demonstrated satisfactorily that the phenomenological analysis of existence revealed man's inability to answer the fundamental question "Why?" (*die Warum-Frage*) in terms of his own or the world's existence.[24] When man is confronted with a clear delineation of the inexorably intramundane dimensions or "spaces" which make up his apprehension of the universe, he can at least know what the alternative answers to the great existential question are. All the answers apart from revelation resolve themselves into two alternatives: idolatry, the divinization of one aspect of the intramundane sphere; or pantheism, the divinization of the whole. Since both these answers are patently unsatisfactory, the way is at least cleared for

59

a consideration of revelation, which is the appearance within the intra-mundane of an unframable supramundane reality.

As a theologian, Heim was deeply and thoughtfully concerned about the unexamined manner in which his neo-orthodox contemporaries used spatial metaphors to talk about God's revelation of himself. Hence his insistence, in the passage quoted above, "that we should define the meaning of the words which we all constantly employ." Heim speaks of how "dialectical theology, in order to illustrate the divine Transcendence, has constantly made use of the spatial metaphor of a plane, which is intersected by a ray from another direction 'plumb down from above' [*senkrecht von oben*, one of Barth's characteristic expressions]." [25] At the heart of his own work is the attempt to clarify what we can possibly mean by the transcendence of God in a post-Copernican world dominated by science, and how divine transcendence differs from intramundane relations of transcendence. Heim tried to do just this with his phenomenological analysis of existence in terms of dimensions or spaces.

Clearly, Bonhoeffer and Heim were talking right past each other. Bonhoeffer refused to acknowledge the valid possibility of existentialist analysis apart from revelation. Heim believed such analysis both possible and necessary.[26]

Bonhoeffer's Theological Personalism

Bonhoeffer's own understanding of I-Thou existentiality is spelled out most fully in his doctoral dissertation, *The Communion of Saints*,[27] written at the time when he was quite consciously involved in the personalist-existentialist framework. The heart of the matter is chapter two, "The Christian Concept of the Person and the Concepts of Basic Social Relation." [28]

"For Christian philosophy," Bonhoeffer says, "the human person comes into being only in relation to the divine person which transcends it, opposing and subjugating it." The person is not the autonomous mind of idealism, but the concretely existing creature of God. The true limit of personhood is neither the self-limitation of the I nor the other-limitation of the Thou, but solely "the absolute distinction between God and man." [29]

Bonhoeffer thus begins by asserting that the boundary of human existence is solely the difference between Creator and creature. He interprets personhood so conceived in thoroughly *ethical* terms, which is a matter of central significance for his thought as a whole and for the "religionless" project in particular. "It is a Christian recognition," Bonhoeffer maintains, "that the person, as a conscious person, is created in the moment when a man is moved, when he is faced with responsibility, when he is passionately involved in a moral struggle, and confronted by a claim which overwhelms him." [30] The only claim which is ultimately decisive in the creation of the moral person is the claim of the *boundary*, i.e., the claim of God who encounters man and calls him into responsible existence.[31]

But now the reality of social existence must be dealt with, for the isolated individual is an idealist abstraction. The chief concern of ethical understanding is man's responsibility for other men: "The individual cannot be spoken of without the 'other' also being thought who has set the individual in the ethical sphere." Bonhoeffer now proceeds to elaborate his own analysis of the human I-Thou or social relationship. If we set aside his theological framework, his analysis of interpersonal existence follows that of Grisebach almost exactly. Thus, "the individual exists only through the 'other' [the concrete Thou]." [32] In the ethical sphere, "the Thou-form is fundamentally different from the I-form. . . . It is a barrier to the subject, it activates a will for which the other will comes into conflict, as an I for a Thou."

Of basic importance is Bonhoeffer's agreement with Grisebach, albeit on theological grounds, that

The transcendence of the Thou has nothing to do with epistemological transcendence. *This is a purely moral transcendence,* which is experienced only by the man who makes a decision, which can never be demonstrated to someone standing outside.[33]

It is impossible to overestimate the significance of the above passage. Here, in Bonhoeffer's earliest writing, we find a clear rejection of any sort of epistemological (and, by obvious implication, metaphysical) understanding of transcendence in favor of a thoroughly ethical interpretation. The interpretation of theological transcendence in ethical terms helps to explain why Bonhoeffer could never get excited about Heim's painstaking attempts to clarify the theological vocabulary of transcendence in phenomenological and metaphysical terms of dimensionality. To Bonhoeffer such efforts were beside the point: The biblical and theological understanding of transcendence has nothing to do with epistemological and metaphysical concepts of transcendence.

In his 1933 lectures on christology at the University of Berlin, Bonhoeffer approached the matter of theological *versus* epistemological-metaphysical transcendence from another interesting angle. Here he poses the issue as the difference between the questions "Who?" and "How?" "The question 'Who?'," he says, "is the question of transcendence. The question 'How?' is the question of immanence." [34] In other words, the problem of transcendence is properly a question of personal ethical encounter, not of epistemological or metaphysical explanation. "The question 'Who?' . . . is the question about the other man and his claim, about the other being, the other authority. It is the question about love for one's neighbour. The questions of transcendence and existence become a personal question."

For Bonhoeffer, of course, the question "Who?" is at bottom a theological question, and therefore not even the Thou of the neighbor in itself but the Thou of God confronting me in the ethical claim of the neighbor is authentic transcendence:

> The question "Who?" expresses the strangeness and otherness of the encounter and at the same time reveals itself as the question of the very existence of the enquirer himself. He enquires about the being which is alien to his own being, about the boundaries of his own existence. Transcendence puts his own being in question. With the answer that his Logos has found its limit man comes up against the boundaries of his existence. So the question of transcendence is the question of existence and the question of existence is the question of transcendence. In theological terms: man only knows who he is in the light of God.[35]

The question "How?" can never deal with existence but only with phenomena; it can never deal with transcendence but only with immanence. Hence Heim's efforts are misdirected.

Throughout his life Bonhoeffer understood Christian theology fundamentally in terms of ethical personalism. When we come to deal specifically with his "non-religious" concept of divine transcendence, we shall find nothing more than a radicalization of this early and life-long insight. Bonhoeffer's insistence that existential or ethical transcendence, i.e., the "over-against-ness" of a concrete Thou, is experienced by the person only insofar as he is a moral participant, and not "objectively," takes its place within the theological affirmation that the transcendence of God, the "over-against-ness" of the divine Thou, is experienced only in faith and not from outside. And, as we shall see, the transcendence of my neighbor's Thou is itself grounded in the basic transcendence of the divine Thou.

Because the divine Thou creates the human Thou, but for no other reason,

this human Thou is real, absolute and holy, like the divine Thou. . . . It is not his person as an I that is holy, but the Thou of God, the absolute will, here visible in the concrete Thou of social life. The other man is Thou only in so far as God makes him this. It is only in God that the claim of the other resides; but for this very reason it is the claim of the other.[36]

With this grounding of the analysis of interpersonal existence in the divine Thou of Christian revelation, we are able to view Bonhoeffer's personalism in its proper perspective. The Thou of the other man calls me into ethical existence as the boundary of my own existence. But the real limit is the divine Thou; the meaning of transcendence is the "over-against-ness" of God. But it is precisely in the concrete Thou of my neighbor that I encounter the divine limit; in responsible experience of my neighbor's "over-against-ness" I experience the transcendence of God. The idea that the concrete ethical encounter with my neighbor is at the same time the concrete encounter with God is absolutely central to Bonhoeffer's thought. It is impossible adequately to understand the "Christianity without religion" project of his last years apart from this theological personalism, in which God establishes I-Thou existence and discloses himself to me in the Thou of my neighbor in the living ethical situation.

Like Grisebach, Bonhoeffer considered the question whether my neighbor's Thou is also an I to be unanswerable on the ethical-existential plane:

I and Thou are not just interchangeable concepts, but they comprise specifically different contents of experience. . . . It is perfectly possible for another man to become for me an object for the contemplation of his life as an I; but I can confront him only as a Thou. . . . My I as a form of Thou can only be experienced by the other I; my I as a form of I can only be experienced by myself. Thus in the experience of a Thou the I-form of the other is never immediately given. . . . So the Thou-form is to be defined as the other who places me before a moral decision. . . . Whether the other is also an I in the sense of the I-Thou relation is something I can never discover.[37]

Bonhoeffer's criticism of Karl Heim's analysis of I-Thou reality focused on Heim's assumption that the I experiences the Thou at least in part analogously, as an "other I." [38]

In Bonhoeffer's thought, however, unlike Grisebach's, the ultimate explanation of the impenetrability of the Thou is theological; even more specifically, it is christological. Nowhere does Bonhoeffer spell this out more clearly than in *Life Together,* written in 1939. Christ is the Mediator between self and neighbor as well as between God and man: "Without Christ we . . . would not know our brother, nor could we come to him. The way is blocked by our own ego. Christ opened up the way to God and to our brother." [39] The objective reality of Jesus Christ establishes both the possibility and the limits of I-Thou knowledge. On the one hand, he alone breaks through the mutual impenetrability of I and Thou. On the other hand, since *he* is the foundation of I-Thou knowledge, he comes between I and Thou. As Mediator, Christ renders I-Thou knowledge mediate; he prevents it from being immediate. Authentic encounter is not the merging of I and Thou, nor is it absorption of one by the other; that is immediacy. It is rather a relationship of free persons which preserves and enhances the integrity of each, a relationship which is secured by the mediation of Christ between self and neighbor:

Because Christ stands between me and others, I dare not desire direct fellowship with them. . . . This means that I must release the other person from every attempt of mine to regulate, coerce, and dominate him with my love. The other person needs to retain his independence of me. . . . Because Christ has long since acted decisively for my brother, before I could begin to act, I must leave him his freedom to be Christ's; I must meet him only as the person that he already is in Christ's eyes. This is the meaning of the proposition that we can meet others only through the mediation of Christ.[40]

The contrast between mediate or christocentric I-Thou encounter and immediate or egocentric relationships is the contrast between the church and the world: "Within the spiritual community there is never, nor in any way, any 'immediate' relationship of one to another, whereas human community expresses a profound, elemental, human desire for community, for immediate contact with other human souls. . . . Such desire of the human soul seeks a complete fusion of I and Thou." [41] Bonhoeffer also expresses the contrast in terms of "spiritual love" and "human love." Human love

is directed to the other person for his own sake, spiritual love loves him for Christ's sake. Therefore, human love seeks direct contact with the other person; it loves him not as a free person but as one whom it binds to itself. It wants to gain, to capture by every means; it uses force. It desires to be irresistible, to rule. [42]

Spiritual love, on the other hand, "comes from Jesus Christ, it serves him alone; it knows that it has no immediate access to other persons." [43]

Spiritual love . . . will not seek to move others by all too personal, direct influence, by impure interference in the life of another. It will not take pleasure in pious, human fervour and excitement. It will rather meet the other person with the clear Word of God and be ready to leave him alone with this Word for a long time, willing to release him again in order that Christ may deal with him. It will respect the line that has been drawn between him and us by Christ, and it will find full fellowship with him in the Christ who alone binds us together. Thus this spiritual love will speak to Christ about a brother more than to a brother about Christ. [44]

Bonhoeffer summarizes the distinction by saying: "Human love produces human subjection, dependence, constraint; spiritual love creates *freedom* of the brethren under the Word." [45]

Bonhoeffer's underlining of the word *freedom* points to a fundamental element in his theological anthropology. He sought in his analysis of the radical "otherness" of the Thou to elucidate the concrete integrity and freedom of both self and neighbor which he believed a christological understanding of persons to demand. This conception of sociality was embodied in his lifelong insistence on respect for personal integrity and a healthy reserve between self and neighbor. In *Life Together* Bonhoeffer speaks of the basic importance to Christian life of allowing others to be free:

65

It is . . . the *freedom* of the other person . . . that is a burden to the Christian. The other's freedom collides with his own autonomy, yet he must recognize it. He could get rid of this burden by refusing the other person his freedom, by constraining him and thus doing violence to his personality, by stamping his own image upon him. But if he lets God create His image in him, he by this token gives him his freedom and himself bears the burden of this freedom of another creature of God.[46]

He goes on to speak of the sacredness of the integrity of the Thou:

The other person . . . has his own right, his own responsibility, and even his own duty, to defend himself against unauthorized interference. The other person has his own secret which dare not be invaded without great injury, and which he cannot surrender without destroying himself. It is not a secret dependent on knowledge or feeling, but rather the secret of his freedom, his salvation, his being.[47]

In the prison writings Bonhoeffer was to condemn with an almost uncharacteristic ferocity what he regarded as the vicious delight which "psychotherapists," "existentialists," and far too many Christian pastors take in ruthlessly laying bare people's inner lives. This attitude, which has pervaded Western society, represented to Bonhoeffer an unchristian and vulgar cheapening of human relationships in the name of "absolute honesty." It attempted to make the Thou "immediately" open to the I, whereas the Thou is an impenetrable limit to the I which must therefore be respected in its freedom and can be known as an I-form only mediately (in Christ) and not in direct encounter. "Unless we have the courage to fight for a revival of wholesome reserve between man and man," Bonhoeffer urged, "we shall perish in an anarchy of human values." [48] Bonhoeffer's analysis of human relationships in terms of healthy reserve plays a role both in his analysis of the modern secular world and in his many-faceted portrait of the mature or "religionless" Christian equipped to affirm and serve that world.

In the writings which make up Bonhoeffer's *Ethics*, dating from the last years of his life before he was imprisoned (1940-43) , he reaffirmed his early ethical-personalist interpretation of Christianity in a more explicitly christocentric manner than in *The Communion of Saints*, but in complete continuity with the argument which we find there. Arguing for a christological understanding of reality as a whole, Bonhoeffer states that "Life is not a thing, an entity or concept; it is a person, a particular and unique person, not in respect of what this person has in common with other persons, but in the I of this person; it is the I of Jesus." [49] Jesus Christ is the foundation and the meeting point of the fact that I encounter the divine Thou precisely and concretely in the Thou of my neighbor:

There is no relation to men without a relation to God, and no relation to God without a relation to men, and it is only our relation to Jesus Christ which provides the basis for our relation to men and to God. Jesus Christ is our life, and so now, from the standpoint of Jesus Christ, we may say that our fellow-man is our life and that God is our life.[50]

Commenting on the strict subordination of the "It" world to the "I-Thou" world because of the person of Christ, Bonhoeffer affirms that "the world of things attains to its full liberty and depth only when it is grasped in its original, essential and purposive relevance to the world of persons." [51] And in a footnote he reiterates the ontological groundwork of his thought, again with reference to Christ as the prototypical person, that "reality consists ultimately in the personal." [52]

Bonhoeffer's dialogical interpretation of reality, which found its focus and justification in the person of Jesus Christ, issued in two of the major themes of his thought. On the one hand it produced an intense lifelong preoccupation with the *church,* that I-Thou social reality in which Christ "exists as community," encountering me in a conscious way in the Thou of my fellow Christian.[53]

On the other hand, the encounter with the divine Thou concretely in the Thou of my neighbor was the existentialist-theological articulation of what might be called Bonhoeffer's *Christian humanism.* We have already touched on the deep respect he had for the freedom and integrity of the Thou, which led to a concern for a healthy reserve among people. His love for man as man, not in the abstract but as concrete persons, shines through all his writings. In *The Cost of Discipleship,* for example, published in 1937, Bonhoeffer said that "God will not be separated from our brother: he wants no honour for himself so long as our brother is dishonoured." [54] If rich theological humanism is important throughout his writings, it dominates the prison writings, where Bonhoeffer affirms with compassion and confidence the coming to maturity of mankind in the rise of modern secularity. Yet to the very end his humanism was a fully *Christian*

67

humanism. He firmly believed that only the revelation of God in Christ establishes true and complete appreciation of the dignity of man. In one of his prison letters to Eberhard Bethge, he affirmed the centrality of I-Thou existence while criticizing some of its pitfalls apart from a christological grounding.[55] In a very brief essay among the prison writings entitled "Contempt for Humanity?" Bonhoeffer set forth his fully Christian humanism succinctly:

> There is a very real danger of our drifting into an attitude of contempt for humanity. . . . We must learn to regard people less in the light of what they do or omit to do, and more in the light of what they suffer. The only profitable relationship to others—and especially to our weaker brethren—is one of love, and that means the will to hold fellowship with them. God himself did not despise humanity, but became man for men's sake.[56]

The last sentence reminds us that Bonhoeffer's humanism was rooted from beginning to end in the God-manhood of Jesus Christ.

I have dwelt at some length on the influence of personalist-existentialist thought on Bonhoeffer for two reasons. (1) As I pointed out at the beginning, it is an influence which has been strangely neglected by interpreters of Bonhoeffer, and therefore there was a purely substantive as well as an interpretative gap to be filled. (2) In the early involvement with existentialism the central themes of Bonhoeffer's theology and the fundamental matter of his theological method emerge quite distinctly. Crucial to the former is his ethical personalism, with its purely ethical-existential understanding of transcendence. As for the latter, we have seen in examining Bonhoeffer's critical relationship to philosophy his Barthian conception of theological method. The early dialogue between Bonhoeffer's "Barthian-theological" existentialism and the philosophically oriented existentialisms was absolutely formative. It was also symbolic of the fact that it is only the theology of Karl Barth which ranks as a more important influence on Bonhoeffer's thought.

Nietzsche

As an appendix to our discussion of existentialist influences on Bonhoeffer, we must look briefly at the impact of one of the "fathers" of existentialism, Friedrich Nietzsche. One of Bonhoeffer's intellectual pursuits during his student days was the "philosophies of life." *Lebensphilosophie* was very much in vogue among German young people of the first decades of the twentieth century.[57] The philosophies of life, above all that of Nietzsche, left a permanent imprint on Bonhoeffer's thought, primarily as an attitude toward the world rather than as a conceptual scheme.

Nietzsche's bold affirmation of the earth and its creatures made a vivid impression on Bonhoeffer's own attitude toward the world. In an address of January 25, 1929, entitled "What is a Christian Ethic?" Bonhoeffer reveals a profoundly perceptive appreciation of Nietzsche. Discussing the ethical freedom and spontaneity of the Christian, Bonhoeffer boldly compares the genuinely free Christian with Nietzsche's Superman:

> The Christian creates new tables [of the Law], a new Decalogue, as Nietzsche said of the Superman. Nietzsche's Superman is not really, as he supposed, the opposite of the Christian; without knowing it, Nietzsche has here introduced many traits of the Christian made free, as Paul and Luther describe him.[58]

Like the Superman, the truly liberated Christian is a man of strength who transvalues conventional values. The difference is that for the Christian, that which is "beyond good and evil" is the gospel of God in Jesus Christ which invades the human moral scene and turns upside down our notions of good and evil. Common to the Superman and the Christian, however, are freedom, strength, maturity, spontaneity, and life-affirmativeness—all made possible by a standing point which is independent and transcendent of the fearful, legalistic slavishness of moral custom.

Bonhoeffer refers to Nietzsche several times in the writings from his last years which comprise his *Ethics*. These references show that to the end of his life Bonhoeffer was in dialogue and debate with Nietzsche on the matter of ethics. It was Nietzsche who called the ethics of Christianity a "slave morality," and Bonhoeffer's own ethical writings can be seen as a creative interpretation of Christian ethics which attempts to refute that charge.[59] But, as we have seen in the early writing "What is a Christian Ethic?" Bonhoeffer does not merely refute Nietzsche's accusation. Even more importantly, he claims Nietzsche's powerful life affirmation for the Christian who has been liberated by the gospel of Christ.

Knowledge of good and evil belongs to man "in Adam":

In the knowledge of good and evil man does not understand himself in the reality of the destiny appointed in his origin, but rather in his own possibilities, his possibility of being good or evil. He knows himself now as something apart from God, outside God, and this means that he now knows only himself and no longer knows God at all. . . . The knowledge of good and evil is therefore separation from God.[60]

The man "in Christ," however, is rooted in the "trans-moral," which is union with God:

The new knowledge of the reconciliation which is accomplished in Jesus, the knowledge of the voiding of the disunion [with God], itself entirely voids man's own knowledge of his own goodness. The knowledge of Jesus is entirely transformed into action, without any reflection upon a man's self. . . . His deed has become entirely unquestioning; he is entirely devoted to his deed and filled with it; his deed is no longer one possibility among many, but the one thing, the important thing, the will of God. . . . Knowing of Jesus a man can no longer know of his own goodness, and knowing of his own goodness he can no longer know Jesus. . . . [Jesus' call is] the summons . . . to return to unity and the origin, to the new life which is in Jesus alone. It is the call of liberation, the call to simplicity and to conversion . . . .[61]

The mature Christian is the world's real Superman, the man who lives at unity with the origin of life and therefore with life itself, the strong man of action. As Bonhoeffer says in an essay of 1932 entitled "Thy Kingdom Come," Christ "does not lead man in a religious flight from this world to other worlds beyond; rather, he gives him back to the earth as its loyal son. Be not otherworldly, but be strong!" [62]

The classical life-affirmative symbol of the giant Antaeus, who drew strength from repeated contact with the earth, fascinated Bonhoeffer throughout his life. In the 1929 address "What is a Christian Ethic?" he recounted the Antaeus legend and "baptized" it for Christian ethics:

A glimpse of eternity is revealed only through the depths of our earth, only through the storms of a human conscience. The profound old saga tells of the giant Antaeus, who was stronger than any man on earth; no one could overcome him until once in a fight someone lifted him from the ground; then the giant lost all the strength which had flowed into him through his contact with the earth. The man who would leave the earth, who would depart from the present distress, loses the power which still holds him by eternal, mysterious forces. The earth remains our mother, just as God remains our Father, and our mother will only lay in the Father's arms him who remains true to her. That is the Christian's song of earth and her distress.[63]

The vigorous this-worldliness represented by the myth of Antaeus was to become a foundation stone in Bonhoeffer's vision of a "religionless Christianity." As Martin Marty has commented, "To Bonhoeffer, Antäus represented earthiness, concreteness, sanity, place, 'ground under the feet' in the Christian theological and ethical quest." [64] Bonhoeffer early and daringly also claimed Prometheus, usually a favorite myth of the humanist against the Christian myth of Adam's fall. The Christian, Bonhoeffer implies, is Prometheus: "It is the eternal right of Prometheus to love the earth . . . ; it is this right which allows him to draw near the Kingdom of God, in a way that the coward fleeing to worlds beyond cannot." [61]

In the active this-worldliness, the (to use a phrase of Albert Schweitzer) "life- and world-affirmation" of *Lebensphilosophie,* particularly that of Nietzsche, is to be found another clue to the "religionless" Bonhoeffer of 1940-45. The passionate assertion of the rights of earthly existence found in the philosophies of life reappears dramatically in Bonhoeffer's positive evaluation of modern secularity (his concept of a world "come of age") , and in his own portrait of the mature Christian of a secular world as a strong person who has been freed by a source "beyond good and evil" to live creatively and actively in and for the world.

Chapter Three
The Impact of Luther

Another formative influence in Bonhoeffer's theological development was his adherence to Lutheran Christianity. He was profoundly molded by the personality and the thought of Luther himself, as well as by the theological emphases and ethos of the Lutheran tradition. Bonhoeffer must always be seen within this context, for it gave to his "religionless Christianity" some of its most distinctive, not to say paradoxical and puzzling, characteristics. Many of the riddles and seeming antinomies in Bonhoeffer's prison writings can be resolved only if he is seen to the very end as a Lutheran churchman. In recent attempts to adapt the "religionless" Bonhoeffer to the liberal-empirical, free-church, nonliturgical tradition especially in American Christianity, there is a constant danger of obscuring the original Lutheran setting of "Christianity without religion," and therefore its full dialectical character.

Two men on the Berlin faculty who were attempting to bridge the gap between the prevailing liberalism and classical orthodoxy, Karl Holl and Reinhold Seeberg, were leaders of the Luther renaissance in the German church of Bonhoeffer's student days. Although Bonhoeffer soon came to criticize Holl's interpretation of Luther,[1] it was in his Luther seminar that he was introduced to and came to love the "rediscovered" Reformer.

Holl saw more deeply into Luther than the liberals did, but he failed to break out of the liberal concentration on Luther's religious subjectivity, to the neglect of his prior grasp of the objectivity of God in

revelation. Holl interpreted Luther's theology as "the religion of conscience" (*Gewissensreligion*), and neglected the highly objective, christocentric focus of Luther's thought.[2]

Bonhoeffer elected to do his work for the degree of licentiate of
theology under Reinhold Seeberg, Holl's partner in the Luther revival. Seeberg's influence on Bonhoeffer's work *The Communion of
Saints* was extensive, especially through his own books on systematic
theology[3] and the history of Christian doctrine.[4] Bonhoeffer and Seeberg were friends and corresponded with each other for a number of
years.[5]

By the time he wrote *Act and Being*, Bonhoeffer had become critical
of Seeberg's theology. Like Holl, Seeberg was a transitional figure between liberalism and the Neo-Reformation theology, and his basic
premises remained those of liberalism. He interpreted Luther in terms
of the primacy of the will: " 'Being in Christ' means the possession of
the new direction of will." "The new I is the new will, which God has
turned into the direction which points to him, and which, being now
in the right direction, does good of its own accord." [6] Bonhoeffer ad-
mired the simplicity and holism of Seeberg's interpretation, but found
it to be mired in the psychologism from which liberal theology was
unable to shake itself free:

> The concept of direction [of the will] does not guarantee the unity of
> the concept of the person. . . . Man must be conceived as a unity before we
> can set him over against the oneness of God. This unity, however, is some-
> thing which a psychological concept, as such, is unable to convey: even
> according to Luther, man is self-impenetrable in his psychology. . . . The
> unity of man, of human existence, is founded solely in the Word of God. . . .
> This is not an empirical datum, but is given to faith as revelation.[7]

Holl and Seeberg had uncovered more of the richness in Luther's
thought than the earlier liberals, but they had failed to uncover the
whole Luther of the Reformation, the Luther who from beginning to
end had his sights fixed firmly on the objective revelation of God in
his Word, Jesus Christ. All the psychological depth and introspection
in Luther is misunderstood if it is detached from its rooting in the
nonsubjective Word of God witnessed in the Scriptures. This was the
discovery of Barth, Bonhoeffer, and the other Neo-Reformation theologians. Only when Luther's grounding in that which was outside him-

self, the Word of God in Jesus Christ, was fully recognized and incorporated, could the Luther renaissance come to full fruition.

Christ and Conscience

A brief look at Luther's christocentric, *extra nos* orientation will show how he transcends the interpretations of Holl and Seeberg and provides a basis for the "theology of the Word" of Barth and Bonhoeffer. I have chosen two representative writings of Luther, *The Freedom of a Christian*[8] and his *Lectures on Romans*.[9] Luther's fundamental and revolutionary theme was the justification of sinful man by faith in the Word of God in Jesus Christ alone, apart from works. The liberal theologians, including Holl and Seeberg, could not fully grasp the highly objective, non-psychologistic character of this principle, because they were dominated by a theological method based on the religious consciousness and not on the biblical revelation which is the source and prior correlative of the religious consciousness. Luther clearly recognized the proper claims of subjectivity and religious experience, but always with reference and in subordination to the external Word of God: "A man must look into his own heart before everything else, and see how it may become godly. But the heart becomes devout and is saved, not by commandments or works, but by the word of God, that is, by His promise of grace, and by faith." [10] In the Introduction to his commentary on Romans, Luther drew an important lesson from the apostle Paul's order of dealing with things: "But do you follow the order of this epistle? Worry first about Christ and the Gospel, that you may recognize your sin and His grace; then fight your sin." [11]

Karl Holl almost entirely neglected Luther's christology. Bonhoeffer, however, realized that christology is the whole key to understanding Luther. Countless references out of Luther's works could be given to show his concentration on the biblical Christ, but the following methodological statement will put the matter in a formal theological context. Commenting on Romans 1:3, 4, Luther says: "The substance, or the object, or (as some say) the subject of the gospel is Jesus Christ, the Son of God." [12] In a passage which almost constitutes a direct reply to Holl's interpretation of Luther's thought as "the religion of conscience," the Reformer shows how the function of conscience is purely negative and is transcended by turning from conscience to Christ:

From our conscience we have surely only accusing thoughts, because before God our works are nothing (unless he himself works in us through his grace). . . . Wherefrom, then, shall we take the thought that excuses us? Only from Christ and in Christ. For when his own heart reproaches a Christian and accuses him by testifying against him that he has done evil, he presently turns away from it and turns to Christ and says: He made satisfaction, he is righteous, he is my defense, he died for me, he made righteousness to be mine, and made my sin his own. And if he made my sin his own, then I have it no longer, and I am free. And if he made his righteousness mine, then I am righteous in the same righteousness as he. But my sin cannot swallow him up but it is swallowed up in the infinite abyss of his righteousness, for he is God himself to whom be praise forever and ever.[13]

Bonhoeffer's analysis of conscience in his *Ethics* follows that of Luther in subordinating it to the revelation in Christ, over against the usual tendency to regard conscience as ultimate and positive. According to Bonhoeffer, "conscience is the sign of man's disunion with himself. . . . It presupposes disunion with God and with man and marks only the disunion with himself of the man who is already disunited from the origin." [14] The knowledge of good and evil is the result of man's fall from original unity with God, and "is therefore separation from God." Conscience, along with shame, is a product of the Fall; it depends upon the knowledge of good and evil. It is a mark of man's disunity, the peculiar sign of his disunity with himself.

Conscience imagines that it is positive and ultimate:

Conscience . . . derives the relation to God and to men from the relation of man to himself. Conscience pretends to be the voice of God and the standard for the relation to other men. It is therefore from his right relation to himself that man is to recover the right relation to God and to other men. This reversal is the claim of the man who has become like God in his knowledge of good and evil. Man has become the origin of good and evil. . . . In conscience man summons himself, who has become evil, back to his proper, better self, to good.[15]

These comments show that Bonhoeffer regarded conscience as rooted in subjectivity, in man's inner self. As long as one views conscience apart from revelation, the subjectivity of conscience is not a defect. As long as the inner man is seen, as in classical philosophical and religious thought, as an autonomous rational nature (*nous*) or as a part of the divine nature (a *logos spermatikos*), then it follows that man's conscience is an ultimate court of appeal—the voice of God.

But Bonhoeffer's point is that in the light of the self-disclosure of God in Christ man's conscience is by no means ultimate and positive. On a biblical-theological reading, man is fallen away from unity with God and therefore from unity with himself. Conscience is not the voice of unity with the divine ground or of rational autonomy, but rather the voice which reminds man of his disunity with God and his conflicts with himself. To be thrown back upon one's conscience is to be thrown back upon one's own subjectivity and therefore upon a desert of violently shifting sands. To have nothing but one's conscience is to be terribly alone:

> The man with a *conscience* fights a lonely battle against the overwhelming forces of inescapable situations which demand decisions. But he is torn apart by the extent of the conflicts in which he has to make his choice with no other aid or counsel than that which his own innermost conscience can furnish. . . . A man whose only support is his conscience can never understand that a bad conscience may be healthier and stronger than a conscience which is deceived.[16]

In a profound sense conscience deceives man, because it pretends to be the voice of God, the final arbiter, when it is really the mark of disunity and conflict. Bonhoeffer believed that far too many Protestant theologians had been taken in by the pretended ultimacy of conscience.

Like Luther, Bonhoeffer insisted that man's ethical existence must be grounded in the objective Word of God in Jesus Christ and not in his own subjectivity. Only the revelation of God can transcend conscience, and it must transcend conscience or man is left in his disintegration. As the discussion of Bonhoeffer's "baptism" of Nietzsche's Superman showed, the Christian, the one whose being is "in Christ," is "beyond conscience." His life is rooted, not in himself (i.e., not in conscience or in custom), but in the Word of God which is the true ontological reality and which comes to him *extra se*. The person who understands his being only in Christ "can no longer know of his own goodness."[17] He has been returned to his origin, to unity with God, in whom the knowledge of good and evil upon which conscience depends is transcended. The Christian is therefore the free man, liberated not only from the legalistic conformity which is the true "slave morality" but even from the tragic and lonely grandeur of conscience. No longer torn apart by the need to consider conscience his ultimate arbiter, the Christian is unshackled for radical, simple obedience to God in the world. Bonhoeffer's teaching on conscience follows directly in the footsteps of Luther, for whom justification solely by the gracious Word of God turned human existence on its head and transvalued man into freedom.

Simul justus et peccator: Dialectic of Radical Obedience

In his criticism of Seeberg's interpretation of Luther, which I cited above, Bonhoeffer points out that Luther recognized the opaqueness of the self in terms of psychological self-understanding. In his lectures on Romans, Luther addresses himself specifically to the idea that a person can be fully conscious of his will: "Who knows or can know, though he imagines that he means to do good and not evil, whether this is really so, since only God will judge this. . . . If some really imagine that they have such an attitude of mind, they make a dangerous presumption, in connection with which most are very cunningly deceived." [18] Seeberg wanted to say that the direction of the will (toward or against God) is for Luther the seat of the unity of the person before God. But according to Luther the unity of the self before God cannot be guaranteed psychologically, but only theologically. Our psychological existence, including our will, is too complex and elusive ever to provide firm ground on which to stand. The *cor curvum in se*—the old Adam—is too powerful even within the Christian for him to place his trust in the achievement of a "new direction of the will." In the light of the Word of God revealed in Christ, to speak of "being in Christ" in terms of the unity of the Christian's will is another example of reliance on works rather than on faith alone. The Christian understands himself only on the basis of God in his revelation, which comes to him from without. The only unshakeable unity he knows is not the vacillating "I-ness" of his own psychology, but his personal being as revealed in the biblical Word. As Barth and Bonhoeffer would put it: The only anthropology is "the-anthropology." Man is fully and properly understood only in the light of the self-disclosure of God.

It was by understanding the self theologically, from outside itself, that Luther developed his famous dialectic of the Christian before God:

We are sinners before ourselves and yet in the reckoning of God we are righteous through faith. . . .

[The Christian] is at the same time both a sinner and righteous (*simul peccator ac justus*), a sinner in fact but righteous by virtue of the reckoning and the certain promise of God that he will redeem him from sin in order, in the end, to make him perfectly whole in hope, while he is in fact a sinner, but he has already begun to be actually righteous, and he always seeks to become more so, always knowing himself to be unrighteous.[19]

"Therefore, I myself with the mind serve the law of God, but with the flesh, the law of sin." (Rom. 7:25.)

This is the most telling passage of all. Notice that one and the same man serves both the law of God and the law of sin, that he is righteous and at the same time he sins. He does not say: "My mind serves the law of God," nor "My flesh serves the law of sin," but he says, "I, this whole man, this person here, stand in this double servitude." He therefore gives thanks that he serves the law of God and he asks for mercy that he serves the law of sin. . . .

The saints in being righteous are at the same time sinners; they are righteous because they believe in Christ whose righteousness covers them and is imputed to them, but they are sinners because they do not fulfill the law and are not without sinful desires.[20]

Here is a subtler and more profoundly theological interpretation of the self than we find in the psychologism of the liberal interpretation of Luther. Man's unity is his forgiveness and "right-wising" by God through the death and resurrection of Christ. Man's conflicts result from the fact that on earth only the firstfruits of Christ's triumph are visible; the old Adam and the devil still war fiercely against Christ until the consummation.

To be sure, the highly dialectical character of Luther's interpretation of Paul, precisely because of its profundity and delicately balanced tension, lends itself to dangers and abuses. Bonhoeffer's best-known work, *The Cost of Discipleship*, is a vigorous attack on the abuse of Luther's *simul justus et peccator* by Lutheranism. The now-familiar phrase "cheap grace" is Bonhoeffer's characterization of what Lutheranism has tended to make of Luther's doctrine of the justification of sinful man:

Cheap grace means the justification of sin without the justification of the sinner. Grace alone does everything, they say, and so everything can remain as it was before. . . . The world goes on in the same old way, and we are still sinners "even in the best life" as Luther said.[21]

Since we are inevitably sinners, runs the undialectical argument of "cheap grace," let us not frustrate ourselves with the problems of obedience, ridden as it is with the ambiguities of all human works. Let us instead make our peace with the world and enjoy our justification before God. But

It is a fatal misunderstanding of Luther's action to suppose that his rediscovery of the gospel of pure grace offered a general dispensation from obedience to the command of Jesus, or that it was the great discovery of the Reformation that God's forgiving grace automatically conferred upon the world both righteousness and holiness. On the contrary, for Luther the Christian's worldly calling is sanctified only in so far as that calling registers the final, radical protest against the world. . . . It was not the justification of sin, but the justification of the sinner that drove Luther from the cloister back into the world.[22]

The true understanding of the *simul justus et peccator* dialectic is in terms of "costly grace," not "cheap grace." The justification of sinful man cost God the obedience, the suffering, and the death of his Son. The proclamation of justification is therefore the call to obedient, costly discipleship, not to the passive basking in the *doctrine* of justification, which is a cheap substitute. That is the difference, according to Bonhoeffer, between Luther and pseudo-Lutheranism. "The only man who has the right to say that he is justified by grace alone is the man who has left all to follow Christ." [23]

Hence Luther's dialectic of the justified sinner is not a panacea for comfortable quietism, but a call to bold action, a call to risk simple obedience. If God has boldly risked his Son to justify sinful man, is not the justified sinner the brave man who in gratitude for so great a gift takes the risk of concrete decision and action in the world? For Bonhoeffer, justification *is* concrete, costly obedience. Throughout his writings he urgently calls the church and the Christian to take the risk of decisive words and actions on behalf of God's world, instead of resting content with the usual vaguely general pronouncements and worldly inaction. In this he was following in the footsteps of the bold Reformer, Martin Luther.

In Bonhoeffer's ecumenical writings we see with special clarity his passion that the church risk speaking a concrete word to the world. His report on the Cambridge Conference of the World Alliance for Promoting International Friendship Through the Churches, which met in September of 1931, concludes with a question which is a lament and a challenge: "When will the time come that Christianity speaks the right word at the right time?" [24] But perhaps his most sustained plea for a concrete Christian message on specific issues was his address to the Youth Peace Conference of 1932, "A Theological Basis for the World Alliance." Here he laid down theological guidelines for the obedient proclamation of the divine commandments to the world:

The church must be able to say the word of God, the word of authority, here and now, in the most concrete way possible, out of knowledge of the situation; otherwise it says something else, a purely human word, a word of impotence. Therefore the church may not proclaim principles, which are always true, but only commandments, which are true today. For what is "always" true is precisely not true "today." God is "always" *God* to us "today." [25]

Bonhoeffer goes on to insist that "only as a concrete word to me is it the Word of God." [26] "A commandment must be concrete or it is not a commandment." Addressing himself specifically to the issue of war and peace, he maintains that the church "should be able to say concretely: 'Engage in this war' or 'Do not engage in this war.' " [27]

The key to Bonhoeffer's argument for a particular word of the church to worldly issues is Luther's central dialectic of the justified sinner. To Bonhoeffer it is precisely the forgiveness of our sins, the justification of sinners by the grace of God, which is the stimulus to confident proclamation of the will of God in explicit situations. By "daring to put the commandment definitely, exclusively and radically,"

the church will recognise that it is blaspheming the name of God, erring and sinning, but it may speak thus in faith in the promise of the forgiveness of sins which applies also to the church. *Thus the preaching of the commandment is grounded in the preaching of the forgiveness of sins.* The church cannot command without itself standing in faith in the forgiveness of sins and without indicating this in its preaching of the forgiveness of sins to all those whom it commands.[28]

Luther's *pecca fortiter*—"sin boldly, but rejoice and believe in Christ more boldly still"—finds expression in Bonhoeffer's unshakeable confidence in the concrete, obedient word spoken with boldness and penitence by those who know themselves to be forgiven sinners.

But not only must the church's *words* risk taking on specific, situational, contemporary form; even more important, its words must be accompanied by and inseparably joined with bold *actions*. In his actions as well as in his words, Bonhoeffer, like Luther, possessed the strength and decisiveness of the justified sinner. Bonhoeffer's bold anti-Nazi actions as a leader in the Confessing Church during the 1930's, including the supervision of a secret and illegal seminary of the Confessing Church at Finkenwalde, early won him the suspicion and later the hostility of the Third Reich. The most dramatic step taken by Bonhoeffer, however, was his participation, *as a matter of Christian vocation,* in the German Resistance, living for three years (1940-43) in constant danger and at the cost of a martyr's death. Bonhoeffer always reflected thoroughly and theologically on every issue before he decided and acted. But once he acted, he acted decisively and with the freedom and strength of one who in utter trust has placed his action unreservedly in the hands of the God who in the costly action of Jesus Christ has forgiven all his sins.[29]

Bonhoeffer's interpretation of Luther's famous dialectic must be seen as an important aspect of his "non-religious interpretation of biblical concepts." It is the distinctively Lutheran expression of the christocentric basis of Bonhoeffer's life affirmation. Bonhoeffer's portrait in the prison writings of the mature Christian of a world "come of age" is above all a portrait of the strong, free person rooted not in himself but in the forgiving love of God in Jesus Christ.

Perhaps the most important implication of Luther's *simul justus et peccator* for our study of Bonhoeffer, however, is its legitimation of the revolutionary theological reconstruction which we find in Bonhoeffer's prison writings. Contrary to some popular impressions, Bonhoeffer did not in any sense abandon the classical Christianity by which he had always lived during those last years. On the contrary, his "religionless Christianity" is the bold affirmation of one whose faith in the God who gives himself to us in Jesus Christ remains unshakeable. Bonhoeffer questioned many things in the prison writings, but he never doubted that the man Jesus is the meaning of the universe.[30]

It was precisely Bonhoeffer's confident trust in the Christ who has "right-wised" sinful man and who has the victory which enabled him to push forward with a radical interpretation of the gospel for modern secular man. Because he was rooted and grounded in the revelation of God in Christ and not in himself, Bonhoeffer was theologically as well as existentially freed for the important work of creative theological revision. "Religionless Christianity" is not the vision of a man whose grasp is slipping, but of one who grasps with all his being "the faith once delivered to the saints" and is thereby liberated and emboldened to participate creatively in the ongoing task of interpreting that faith to the world. Bonhoeffer pleaded in his last days for the church to "come out of its stagnation. We must move out again into the open air of intellectual discussion with the world, and risk saying controversial things, if we are to get down to the serious problems of life." [31] In his embryonic projection of a "Christianity without religion" for a world "come of age" he was doing just that, taking the risk with the strength and freedom of the forgiven sinner. "Religionless Christianity" is Bonhoeffer's final expression of Luther's *simul justus et peccator* dialectic.

Clearly, Bonhoeffer's interpretation of Luther on conscience and justification has fundamental implications for the working out of a Christian ethics. We shall examine Bonhoeffer's ethical reflections in Chapter Nine. Two central influences of Luther and the Lutheran tradition on Bonhoeffer's theology are his doctrines of Christ and the Church, which will be discussed separately and in some detail in Chapters Six and Seven because of their fundamental and overarching importance in his thought.

There are certainly other significant aspects of Luther's influence on Bonhoeffer which I have not selected because other interpreters have already ably discussed them. I have focused on two areas, the problem of conscience and the dialectic of justification, both because I believe them to be important to an understanding of Bonhoeffer's theology and because I have not seen them emphasized in quite the way I think they deserve to be emphasized. Regin Prenter's "Bonhoeffer and the Young Luther" is an excellent comparison of Luther and Bonhoeffer in terms of "the way they have correlated the theology of the cross with the theology of the Word." [32] Pertinent to our discussion of the dialectic of justification in Luther and Bonhoeffer is the following statement by Prenter:

> Every theology of the Word which does not require a theology of the cross as correlate is docetic. It transforms Christ, the content of the Word, into a principle of grace, and thus transforms faith into an intellectual acceptance of this principle. This is a *theologia verbi* as a *theologia gloriae*. Both the young Luther and Bonhoeffer combat such a theology of the Word with their *theologia crucis*. In the name of the authentic faith in the Word of the crucified one they must affirm that there is no faith . . . without obedient discipleship.

Prenter adds: "Only on this basis does it seem to me that we can fully understand those thoughts of the later Bonhoeffer on the non-religious interpretation of the gospel in a world come of age." [33]

John A. Phillips, in *Christ For Us in the Theology of Dietrich Bonhoeffer,* likewise has provided us with valuable material on the relationship of Bonhoeffer to Luther. He discusses Holl and Seeberg, the former especially with regard to his interpretation of Luther.[34] Of particular interest, however, is Phillips' treatment of the Lutheran character of Bonhoeffer's christology.[35] Perhaps Phillips' most singular contribution to the illumination of the Luther-Bonhoeffer relationship is his examination of the dialectic of justification and obedient discipleship under the heading of Bonhoeffer's use of Luther's "tropological (i.e., christological-devotional) interpretation" of Scripture.[36]

Finally I must mention William Kuhns, *In Pursuit of Dietrich Bonhoeffer,* within the context of our examination of the impact of Luther. Kuhns's exposition has the merit of weaving in Luther and Lutheran themes throughout the whole of his study, providing brief accounts of Luther's position on various issues relevant to Bonhoeffer's outlook on those issues. Kuhns emphasizes the ways in which Bonhoeffer built squarely upon Luther but went beyond Luther's own answers in the light of dramatically changed historical circumstances: He speaks of "the dependence upon, yet the reach beyond Luther's theology." [37]

Bonhoeffer's Lutheran Precursor: Sören Kierkegaard

Out of the Lutheran tradition in the nineteenth century came the brilliant Dane whose fresh insights into the meaning of the biblical faith and the Reformation became the major source of twentieth-century Neo-Reformation theology. Some features of Kierkegaard's thought peculiarly reflect and creatively carry forward the heritage of Luther and Lutheranism. Very strikingly, certain of these Kierke-gaardian emphases within Lutheranism reappear in a singular manner in Bonhoeffer's vigorous attempts, a century later, also to explore new and neglected insights in the theology and tradition of the German Reformer.

In comparing the Lutheranism of Kierkegaard and Bonhoeffer, we are on firmer ground to speak of *parallels* rather than of direct influence.[38] But the parallels are significant, and in their light those important differences which remain between the two men are not so pronounced as even Bonhoeffer thought they were.

The most important theme which Kierkegaard and Bonhoeffer share is their unusual emphasis upon *active obedience* within the framefork of the central Lutheran doctrine of justification by faith alone. We have seen how for Bonhoeffer it is precisely Luther's dialectical understanding of man before God as *simul justus et peccator* which demands creative action rather than quietistic acceptance. Just as Bonhoeffer in *The Cost of Discipleship, Ethics,* and the prison writings sought to call the German Protestantism of the 1930's and '40's away from a one-sided, passive interpretation of *sola gratia,* so Kierkegaard in writings such as *Works of Love, Training in Christianity,* and *The Attack upon "Christendom"* had done on behalf of his fellow Danish Lutherans a century before. Although his approach was from Bonhoeffer's point of view too individualistic and (increasingly in his later years) ascetical, Kierkegaard stands out sharply from the prevailing Lutheranism of his day in his activistic portrayal of faith as the highest of human passions and in his radical insistence upon taking the concrete demands of Christ in the Gospels with utter seriousness. In his writings Kierkegaard relentlessly indicted the easy identification of Christianity with right belief and bourgeois civility; in his life, he set himself the arduous task of striving to conform himself to Christ in deed as well as in word.

Both Kierkegaard and Bonhoeffer were deeply perceptive Lutheran thinkers who saw keenly, each in his own age, how the Lutheran tradition had made Luther's insights concerning justification by faith into a sterile concept of correct doctrine on the one hand, and a rationalization of "cheap grace" on the other. If the dominant problem of the sixteenth century was righteousness by works, that of the nineteenth and twentieth centuries was a corruption of faith by which in Kierkegaard's words, "all are Christians" in an easygoing manner. Each man sought, in his life as well as in his thought, to redress the balance by reclaiming what he considered to be neglected implications of Luther's interpretation of the gospel.[39] We have seen how intensely Bonhoeffer held together both sides of the New Testament dialectic of faith/obedience. Kierkegaard likewise set it forth again and again with vigor, perhaps never more passionately than in *The Attack upon "Christendom"*:

> When of the individual Christ requires faith, then (and with this we have a sharper definition of what He understands by faith), then by reason of the situation this is not feasible without coming into a relationship with the surrounding world which perhaps involves mortal danger.[40]

For Kierkegaard, faith is passionate personal appropriation of the Person of Christ in his true objectivity, which is identical with striving throughout one's life to conform oneself wholly and obediently to his demands, always recognizing in "fear and trembling" that all is of grace and that one stands before God only as a forgiven sinner. It is not the "cheap grace" of mere adherence to correct doctrine and the comfortable adjustment of Christ to one's own pattern of living. Such a view of the relationship between faith and obedience was reaffirmed in a remarkably parallel way in the writings of Bonhoeffer.

Another fascinating parallel between Kierkegaard and Bonhoeffer is the *Menschlichkeit* which each shared with Luther in a way which was uniquely his own. There is a remarkable *humanism,* a rich love of things human for their own sake, in Kierkegaard's outlook which has been unfortunately obscured in Kierkegaard interpretation in favor of the image of the "melancholy Dane" who denied himself his only true earthly love, countered the wisdom of the world with the foolishness of Christ in an extreme fashion, and dwelt on suffering and renunciation as marks of the serious Christian. Yet all this must be seen as one-half of Kierkegaard's intense version of the dialectic of Christian existence. His "hard sayings" about Jesus' demands that the Christian hate himself and his family and live a life of cross-bearing and sacrifice are often misunderstood because they are lifted out of this rigorously dialectical context.[41] For Kierkegaard, as for Bonhoffer, the two sides, faith and worldliness, were never to be divorced from each other. Although neither in his writings nor in his life was Kierkegaard able to hold together this dialectic as successfully as Bonhoeffer, the theme of their interplay resounds throughout his writings and is by no means absent from his life.[42] Here is a typical statement:

> Everyone for himself, in quiet inwardness before God, shall humble himself before what it means in the strictest sense to be a Christian, admit candidly before God how it stands with him, so that he might yet accept the grace which is offered to everyone who is imperfect, that is, to everyone. And then no further; then for the rest let him attend to his work, be glad in it, love his wife, be glad in her, bring up his children with joyfulness, love his fellow men, rejoice in life. If anything further is required of him, God will surely let him understand, and in such case will also help him further.[43]

Kierkegaard's provocative dwelling on the very hardest sayings of Jesus about self-hatred and self-sacrifice must be seen as the radical "break with immediacies" which characterizes the Christian—a break which is not essentially ascetical but dialectical. With this basic approach Bonhoeffer fully agreed. Perhaps the best description is still the "knight of faith" in *Fear and Trembling*, the person who is willing to give up the dearest earthly things in obedience to God, and precisely in so doing rejoices in and affirms the earth and human relationships more passionately than ever before.[44] For Kierkegaard as for Bonhoeffer, the Christian, in the words of the apostle Paul, "has nothing and yet possesses all things." He puts himself at God's disposal, to use Bonhoeffer's terms, in both suffering and blessing.[45]

Kierkegaard's humanism appears in abundance throughout his writings. In terms of his famous categories or "stages on life's way," the aesthetic, the ethical, and the religious, he explicitly affirmed that the person who truly moves out of the purely aesthetic into the ethical-religious in no sense turns his back on or denies the aesthetic but rather enriches it by appreciating it from a fuller perspective. As one who himself participated thoroughly in "aesthetic existence" from its coarsest to its most refined, its most cynical to its sublimest aspects, Kierkegaard, like Bonhoeffer, remained to the end of his days an intense appreciator of the sensual and sensuous life of man and of the beauty which man has created in the arts. Kierkegaard loved the pagan Socrates second only to Christ, looking upon him as the noblest and wisest of human beings. He extolled the purely human achievements of the ancient Greeks in knowledge, ethics, art, and politics, and often contrasted his own so-called "Christian" era very unfavorably. Kierkegaard often described himself as a "poet," who among other things sang the praises of the heroes, the best, of mankind. One of his sharpest criticisms of his own age was that it lacked passion; like Bonhoeffer, Kierkegaard much preferred even diabolical zest and intensity to what he called "shopkeeping souls." Kierkegaard, who regarded Christian faith as the highest, most intense of all human passions, would have agreed wholeheartedly with Bonhoeffer's criticism of those who think that Christianity means "the restraint of passion." [46] Kierkegaard's profoundest analogies in his writings are taken from romantic and conjugal love, which he regarded as the deepest of human relationships and the most inexhaustible parables of the relationship between God and man.

Kierkegaard's individualism, which Bonhoeffer along with many others finds too extreme, nevertheless produced certain insights into interpersonal relationships which show up as significant features of Bonhoeffer's outlook. Kierkegaard possessed a highly sensitive respect for the freedom and inviolability of other persons which was also very characteristic of Bonhoeffer. Bonhoeffer's accent on the importance of "healthy reserve" between persons and his distaste for prying about in people's personal lives took the form in Kierkegaard's writings of an awed respect for *silence:*

> The fact that men through rumor, through village gossip, are accustomed inquisitively, frivolously, enviously, maliciously perhaps, to learn of their neighbor's faults—that debases men. It would certainly be desirable if men once more learned how to be silent.[47]

This side of Kierkegaard's *Menschlichkeit* also appears in his affirmative recognition of the fundamental importance of healthy self-respect in Christian love, a theme which Bonhoeffer explicitly took up in his own concept of "selfless self-love." Kierkegaard's remarks in *Works of Love* about "selfless self-love" afford an excellent example of the dialectical character of his other statements about self-renunciation and sacrifice: "This word ['Thou shalt love thy neighbor as thyself'] . . . does not wish to teach a man that he ought not to love himself but, on the contrary, simply wishes to teach him the proper kind of self-love." [48]

In the themes of faith as active obedience and rich humanism Kierkegaard and Bonhoeffer share to a striking degree (more than Bonhoeffer himself realized) as theologians who recovered and carried forward neglected treasures in Luther and the Lutheran tradition.

Chapter Four

Karl Barth and the Nature of Theology

The major theological influence on Bonhoeffer was Karl Barth. Bonhoeffer was a theological student during the period when Barth was shaking continental theology to its foundations, and he remained a lifelong friend of Barth's. Although Bonhoeffer very early became keenly aware of what he considered to be inadequacies in Barth's theology,[1] he nevertheless remained dominated by Barth's understanding of the nature and method of theology. Bonhoeffer's notion of a "religionless Christianity" would never have occurred to him in the form it did if it had not been for his thorough grounding in Barth and the modern interpretation of Reformation theology in Europe. His experience of utter secularity would not of itself have produced his distinctive vision of a "Christianity without religion."

Barth and Bonhoeffer

Bonhoeffer's only regret about his otherwise superlative formal theological education was that he had never studied under Karl Barth, although he had been propounding Barth's theology almost from the beginning. During the summer between his return from a year in America as Sloane Fellow at Union Theological Seminary in New York (1930-31) and his assumption of duties as a lecturer in systematic theology at the University of Berlin, Bonhoeffer spent a short time in Bonn to hear Barth for the first time. In a letter to his friend Erwin Sutz, written from Bonn on July 24, 1931, Bonhoeffer remarked, "I don't think that I have ever regretted anything that I have failed to do in my theological past as much as the fact that I did not come here earlier." [2]

Bonhoeffer made up for the lack by reading and above all by personal friendship with Barth, a friendship which lasted to the end of Bonhoeffer's life. In his introductory notes to the first section of Bonhoeffer's miscellaneous writings, Edwin H. Robertson significantly observes that "none of Barth's actual students absorbed more of his teaching" [3] than Bonhoeffer. To this statement I would add that neither did any of Barth's actual students develop his theological insights more creatively than Bonhoeffer. Bonhoeffer's profound indebtedness to Barth and his revolutionary development of Barth's themes lie at the heart of the "religionless Christianity" project.

Bonhoffer had been reading and expounding Barth's theology for several years when he first met him in 1931. His first impression of Barth as a person has been that of countless theological students since that time who have studied under Barth:

It is important and surprising in the best way to see how Barth stands over and beyond his books. There is with him an openness, a readiness for any objection which should hit the mark, and along with this such concentration and impetuous insistence on the point, whether it is made arrogantly or modestly, dogmatically or completely uncertainly, and not only when it serves his own theology. . . . I have been impressed even more by discussions with him than by his writings and his lectures. For he is really all there. I have never seen anything like it before and wouldn't have believed it possible.[4]

The first exchange of letters between Bonhoeffer and Barth took place in 1932-33. Bonhoeffer's deep admiration for Barth, and particularly for the rightness of his approach to theology, is apparent:

I feel with you, it is hard to say why, in a strange way quite certain that the way in which you see things is somehow right. When I am talking with you, I am brought right up against the thing itself, whereas before I was only continually circling round it in the distance, and that is for me a quite unmistakable sign that here I've somehow got to the point.[5]

Significantly, Bonhoeffer apologizes to Barth for burdening him with "my perhaps too obstinate and—as you once said—'godless' questions." This statement symbolizes two aspects of Bonhoeffer's theological relationship to Barth. In the first place, the younger man was continually *questioning* Barth's theology, and he continued to question it with increasing boldness until the end of his life. Bonhoeffer was too independent a thinker ever to be slavish and purely imitative in his use of Barth's thought. In the second place, Barth, perhaps half jestingly but pointedly, described Bonhoeffer's questions as "godless." It is difficult to imagine what the questions were or why Barth called them "godless"; but his choice of adjective was prophetically pertinent in the light of Bonhoeffer's prison writings.

Of course Barth, the great critic of religiosity, did not use the word "godless" to mean "irreligious" or "impious"; rather, he meant "unbelieving" or "secular." Because all reality is ontologically constituted by the Incarnation, it is impossible, from a fully Christian theological perspective, to recognize as ultimately significant questions which assume that one can stand outside the revelation in Christ. Such questions assume that there are "religious" and "profane," "sacred" and "secular" spheres of reality side by side, whereas there is only one reality, the reconciliation of all being in Christ.

Barth has always insisted that since the Christian believer is the per se godless and unbelieving person to whom the impossible (faith) has happened, unbelief ("godlessness") has already found a proper hearing in the self-understanding of faith, and therefore cannot be taken seriously in itself.[6] To treat godlessness as ultimately serious is to act as if Christ has not come and objectively overcome unbelief on behalf of all men. When he understands existence in terms of the revelation in Jesus Christ, the Christian knows himself to be a godless person like everyone else. But he also knows that Christ has judged, forgiven, and triumphed over the unbelief of all men, although in the mystery of his grace he has opened the eyes only of some to behold in faith what is true for all. Hence god-lessness, the attempt to exist without God, is a "possible impossibility," to use a Barthian-type paradox. People imagine that to be without God is a genuine possibility; but if revelation is an actuality, then godlessness per se is an impossibility, since it has already been objectively "placed" within the reconciliation of all men in Christ. Faith, on the other hand, is an "impossible possibility." It is impossible that godless man can believe, and yet by the miracle of the Holy Spirit some persons do believe.

Bonhoeffer may have been raising "possible but impossible" questions which assumed that one could stand outside the reality of revelation and take unbelief seriously. If such is the case, we have evidence here that even the early Bonhoeffer was compelled to ask the questions which secular man asks about Christianity, and not only those which are demanded by obedient theological exegesis within the church. He did not fail, in the final analysis, to see the dangers implicit in Barth's revelational umbrella. Bonhoeffer, like many others then and since, came to believe that the question of *communicating* the gospel to the world was not to be solved so handily. By understanding the working of God's grace so largely on the divine and miraculous side, Barth tended, in his *Church Dogmatics,* to play down the responsibility of the church to interpret its message to the world. Hence his theology has a markedly intramural, ecclesiastical outlook, in which the world's questions are already assumed to have been dealt with satisfactorily within the church's own confession.

One of the most striking features of Bonhoeffer's creative advance on Barth is the fact that beginning exactly where Barth began, with the understanding of all reality solely in terms of revelation, he saw the urgent necessity of interpreting that vision of reality in radically contemporary terms—something which Barth never felt to be either urgent or necessary. "Godless" questions plagued Bonhoeffer increasingly toward the end of his life, because, turning Barth upside down, as it were, he believed that the reconciliation of all men in Christ demanded precisely that the "godless" world, the secular world "come of age," be taken more seriously than ever before.

The truly close personal relationship between Bonhoeffer and Barth comes to light dramatically in their correspondence shortly after Bonhoeffer had gone to Britain to be pastor of a German-speaking congregation in London for a year. It was 1933, and the political situation in Germany had become ominous. Both Bonhoeffer and Barth had seen the handwriting on the wall almost from the first and were extremely anxious for the fate of church and country. Bonhoeffer did not ask Barth's advice before he went to London, because he knew that Barth would urge him in the strongest possible terms not to leave the church in Germany in its time of crisis. The young pastor waited until he arrived in London before he wrote. His penitence over deliberately failing to consult Barth reveals how deeply attached

Bonhoeffer was to the older man, and how strongly he valued his counsel:

I knew that I would have to do what you told me and I wanted to remain free. . . . I know now that that was wrong, and that I must ask you to forgive me. For I have now made up my mind "freely" without being able to be free in respect of you.[7]

Barth's reply was as Bonhoeffer had expected: He chastised him rather vigorously for "abandoning his post." Yet the very frankness and ferocity of Barth's letter reveal how deeply the older man cared for his young friend: "If I were not so attached to you, I would not let fly at you in this way." [8] The evangelically persuasive fervor of Barth's reply also indicates the high regard in which he held Bonhoeffer as a Christian theologian and church leader: "You are a German, . . . the house of your church is on fire, . . . you must return to your post by the next ship." [9] Barth's esteem for Bonhoeffer's ability was to grow with the years.[10]

Bonhoeffer did not return to Germany immediately as Barth had urged. He worked in London for a year. Characteristically, however, he spent the year in Britain working tirelessly to publicize and gain support for the plight of the church in Germany. He became a friend of the distinguished ecumenical leader, the Right Reverend G. K. A. Bell, Bishop of Chichester, and the two men did all in their power to inspire informed ecumenical concern and action on behalf of the beleaguered Confessing Church.[11]

In dealing with Barth's theological influence on Bonhoeffer, we must keep in mind two things. First, the writings which helped mold Bonhoeffer's own outlook are those which Barth produced before about 1935. This means that Bonhoeffer was familiar with Barth's explicitly dogmatic work only in its formative stages (ca. 1924-35). Bonhoeffer read enthusiastically Barth's book on Anselm, which Barth himself regarded as the turning point in his transition from "dialectical" to "dogmatic" theology.[12] But of the definitive *Church Dogmatics* Bonhoeffer had read only the first volume (*Prolegomena*) and perhaps the second volume (*The Doctrine of God*) by the end of his life.[13] It is clear from Bonhoeffer's early writings, however, that he had a firm grasp of the fundamental theological con-

ception and methodology which have undergirded Barth's whole dogmatic enterprise, and claimed them formally as his own.[14]

It is no less clear, however—and this is the second point which needs
to be made—that from beginning to end Bonhoeffer was a quite independent theologian who even as a very young man freely criticized the material developments within Barth's theology and offered
a distinctive alternative of his own.[15] Bonhoeffer's originality is
as marked as is his indebtedness to Barth. He took over Barth's
understanding of the nature and method of theology, but he developed
it in his own way, attempting to correct Barth on the basis of the
latter's own method.[16]

Bonhoeffer, then, must be seen as a "Barthian," if by that we mean
simply that he was directly indebted to Barth for his understanding
of theology and its method, a crucially important form of indebtedness
indeed. He is not a "Barthian," if by that is meant a slavish imitator
of the matter or content of Barth's theology. In tracing the background
and development of the themes in Bonhoeffer's theology which culminated in the "Christianity without religion" project, we must bear
in mind both his deep indebtedness to and his independence of
Barth.

Bonhoeffer's independence of Barth can be seen biographically.
Their paths always seemed to cross going in opposite directions.[17]
The early Barth was the "worldly" theologian of *The Epistle to the
Romans,* while the young Bonhoeffer of *The Communion of Saints*
and *Act and Being* was very "churchly." Barth began with preaching
and biblical exegesis and moved into dogmatics; Bonhoeffer began
with a predominant interest in dogmatics and moved into ethics,
exegesis, and sermon. Barth started with the general problem of
revelation and moved toward christology and ecclesiology; Bonhoeffer
started with an ecclesiological approach to christology and came to
a "secular" interpretation of revelation.

Vocationally the beginnings and endings of the two men were different, and this also contributed to their exchange of positions on
the matter of church and world. Barth was a pastor who became a
theologian; Bonhoeffer, a theologian who became a pastor. Barth
tended to move from the role of participant to that of spectator; Bonhoeffer's life took the opposite direction. Hence Barth began as the
prophet of judgment on religion and became preoccupied with the

church; Bonhoeffer began with an intense interest in the church and ended with a radical concern for the world.[18]

Theological Presuppositions and Method

The focus of Barth's basic impact on Bonhoeffer's thought, as I have indicated already, is his conception of the nature and method of theology. There are three divisions of theology, according to Barth, of which dogmatic theology forms the center:

> We might quite justifiably speak of theology as such and as a whole, that is, of the unity of biblical, dogmatic and practical theology. And in this unity there is certainly no question of precedence. Yet there is in it, . . . and not as a sum of the whole, a concrete centre which is constituted by dogmatics. In biblical theology it is a question of the foundation, in practical theology a question of the form, but in dogmatic theology—in the transition from the one to the other—a question of the content of Church preaching, its agreement with the revelation attested in Scripture.[19]

Thus dogmatics is theology's "midway position between the Bible and the Church." [20]

Barth defines dogmatics as follows: "Dogmatics is the self-test to which the Christian Church puts herself in respect of the *content* of her peculiar language about God. Our object, the *proper* content of this language, we call 'dogma.' " [21] Dogma is "the agreement of Church proclamation with the revelation attested in Holy Scripture." [22] The aim of dogmatic theology, then, is constantly to test the present-day language of the church by the source, norm, and object of all the church's language, the revelation of God to which the Bible witnesses.

What are this source, norm, and object by which everything the church says and does is to be measured? "The *criterion* of Christian language," says Barth, "in past and future as well as at the present time, is . . . the *essence of the Church,* which is *Jesus Christ, God* in His gracious approach to man in revelation and reconciliation." [23] The all-controlling object of dogmatic reflection is simply and totally the man whom the Scriptures declare to be the Word of God made flesh. Hence dogmatics may quite accurately be said to be *christology:*

> In the account which Church proclamation and dogmatics have to give of the work and activity of God their business is wholly with the work and

95

activity of God in His Son Jesus Christ. It is in Him and Him alone that the Father is revealed. It is He and He alone whom the Holy Spirit reveals. Therefore dogmatics must actually be Christology and only Christology.[24]

As a reflective enterprise with a specific task and object, dogmatic theology takes its place as a distinctive human intellectual discipline. It is, in fact, a *science:*

If theology lets itself be called and calls itself a "science," it thereby declares that—1. Like all other so-called sciences, it is a human effort after a definite object of knowledge. 2. Like all other sciences, it follows a definite, self-consistent path of knowledge. 3. Like all other sciences, it is in a position of being accountable for this path to itself and to every one—every one who is capable of effort after this object and therefore of following this path.[25]

The fact that it deals with the very Word of God to man does not make dogmatics "divine" in contrast to all other sciences conceived as merely "human" or "mundane." Theology is simply and modestly a human inquiry, alongside but not above all other human inquiries. It is peculiarly *theological* science because of the object of its inquiry: Jesus Christ as the self-disclosure of God to man. Like any science worth its salt, dogmatics strives to let its inquiry be wholly determined by its object. Dogmatic method is not *a priori* but *a posteriori*: It arises out of this total determination by its object.

At the same time, the fact of its determination by the act of God in Jesus Christ as attested by the Scriptures means that dogmatic science is peculiarly a function of the *church:* "The Church tests herself by essaying dogmatics. To the *Church* is given the promise of the criterion for Christian faith, namely, the revelation of God. . . . Dogmatics is impossible outside the Church." [26] Hence the title of Barth's great theological effort, *Church Dogmatics*. Unlike Schleiermacher, Barth understands dogmatics to be, not a confessional or denominational, but an ecumenical task: "Where dogmatics exists at all, it exists only with the will to be a Church dogmatics, a dogmatics of the ecumenical Church." [27] As a function of the church, dogmatics is furthermore intrinsically a function of *faith:* "Dogmatics is only possible as an act of faith, in the determination of human action by listening, and as obedience towards Jesus Christ." [28]

As we have seen, the task of dogmatics is not simply to report what the church believes (Schleiermacher), but to hold up its belief to the norm of the revelation of God *attested in Scripture*. Dogmatics, with its "midway position between the Bible and the Church," has what Barth calls a "biblical attitude" as well as a "church attitude," and its biblical outlook is absolutely fundamental. Explaining the meaning of a "prolegomena" to dogmatics (Vol. I of the *Church Dogmatics,* of course, comprises Barth's prolegomena) as "an account of the path to knowledge to be trodden by dogmatics," [29] Barth states:

Thus understood the theme of the prolegomena to dogmatics is clearly in essentials none other than that which Old-Protestant theology, in its defence against Catholicism and also, soon after, against the inroads of Modernism, dealt with under the title *De scriptura sacra*. In fact we shall see that the main proposition in the doctrine of the Word of God, which we shall try to evolve in what follows, will materially be none other than that of the authority and normativity of Holy Writ, as the witness to God's revelation and as the presupposition of the Church's proclamation.[30]

The assumption that the sole matter of dogmatics is the Holy Scriptures cannot be justified theoretically, but only practically:

That dogmatics cannot be "dogmatics" in the sense of the Roman Catholic Church, i.e. not an unfolding of the revealed truths immanent in the Church, and not *Glaubenslehre* in the sense of Protestant Modernism (the exposition of the faith of the men united in the Church) —that we have decided by our opposition, which, in view of the Biblical sign, must be made good only factually and not by proof. By this opposition we declare that the *possibility of visualising the Word of God as an entity different from Church proclamation is given to us . . . in the fact that in the Church the Bible is read, and we relate ourselves to this fact,* when, not in a Catholic and not in a Modernist, but just in a Protestant way, i.e. in opposition, we take practical account of *this* possibility. By this opposition, which, of course, we take for granted in every form, we assert that dogmatics, as the inquiry about the Word of God in Church proclamation, must be the critical inquiry as to the agreement of Church proclamation, not with any norm of human truth or human value . . . , nor with a standard of divine truth already known and proclaimed by the Church herself . . . but *with the revelation attested in Holy Scripture*. That is the concrete meaning of the inquiry to be set up in dogmatics concerning the Word of God.[31]

In the early volumes of his *Dogmatics* Barth quite explicitly sets forth his "evangelical" understanding of church dogmatics in clear opposition to both Catholic and liberal Protestant ("Modernist") views of dogmatics. Of particular importance is his sharp disagreement with the tradition of liberal theology out of which both he and Bonhoeffer sprang. The rejection of the "religious experience" approach of liberalism and the reaffirmation of the Reformers' concentration on Scripture as the witness to the objective reality of God in Christ is a hallmark of the Neo-Reformation theology of Barth and Bonhoeffer. "Ultimately," Barth says, "everything depends upon whether a dogmatics is scriptural." [32]

Barth describes the "biblical attitude" of dogmatics as follows:

As from the absolute authority of Holy Scripture as the Word of God there results the relative authority of the biblical Canon, so from the absolute requirement of the obedience of faith to the prophetic and apostolic witness there results the relative requirement of a basic mode of thinking and speaking which corresponds with this obedience of faith. This is what we have to describe and understand as the biblicism or biblical attitude of dogmatics.[33]

The task of dogmatics must be to institute "a kinship between the outlook, approach and method of the biblical writers and those of the Church preacher. . . . The teaching Church cannot listen afresh to the Word of God except in a fresh adoption of this biblical attitude." [34]

Dogmatics must be based solely upon the most thoroughgoing biblical exegesis as its foundation and *sine qua non*; at the same time, dogmatics is to be distinguished from exegesis:

Biblical exegesis is the decisive presupposition and source of dogmatics. Indeed, we can and must go further and say that it is the task of dogmatics, not to leave the teaching Church to its own devices, but constantly to recall it to the work of biblical exegesis. But dogmatics in itself is not biblical exegesis. It is the examination, criticism and correction of the proclamation to which the teaching Church addresses itself on the basis of Holy Scripture, not merely by reproducing and explaining it, but also by applying and thus in some measure producing it. What is really demanded of dogmatics is that this examination, criticism and correction should be carried out with the same biblical attitude of thought and speech to which Church proclamation is called. Self-evidently, it will have to keep the text of the Bible continually and constantly in view in its content. Therefore . . . it will be continually and consistently occupied with its exegesis. Often enough, it will have to hark back to it directly, thus taking up again the immediate and detailed work of exegesis. Nevertheless this is not its special and peculiar function.[35]

As the medium between Scripture and church, dogmatics cannot be *simply* biblical exegesis; but as the testing of the church's message by the criterion of the Word of God attested in Scripture, dogmatics must be thoroughly and knowledgeably biblical before all else:

What has to be said is that dogmatics has no freedom to be an autonomous branch of Church theology in independence of the witness of Scripture. It cannot give its own witness from its own sources. In Church proclamation and the special questions and concerns of the teaching Church in every age, there can be no question of anything other than the repetition and confirmation of the biblical witness. Thus dogmatics has no freedom to decline to allow its thought to be formed by the prototype of the biblical witnesses. It has no freedom to become a historical or psychological, political or philosophical dogmatics. It may or may not be directly concerned in exegesis. It may or may not make actual textual references. But necessarily it takes the form of its thought from its submission to the biblical *Deus dixit*. And it can acquire this necessary form of thought only from confrontation with the biblical text.[36]

Dogmatics is the human science which is wholly determined in its nature and method by the Word of God revealed in Jesus Christ as witnessed by the Scriptures. "It has no freedom," Barth maintains, "to become a historical or psychological, political or philosophical dogmatics." Barth accordingly rejects both the natural or philosophical theology of Roman Catholicism and the attempt of both liberalism and some of his fellow neo-orthodox theologians (especially Bultmann, Gogarten, and Tillich) to begin with an independent anthropology as the basis for theological reflection. Both Catholic natural theology and Protestant "pre-understanding" proceed from the mistaken premise that dogmatics must or even can begin with the question of *possibility*. As reflection entirely determined by the concrete, available data of biblical testimony, dogmatics deals only with *actuality*. The interest of dogmatic theology, says Barth, lies not in exhibiting a "point of connection" with the divine message to man, but purely in the divine message published and apprehended. Moreover, her epistemological question can *not* run: How is human knowledge of revelation *possible?* (as if it were a question whether revelation is known! as if it were to be expected from an investigation of human *knowledge* that we would see into the possibility of knowing divine *revelation!*). *But* it runs, What is man's *real* knowledge of divine revelation? (the presupposition being that revelation creates the needful "point of connection" in man, itself and on its own initiative).[37]

Hence responsible dogmatic science, like the rest of the contemporary sciences, will base itself squarely on the actual data which determine its peculiar sphere of inquiry—revelation and the knowledge of revelation in faith—and will simply refuse "to discuss the basis of its ground, questions such as *whether* God is, *whether* there is such a thing as revelation, etc." [38]

Barth's description of the approach of both liberal and (chiefly) Bultmannian theology to dogmatics in terms of possibility is important to an understanding of the background to Bonhoeffer's criticisms of his existentialist contemporaries. For modernism—including its "neo-orthodox" adherents such as Bultmann and Tillich—

the Church and faith are to be understood as part of a larger essential context, and dogmatics as part of a larger scientific problem-context, from the general structural laws of which we are to read off its special epistemological conditions, and to recognise its special scientific claims. This problem-context is, however, that of an ontology; and ever since Descartes that must mean a comprehensively explicated self-interpretation of man's existence, such as will, among other things, also help at the right point to the preliminary understanding of an existence in the Church, i.e. in faith, and so to a preliminary understanding and criterion of theological knowledge.[39]

Bultmann's Heideggerian existentialist "pre-understanding" and Tillich's Schelling-inspired ontology do precisely what Barth here describes: They set up a conceptual and ontological framework within which to place the biblical revelation, faith, and the dogmatic questions. Such a view recognizes, Barth says, that the gospel is a certain determination of human reality. But because it interprets this determination as a human possibility, "it fails to see that such a determination of human reality only proceeds, and is to be perceived as proceeding, from something outside all human possibilities, i.e. from God acting." [40]

Dogmatics, then, must sharply reject philosophy and metaphysics insofar as they claim to be independent insights into its own proper subject matter. Dogmatics is free, however, to use philosophical and metaphysical concepts in its task, so long as it clearly defines them and strictly subordinates them to its own mode of reflection. The use of personalist-existentialist conceptuality by both Barth and Bonhoeffer is an important example of their own theological incorporation of philosophical concepts. As Barth states, "concepts of a pure metaphysics may become concepts of proclamation." [41] "But by the context," he continues—i.e., the sole determination of the dogmatic sphere by Jesus Christ as proclaimed by the Scriptures—"is decided the legitimacy of the occurrence of all concepts, even those that appear clearly to belong to proclamation." [42]

The task of dogmatics is the criticism of church teaching by the obedient elucidation of the revelation of God attested by Scripture. The other two forms of theology are biblical theology, which engages in the foundational work of exegesis, and practical theology, which works out the concrete forms which theology takes in the church. These three modes of theological thought exhaust the church's theological task. Is there any place, then, for apologetics or polemics? Not as separate disciplines, replies Barth:

> There is no dispute about the fact that dogmatics too, together with the Christian Church generally, has to speak all along the line as faith opposing unbelief, and that to that extent all along the line her language must be apologetic, polemical. But there has never been any other *effective* apologetic and polemic of faith against unbelief than the unintended one (impossible to intend! purely experiential!) which took place when God himself sided with the witness of faith.[43]

"Apologetics and polemics," Barth summarizes, "can only be an *event*, they cannot be a *programme*." [44] The obedient explanation and elucidation of the actuality of God's self-disclosure in Christ according to the Scriptures is all that is necessary in theology. If this task is performed faithfully and intelligently, the theologian has done all he can to "build bridges" to or argue with non-Christian man. God himself will open the eyes of some who hear the testimony.

Throughout his career Bonhoeffer shared with Barth all the features of the concept of Christian theology which I have illustrated from Barth's *Dogmatics*: christocentricity, ecclesiocentricity, biblicism, reasoning only from the actuality of revelation, and the corresponding rejection of apologetics and polemics. The visionary thoughts of the prison writings, not to mention the theological development preceding them, are incomprehensible apart from this understanding of the nature and methodology of the theological enterprise.

Bonhoeffer, following Barth, grounds all his reflection solely upon the concrete actuality of God in his revelation in Christ, over against philosophical theology and existentialist "pre-understanding." From *The Communion of Saints* to *Letters and Papers from Prison* his theology is determined "as a whole and in all its parts" (to use a phrase of Barth's to describe the christological character of dogmatics) [45] by the biblical witness to Jesus Christ, whether he is writing on the doctrine of man, the ecumenical movement, ethics, politics, or history.

Correspondingly, Bonhoeffer always rejected apologetics and polemics as independent aspects of the theological task. Faithful dogmatic reflection contains "built-in" apologetics and polemics, as it were. The "non-religious interpretation of biblical concepts" was not apologetics. It was rather Bonhoeffer's attempt, again, to be more faithful to Barth's theological task than he believed Barth was himself: to expound the biblical witness to Jesus Christ intelligibly and in the fullness of its revolutionary implications, both to the Christian community and to the increasingly "non-religious" people of a secular world.

Chapter Five
Revelation and Religion

Bonhoeffer

Bonhoeffer's experiences of and reflections upon modern secularity during the last years of his life raised a question that "is bothering me incessantly; . . . what Christianity really is, or indeed who Christ really is for us today." The whole history of Christian theology and preaching has been built upon what Bonhoeffer calls (after his teacher Reinhold Seeberg) the "religious a priori" of man, which at one point he identifies simply with "inwardness and conscience." Christianity has been traditionally considered the true pattern of *religion*. But now, says Bonhoeffer, writing in 1944, "we are moving towards a completely religionless time; people as they are now simply cannot be religious any more." What *is* Christianity in this "religionless" world upon which we are entering? What "if one day it becomes clear that this a priori does not exist at all, but was a historically conditioned and transient form of human self-expression"? [1] Bonhoeffer believes that that day has already dawned.

If the church clings to the "religious a priori" as the basis of its gospel, it will find itself, says Bonhoeffer, equating the elect with those whom the evangelist catches in a weak moment, with the nostalgically "neo-medieval," or with the intellectually dishonest. In other words, the "chosen few" will be those with particular psychological attitudes conducive to "religiousness": the naturally pious, the romanticist born out of his time, or the emotionally unstable.

Rejecting this solution, Bonhoeffer raises again and in an even more pertinent way the question, What is Christianity in a "non-

103

religious" world? "How can Christ become the Lord of the religionless as well?" [2] If the "religious a priori" was merely a historical garment for Christianity, what is "religionless" Christianity? Questions immediately arise, such as the nature and function of the church in a "religionless" world and the problem of speaking of God in a "non-religious" way.[3]

In raising the question of talk about God, Bonhoeffer introduces a second meaning to the word "religion." Up to this point he has been speaking of "religion" as a built-in "need for God" in each person's inner life, of which the clues are "inwardness and conscience." [4] Now Bonhoeffer introduces the idea of "religion" as *metaphysical ideas of God*. "Religion" in this sense, as tied up with a metaphysical object called "God," leads directly to the problem of divine transcendence.

Bonhoeffer therefore seems to think of "religion" in two ways: (1) as the psychological attitude of a private *subject*; and (2) as one of a host of expressions of that subject's relation to a metaphysical *object* (God). "In my view," states Bonhoeffer, "[to 'interpret in a religious sense'] means to speak on the one hand metaphysically, and on the other hand individualistically." [5] Both elements in this dipolar phenomenon called "religion" are historical moments which are passing away.

Bonhoeffer's personal observations on particular manifestations of "religion" are illuminating. During both his sojourns in the United States he was continually impressed by what Alec R. Vidler has more recently called "the appalling religiousness of America." [6] Reporting on his year as Sloane Fellow at Union Theological Seminary (1930-31), Bonhoeffer had this to say about the difference between the German and the American seminarian: "If the first sermons of the German student serve for him to hand on his dogmatics as quickly as possible, they serve for the American student to display before the congregation the whole of his religious experience." [7] And in his essay "Protestantism Without Reformation," Bonhoeffer assessed American Christianity in more formal theological terms:

American theology and the American church as a whole have never been able to understand the meaning of "criticism" by the Word of God and all that signifies. Right to the last they do not understand that God's "criticism" touches even religion, the Christianity of the churches and the sanctification of Christians, and that God has founded his church beyond religion and beyond ethics. A symptom of this is the general adherence to natural theology. In American theology, Christianity is still essentially religion and ethics.[8]

Here the reality, not only of the gospel, but also of the church, is "beyond" both religion and ethics. I have discussed in previous chapters the "trans-moral" basis of the Christian life in Bonhoeffer's thought. Here too is Bonhoeffer's consistent rejection of natural or philosophical theology, following Barth. Both theologians saw the various forms of philosophical theology as bound up with an interest in "religion," either on the metaphysical level (as in Catholic natural theology) or in terms of analysis of the religious subject (as in liberal and existentialist Protestant "religious a prioris" or "anthropological pre-understandings").

Still more decisively revealing of Bonhoeffer's personal attitude toward "religion" are observations which he set down in a diary that he kept during his second brief stay in America during the summer of 1939. The entry for June 16 records how he has spent the whole day in a library in New York City looking though copies of *The Christian Century.* He mentions a report on the "lack of religion" (*Areligiosität*) of American college students; they are described in the article as "disinterested." Bonhoeffer comments: "That must happen if one doesn't eventually realise that 'religion' is really superfluous." Two days later he worshiped at Riverside Church, the "cathedral" of American liberalism. Afterward he described the "whole thing" as "a respectable, self-indulgent, self-satisfied religious celebration," as "idolatrous religion" (*Religionsvergötzung*).[9] He asks: "Do people not know that one can get on as well, even better, without 'religion'—if only there were not God himself and his Word? "[10]

The key passage among Bonhoeffer's personal reflections on the phenomenon of "religion," however, is a statement which he made in a letter to Bethge of June 25, 1942, after he was fully involved in the German Resistance movement:

Again and again I am driven to think about my activities which are now concerned so much with the secular field. . . . I feel the resistance growing in me against all religiosity [*alles "Religiöse"*], sometimes reaching the level of an instinctive horror—surely, this is not good either. Yet I am not a religious nature at all [*Ich bin keine religiöse Natur*]. But all the time I am forced to think of God, of Christ, of genuineness, life, freedom, charity— that matters for me. What causes me uneasiness is just the religious clothing [*die religiösen Einkleidungen*]. Do you understand? This is no new concept at all, no new insights, but because I believe an idea will come to burst upon me I let things run and do not offer resistance. In this sense I understand my present activity in the secular sector.[11]

In this letter Bonhoeffer explicitly states that it is his purely secular activities—as an employee of the German Military Counter-Intelligence and a Resistance worker—which are stimulating and troubling his thoughts on the whole phenomenon of "religion." He goes on to speak of his "resistance" to all forms of "religiosity," a resistance which sometimes intensifies into "an instinctive horror."

Bonhoeffer's continued resistance to religiousness reappears in the prison letters, where he speaks of his awkwardness with "religious people" and launches a violent attack on the "religious prying" of Christian pastors and apologists and their "secularized offshoots," the "psychotherapists" and the "existentialists."

Bonhoeffer confesses that he himself is not a "religious" person by nature. At the same time, the things that really count for him are "God, . . . Christ, . . . genuineness, life, freedom, charity." It is important to stress that these themes, the nucleus of Christianity and Christian life for Bonhoeffer, are for him "non-religious." We see here his lifelong concentration on the centrality of Christ as the way to God, personal authenticity of belief and spontaneity of action, love of earthly life, and concrete concern for the neighbor. The realities of God, Christ, genuineness, life, freedom, and charity continued to be at the heart of Bonhoeffer's outlook in the prison writings. There he wrestled with the problem of translating these Christian realities into fully secular, "non-religious" terms for a world which had outgrown "religion."

It is not, then, the essence of Christianity which is at stake, for the gospel is not "religious." What bothers Bonhoeffer is "the religious clothing" which Christianity wears. This garment of "religion" is characterized by a metaphysical apprehension of God as a *deus ex machina* and by those attitudes and activities characterized by the term "religiosity."

The passage from Bonhoeffer's letter of 1942 concludes by pointing out that these "non-religious" thoughts on Christianity are "no new concept at all, no new insights." As a Barth-inspired theologian, Bonhoeffer shared from the beginning Barth's critical views on the phenomenon of "religion." At the same time, along with Barth, he had assumed the inevitability and even the rightful place of "religion" within Christianity. Where Bonhoeffer went beyond Barth and his own earlier views was in his growing conviction, during the war years, that "religion" was no longer inevitable in human affairs; that "people as they are now simply cannot be religious any more." Bonhoeffer seems to have been groping with the idea in an extremely inchoate form in this letter of 1942, but it was to emerge with definiteness in the prison writings. Written a year before his arrest, the letter symbolizes the decisive impact of full-blown secularity on Bonhoeffer's consciousness, an impact which bore fruit in his "religionless" proposals.

In prison letters dated May 5 and June 8, 1944, Bonhoeffer undertook to criticize the efforts of certain other leading German-speaking theologians who deal with the problem of "religion." His criticisms of the attempts of his contemporaries to interpret Christianity as in some sense "beyond religion" shed light in a negative way on the path Bonhoeffer himself was pursuing, and place him within the context of modern Neo-Reformation critiques of "religion."

Rudolf Bultmann

Bonhoeffer acknowledges that Bultmann, in his program of demythologizing the New Testament, has recognized the problem of "religion," but contends that he has gone about solving it in the wrong way. Bultmann has not really broken with the liberal tradition, because he is still attempting to separate the "essence" of the gospel from its outer wrapping, however differently he may do it from, say, Harnack. "Bultmann's approach is fundamentally still a liberal one (i.e. abridging the gospel)," comments Bonhoeffer, "whereas I am trying to think theologically." [12]

Bonhoeffer, unlike some other interpreters of Bultmann, did not think that Bultmann had gone too far; he believed that he had not gone far enough. Bultmann's demythologizing still leaves us with the "religious" problem: "It is not only the 'mythological' concepts, such

107

as miracle, ascension, and so on (which are not in principle separable from the concepts of God, faith, etc.) , but 'religious' concepts generally, which are problematic." [13] The real problem in a secular world is to interpret and proclaim *both* God and miracles, i.e., kerygma and myth, "non-religiously."

In the second of two letters which discuss Bultmann, Bonhoeffer makes the same point in a positive way: "The full content, including the 'mythological' concepts, must be kept—the New Testament is not a mythological clothing of a universal truth; this mythology (resurrection, etc.) is the thing itself—but the concepts must be interpreted in such a way as not to make religion a precondition of faith." [14]

The notion that the biblical mythology is "the thing itself" and not the dispensable medium of eternal principles or even of authentic existential self-understanding is an expression of Bonhoeffer's doctrine of Scripture, which we shall examine in detail in the chapter on "Biblical Hermeneutics." The fallible, time-bound words of the Bible are in their very particularity and historicity the concrete Word of God to us. We cannot get "behind" the biblical witness to abstract universal truths (liberalism) or to a theory about what it "really" is (Bultmann) ; the witness itself is all the truth we possess or need to possess. This biblical truth, to use Emil Brunner's phrase, is "truth as encounter": the living presence of God who speaks to man wholly within the events of his history, and who through his Spirit makes past and future generations contemporary with those revelatory events. Biblical truth, as Bonhoeffer was fond of saying (along with Kierkegaard and Barth), is universal only by being intensely particular; it is eternal only by being fully historical. Hence the mythology of the Bible, right along with the simply historical and the didactic, must be seen as "the thing itself" and not merely as a veil shrouding the essence of the gospel: the mythology is part of its essence. This is Bonhoeffer's intimate and highly concrete dialectic of the relation between God and man, which we shall also see in his doctrine of Christ and the church.

It is essential to remember that Bonhoeffer does not mean that the Bible is all of a piece, either historically or theologically. There are "degrees of knowledge and degrees of significance," to use his own words; and his difference from Barth on such matters as the significance of the "myth" of the Virgin Birth of Christ indicates a definite selectivity about what is central and what is peripheral in the Scriptures. Bonhoeffer means rather (1) to safeguard the utterly historical, "event" character of the revelation of the true God, and his real entrusting of the word of salvation to human flesh in Jesus Christ and his witnesses, which is secured only by an obedient attentiveness to the actual words of Scripture as a whole; and (2) to insist that authentically theological reflection must take its rise solely from the Bible itself, which must be taken as a whole in order to discover the actual priorities which the text itself establishes and demands. The all-determining centrality of the Incarnation and the wholly peripheral importance of the narrative of Jesus' birth, for example, are priorities established by the New Testament itself.

Bultmann, like the liberals, brings priorities to the Bible from outside rather than allowing it to set out its own. One of these is the distinction, not between mythology and history, but between mythology and a particular theory of the "essence" of the New Testament proclamation, the kerygma. Bultmann has determined in advance, on the basis of existentialist philosophy, what the "essence" of the New Testament proclamation is, and proceeds to extract it from its setting in the first-century Jewish and Hellenistic mythological world views. Bonhoeffer insists that this is an aprioristic abridgment of the gospel.

We must understand the gospel on its own biblical terms and therefore as a whole. Just here is the platform on which Christian theology must stand even in a "non-religious" world. Seen in this light, it is not just the mythological New Testament world picture which is problematic but the "religious" presuppositions of the biblical language as a whole, including the kerygma itself. Hence excising the mythology is not enough. The entire New Testament must first be freed of any "religious" preconditions and then entirely reinterpreted "non-religiously." This is the "non-religious interpretation of biblical concepts," which Bultmann's demythologizing fails to reach.

Two interpreters of Bonhoeffer have pointed out that his brief assessment of Bultmann's work in *Letters and Papers* is mistaken in its critical judgment. John Godsey warns that "we must question whether Bonhoeffer really understood Bultmann's view of 'demythologizing' when he considers it a typical liberal reduction process aimed at eliminating myth in order to expose the essence of Christianity.

Here Bonhoeffer clearly misunderstands the *intention* of Bultmann, who has repeatedly declared that he is not interested in eliminating the mythological elements, but in *interpreting* them." [15] According to Gerhard Ebeling, "Bonhoeffer's reproach that Bultmann succumbs to the typical liberal reduction process fails to recognize Bultmann's express intention." [16] Both men, however, raise the question as to whether Bultmann has in fact succeeded in carrying out his intention, and we must now turn to that question.

In the original essay on demythologizing, "New Testament and Mythology," Bultmann declared that "our task is to produce an existentialist *interpretation* of the . . . mythology of the New Testament." [17] His later writing entitled *Jesus Christ and Mythology* makes this intention even more explicit. He defines demythologizing in this way: "Its aim is not to eliminate the mythological statements but to interpret them. It is a method of hermeneutics." [18] Bultmann believes that liberalism went wrong precisely because it did attempt to *eliminate* the mythology.

At other times, however, Bultmann expressly speaks of the need to *eliminate* the mythology of the New Testament. In the original essay, which is all Bonhoeffer had read of Bultmann's program, he declares quite explicitly: "The question is simply whether the New Testament message consists exclusively of mythology, or whether it actually demands the *elimination of myth* if it is to be understood as it is meant to be." [19]

The contradiction in Bultmann's intentions is only an apparent one resulting from the imprecision of his language. Stated precisely, he seeks to *reinterpret* the myths of the New Testament by *eliminating* their *purely mythical* character. He is in quest of the human understanding of existence which myths symbolize: "The real purpose of myth is not to present an objective picture of the world as it is, but to express man's understanding of himself in the world in which he lives. Myth should be interpreted not cosmologically, but anthropologically, or better still, existentially." [20] By constructing myths, ancient man objectified his understanding of his existence in terms of a supernatural reality or event. The job of demythologizing, then, *is* to *reinterpret* the New Testament myths by discovering what they were trying to say about human existence. But this reinterpretation proceeds by *eliminating* the myths *as myths*. Hence Bultmann's

110

method is both a reinterpretation and an elimination, the latter being part of the total procedure which bears the name of the former.

To cite one example of Bultmann's method: The resurrection of Jesus is a mythological event; yet the resurrection faith is at the center of the kerygma. For Bultmann the existential truth of the resurrection is the victory over sin and death in the life of the person who in faith understands the meaning of the cross for him. The myth of the resurrection, on the other hand, is the belief in the transmutation of Jesus' physical body on the third day after his crucifixion. Bultmann would say that to get at the truth of the resurrection, to reinterpret it, requires eliminating the resurrection myth viewed as an objective supernatural event in the world, as the New Testament stories of the empty tomb picture it.

Against Bonhoeffer, it may truly be said that to some degree Bultmann's "existentialist" interpretation of the New Testament comes very close to what Bonhoeffer in fact produces in his "non-religious interpretation of biblical concepts." The two-volume work *Theology of the New Testament* is an excellent example of Bultmann's method, and bears comparison with some of Bonhoeffer's "religionless" material. Here Bultmann systematically reinterprets the major New Testament (chiefly Pauline and Johannine) concepts, many of which are originally mythological in form, in what can genuinely be called fairly "secular" terms.[21]

When Bultmann's position has been carefully defined to show what his actual intentions and results are, however, we must still acknowledge the crucial validity of Bonhoeffer's basic criticism that "it is not only the 'mythological' concepts, such as miracle, ascension, and so on (which are not in principle separable from the concepts of God, faith, etc.), but 'religious' concepts generally, which are problematic." This is a key sentence which discloses the fundamental distinction between "existentialist" and "religionless" interpretation.

Contrary to Bonhoeffer, Bultmann does not appear to consider certain "religious" conceptions ultimately problematic. He retains as "non-mythological" such New Testament conceptions as the Word of God, divine action in history, and, most decisively, the conception "God" itself. It is clear from his writings that for Bultmann certain New Testament ideas *are* "in principle separable" from the mythological ones, and can in fact continue to be used.[22] Bultmann believes,

111

over against Bonhoeffer, that certain " 'religious' concepts" are still legitimately used in a "come-of-age" world, particularly the apex word "God." Bultmann, like Bonhoeffer, is passionately devoted to rendering the gospel relevant and intelligible to modern man, but clearly he does not consider certain traditional "religious" conceptions to be the insuperable stumbling block that Bonhoeffer does.

To Bonhoeffer the very word "God" itself is perhaps the most meaningless "religious" term to secular man. The crucial notion of divine transcendence is under greater suspicion in *Letters and Papers* than in Bultmann's writings. Bultmann, however, like Bonhoeffer, decisively rejects any sort of mythological or metaphysical understanding of God's "over-against-ness." The thought of both is strongly influenced by the I-Thou conception of transcendence as the concrete "standing-over-against-the-self" of an "other" whom man encounters through his ethical encounters with other men.[23] But Bonhoeffer always began from the biblical testimony that the man Jesus is very God, and therefore in his "religionless" christology he could focus on this human being in all his individuality and reinterpret his Godhead, the transcendent dimension, in terms of his actions. For Bultmann, on the other hand, the man Jesus himself is largely unknown, and Christianity is the kerygma which proclaims the activity of God and a new understanding of human existence on the basis of Christ's cross. Hence in Bultmann's thought we are left with a God who is separable from the man Jesus at the very center of faith, and correspondingly with the problem for secular man of transcendence as a "religious" sphere "out there." [24]

This difference, then, exists between "non-religious" and "existentialist" interpretation of the New Testament: The former regards *all* "religious" presuppositions, both "mythological" and "non-mythological," as entirely problematic in the modern world; while the latter distinguishes between "mythological" and "non-mythological" religious ideas, regarding only the "mythological" as incredible to modern man and therefore reinterpreting them existentially. Such a difference is not absolute, since Bultmann subjects "non-mythological" religious conceptions such as God and faith to extensive reinterpretation even as he continues to use them; while Bonhoeffer tends in his "non-religious" interpretation of Christianity toward the reduction of the major biblical themes to a "non-mythological" as well as a "non-religious" essence. Bultmann cannot avoid the large contemporary question mark which stands even over so-called "non-mythological" New Testament ideas. Desiring to retain "the full content" of the biblical message, albeit "non-religiously," Bonhoeffer acknowledges in practice if not in theory that it is exceedingly difficult to reinterpret the "mythological" elements in "secular" terms.[25]

I have devoted detailed attention to Bonhoeffer's criticisms of Bultmann and to Bultmann's own position on the matter of "religion" because of an important trend in current Bonhoeffer interpretation. Leading interpreters of Bonhoeffer like Ronald Gregor Smith and Gerhard Ebeling, who are essentially Bultmannian in their orientation, believe that the "religionless" Bonhoeffer is closer to Bultmann than to any other contemporary theologian. Behind the differences in presuppositions and method, they contend, the two thinkers are remarkably similar in their reinterpretation of the gospel for modern man. I have tried to indicate some of the similarities as well as the fundamental differences between Bonhoeffer and Bultmann. With Bultmann occupying the center of European theological discussion in recent years, this link with Bonhoeffer becomes highly significant in the contemporary quest for a "Christianity without religion." [26]

It is intriguing to speculate as to whether Bonhoeffer would have found Bultmann's approach more congenial had the two of them been able to engage in theological dialogue after the war. Bonhoeffer is known to have welcomed the publication of Bultmann's programmatic essay with qualified enthusiasm.[27] Bultmann, on the other hand, is in agreement with Bonhoeffer's analysis of the modern world as "come of age," and endorses the views set forth in R. G. Smith's book *The New Man,* which is fundamentally Bonhoeffer-inspired.[28]

Interestingly enough, some "post-Bultmannian" criticisms of Bultmann have suggested, along with Bonhoeffer, that Bultmann has "not gone far enough." Reversing Bonhoeffer's criticism, however, they maintain that Bultmann has stopped short at "neo-orthodoxy" and has failed to carry through consistently to a "neo-liberalism." Fritz Buri and Schubert Ogden are leading representatives of the "left wing" of Bultmann's students and interpreters, who maintain that to stop short at demythologizing, as Bultmann does, is illogical and arbitrary theological method.[29] Bultmann's clinging to the historical uniqueness and particularity of the kerygma is inconsistent, they say, with his basic presuppositions. The New Testament, insist Ogden and Buri, must also be "dekerygmatized," the kerygma being seen as the paradigm of a universal possibility of authentic existence and not as a surd historical event to which all salvation must be consciously anchored.

Clearly we are at the opposite end of the spectrum here from Bonhoeffer's attempt to "go beyond" Bultmann. For Bonhoeffer it was precisely the objectivity of the scandalously particular, historical event of Jesus Christ which remains when human "religiousness" (a particular form of "self-understanding") has disappeared; the problem is simply to reinterpret the event "non-religiously," which Bultmann has achieved only partially. For Ogden and Buri, on the other hand, the objective event of Christ is precisely the difficulty with Bultmann's whole enterprise. From the point of view of our present context, we may say that they dissolve the historical Christ-event into a general "religious" possibility (i.e., into a certain form of human self-understanding).

When all allowances have been made for their common concern to grapple seriously with the "loss of religion by man come of age" and the meaning of the New Testament in such a situation, fundamental differences remain between Bultmann and Bonhoeffer in their understanding of the gospel and theology, and indeed in their understanding of twentieth-century man, which are not to be glossed over as easily as they sometimes seem to be by those who interpret the later Bonhoeffer in "liberal" terms.

Paul Tillich

Only one reference to Paul Tillich's approach to "religion" appears in *Letters and Papers,* in the letter of June 8, 1944. Here Bonhoeffer criticizes Tillich for attempting the futile task of convincing the world, despite appearances to the contrary, that it is "religious" through and through.[30] Tillich makes the older liberal mistake, according to Bonhoeffer, of trying to establish a place for "religion" in the world. While brilliantly critical of the subtle and often unconscious idolatries of "bad religion" in the modern world, he tries to discern "religion" itself (ontological "ultimate concern") in every activity of man; he attempts to tell secular man that he is inescapably "religious," if only he will recognize it.[31] To Bonhoeffer this is nothing but a modern continuation of traditional Christian apologetics, building a bridge to Christian faith on the "religious a priori." Is Tillich after all so different from Justin Martyr or Clement of Alexandria? Bonhoeffer might well have been asking. In a world "come of age," in a "religion-less" world, such appeals are futile.

"Of course," Bonhoeffer goes on to say, "*the world must be understood better than it understands itself,* but not 'religiously.' " [32] A truly "religionless" Christianity is the only thing which can understand the world better than the world understands itself. Any attempt to understand the world "religiously," even Tillich's sophisticated and compelling theological reconstruction, does not genuinely achieve a better understanding of the world, but only a new form of an outdated one. One of the key characteristics of a world "come of age" is its increasingly "non-religious" (secular) self-understanding. It quite naturally rejects any attempt to interpret it as permeated with "religiousness," since that is precisely what it has "outgrown." To interpret the modern world "religiously" is to misunderstand it and to subvert its maturity.

Bonhoeffer concludes the letter in which he criticizes Tillich by saying, "the world's coming of age is no longer an occasion for polemics and apologetics, but *is now really better understood than it understands itself, namely on the basis of the gospel and in the light of Christ.*" [33] Here Bonhoeffer rejects both the polemical approach to secularity of much Christian orthodoxy and the decidedly world-appreciative apologetical approach of someone like Tillich. It is significant that Bonhoeffer does not conceive the Christian approach to the modern world in either polemical or apologetical terms. He inherited Barth's belief that the task of theology is simply the obedient exposition of the biblical testimony to Jesus, and that apologetics and polemics are unnecessary. Yet he was more faithful to the expository task than Barth, since he saw the urgent need to elucidate the Scriptures in a radically "non-religious" way in a world which has become secularized.

Bonhoeffer's "non-religious" interpretation, then, is not apologetics; this point must be emphasized, because the Anglo-Saxon reader in particular tends to understand it in this way. "Apologetic theology," in Tillich's own words, "is 'answering theology.' It answers the questions implied in the 'situation' in the power of the eternal message and with the means provided by the situation whose questions it answers." [34] Bonhoeffer's view of theology is strikingly different. He repeatedly insists that Christ "did not 'come' to answer our unsolved problems." [35] The business of theology is not to answer the questions raised by the "situation"; it is simply to expound faithfully the biblically witnessed revelation of God in Christ. The crucial point for Bonhoeffer is that the church must expound the biblical message *intelligibly,* which means in the language of the day. The Bible itself simply uses the language of the places and times in which it was written. Similarly, the biblical expositor or theologian living in the twentieth century must communicate the Word of God in terms which the twentieth century can understand; otherwise he is not engaged in true exegesis, the interpretation of the meaning of the text. The decisive thrust of Bonhoeffer's project is that the present and future world is no longer "religious," and that therefore the task of the church and the theologian is the "non-religious interpretation" of the Scriptures. It is a matter of interpreting the Word of God in a way which will not hinder the church's unchanging commission to proclaim the gospel. As we shall see below, Bonhoeffer's fundamental criticism of Barth is that the latter saw the dimensions of the loss of "religion" in the modern world but failed to carry through to a correspondingly "non-religious" exposition of the Scriptures. Even more than Barth, Bonhoeffer believed, has the church as a whole failed signally to grasp the radical transformation of human self-understanding in modern secular civilization.

The only way to understand the world better than it understands itself is "on the basis of the Gospel and in the light of Christ." Such a statement is entirely consistent with the thoroughgoing christocentricity of Bonhoeffer's whole theological development. The world "come of age" must be understood christologically. The all-sufficiency of christology to the very end of Bonhoeffer's life is another sharp difference between Bonhoeffer and Tillich. Tillich begins with "religion" and moves to Christ, in the German liberal tradition of Schleiermacher. Bonhoeffer begins and ends with Christ, and in so doing discovers that "religion" is not essential to the gospel. Tillich seeks to understand the world "religiously," but the world, says Bonhoeffer, is "non-religious." Bonhoeffer seeks to understand the world christologically, for Christ himself and reality seen in him are "non-religious."

Would Bonhoeffer have modified his criticism of Tillich in the light of the latter's postwar writings? The Tillich whom Bonhoeffer knew was the religious socialist of the 'twenties in Germany. The more recent Tillich became more profoundly aware of the problem of irreligion, and in his conceptions of the "God above the God of theism" and the "New Being" which appears in Jesus understood as the Christ he sought to transcend both "religion" and "irreligion." [36] Whether Bonhoeffer would consider even this attempt radical enough for a "religionless" world, however, is a very real question. Tillich's fundamental presuppositions consist in a "religious ontology" in the classical metaphysical tradition of Augustinianism and German idealism. Bonhoeffer would almost certainly still question whether "religionless" man is addressable even in the "crypto-religious" terminology of "ultimate concern," and especially in the erection of a metaphysical structure into which the biblical faith is inserted.

Nevertheless, there have been attempts to synthesize the insights of Tillich and the "religionless" Bonhoeffer, notably John A. T. Robinson's *cause célèbre, Honest to God.*[37] Bishop Robinson's central theme is Tillich's doctrine of God as "the ultimate depth of all our being, the creative ground and meaning of all our existence." [38] On this basis Robinson presses for a thoroughly secular understanding of transcendence. Transcendence is the dimension of "depth" in the world, supremely manifest in ordinary personal relationships. Robinson believes that Tillich's greatest contribution to theology is "the reinterpretation of transcendence in a way which preserves its reality while detaching it from the projection of supranaturalism." [39] As we shall see in examining Bonhoeffer's "non-religous" interpretation of divine transcendence, which is grounded in his I-Thou apprehension of reality, he sought to do precisely what Robinson attributes to Tillich, albeit along sharply different lines.

Bishop Robinson fuses this "secular" doctrine of God and transcendence with Bonhoeffer's "non-religous" reinterpretation of Christianity. In his chapter on christology, Robinson interprets Bonhoeffer's "religionless" doctrine of Christ in Tillichian terms: "Jesus is 'the man for others,' the one in whom Love has completely taken over, the one who is utterly open to, and united with, the Ground of his being. And this 'life for others, through participation in the Being of God,' *is* transcendence." [40] The human example of Jesus is our clearest window into the character of the dimension of depth in all existence.

The fundamental differences outlined earlier in this section, however, cannot easily be reconciled. Tillich interprets reality, including Christ, in terms of religion and ontology; Bonhoeffer sees everything in the light of the biblically attested Christ, and dispenses with "religion" and metaphysics. Quite unlike Bultmann's position, Tillich's system would tend almost invariably to swallow up Bonhoeffer's insights, thereby transforming them into something different and blunting their radicality. Bishop Robinson's amalgam of the christologies of Tillich and Bonhoeffer, for example, mutes the stark humanization of the divine transcendence which characterizes Bonhoeffer's christology. Jesus is not "the one who is utterly open to, and united with, the Ground of his being." This man Jesus himself *"is"* the "Ground of being": His actions and sufferings are the actions and sufferings of God himself. The being of the man Jesus is the meaning of the world. This figure of the gospels whose being is entirely being-for-others, this man who lives in humiliation and weakness and rejection because he lives only for others, is all in the world we know of God. All we see of God is his utter humanity for our sakes. To begin with "the Ground of being" is unbiblical and "religious." The fully secular man can understand only the biblical God, the one who lives as a human being and suffers by our side, because the very meaning of "secular" is "de-divinized" or "de-religionized," and therefore fully humanized. The issue between Bonhoeffer and Tillich is the issue between Luther and Schelling, between biblicistic christocentricity and metaphysical idealism, between the concretely human and the ubiquitously divine.

Karl Heim

The same letter which discusses Tillich also makes brief mention of Bonhoeffer's old teacher at Tübingen, Karl Heim. Bonhoeffer is writing to Bethge of major attempts by twentieth-century theologians to come seriously to grips with the problem of "Christ and the world that has come of age." He discusses briefly the strengths and weaknesses of the older liberal theology in answering the question. Its strength, he maintains, lay in its courageous refusal to "put the clock back," in its willingness to accept the modern world and to try to deal with it. In his "religionless Christianity" for a secular world Bonhoeffer sought to carry forward this true insight of the liberal program.

"The weakness of liberal theology," Bonhoeffer goes on to say, "was that it conceded to the world the right to determine Christ's place in the world"—a mistake which Bonhoeffer sought to avoid through his thoroughly biblical-christological presuppositions and method. He then takes up the overthrow of liberal theology and the recovery of authentically biblical and Reformation principles during the 'twenties and 'thirties of this century. Under this heading he mentions Heim, Althaus, Tillich, and Barth. Bonhoeffer finds the first three of these Neo-Reformation theologians guilty of "sailing, though unintentionally, in the channel of liberal theology," i.e. of "leaving clear a space for religion in the world or against the world." [41] As we have just seen, Bonhoeffer regards this attempt to carve out a niche for "religion" as the fundamental weakness of the liberalism which these theologians displaced. At bottom they are still allowing the world "the right to determine Christ's place in the world."

How did Karl Heim make this "liberal" mistake? We have seen that Tillich attempts to make a place for "religion" in the world come of age by interpreting its very secularity "religiously." Heim, on the other hand, sought by a rigorous phenomenological analysis of existence in terms of "I," "Thou," and "It," to demonstrate intellectually that modern man is faced with a decisive either/or between the Christian and the various secular world views. Much of his life work was devoted to elucidating the Christian view of the world in modern terms and the fundamental nihilism of nontheistic attitudes toward life.[42]

Theologically and temperamentally, however, Heim had his roots in the German pietist tradition. What resulted was a call not only to the either/or of opposing worldviews, but also, as Bonhoeffer puts it, to "despair or Jesus": "Heim sought, along pietist and methodist lines, to convince the individual man that he was faced with the alternative 'despair or Jesus.' He gained 'hearts.' " [43] Clearly Bonhoeffer believed that the dominant either/or which emerged in Heim's attempt to deal with "Christ and the world that has come of age" was the pietist "decision" to make Christ Lord in one's personal life. Despite the important philosophical underpinning of Heim's theological effort, Bonhoeffer saw this as the intellectual and evangelical attempt to preserve a place for God in the "inner life" of man—and "inwardness" is one of the two marks of "religion" over against the biblical view of man. Heim continued the liberal error of allowing the world "the right to determine Christ's place in the world," of "leaving clear a space for religion in the world or [in Heim's case] against the world." With his admirably thorough knowledge of modern science, Heim allowed science the right to assign faith to "non-objective" and "suprapolar" space, beyond the reach of scientific language and method: "Not only the ego but also the reality of the personal God in fact belongs to a dimension which is different from those of everything which is accessible to scientific investigation." [44] The space Heim cleared for subjective "religion" against the world was the logically unassailable, isolable human ego:

I myself am neither in my body nor above it nor beside it. I am on this side of all objectivity, and consequently outside all three-dimensional space. . . .
I distinguish your self, your "soul," from the destiny which God has imposed upon you, just as I distinguish my own self, my own "soul," from the temporary role which God has assigned to me for this brief lifetime.[45]

On the objective, metaphysical side of "religion," God's transcendence was safeguarded by removing his "otherness" from the world of space and time and even from the polarities of "I" and "Thou":

Ultimately there is only one question upon the answer to which everything depends and to which all the fundamental problems of our thought and life may be reduced. This is the question whether there in fact exists that suprapolar space of which we have repeatedly spoken . . . , or whether this suprapolar space is an illusion, so that we are confined within the polar space [of I-It and I-Thou] with all our perceptions, conceptions and cognitions.[46]

Bonhoeffer's criticisms of what he calls "methodism" are severe. While he has too much regard for the theological stature of his former teacher to level his attack directly at Heim's position, it is clear that Heim is in some way representative of a general approach by Chris-

120

tians to the "come-of-age" world which Bonhoeffer considers wide of the mark. His bitterest remarks in the prison writings are reserved for those modern Christian apologists who attempt to salvage man's inner life for God by showing him the misery of his existence without God. In the face of the steady retreat of "God" to the periphery of man's concerns, pietism and "methodism" make the desperate bid to cling to him as the "answer" to the ultimate questions which confront the individual man: birth, suffering, meaninglessness, and death. To Bonhoeffer these efforts are dedicated to the futile task of "leaving clear a space for religion in the world or against the world." The alternative "despair or Jesus" is not a viable one for the citizen of the "world that has come of age." [47]

Bonhoeffer's description of "religion" as metaphysical and individualistic is particularly relevant to what has been said above about Karl Heim. We must always keep in mind Bonhoeffer's fundamental debt to Heim and others for the central strain of I-Thou personalism throughout his theological development. But Heim interpreted the "life of dialogue" metaphysically, while Bonhoeffer rejected the metaphysical completely for the social and ethical in his understanding of the I-Thou relation. This divergence appears sharply in their ideas of divine transcendence, Heim speaking of "suprapolar space" and Bonhoeffer simply of Jesus' selfless existence for others. Heim's understanding of dialogical philosophy could never have led to a "religionless" theology; given the proper setting, Bonhoeffer's almost demanded it.

The second characteristic of "religion"—individualism or "inwardness"—has been seen to be the other element in Heim's theology. Bonhoeffer believed that this appeal to a "religious a priori," to a contact point in man's inner life such as a non-objectifiable ego, is both unbiblical and impotent in an increasingly "non-religious" world.

Karl Barth

It is highly fitting that most of Bonhoeffer's fragmentary criticisms of fellow theologians should be directed at Karl Barth. Reading between the lines, as it were, we can see the student who owes so much to his mentor and yet believes that at certain points the latter's doctrine is inadequate. Only a man who was so deeply indebted to Barth, as was Bonhoeffer, could have perceived so sympathetically and incisively the deficiencies of his theology.

Bonhoeffer believed that Barth's greatest achievement was his having been the first theologian to criticize the whole concept of "religion." As he says in the letter of June 8, 1944, Barth "brought in against religion the God of Jesus Christ, *'pneuma* against *sarx.'* " [48] Here was the first realization that liberal theology was fundamentally misguided in its attempt to claim everything for "religion." Here was a *"Nein!"* beside which Bultmann's and Tillich's critiques of "religion" looked like a bit of liberal face-lifting.

Barth's *Epistle to the Romans,* one of the truly revolutionary writings in the history of theology, can be seen as a sustained prophetic criticism of "religion." *The Epistle to the Romans* is an amazing foreshadowing of almost all the "religionless" themes of *Letters and Papers from Prison.* In certain important ways, Barth began where Bonhoeffer ended—and vice versa. The young Barth was the fiery prophet of a new order in Christianity; the young Bonhoeffer was a scholarly dogmatic theologian. Over the course of their lifetimes their roles were reversed. Now Bonhoeffer, speaking to us in death, is the unsettling prophet of a new Christian order, and Barth is the preservative dogmatician. *Romans* is fragmentary, inconsistent, and movingly impassioned in the same way as *Letters and Papers. Romans* represents the beginning of a new movement in Christian thought and life; *Letters and Papers* represents one legitimate outcome of that movement, as well as its transformation.

The crucial difference between the critique of "religion" in the commentary on Romans and in the prison writings is their respective starting points. Barth's fundamental theological assumption was Kierkegaard's "infinite qualitative distinction" between time and eternity.[49] To the early Barth the Bible witnessed to God's utter separation from and lordship over the world. Nowhere does he push this time/eternity dichotomy as rigorously or as thoroughly as in *Romans,* where the extreme dialecticism and actualism which Bonhoeffer criticized in *Act and Being* render God's relationship to the world highly tangential. The time-eternity duality which emerges is strongly Neo-Kantian in its epistemological foundation and almost Platonistic in its radical separation of God and the world.

Bonhoeffer pressed from the beginning for the intimate *togetherness* of God and man in Christ and the church, over against Barth's sharp division of divine and human. Bonhoeffer not only maintained this premise to the end: He pushed the union of God and the world in Christ to its logical conclusion in the prison writings. The difference between *The Epistle to the Romans* and *Letters and Papers from Prison* can be expressed in the classic Reformed and Lutheran formulas which we shall have occasion to examine in the next chapter: The theme of *Romans* is *finitum non capax infiniti;* that of *Letters and Papers, finitum capax infiniti.* The striking thing is that from these different thematic lines Barth and Bonhoeffer ended up at nearly the same place.

The Epistle to the Romans is the charter document of the critique of "religion" in our day; its definition of and attitude toward "religion" have become a hallmark of Neo-Reformation theology generally. Bonhoeffer's own critical stance toward "religion" places him squarely in the theological movement begun by Barth. Undoubtedly Bonhoeffer was inspired, as his own words suggest, by *Romans.*

"Religion" is a purely human achievement, albeit the highest one; revelation is solely an unmerited action of the otherwise unknown God. So runs the general theme of Barth's commentary on the Letter to the Romans. As the pinnacle of human aspiration, "religion" is subject above everything else to the sin of pride. More than once Barth uses the phrase "the criminal arrogance of religion." [50] The paradox of "religion," seen in the light of divine revelation, is that precisely as *man's* highest and most self-satisfying work, it is of all his endeavors the most permeated with awareness of the death and judgment which hang over every human enterprise. Only in terms of driving man to a confrontation with his finitude and guilt is "religion" even a *praeparatio fidei.* It does not give man knowledge of God: "Religion compels us to the perception that God is not to be found in religion." [51]

"Religion" is idolatry. It "is the crowning of all other passions with the passion of eternity, the endowment of what is finite with infinity." [52] We have seen, in discussing Bonhoeffer's conception of a world "come of age," that the chief characteristic of that world is the death of "religion," which means in part the death even of idolatry. According to Bonhoeffer (following Barth), idolatry is a "religious" phenomenon; with the decay of "religion" in a mature world, idolatry is replaced by nihilism.

Bonhoeffer characterizes "religion" as inwardness (inner dispositions of man disclosed to him in the private dimension of his life which provide a "contact point" with the transcendent: piety, conscience, etc.) and metaphysics (God as the *deus ex machina* and the stopgap for human knowledge). In *Romans* Barth attacked the nineteenth-century equation of Christian faith with religious piety: "Faith . . . is never identical with 'piety,' however pure and however delicate." [53] He also rejected the "religious" attempt to make God a metaphysical entity: "God is no 'thing-in-itself,' no metaphysical substance in the midst of other substances." [54] And again: "The boldest speculations of religion . . . stick fast . . . in some endeavour to stretch nature to supernature or to metaphysics." [55] Following Barth, Bonhoeffer was a lifelong foe of "inwardness" and theological metaphysics.

In considering Bonhoeffer's critique of "religion," we noted that he regarded "religion" as "non-necessary," i.e., as a temporary historical phenomenon which in our day has already begun to disappear. We find expressions of this nature in Barth's *Romans:* " 'Religion' . . . [is] a speciality of certain special circles and epochs and tempera-ments." [56] He goes on to raise the rhetorical question, "What human passion is more obviously temporary than the passion of religion?" [57] Barth was to elucidate and make more emphatic the "non-necessity" of "religion" in his developed critique of "religion" in the *Church Dog-matics.*[58]

Both Bonhoeffer and Barth reject the usual dichotomy between "re-ligious" and secular, holy and profane, spheres of life. In *The Epistle to the Romans* Barth was already analyzing "religion" as "a thing in the midst of other things. . . . A dualism controls the whole world of religion." [59] "In religion," he went on to elaborate, "dualism makes its appearance. . . . Religion breaks men into two halves. One half is the *spirit* of the inward man. . . . The other half is the *natural* world of my members." [60] The identification here of "religion" with the soul (spirit) and with inwardness should be noted. Biblical faith sees man as a whole, according to Barth, and this holistic anthropology plays a prominent role in Bonhoeffer's "Christianity without religion" project. In the light of the gospel there is only one division that mat-ters: the division between God and man.

Finally, like the Bonhoeffer of *Letters and Papers,* the Barth of *Romans* proclaimed the *death* of "religion." In Bonhoeffer's thought, however, the death of "religion" is in the indicative: as a matter of fact, "religion" is dying or dead. Barth, on the other hand, made the death of "religion" an imperative: "If religion be understood as a concrete, comprehensible, and historical phenomenon in the world of men and of sin and of death—it must be abandoned." [61] The reason that the death of "religion" is mandatory and not declarative in Barth's view has to do with what has turned out to be a disagreement with the "religionless" Bonhoeffer over the meaning of a world "come of age." To Barth the modern world is still incurably "religious," filled with idolatries whose faces alone have changed; hence the demand that "religion" (which is nothing but idolatry) die, in order to confront man with the true God. The Bonhoeffer of the prison writings, on the other hand, makes the revolutionary suggestion that "religion" and therefore even idolatry are dying. For Barth the entry of the gospel into human affairs demands that "religion" be shattered. For the later Bonhoeffer, the problem is rather how the gospel is to make sense to a world in which "religion" has already been shattered.

Even as he demanded that "religion" had to die, Barth maintained its inevitability even within Christianity: "Religion is the unavoidable reflection in the soul—in experience—of the miracle of faith which has occurred to the soul." [62] Later on he made the remarkably affirmative statement that "Religion is the ability of men to receive and to retain an impress of God's revelation." [63] "Religion" is an utterly human work and therefore subject to judgment and death; but it is also the usual "container," as it were, for revelation and for the life of response to revelation. Barth later clarified his negative and positive assessments of religion in his *Dogmatics* under the headings "false religion" and "true religion." [64] "Religion" per se is always false because it is always a purely human attempt to storm heaven; it is unbelief. But "religion" can be rendered "true" by being the vessel of revelation. We can speak of Christianity as "true religion" in the same sense that we can speak of a justified sinner. "False religion" is destroyed by the revelation of God, but that revelation transforms and sanctifies the vessels of "religion" (piety, prayer, the sacraments, the communal religious life) and makes of them "true religion."

The early Bonhoeffer, following Barth, had some positive things to say about "religion." Interestingly enough, we find Bonhoeffer to have been less critical of applying the word to Christianity than was Barth.

With his concern for the concrete, material relationship of revelation to the church, he was willing to use the word "religion," when properly understood, to mean the same thing as "faith." This was in explicit contrast to Barth, who (along with the dialectical theologians generally) set faith over against "religion" as the essential over against the nonessential response of man to God.

In *Sanctorum Communio* Bonhoeffer defined "religion" as "the touching of the human will by the divine, and the overcoming of the former by the latter with resultant free action." [65] Bonhoeffer's willingness to grant so much to "religion" as a general term, despite his Barthian position at that time, attests perhaps to the liberal influence of his Berlin teachers such as Seeberg (his thesis supervisor) and Harnack. An important passage from *Act and Being* makes explicit Bonhoeffer's early views on the matter of "religion":

It must be plainly said that within the communion of Christ faith takes shape in religion, that therefore religion is here called faith, that, as I look on Christ, I may and must say for my consolation "I believe"—only to add, of course, as I turn to look on myself, "help Thou my unbelief." All praying, all searching for God in his Word, all clinging to his promise, all entreaty for his grace, all hoping in the sight of the Cross, all this for reflexion is "religion," "faith-wishfulness" [Barth]; but in the communion of Christ, while it is still the work of man, it is God-given faith, faith willed by God, wherein by God's mercy he may really be found.[66]

For Bonhoeffer, in the passage quoted, there is such a thing as "true religion," precisely in Barth's later sense of the word: i.e., "religion" transformed and "justified," sinful though it be, by the revelation of God in Christ.

Barth and the early Bonhoeffer tended to talk of "religion" which can be "true" chiefly in terms of piety and ecclesiastical practices. Worship, the sacraments, prayer and acts of devotion, religious fellowship, and even peculiarly "religious" experience can presumably become "true" when they are informed by the grace of God in Christ. It seems to be the subjective side of "religion"—inwardness, conscience, piety—which can become a vessel of grace.

Barth and Bonhoeffer had nothing of a positive nature to say about the possibility of the objective side of "religion," the metaphysical God, being transformed into "true religion." The reason, of course, is that "religion" begins and ends with God; therefore the concept or "image" of God is the central issue. While "religious" piety as a purely human work must die, it is capable of resurrection by God. "Religious" practices are always relative and changing matters which can be transformed for good or for ill. A faulty apprehension of God as a metaphysical being outside time and space who fills the gaps in our knowledge and descends to our aid in the "boundary-situations" is fundamentally and unequivocally wrong, however, since everything depends upon who God really is. Both Barth and Bonhoeffer agreed with Pascal that the God of the philosophers (and of much popular belief) is not the God of Abraham, Isaac, and Jacob. The metaphysical image of God must die completely and make way for the image of the true and living God: Jesus Christ as proclaimed by the Scriptures. The subjective side of "religion" can be transformed and made "true" by the work of its true "object," the living God in his revelation. The objective dimension of "religion" is irredeemable, since there can be only one true "object," the God who is unknown apart from his own gracious self-disclosure in Christ.

The two theologians always insisted emphatically, of course, that "religious" experience and practices have no claim, and far less a monopoly, on God's revelation. They pointed vigorously to the constant danger of piety's becoming an end in itself, a simply human work, and therefore idolatry or unbelief. They were careful to define the essential response to God, faith, in holistic terms, as a total human (not "religious") relationship to God grounded entirely by God and even capable of being psychologically "unconscious" from a subjective point of view. Barth and Bonhoeffer strenuously resisted the liberal habit of describing faith in psychological terms. Faith is a reality independent of psychological considerations. "Religion" and its practices, on the other hand, can and should be easily described in psychological terms. The dependence of "religion" upon the relativities of psychological makeup and temperament lies in part at the root of both Barth's and the "religionless" Bonhoeffer's suggestion that "religion" is a "non-necessary" or "non-essential" phenomenon. Historically the human psyche has been capable of striking differences from culture to culture, age to age, and individual to individual.

The earlier Bonhoeffer, then, believed that God in Christ can and does transform our "religious" attitudes into what can genuinely be called "true religion." Yet the later, "religionless" Bonhoeffer declared that these same attitudes are in the process of disappearing almost entirely. The objective, "metaphysical" side of "religion," which was irredeemable anyway, is now long dead except for vestiges such as the common acknowledgment of a "supreme Being," a phenomenon which is increasingly nothing more than a cultural way of speaking. But "religion" as "inwardness" is now decaying also—that side of "religion" which is capable of being rendered "true." Here is the present dilemma for Christianity.

The Epistle to the Romans was the noisiest of Barth's opening guns in the neo-orthodox attack on "religion" in the name of revelation. Where, then, did Barth fail? Bonhoeffer replies: "It was that in the non-religious interpretation of theological concepts he gave no concrete guidance, either in dogmatics or in ethics." [67] Having shattered "religion," having performed the negative task of prophetic criticism, Barth failed to understand its full implications and hence offered nothing constructive along "non-religious" lines. What he did come up with to take the place of "religion" is what Bonhoeffer calls a "revelation-positivism" (*Offenbarungspositivismus*). The "positivist doctrine of revelation . . . says, in effect, 'Like it or lump it': virgin birth, Trinity, or anything else; each is an equally significant and necessary part of the whole, which must simply be swallowed as a whole or not at all." Authentically biblical and evangelical faith is not like that, argues Bonhoeffer: In the Scriptures we find many gradations and nuances of both discernment and importance. By throwing the Bible in our laps, as Barth seems to do, he sets up "a law of faith, and . . . mutilates what is—by Christ's incarnation!—a gift for us." By focusing so exclusively on the "law of faith" and the church's inner life, Barth leaves "the world . . . to its own devices, and that is the mistake." [68]

In the chapter on "Biblical Hermeneutics" we shall discuss Barth's "scholastic" tendency to treat biblical faith as a seamless fabric of classical doctrines which form the *depositum fidei* of traditional Catholicism and Protestant orthodoxy. We shall contrast with this outlook the more authentically Reformation and evangelical insight into the Scriptures held by Bonhoeffer (and by Emil Brunner): the sensitive recognition of central and peripheral elements in the faith of the Bible, and a reticence about speculating behind the concrete biblical word. The issue between Bonhoeffer and Barth will be examined specifically with

reference to the doctrine of the Virgin Birth of Christ. What the Bonhoeffer of the prison writings calls Barth's "revelation-positivism" is
simply and precisely this "neo-scholastic" presentation of Christian
faith. The Barth of the *Church Dogmatics,* the mature, constructive
Barth, views revelation, according to Bonhoeffer, as something all of a
piece. The full range of orthodox Christian dogma ("virgin birth,
Trinity, or anything else"), as based in Holy Scripture and interpreted
by creeds and councils, "must simply be swallowed as a whole or not at
all." Revelation as thus posited becomes "a law of faith." Everything
must either be accepted as "an equally significant and necessary part of
the whole" or "not at all." Paul Tillich expresses a very similar criticism of Barth when he says that Barthian theology is "thrown at those
in the situation—thrown like a stone." [69]

Bonhoeffer counters Barth's "positivism" with his characteristic concern for the concreteness and dynamism of the biblical revelation. The
Bible, he states, does not view revelation as a monochromatic reality
which stands anomalously over against man; it recognizes "degrees of
knowledge and degrees of significance." Revelation confronts man
amid the concreteness and ambiguity of his historical situation; hence
it cannot be demanded of man that the dogmas which interpret and
focus the revelation "be swallowed as a whole or not at all." Barth, the
theologian of grace par excellence, curiously tends to make the self-
disclosure of God a law rather than "what is—by Christ's incarnation!
—a gift for us." To handle the church's dogmas as a kind of law confronting man renders the revelatory gift no longer a gift; it becomes an
alien and arbitrary and, in a world come of age, an archaic power pos-
sessing a grace-less severity. In the last analysis, Bonhoeffer maintains,
Barth fails modern man by replacing "religion" with a fideism which
only a few even inside the church understand and can still believe.

Bonhoeffer considered Barth's thology a half-way house. Barth understood the problem of "religion" but did not understand the radical
implications of this problem for theological reconstruction in the present age. His theological solution, according to Bonhoeffer, was a stopgap between an orthodox restoration and a radical reconstruction. The
church seemed to Bonhoeffer so to absorb Barth that he did not really
concern himself with *communicating* the gospel to the world; hence
his preoccupation with endlessly weighing and sifting every detail of
the church's classical teachings, and his relative indifference to the

problem of the church's language in terms of the non-Christian, "non-religious" world.

Barth's theological presuppositions and method were on the right track, said Bonhoeffer, and the younger man was well aware of his own indebtedness. But Barth refused to give any "concrete guidance" on "the non-religious interpretation of theological concepts." Having shown the wholly problematic character of "religion," Barth offers nothing to replace it but a "neo-scholastic" fideism, which is perhaps workable for the church (although even this is seriously arguable, since the Christian is at the same time a secular person), but which leaves the world "to its own devices." "And that," Bonhoeffer comments, "is the mistake." Barth had the "right" theology—biblical and christocentric—but he failed to translate it into "non-religious" terms for the sake of a world "come of age" (and of the Christian, insofar as he belongs inescapably to that world). The task of translating Barth's basically correct approach to the interpretation of the gospel into the "non-religious" language of a secular world fell to Bonhoeffer.

The question may again be asked whether Bonhoeffer's criticisms would not have been modified in the light of Barth's post-war writings. Perhaps more significantly than the other theologicans discussed in this chapter, Barth's thought, in its ceaseless and genuinely open-ended ferment, altered to some degree. There are certain respects in which he came remarkably close to Bonhoeffer theologically, quite consciously appropriating some of the latter's insights. A good example of this is Barth's book *The Humanity of God,* in which he criticizes his own one-sided emphasis in his early years on the complete "otherness" of God. His deepening insight into the christological basis of theology, he says, has caused him more and more to realize that Jesus Christ is God's "togetherness" with man. In Christ we know that God is truly *man's* God, the graciously initiating partner in an eternal covenant with the human race. Theology is then more properly to be spoken of as "The-anthropology," and Christians must speak boldly of "the humanity of God." All these are themes which were there from the beginning in Bonhoeffer's christology.

At the same time, the Barth of *The Humanity of God* is quite explicitly critical of Bonhoeffer and the thinking inspired by his prison letters, although nowhere does he mention him by name. Barth rightly sees that the issue, on the theological level, is the problem of the "non-religious interpretation of biblical concepts": "The question of *language*, about which one must speak in reference to the so-called 'outsiders,' is not so burning today as is asserted in various quarters. This is true in the first place because, . . . thinking in terms of the humanity of God, we cannot at all reckon in a serious way with *real* 'outsiders,' with a 'world come of age,' but only with a world which *regards* itself as of age (and proves daily that it is precisely not that) ." [70] In the light of Jesus Christ, *all* men, Christians and secularists alike, stand together before God simply as judged and forgiven sinners.

Barth recognizes that not only is secular man really an "insider," but Christian man is also an "outsider," a contemporary "non-religious" person. Just for that reason, however, there is no need for a special "translation" of the gospel into contemporary terms:

Thus the so-called "outsiders" are really only "insiders" who have not yet understood and apprehended themselves as such. On the other hand, even the most persuaded Christian, in the final analysis, must and will recognise himself ever and again as an "outsider." So there must then be no particular language for insiders and outsiders. Both are contemporary men-of-the-world—all of us are. [71]

Bonhoeffer, of course, never regards secular man as "a *real* 'outsider,' " as Barth seems to suggest. For Bonhoeffer as well as for Barth, all men are caught up, whether consciously or unconsciously, in the saving reality of Christ. It is simply that Bonhoeffer appears to have been more passionately concerned than Barth that as many persons as possible should understand and become joyously conscious of their reconciliation in Christ. In this "missionary" zeal Bonhoeffer would seem to have been on good New Testament ground. It also reflects his concern for the "penultimate" over against Barth's tendency to talk only of the "ultimate." Ultimately, secular man stands before God simply as a sinner, and is saved only by the grace of God in Christ; but penultimately he is a person who is predominating in the modern world—often a good person who strives for many of the same values as Christians—and who, like any other human being in all times and places, is entitled to have the gospel proclaimed in his own (in this case, "non-religious") language so that he too may become conscious of so great a gift. Even Barth, as we have seen, recognized that the task of the preacher and the theologian is not simply to "repeat the Bible";

this is not hermeneutics. Bonhoeffer took the hermeneutical task more seriously than ever before in the prison writings.

To the charge that his theology is a "revelation-positivism," Barth replies with the slightly condescending humor of the Grand Old Man:

A little "non-religious" language from the street, the newspaper, literature, and, if one is ambitious, from the philosopher may thus, for the sake of communication, occasionally indeed be in order. However, we should not become particularly concerned about this. A little of the language of Canaan, a little "revelation-positivism," can also be a good thing in addressing us all and . . . will often, though not always, be still better understood even by the oddest strangers.[72]

It is interesting that Barth interprets "revelation-positivism" to mean simply "the language of Canaan," i.e. the biblical language. But that is not what Bonhoeffer meant by the term: He meant rather what Barth has *done* with "the language of Canaan"—and what he has failed to do.

Thus even the more recent Barth, as represented by *The Humanity of God,* could not take "the world" as seriously as did Bonhoeffer. Barth's remarks on the "insider" and the "outsider" reflect basically the same stance as the following statements in the first volume of the *Church Dogmatics,* written a quarter of a century earlier:

Language about God is the language of the *per se* faithless and anti-faith reason of man.[73]

The conflict of faith with unbelief can only be important in the case and form in which it is a conflict of faith with itself; because in faith itself unbelief has somehow reported itself verbally and claims a hearing . . . .[74]

The pivotal point from the beginning in later, dogmatic Barthian theology is the reconciliation of all things in Christ. Barth's dogmatic procedure has for one of its cornerstones the principle that Christian theology cannot begin with an independent anthropology (as Bultmann does) but only with a christological anthropology. Bonhoeffer himself, speaking very much as a Barthian, put it succinctly: "There is no man 'in himself.' . . . Man is the man who was accepted in the incarnation of Christ, who was loved, condemned and reconciled in Christ." [75] Hence Barth's "failure" to "take the world seriously." It is because in Christ all men have been judged and reconciled, and therefore to talk about "the world" as an independent entity with a life of its own is meaningless.

It is precisely at this point, however, that the fundamental divergence between Bonhoeffer and Barth appears. Barth begins with the reconciliation of all things in Christ and concludes that "godlessness," the world "come of age," cannot be taken seriously. Bonhoeffer begins no less strongly from precisely the same premise and concludes that "the world" must be taken more seriously than ever before. Both conclusions are in fact possible from the initial conviction that "Man is the man who was accepted in the incarnation of Christ." The road the later Barth pursues is the affirmation of the church in all its churchliness. The later Bonhoeffer, on the contrary, presses for the affirmation of the world in all its worldliness.

While criticizing Barth for presenting Christian dogmas as a "law of faith," Bonhoeffer nevertheless recognized the important need for the preservation and constant renewal by the church of the great historical beliefs of Christianity—Incarnation, Atonement, Resurrection, Ascension, etc.—even in a "religionless" world. Here he introduced his notion of the *Arkandisziplin,* the "secret discipline," of the church, which will be discussed in Chapter Seven.

Chapter Six

The Humanity
of God in Christ

The one word which best sums up Bonhoeffer's entire theological development is *christology*. It is the golden thread which ties together his works from first to last. In an early article, written while he was in the United States and setting forth a fairly straightforward Barthian approach to the doctrine of God, Bonhoeffer spoke of Christ as "the personal revelation, the personal presence of God in the world." [1] In the exegetical work *Creation and Fall*, first published in 1933, Bonhoeffer stated that " 'Jesus Christ' is the name of God. This is highly anthropomorphic and highly objective at the same time." [2] In the later, transitional writings which make up his *Ethics*, Bonhoeffer was to affirm that "God is God become man [*der Menschgewordene*]." [3] And in the final, "religionless" *Letters and Papers from Prison*, Bonhoeffer asked the question "Who is God?" and replied, "Encounter with Jesus Christ. The experience that a transformation of all human life is given in the fact that 'Jesus is there only for others' [*"für andere da ist"*]." [4]

Indeed, the absoluteness of Bonhoeffer's christocentricity parallels that of the later Barth as does no other modern christology. Jesus Christ as the object of all theology is the key to the "Christianity without religion" of the prison writings no less than to Bonhoeffer's earlier writings. The christology of the "non-religious interpretation" is in fact a perfectly consistent outcome of his whole christological development. "How intensely Bonhoeffer's theological outlook took its bearings from Jesus Christ," writes Gerhard Ebeling, one of his most astute interpreters, "requires no substantiation." [5]

Finitum capax infiniti

Bonhoeffer espoused the christological method in theology which Barth articulated, going on to give it expression as the very bedrock and structure of all his own theological works. Yet it is precisely on the matter of christology that Bonhoeffer differed sharply from the early Barth. "Just because they are both theologians whose foundations are so radically Christological," writes Ebeling, "the differences between them necessarily stand out most clearly in Christology." [6]

In discussing Bonhoeffer's christology with reference to Barth's, it is important to distinguish between the "early" and the "later" Barth, for Bonhoeffer's quarrel was basically with the "early" Barth. In the first part of Barth's revolutionary theological career (1915-31), he was the dialectical, existentialist theologian who began with Kierke-gaard's "infinite qualitative distinction" between God and man in exegeting the Scriptures. During this early period, however, he came increasingly to define the task of theology in exclusively theological, classical-dogmatic, christological terms. The publication of the first part of the first volume of the *Church Dogmatics* in 1932 embodied this "new beginning" [7] in his theology. It must be remembered that it was the "early" Barth with whom Bonhoeffer was thoroughly conver-sant. Although Bonhoeffer also knew intimately the dogmatic-theologi-cal direction which Barth was taking during the later 'twenties and the 'thirties, the circumstances of the church struggle in Germany, the war, and his untimely death prevented him from ever reading more than probably the first volume of Barth's *Dogmatics*.[8] In addition, of course, most of Barth's theological system has been published only since the end of the war. All this is relevant to a comparison of the views of Bonhoeffer and Barth on the matter of christology.

Bonhoeffer's objections to Barth's early christology were the focal point of his internal criticisms of dialectical theology generally. The main charge Bonhoeffer brought against Barthian dialectics was that of *formalism*. Dialectical theology, Bonhoeffer claimed, was rooted epistemologically in Neo-Kantian transcendentalism. In his early writ-ing *Act and Being* he defined "genuine transcendentalism" as "the reference of thought to something transcendental" without "its having

135

that something at its disposal." [9] Since knowledge cannot encompass the transcendent in ontological categories, "questions of being are unknown to genuine transcendentalism." Hence truth is not found in the reflection of being in the mind (ontologism), but in the act of knowing. In this way "the concept of being is resolved into the concept of the act." [10] This approach to knowledge is formalism (as opposed to realism) or actualism (in contrast to ontologism).

The early, dialectical Barth propounded a formalistic theology, a theology of pure act: "The conceptual world of Karl Barth," wrote Bonhoeffer in *Act and Being*, "leans toward the transcendental theory." [11] John Godsey, in his study of Bonhoeffer's theology, has a good description of Barth's early actualism. His theology, Godsey states, presupposed

a purely formal understanding of the freedom of God, and it follows that theological thinking must remain fundamentally profane thinking. God remains free from every grasp of the knowing ego and thus moves into the non-objective sphere; that is, God always remains Subject and shuns every attempt of men to know him as an object. Thus man can speak of God only indirectly, which is to say, dialectically. . . . Human existence must be thought of in terms of God-effected decisions, and it becomes problematic how the human being is to be thought of in continuity.[12]

Barth's attempt, following Kierkegaard, to preserve the freedom and majesty of God over against every effort of sinful man to domesticate him led to a method which described God's activity in negations. God was *unverdinglich*—not at our disposal—and his revelation to us highly contingent. Just when man thinks he has grasped hold of God in his revelation, he has then surely not grasped him. Hence there is no continuity about God's self-disclosure in history; it is "atomized in pure acts," as Eberhard Bethge interprets Barth's early dialectic.[13]

Applying this formalistic method to christology itself, Barth affirmed as late as in the first volume of the *Church Dogmatics* that "the essence of the Church [Jesus Christ] is *actus purus, divine* action beginning with itself . . . ; free *action*, not a continuously present relation." [14] Replying to the liberal notion that the *humanitas Christi*, the man Jesus as such, is the revelation of God, Barth stated that

the power and the continuity in which the man Jesus of Nazareth, according to the testimony of the evangelists and apostles, was in fact the revealed word, consisted here also in the power and continuity of the divine action in this form and not in the continuity of this form as such. . . . Manifestation is clearly not in itself or directly ascribed to His existence as such. . . . The divinity is not so immanent in the humanity of Christ as not also to remain transcendent over it.[15]

To be sure, in other places throughout volume one of the *Church Dogmatics,* as well as in his earlier works, Barth came down firmly on the side of the utter corporeality of God's revelation in Christ.[16] But this corporeality of "the Word made flesh" was always seen as utterly contingent on the sovereign freedom of God alone. The Incarnation thus appeared to be a *formal* unity of God and man, sustained entirely by the divine act and not at all by the obedience of Jesus' humanity. At times Barth spoke of the *form* of the Incarnation (the *humanitas Christi*) as if it were an empty container filled by the divine Word: "It is *not the form* that reveals, speaks, comforts, works, helps, *but God in the form.*" [17]

The scales must be tipped in favor of the transcendentalistic side in Barth's earlier understanding of the Incarnation. One of his definitions of revelation, synonymous with Jesus Christ, further attests to Barth's emphasis on the divine freedom over against man. He declares that "revelation itself is nothing else than the freedom of God's grace, . . . the event in which God, being free, allows this free grace scope to operate." [18] This way of speaking christologically is simply abstract and insufficiently biblical. Barth was definitely committed to a thoroughly christocentric understanding of the nature and method of theology when he wrote the first volume of his *Church Dogmatics,* but even here he had not entirely freed himself from his earlier actualism for a genuinely historical, concrete grasp of the Incarnation.

Acknowledging the importance of Barth's reaffirmation of the sovereign majesty of God, Bonhoeffer nevertheless felt that Barth's methodological application of this principle to christology resulted in an abstraction. Among Bonhoeffer's theological theses offered for graduation from the University of Berlin in 1927 is one which predicates that "the dialectic of so-called dialectic theology has logical and not real character, and thus runs the risk of neglecting the historicity of Jesus." [19] In an article on Bonhoeffer's *Act and Being,* which deals specifically and critically with Barth's actualism, Franklin Sherman succinctly paraphrases Bonhoeffer's questions to Barth:

Is the freedom to speak or not to speak, the freedom to give or to withhold himself from man, really the freedom of the God we know in Christ? Has not Barth fallen into the error of dealing with possibilities—with what God can or cannot do, might or might not do—rather than cleaving to the *reality* in which God has in fact revealed himself? [20]

Thus Bonhoeffer countered Barth's actualism with realism. Barth's dialectical method broke apart on the side of negation. God's relation to the world is so utterly free that his freedom becomes an abstraction. Barth, who was later to accuse Calvin of having attempted to go behind the revelation in Christ in his doctrine of election,[21] fell at an early stage into the same pitfall on the matter of divine sovereignty. Desiring to begin with the revelation in Christ, he nevertheless attempted to speak within this framework of God *a se;* Bonhoeffer preferred to speak only of God *pro nobis.* For Barth, Jesus Christ meant an event in God's freedom; for Bonhoeffer, the utter availability of God:

In revelation it is a question less of God's freedom on the far side from us [*jenseits*], i.e. his eternal isolation and aseity, than of his forth-proceeding [*Aussichheraustreten*], his *given* Word, his bond in which he has bound himself, of his freedom as it is most strongly attested in his having freely bound himself to historical man, having placed himself at man's disposal. God is not free *of* man but *for* man. Christ is the Word of his freedom. God *is there* [*ist da*], which is to say: not in eternal non-objectivity [*Nichtgegenständlichkeit*] but . . . "haveable" ["*habbar*"], graspable [*fassbar*] in his Word within the Church.[22]

The issue between Bonhoeffer and the early Barth on christology can be viewed from a historical perspective as a modern version of the classical Lutheran-Reformed debate. *Finitum non capax infiniti* is the traditional Calvinist doctrine of revelation: the finite cannot contain the infinite. The glory of the sovereign God does not enter entirely into this sinful world. Barth the modern Reformed theologian affirmed this doctrine in his early career by means of a formal, actualistic, abstract understanding of God's freedom. Luther, on the other hand, had affirmed that *finitum capax infiniti:* the finite does have the capacity for the infinite. "God's glory is total freedom not from, but for, man." Bonhoeffer, a modern representative of the Lutheran tradition, espoused this doctrine in terms of a material, realistic, concrete interpretation of God's freedom. Bethge interprets Bonhoeffer's Lutheran understanding of the Incarnation in this way:

> There is no God, Bonhoeffer emphasizes, other than the incarnated one. . . .
> God's free majesty we do know in the assuming and accepting of man in Christ. . . . Whether there might be some different majesty of God we do not know, and we should even refrain from interesting ourselves in it in order to worship the real and concrete majesty of God.[23]

Contrasting the starting points of Barth and Bonhoeffer, Bethge concludes that "while Barth, in order to save God's majesty, started by pushing God away, Bonhoeffer starts by drawing him in—in order to save the same majesty of God." [24]

In the first volume of the *Church Dogmatics*, it is true, Barth explicitly rejected his earlier *finitum non capax infiniti* in favor of the more accurately theological expression *homo peccator non capax verbi Domini:*

> The statement *finitum non capax infiniti* . . . really could not prove what is to be proved. If the real experience of a man addressed by the Word of God were to speak against this statement, this statement would have to go, as every philosophical statement in theology must go which contradicts this experience. . . . We shall not say *finitum,* but we shall say *homo peccator non capax*—and we shall not continue *infiniti,* but *verbi Domini.*[25]
>
> "Th' eternal Good's your brother." And that is exactly what is so far from being obvious; what is rather miraculous; and not only and primarily as a miracle of all power, as the mystery in which the statement *finitum non capax infiniti* is dissolved. That, of course, is also the case. But it is not the dissolution of this statement that is the mystery of the revelation of God the Son, it is the dissolution of the other, far more incisive statement, *homo peccator non capax verbi divini.* God's power to establish intercourse with us is, of course, also, though in the long run not decisively, called in question by the fact that He is infinite while we are finite. . . . But then this possibility in God is decisively called in question by our being God's enemies.[26]

It is true that the old Lutheran and Reformed formulas *finitum capax* and *finitum non capax* have an abstract, philosophical form which may be misleading. To one standing outside the theological context, they seem to be preoccupied with the metaphysical problem of the relation of finite to infinite rather than the properly theological problem of the relation of sinful man to the living God. Nevertheless, it must be said, first of all, that in the theological sphere of Lutheran and Reformed dogmatics *finitum* was simply assumed to contain the concept of sinfulness as well as of finitude. Likewise *infiniti* was not the abstract deity of philosophy but the living God of the Bible (however laden he was in Protestant scholasticism with metaphysical attributes).

Secondly, and even more importantly, the old dogmatic formulas symbolize, however inadequately, the historical christological differences between Bonhoeffer and Barth, differences to which Barth's later substitution simply does not apply. Obviously Bonhoeffer would have agreed wholeheartedly that *homo peccator non capax verbi Domini;* no less than Barth did he assert that all is of grace. But that is not the issue in the christological question of Barth's early formalism versus Bonhoeffer's lifelong realism. The issue there is rather how dogmatics is to describe or interpret the Incarnation. Is it the wholly free, tangential act of an eternal, isolated God in the form of the man Jesus; or is it this Person whom we encounter in the Scriptures simply and concretely as fully God and fully man? For Bonhoeffer, Jesus Christ is both the wholly gracious God and the wholly obedient man. Here *finitum capax infiniti:* In the grace and purpose of God this finite man, born into a fallen humanity, is at the same time the revelation of the infinite and sinless God. God freely gives himself unstintingly to man in Christ. In Barth's early view, on the other hand, God withholds himself in part, as it were, from man, even in the Incarnation: *finitum non capax infiniti.*

The classical Lutheran-Reformed debate created a distinctive christological outlook within each communion. In some of the Confessions and in the dogmatic treatises of the two traditions we can clearly see the "Antiochene" tendency of Reformed christology, the tendency to separate the eternal Logos in some degree from the man Jesus, thereby endangering the concrete reality of the Incarnation and creating a "hidden side" of God which looms threateningly behind the open revelation in Christ (as seen, for example, in the doctrine of predestination) ; and the "Alexandrine" direction of Lutheran christology, the tendency to fuse the Logos and Jesus so intimately as to run the risk of blurring the distinction and making of Christ a divine metamorphosis rather than an Incarnation.

The mistake of these traditional christologies, both Lutheran and Reformed, was that they tried to interpret the Incarnation in terms of the question "How?": "How can the infinite and eternal God relate himself to a finite man?" Bonhoeffer cut right through the problem by asserting that the proper christological question is not "How?" but "Who?": "Who is this actual person whom the Scriptures proclaim both man and God?" Significantly, Barth's own shift from his early preoccupation with the "infinite qualitative distinction" between God and man to the dogmatic premise that "Jesus Christ is the reality of revelation" brought him increasingly to speak of the Incarnation in terms of the question "Who?"

The "Who?" versus "How?" questions with regard to the Incarnation suggest another and perhaps more serious defect in the use of the classical Lutheran and Reformed formulas: They suggest that the problem of interpreting the Incarnation is that of bringing together an infinite God and a finite man. There is certainly this danger. Yet the formulas have the value of giving the early debate between Bonhoeffer and Barth its proper setting within the history of christological reflection. Furthermore, by beginning solely with the whole person Jesus Christ, Bonhoeffer did in fact come down, although far more biblically and convincingly, on the side of *finitum capax infiniti;* by beginning with the utter transcendence of God, Barth definitely began on the side of *finitum non capax infiniti.*

The importance of Bonhoeffer's Lutheran understanding of the Incarnation, in contrast to the Reformed interpretation of the early Barth, cannot be overstressed. *Finitum capax infiniti* could well be the theological motto of Bonhoeffer's whole theological development. His writings show him pushing this "material" doctrine of the Incarnation in an ever more concrete direction with creative passion and rigor. Here is the key to Bonhoeffer's whole theological method, including the final "non-religious interpretation of biblical concepts": God is God become man, the man Jesus Christ, and that is all we can concern outselves with as men. The only majesty, sovereignty, glory, and freedom of God which we know are what he has revealed in Jesus Christ. God is God-turned-toward-man in the Incarnation. He is "haveable," "graspable" in the concrete, historical affairs of men, not "eternal non-objectivity," related to the world only formally and tangentially through bare acts.

Bonhoeffer's protest against the early Barth's abstract doctrine of God reflects his life-long passion for *concreteness,* which we noted earlier in discussing the influence of personalist-existentialist philosophy. In understanding the factors contributing to his concern for concrete reality, it will be especially helpful to remember also Bonhoeffer's love of *Lebensphilosophie,* particularly Nietzsche's passion for the earth, and his interest and training in sociology. But these are always means for Bonhoeffer which help to interpret the central concreteness of the Incarnation itself. Bethge states that

he holds his eyes entirely on the revelation in Christ, in order to discover and describe its concreteness. . . . Concreteness is to be understood not as an addition or second activity but as a genuine attribute of revelation itself.[27]

The problem for Bonhoeffer was not how to make the gospel concrete; the gospel was intrinsically concrete. The problem was how to express and elucidate that concreteness. Christ the revelation of God is supremely concrete. God is to be found only in concrete reality, not hidden behind it and discovered by a process of abstraction, because "for Bonhoeffer revelation means nothing beyond, but an entity in, this historically and sociologically shaped world." [28] Hence the cruciality of the Lutheran *finitum capax infiniti* in Bonhoeffer's thought: It attests that revelation is utterly concrete.

Concern for concreteness is concern for personal-social existence and continuity. Bonhoeffer believed that Barth's actualism could not secure these things. Everything human was seen as so radically contingent, so utterly under the "question-mark" of the gospel,[29] that God's relation to the world was a discontinuous series of sheer acts. The vertical dimension was emphasized to the impoverishment of the horizontal in Barth's christology.

Christ *pro me*

Bonhoeffer's lectures on christology at the University of Berlin in 1933, preserved for us by Eberhard Bethge from student notes, not only bring together into an ordered unity the various christological themes which we have touched upon, but also foreshadow in a remarkable way the main concerns of Bonhoeffer's "non-religious interpretation" of christology. Furthermore, they reveal more dramatically than any other of Bonhoeffer's works that from the early years of his theological career, despite his indebtedness to Barth, he was a strikingly original, independent, and imaginative interpreter of Christ who demands careful consideration in his own right.

Theology is christology, states Bonhoeffer (following Barth), the science of the Logos of God who is at the same time a human being. We encounter a familiar theme from our discussion of Bonhoeffer's personalism in his assertion that it is only the divine Logos, which comes to us from outside ourselves and as a person, which is transcendent in the real (rather than merely logical) sense. The purely immanent logos of man, and even the otherness and impenetrability of the human Thou considered in itself (Grisebach), fail to transcend the individual human ego except in terms of a conceptual possibility which in the end turns back upon that same ego. Christological science alone deals with genuine transcendence:

This Logos is the Logos of God, whose transcendence makes christology the crown of learning and whose coming from outside makes it the centre of scholarship. The subject remains transcendent and yet the Logos with whom we are concerned here is a person. This man is transcendent. . . . There is no proof by which it [christology] can demonstrate the transcendence of its subject. Its statement that this transcendence, namely the Logos, is a person, a man, is a presupposition and not subject to proof. A transcendence which is allowed to be subject to proof instead of being the presupposition of thought is simply reason coming to an understanding of itself.[30]

Bonhoeffer expresses the difference between christology and other sciences, between transcendence and immanence, in terms of the two questions around which his christology lectures polarize: "The question 'Who?' is the question of transcendence. The question 'How?' is the question of immanence." [31] Bonhoeffer's *Christologie* is one of the most precise articulations to be found in his writings of the "christological personalism" which is the basis of all his thought. Only a person can be authentically transcendent to me: transcendence is a personal-ethical, not an epistemological, concept. But more than this: Only the person who is also the Logos of God is the truly transcendent one who makes my neighbor also genuinely "other" than I. Philosophy—epistemology and metaphysics—properly asks the question "How?" But that is the question to ask about immanence, about relations among phenomena. Only christology legitimately asks the question about transcendence, because it asks the person-question "Who?" Throughout his christology lectures, Bonhoeffer criticizes traditional christological thought for failing to focus resolutely on the question "Who?" and yielding time and again to the temptation to ask "How?" questions of Christ. Two examples from the history of theology are the persistent attempt to discuss the Incarnation with the question "How could God become man?" instead of the proper question "Who is this person whom the New Testament proclaims as both God and man?" and both the Roman Catholic and the Reformation attempt to ask and answer the question "How is Christ truly present in the bread and the wine of the sacrament?" [32]

The tenacious "christological personalism" of Bonhoeffer's approach to theology meant for him being content to listen obediently to what the Scriptures say of the man Jesus Christ, with all the enigmas, the ambiguities, the unanswered questions, and the offenses of the biblical picture of this man. We shall see, in discussing Bonhoeffer's "non-religious" christological interpretation, that it is simply a drawing out of the secular implications of this completely biblical and personalistic understanding of transcendence which finds its sole *locus* in the Jesus of the New Testament.

Like Barth, Bonhoeffer insists that christological science can only be a function of the *church:* "The christological question can be put scientifically only in the context of the church. It can only be put where the basic presupposition, Christ's claim to be the Logos of God, has been accepted." [33] The christological premise of all thought about transcendence is apprehended only in faith, and faith is the gift granted by God to the Christian community. We shall examine in the next chapter Bonhoeffer's vividly concrete christological understanding of the church.

The question "Who?" which looks for its answer solely to the flesh-and-blood figure of the New Testament, means that christology is utterly *concrete* in its orientation. We have seen this emphasis in discussing Bonhoeffer's christology with reference to that of the early Barth. In *Christ the Center* Bonhoeffer asserts that "God in timeless eternity is not God, Jesus limited by time is not Jesus. Rather, God is God in the man Jesus. In this Jesus Christ God is present. This one God-man is the starting point of christology. . . . Space and time determine not only the humanity, but also the Godhead of the God-man." Traditionally christology has wrongly phrased the question of the Incarnation as the question of how to bring together an eternal, infinite God and the temporal, finite man Jesus. With Bonhoeffer's concrete biblical question "Who?" "the whole problem of christology is shifted. For here the point at issue is not the relationship of an isolated God to an isolated man in Christ, but the relationship of the already given God-man to the likeness of man." [34] Bonhoeffer "fleshes out" his attempt to answer the question "Who?" throughout the christology lectures, and centrally in his discussion of the problem of the "historical Jesus," to which we shall come a bit later.

What do we discover about the "being" of Jesus Christ when we restrict ourselves to the biblical-theological question "Who?" and look only to the Scriptures for the answer? We discover that

Christ is Christ not as Christ in himself, but in his relation to me. His being Christ is his being *pro me*. This being *pro me* is in turn not meant to be understood as an effect which emanates from him, or as an accident; it is meant to be understood as the essence, as the being of the person himself. This personal nucleus itself is the *pro me*. That Christ is *pro me* is not an historical or an ontical statement, but an ontological one. That is, Christ can never be thought of in his being in himself, but only in his relationship to me. That in turn means that Christ can only be conceived of existentially, viz. in the community. Christ is not a Christ in himself and additionally still in the community.[35]

This passage is highly significant. Here, in these lectures delivered in 1933, Bonhoeffer enunciates a christological idea which is simply reproduced in slightly different terminology in the "religionless" christology of the prison writings. That the very being of Christ is his being-for-man is the essence of Bonhoeffer's christology. We have examined this conception in terms of his insistence, over against the early Barth, that the only God about whom we can say anything is the God-for-us who is Christ. God is concretely "haveable" in his revelation in Jesus; in his sovereign freedom he binds himself inextricably to man and gives himself over to him. In *Christ the Center* we now find this idea spelled out quite specifically in terms of the doctrine of Christ.

For Bonhoeffer, christology must be thoroughly determined in all its parts by what the biblical witness actually says; to go behind this is to raise the illegitimate question "How?" In the Bible the being of the God-man is his being-for-us. There is no Christ "in himself," whose substance is eternal aseity but who *per accidens* (i.e., ontically or historically) gives himself to us. The Bible knows only the Christ who in his inmost essence (i.e., ontologically) is *pro me*.

When we examine the "non-religious" christological interpretation, we shall see that the "secular" Christ is precisely the man *pro me*. The term Bonhoeffer will use in *Letters and Papers* to describe the being of Christ is *"für-andere-da-sein"*: Christ is the one whose very being is his "being-there-for-others." All that we know of God is the "being-there-for-others" which characterizes the Jesus of the Gospels. It is important to bear in mind that the "non-religious" concept of Jesus as "the man for others" is in no sense humanist or ethical reductionism. The whole biblical-theological framework of such writings as *Christ the Center* lies behind it to the very end.[36]

One of Bonhoeffer's most characteristic christological metaphors, which runs through his theology from beginning to end, is the image of Christ as "the center of life" or as "God at the center of life." Bonhoeffer was always fascinated by the polarity of center (*Mitte*) and boundary (*Grenze*). From personalism and existentialism he took over the idea of the limits or boundaries of each person's existence. For Bonhoeffer, God as the Thou who encounters me in the concrete existence of my human neighbor is the true boundary of life and therefore that which alone transcends my finite ego. Every philosophical form of transcendence is purely logical, not real, because the boundaries imposed are merely the self-imposed boundaries of a limitless ego.

But God as the true boundary encounters me at the center of my life, in concrete, daily ethical meetings with my neighbor. There is a false understanding of "God as the boundary" which the "religionless" Bonhoeffer, as we have seen, criticized as a fundamental characteristic of "religion." "Religion" misunderstands what is meant by saying that God is the boundary of life: God becomes the *deus ex machina* who comes to our aid at the "boundary-situations" of our life—emergency, sin and guilt, suffering, and death—or the stopgap who fills up the gaps or "borders" of our knowledge. The biblical testimony to God, says Bonhoeffer, is quite the reverse: God is the true boundary who meets me squarely at the center of my life, in strength and health and blessing and knowledge as well as in sin, suffering, death, and ignorance. What is more, it is at the center of life, not at its borders, that we are to look for the true meaning of who God is.

God at the center of life is Jesus Christ:

> The nature of the person of Christ is to be temporally and spatially in the centre. The one who is present in Word, sacrament and community is in the centre of human existence, history and nature. It is part of the structure of his person that he stands in the centre. . . . Christ is the mediator as the one who is there *pro me*. That is his nature and his mode of existence. He is in the centre in three ways; in being-there [*Dasein*] for men, in being-there for history and in being-there for nature.[37]

Bonhoeffer goes on in his christological lectures to examine briefly the nature of Christ's "centeredness" in human existence, history, and nature. It is important to notice in the above passage how he links Christ's being "at the center" with his being *pro me*, his "being-there." Christ's being at the center of life is not an accident, but the very substance, of his being.

In the latter part of the christology lectures Bonhoeffer turns from the "present Christ," *Christus pro me*, to a consideration of the "historical (*geschichtliche*) Christ." In an extremely important section he now deals with the problem of the "historical Jesus." In the thoroughgoing "humanization" of the Figure of the Gospels by the "religionless" Bonhoeffer some interpreters have seen a call for a "new quest" of the "historical Jesus." In this connection Bonhoeffer's position of 1933, from which no evidence shows him to depart in the last years of his life, becomes centrally significant.

Bonhoeffer's interpretation of the "historical Christ" begins with a critique of the liberal "quest of the historical Jesus." His criticisms of liberalism at this point are of interest not only in understanding his own approach to the problem of the historicity of Christ, but also as an explicit rejection of the christological views of his Berlin teachers, notably Harnack.

"We have so far spoken," Bonhoeffer begins, "of the present Christ; but this present-historical (*geschichtliche*) Christ is the same person as the historical (*historische*) Jesus of Nazareth. . . . There can be no isolation of the so-called historical Jesus from the Christ who is present now." [38] The affirmation of the unity of the "Jesus of history" and the "Christ of faith" runs directly counter to the older liberal attempt to separate the two and to claim only the former as the real object of religious interest. "The attempt of liberal theology," Bonhoeffer goes on to say, "to distinguish a synoptic Jesus from a Pauline Christ is historically and dogmatically doomed to failure. Dogmatically, for if this separation of Jesus from Christ were possible, the proclamation of the church would become an illusion. Historically, because liberal theology up to 1900 can be described as an indirect, unintentional, and therefore all the more impressive, confirmation of the need for a dogmatic basis. The results of liberal theology are its own destruction," because "liberal theology stands and falls first of all by the separation of Jesus from the Christ." [39]

The quest of the historical Jesus, Bonhoeffer observes, ended in failure. Along with Barth, Bultmann, Brunner, and the other Neo-Reformation theologians, Bonhoeffer considered the more recent advances in New Testament criticism—Johannes Weiss and Albert Schweitzer on New Testament eschatology, the "history of religions" school on the cultic apprehension of Jesus as a Savior-God by the primitive church, and the form-critical analysis of the Gospels as fundamentally mosaics of the early community's proclamation and life—to have shown both the irrelevance and the impossibility of a "quest of the historical Jesus."

Bonhoeffer seems to have the work of the "history of religions" school particularly in mind when he says that "from now on the *historical* (*historisch*) interpretation of the New Testament can justifiably be pursued only after serious consideration of the presupposition that Jesus is the proclaimed *Kyrios Christos*." This historical conclusion brings us to two alternatives:

either to remain on the historical plane and to treat the *Kyrios-Christos* cult as one of a number of similar cults; or, to pass from historical to dogmatic study. The historical plane has shown that Jesus cannot be separated from the Christ. It is no longer possible to contrast a religion of Jesus, in which only the Father plays a role, with a cult of Christ. Thus any theology which makes this distinction its starting point is impossible.[40]

Obviously Bonhoeffer himself chooses to press on to the dogmatic-theological implications of these historical findings. The historical presuppositions of dogmatics are "the unity of the present and of the historical (*geschichtliche*) Christ, the unity of the Jesus of proclamation and the Jesus of history."

Facing squarely one of the knottiest and most-discussed of modern christological problems, Bonhoeffer states: "Dogmatics needs to be certain of the historicity of Jesus Christ, i.e. of the identity of the Christ of preaching with the Jesus of history." [41] Can historical science itself provide christology with this certainty? Bonhoeffer replies that it cannot, and his own answer to the problem is strongly Kierkegaardian and Barthian:

It is a characteristic of historical scholarship that it never reckons with the individual fact as the absolute. Nothing ever depends on the individual fact. . . . But the historically (*geschichtlich*) fortuitous fact of the life and death of Jesus must be of basic and absolute significance for the church. If he did not live, the church is doomed. If the church is not sure of this, it is at an end.

But is historical scholarship indeed capable of demonstrating conclusively either that Jesus lived or that he did not? No, replies Bonhoeffer: "History can never absolutely deny the existence of Jesus Christ. It can only cast doubt on it or make it appear improbable. As a subject for historical investigation, Jesus Christ remains an uncertain phenomenon; his historicity can neither be affirmed or denied with absolute certainty." [42] As a matter of fact, Bonhoeffer goes on to say,

Absolute certainty about an historical fact can never be acquired by itself. It remains a paradox. Nevertheless it is constitutive for the church. That means that for the church an historical fact is not past, but present; that what is uncertain is the absolute, what is past is present, and what is historical (*das Geschichtliche*) is contemporaneous (Kierkegaard). Only where this contradiction is tolerated is the historical absolute. This statement, that what is historical is contemporaneous, what is hidden is open, is made possible only where what is historical, what is hidden, has made itself contemporaneous and open, i.e. in faith in the miracle of God in the resurrection of Jesus Christ.[43]

Only in faith can we leap over Lessing's "ugly broad ditch" and affirm the paradox that a particular, problematic event of history has absolute significance. And faith receives its "sufficient reason" directly from "the witness of the Risen One to himself, through which the church bears witness to him as the Historical One. By the miracle of his presence in the church he bears witness to himself here and now as the one who was historical then." "The confirmation of historical investigation," Bonhoeffer concludes, "is irrelevant before the self-attestation of Christ in the present." [44]

Bonhoeffer's remarks in *Christ the Center* about the "historical Christ" make it clear, it seems to me, that when in the prison writings he came to talk of Jesus in what seem to be purely this-worldly terms, he was in no sense returning to the older liberal "quest of the historical Jesus." The "religionless" Jesus is not the pinnacle of humanity, the ethical hero. He is this same fully biblical-theological Christ of the christology lectures, now interpreted in "secular" language insofar as possible. Even in the "non-religious interpretation" of christology, Bonhoeffer's Jesus is the whole Christ, the *Kyrios Christos* of the New Testament who is both the ancient-historical figure and the risen Lord who encounters me in the present as the one whose being is *pro me*. What we do find in the prison writings, but also throughout Bonhoeffer's writings of the 1930's, is a vivid preoccupation with the concrete Jesus portrayed in the four Gospels, the man who in living human situations reveals himself to the eye of faith as the one who "exists for others." But for Bonhoeffer the Jesus of the Gospels, so powerfully alive, is not the "historical Jesus" in the liberal sense, but the historic Christ as the New Testament saw him and proclaimed him.

One further topic of importance to our discussion is the theme of the humiliation of Christ. In treating of Christ as the center of history, Bonhoeffer asserts: "The meaning of history is swallowed up by an event which takes place in the depth and secrecy of a man who is crucified. The meaning of history becomes evident in the humiliated Christ." [45] Stating the matter in terms of the being of the person of Christ, Bonhoeffer expresses himself in words which are startlingly similar to remarks on the same subject, now within a "religionless" framework, in the prison writings:

Jesus Christ is not God in a divine *ousia;* he is not God in a demonstrable and describable way; he is God in faith. There is no such thing as this divine essence. If Jesus Christ is to be described as God, then we may not speak of this divine essence, of his omnipotence and his omniscience, but we must speak of this weak man among sinners, of his cradle and his cross.[46]

The parallel passage in *Letters and Papers* is as follows: "God . . . is weak and powerless in the world, and that is precisely the way, the only way, in which he is with us and helps us. . . . Christ helps us, not by virtue of his omnipotence, but by virtue of his weakness and suffering." [47] In *Christ the Center* Bonhoeffer sums up his viewpoint succinctly by saying, "When we consider the Godhead of Jesus, then above all we must speak of his weakness." [48] The possibility of interpreting "non-religiously" this statement of 1933 awaited only the catalyst of Bonhoeffer's wartime experiences. Bonhoeffer's almost exclusive emphasis on the humiliation of the earthly Christ—his weakness, powerlessness, and suffering—reflects his Lutheran christological heritage, for it was Luther who much more than Calvin dwelt on the helplessness of the child in the manger and the man on the cross. Luther gloried in the paradoxical affirmation that this utterly humiliated man is all we know of God in the world.

A significant aspect of *Christ the Center* is Bonhoeffer's understanding of the Bible and his exegesis of the biblical testimony to Christ. We shall reserve this topic for the chapter on "Biblical Hermeneutics."

Bonhoeffer's christology lectures reveal dramatically that he was a quite independent and original Barth-inspired theologian. In these lectures, delivered only a year after the publication of volume one, part one of Barth's *Church Dogmatics,* we find developed a vigorous christology which is in no sense merely "Barth warmed over." The young Bonhoeffer's christology is at once more concrete, more churchly, and more "evangelical" than that of Barth during the same period. It is more concrete because it is more rigorously and modestly biblical. It is more churchly, because Christ is bound inextricably and quite concretely to his church. And it is more "evangelical," because Bonhoeffer, as we shall see in the chapter on his use of the Bible and have already noted in discussing his criticisms of Barth in the previous chapter, is willing to leave certain doctrines connected with the Incarnation (e.g., the Virgin Birth) in the realm of the problematic and peripheral. In the early 1930's Barth still remained too dominated by transcendentalism to be sufficiently concrete in his christological reflection. The same transcendental bias also prevented him from affirming the wholly intimate relation between Christ and the church which we find in Bonhoeffer. At the same time, and somewhat curiously and "un-evangelically" from the standpoint of fellow Neo-Reformation theologians like

Emil Brunner and later Bonhoeffer himself, Barth came rather quickly to elevate the doctrine of the Virgin Birth of Christ to a central place in christology, to speculate at great length on such matters as the "essential" Trinity, divine election, and the ontological status of evil, and in general to take an increasingly conservative attitude toward the retention of various traditional elements in the Christian proclamation.[49]

This-worldly Transcendence

In his "Outline for a Book" in the prison writings Bonhoeffer asks the question, "Who is God?" He regards the answer which he begins to sketch in to be the "basis" for the "interpretation of biblical concepts." [50] A "secular" doctrine of God is the touchstone of "religionless Christianity."

In "non-religious" terms, the doctrine of God means a this-worldly concept of divine transcendence. It is the meaning of God's "otherness" in a "world come of age" which is the axis around which everything else revolves. In a discussion of Bonhoeffer's idea of transcendence, two poles must constantly be kept in mind: the negative metaphysical and the positive theological poles. On the negative side, one of the characteristics of "religion," according to Bonhoeffer, is the orientation of the human subject toward a metaphysical object called "God." In the metaphysical dimension of "religion," God is a "working hypothesis" or *deus ex machina* to explain lacunae in human knowledge and self-sufficiency. The metaphysical god of "religion" is the stop-gap at the boundaries of thought and life.[51] This is precisely the criticism Bonhoeffer levels at Christian apologetics in a "religionless" world. The first thing to keep in mind, then, in discussing divine transcendence, is that he totally rejects the attempt to posit God as a metaphysical being beyond time and space, a "working hypothesis," a *deus ex machina*. He regards such an apprehension of God as doomed to an infinite and ignominious regress in a world which has "come of age." *Metaphysical* transcendence is not permissible in an authentically "non-religious" understanding of God.

Clearly Bonhoeffer's opposition to a metaphysical conception of God was nothing new by the time he wrote *Letters and Papers*. From the beginning he had joined Barth in combating vigorously the whole enterprise of metaphysical or "natural" theology as a way to God. Bonhoeffer brought to his "non-religious" project a resolutely non-metaphysical notion of divine transcendence, and it was made to order for a world "come of age" as he conceived that world.

The "beyond" ("*Jenseits*") of God, then, is not God the *deus ex machina,* the "working hypothesis" rung in at the boundaries of life. The transcendence of God is to be understood rather by Bonhoeffer's lifelong and characteristic metaphor, "God at the center of life." The unified witness of Old and New Testaments to God's transcendence is to be found in this conviction. *"I should like,"* says Bonhoeffer, *"to speak of God not on the boundaries but at the centre,* not in weaknesses but in strength; and therefore not in death and guilt but in man's life and goodness."* [52] Bonhoeffer insists that God is to be found in the midst of our strength and life and prosperity. Here is the affirmation, now within the context of a doctrine of God, of the healthy-minded "nihilism" characteristic of a mature secular world. It is part of the theological basis for affirming the "good man without God" who still finds joy and meaning in life. The God of the Bible encounters man in the midst of his worldly activities, at his strongest point, and therefore Christianity still has Good News to proclaim to the decent, life-accepting and life-affirming, "non-religious" man of the present and the future. The god of "religion" has to do only with the boundaries, the crises, of life; this god has nothing to say to those who have learned to live manfully with the borderline situations.

Bonhoeffer goes on explicitly to disavow metaphysical transcendence: "The transcendence of epistemological theory has nothing to do with the transcendence of God." Bonhoeffer remarks in another place that "since Kant" God "has been relegated to a realm beyond the world of experience." [53] Kant's removal of God from experience on the basis of a thoroughgoing critique of reason was quite beside the point, and is wrongly used as an explanation or a defense of the transcendence of God. Epistemological theories such as Kant's, equally with their metaphysical predecessors, are simply not descriptions of what the Scriptures and Christian faith mean by the transcendence of God. Divine transcendence is a theological category, and within that framework an ethical and social concept; it is in no sense an epistemological idea. Kant's God is simply the "working hypothesis" by which to account for the data of the practical reason. As the Neo-Kantians showed, such a God can be completely absorbed into human reason (Hermann

153

Cohen) or treated as a useful fiction (Hans Vaihinger). In no sense is he the concrete reality who confronts me at the center of my external, worldly existence in the claim of the neighbor. In the quest for knowledge, as in daily I-Thou experience, God is at the center of what we already know; he is the "beyond" in the fullness of our life and in the assured results of our knowledge.[54]

God's "otherness" must be viewed solely in theological terms. Here the other, positive, pole of Bonhoeffer's idea of transcendence comes into play: his utter christocentricity. God's transcendence is to be understood in terms of the man Jesus, in the proclamation that Jesus is the Christ. Again, this was nothing new in Bonhoeffer's theology. What was new was his willingness to restate his original position in what he believed to be wholly "non-religious" terms. In the prison writings we are still dealing with the Bonhoeffer who always interpreted God's transcendence in concrete, social, ethical, I-Thou terms. From the beginning, too, it was the man Jesus who was the *locus* of Bonhoeffer's non-metaphysical interpretation of divine transcendence. The "enfleshed" God is the only God we know; whatever is to be said of God's transcendence is what we can say of the biblical Christ. The man Jesus provides us with a norm which is concrete and ethical.

Being-there-for-others

It is when we ask about the focus of divine transcendence, the point in the center of life which is the criterion for all other manifestations of the "beyond" of God, that we come to the crucial significance of Bonhoeffer's christocentricity for "religionless Christianity." In the letter of May 25, 1944, he says it as succinctly as possible: "Jesus Christ . . . is the centre of life." [55] The "beyond" of God in the center of life is found definitively in Jesus Christ.

It is with regard to Bonhoeffer's christological grounding of God's transcendence that we find the *Ethics* illuminating: "Whoever sees Jesus Christ does indeed see God and the world in one. He can henceforward no longer see God without the world or the world without God." It is to Christ, and Christ alone, that we look to see God. Any apprehension of the "beyond" of God is an apprehension of the "beyond" which we see manifested in the man Jesus. Christ means that God is to be found in the midst of the world *and nowhere else*. When we see the man Jesus we see both God and the world, and thus we understand that for us there is no "God" on the one hand and "world" on the other, but only God-in-the-world: "There is no man 'in himself,' just as there is no God 'in himself'; both of these are empty abstractions. Man is the man who was accepted in the incarnation of Christ, who was loved, condemned and reconciled in Christ; and God is God become man." [56]

That also describes another facet of christological transcendence: the Barthian emphasis that the world is already reconciled in Christ. Because Bonhoeffer understands the world only in the light of its reconciliation in Christ he can speak only of a this-worldly divine transcendence: "It is now essential to the real concept of the secular that it shall always be seen in the movement of being accepted and becoming accepted by God in Christ." [57] The "beyond" of God is not only God-*in*-the-world *revealed* in Jesus; it is God-*and*-the-world *reconciled* in Jesus. In Christ we not only see God in the center of life; we also see God as the reconciler of life. Divine transcendence is revealed in Christ, and it is revealed as reconciliation. The "beyond" of God is reconciliation at the center of life.

What does reconciliation mean in the "non-religious" terms of a world "come of age"? It means, according to Bonhoeffer, the "being-there-for-others" which is the being of Jesus as proclaimed by the New Testament. Bonhoeffer speaks of God in "secular" terms as "the experience that a transformation of all human life is given in the fact that 'Jesus is there only for others' [*"für andere da ist"*]. His 'being there for others' is the experience of transcendence." [58] These fragmentary sentences from Bonhoeffer's "Outline for a Book" get at the heart of the meaning of divine transcendence in a world "come of age." He goes on to say that Jesus' being-for-others stems from a freedom from self. Jesus maintains his freedom to be for others even to the point of suffering and death. This is the transcendence which we see in Christ, and not some metaphysical doctrine of substance. In this freedom from self, says Bonhoeffer, is to be found all that we can know of God's omnipotence, omniscience, and ubiquity. The theme, rooted in his biblical christocentricity, that Jesus' being-there-for-others is the sole being of God in the world, finds a ready conceptual framework in Bonhoeffer's I-Thou approach to reality. Encounter with God solely in terms of concrete encounter with my neighbor has its basis and para-

155

digm in encounter with the New Testament picture of the Man for others.

How is the human response to the humanity of God which is Jesus to be understood in a "non-religious" way? Faith, Bonhoeffer says, is participation in Jesus' freedom to be for others. Our relation to the God whose transcendence is the reconciliation seen in Jesus' freedom to live for others is "not a 'religious' relationship to the highest, most powerful, and best Being imaginable—that is not authentic transcendence—but our relation to God is a new life in 'existence for others' ["*Dasein-für-andere*"], through participation in the being of Jesus." [59] God's transcendence is manifested, not in "religion," but in a new orientation of human being toward life: existing for others after the pattern and in the power of Jesus' utterly selfless life.

But a world "come of age" is still, in theological perspective, a fallen world. For this reason the new life which is participation in the transcendence which is reconciliation-through-Christ, is experienced chiefly as powerlessness and suffering. God at the center of life is revealed most clearly and decisively in the cross of Christ. "God lets himself be pushed out of the world on to the cross. He is weak and powerless in the world, and that is precisely the way, the only way, in which he is with us and helps us. . . . Christ helps us, not by virtue of his omnipotence, but by virtue of his weakness and suffering." [60]

To Bonhoeffer this is the decisive difference between Christianity and the religions; this is what enables Christianity to speak even to a "religionless" world. In a powerful and significant paragraph he depicts this difference and its implications for a "non-religious" gospel:

Man's religiosity makes him look in his distress to the power of God in the world: God is the *deus ex machina*. The Bible directs man to God's powerlessness and suffering; only the suffering God can help. To that extent we may say that the development towards the world's coming of age outlined above, which has done away with a false conception of God, opens up a way of seeing the God of the Bible, who wins power and space in the world by his weakness. This will probably be the starting-point for our "secular interpretation." [61]

Here we find another hint that Bonhoeffer regards the secularization of the world, its "coming of age," as part of the divine purpose. Clearly he sees the modern rejection of false (i.e., metaphysical or *deus ex machina*) conceptions of God as a *praeparatio fidei* of the best sort.

A passage in the *Ethics* deals from a historical perspective with God's transcendence as his weakness and powerlessness in the world:

The relationship of the Church with the world today does not consist, as it did in the Middle Ages, in the calm and steady expansion of the power of the name of Christ, nor yet in an endeavour, such as was undertaken by the apologists of the first centuries of Christianity, to justify and publicize and embellish the name of Jesus Christ before the world by associating it with human names and values, but solely in that recognition of the origin which has been awakened and vouchsafed to men in this suffering, solely in the seeking of refuge from persecution in Christ. . . . It is not that a "Christian culture" must make the name of Jesus Christ acceptable to the world; but the crucified Christ has become the refuge and the justification, the protection and the claim for the higher values and their defenders who have fallen victim to suffering. It is with the Christ who is persecuted and who suffers in His Church that justice, truth, humanity and freedom now seek refuge; it is with the Christ who found no shelter in the world, the Christ who was cast out of the world, the Christ of the crib and of the cross, . . . who thereby for the first time displays the full extent of his power.[62]

This passage appears in the context of Bonhoeffer's observations on the fact that Germany's crisis of the 1930's and '40's had caused "men of liberal culture," secular defenders of truth and justice and human dignity, to seek refuge in the name of Jesus Christ. We have already examined these reflections of his as a consideration of the "unconscious Christianity" (the "recognition of the origin") of the "good man" of a world "come of age." Bonhoeffer seems to be saying that in a fallen world such decent persons will at some time suffer for their goodness. Precisely in this suffering, this experience by the strong of powerlessness and weakness, such persons are most likely to become aware of the divine transcendence. God in the center of life is the suffering and powerless God revealed in Jesus Christ. Paradoxically, the reconciliation effected by Jesus' being there for others even to the point of suffering and death is all we know of God's power and majesty. It is futile, says Bonhoeffer, to seek after God's power in a majestic, all-powerful metaphysical being who descends as a *deus ex machina* to help his creatures in their ignorance and failure. One of the apostle Paul's great themes expresses the true *locus* of divine transcendence and power as

157

Bonhoeffer understood it: "My strength is made perfect in weakness" (II Cor. 12:9).

I will summarize briefly our discussion of this-worldly transcendence and "humanized" christology in Bonhoeffer's "religionless" thought. The "beyond" of God is not to be understood as *metaphysical* transcendence. It is rather *kerygmatic* transcendence, with the man Jesus as the embodiment of whatever we know about divine "otherness." The God who is to be understood in the man Jesus is "at the center of life." As Bonhoeffer states in epigrammatic form: "The beyond is not what is infinitely remote, but what is nearest at hand." [63] The "beyond" of God is the "other" right in the midst of everyday human relations and tasks; in the midst of health and joy and prosperity and not only (as the *deus ex machina*) in failure and misery. God's transcendence in the realm of knowledge is the "beyond" in what man knows, not the stopgap in what he does not know. Bonhoeffer emphasizes this strongly when he states on one occasion of Christ that "he certainly did not 'come' to answer our unsolved problems," [64] i.e., to be a stopgap.

At the center of life, in Christ, we see that there is no such thing as "God" and "world" in abstraction, as "religious metaphysics" would have us think. There is only God-and-world. But in Christ we understand God-and-world as reconciliation at the center of life. The divine transcendence is the reconciliation of God-and-world. Since transcendence finds its embodiment in Jesus, we look to this man to understand how it is to be equated with reconciliation. In Jesus reconciliation means freedom from self and being there for others. Participation in this freedom to be for others, which is the being of God, is faith. Our relation to God, then, is new life and not "religion"; it is freedom to act responsibly for my neighbor's good, and not a "religious" attachment to a metaphysical being.

But transcendence as existing for others involves weakness, powerlessness, and suffering in a fallen world. Thus transcendence is displayed most clearly in the Christ who suffers and dies on the cross. All those in a "non-religious" world who out of full human responsibility for others experience weakness and suffering participate in the cross and hence in the transcendence of God.

In the "Outline for a Book" Bonhoeffer sets his christological understanding of transcendence within the context of the history of religions.

His statement admirably summarizes our discussion of this-worldly transcendence:

God in human form—not, as in oriental religions, in animal form, monstrous, chaotic, remote, and terrifying, nor in the conceptual forms of the absolute, metaphysical, infinite, etc., nor yet in the Greek divine-human form of "man in himself," but "the man for others," and therefore the Crucified, the man who lives out of the transcendent.[65]

Chapter Seven

The Dialectical Reality of the Church

The Christopersonal Community

Bonhoeffer's criticism of Barth and concrete understanding of the Incarnation find their focus in the doctrine of the church. For Barth "the Church is not constantly, continuously the Church of Jesus Christ, but such she is in the event of the Word of God being spoken to her and believed by her." [1] Bonhoeffer believed this purely actualistic ecclesiology to be lacking in seriousness about the utter concreteness and continuity of the Incarnation. His christology found its fundamental expression in ecclesiology. God's majesty is safeguarded, not by abstracting him from the world, but by the doctrine of the church. Transcendence is a social, not a metaphysical, category. Man encounters God in the encounter with other persons in community:

The person in his concrete life, wholeness and uniqueness, is willed by God as the ultimate unity. Social relations must therefore be understood as built up interpersonally upon the uniqueness and separateness of persons. . . . The basic social category is the I-Thou relation. The Thou of the other man is the divine Thou. So the way to the other man is also the way to the divine Thou, a way of recognition or rejection. [2]

God's transcendence is not a dialectical negation, but the limit or boundary experienced in the concrete encounter of person with person, of I with Thou. "There is no God," says Bonhoeffer, "that 'there is.'

God 'is' in the personal reference, and (his) being is his being a person (*und das Sein ist sein Personsein*)." [3] Franklin Sherman, in his article "Act and Being," sums up Bonhoeffer's understanding of transcendence with relation to ecclesiology:

> It is in meeting my neighbor, that is, in encountering him as person within the personal community of the church, that I encounter my limit in its most tangible form. The undeniable objectivity of the other man, both in his claims and in his gifts, at last convinces me that the meaning of my life does not arise from within me, but comes to me from outside of me.[4]

As Sherman rightly recognizes, for Bonhoeffer the church is the sphere of genuine encounter with God because here the neighbor himself is not recognized as the ultimate boundary of life (Grisebach), but Christ in the neighbor. The neighbor's Thou is the concrete vehicle of the divine Thou meeting me in grace and judgment.

Bonhoeffer's early conviction that divine transcendence is not an epistemological but a personal-social category is fundamental, as we saw in examining the influence of personalism and existentialism, to a grasp of his final "Christianity without religion" project. In *Letters and Papers* he declared that "the transcendence of epistemological theory has nothing to do with the transcendence of God." [5] Bonhoeffer looked neither to transcendentalism nor to ontologism, but to the phenomenological personalism of thinkers like Buber, Heim, Heidegger, and Grisebach for the philosophical tools by which to understand divine transcendence and revelation. His passion for concreteness, for realism, drove him to affirm the empirical church, the personal community of neighbors-in-Christ, as the *locus* of encounter with God in his revelation. Bonhoeffer first explored this concept of ecclesiology in his doctoral dissertation *The Communion of Saints,* developed it theologically in *Act and Being,* and worked it out practically in his later writings.

God is encountered in his fullness as a person in the person of Jesus Christ: *finitum capax infiniti.* But even this, taken as a formal principle, is too abstract for Bonhoeffer. Christology finds concrete expression in ecclesiology. We saw in examining Bonhoeffer's christology lectures that it is of the very being of Christ to exist *pro me.* For Bonhoeffer this means that the church is intrinsic to an understanding of the Incarnate One:

161

Christ can never be thought of in his being in himself, but only in his relationship to me. That in turn means that *Christ can only be conceived of existentially, viz. in the community.* Christ is not a Christ in himself and additionally still in the community.[6]

Bonhoeffer called the church "Christ existing as community" (*Christus als Gemeinde existierend*) [7]—a bold definition driving home the point that it is only in concrete encounter with other persons in community that I encounter the person of Christ as the authentic limit of my life. "The being of revelation," says Bonhoeffer,

does not lie in a unique occurrence of the past, in an entity which in principle is at my disposal and has no direct connection with my old or my new existence, neither can the being of revelation be conceived solely as the ever-free, pure and non-objective act which at certain times impinges on the existence of individuals [Barth's early position]. No, *the being of revelation "is" the being of the community of persons, constituted and embraced by the person of Christ....*[8]

We shall examine this striking identification of the being of revelation (which for Bonhoeffer, of course, means the being of Jesus Christ) with the being of the church a little later in this section.

Barth's central theme was the Incarnation, and through him it became Bonhoeffer's overriding and integrating theological idea. But Barth's early dialectical method rendered the revelation in Christ abstract and individualistic. Bonhoeffer turned instead to a method of interpreting Christ which was highly concrete and social. The actual, visible church is the form of Christ in the world: "As a concrete, historical community, in spite of the relativity of its forms, its imperfect and unpretentious appearance, the empirical church is the Body of Christ, the presence of Christ on earth." [9] Here precisely Bonhoeffer again displays striking originality within the "theology of the Word" movement. John Godsey points this out in the Introduction to his study of Bonhoeffer:

Although Bonhoeffer shared with the dialectical theologians their desire to recapture the Reformation understanding of revelation, he was critical of their method, which he believed was ultimately individualistic and abstract. In contrast, Bonhoeffer advocated a theology that did justice to the fact that revelation is bound to the church. That is, God's revelation has a spatial component as well as a temporal one, and so, while the dialectical theologians were concentrating on the problem of faith and history, Bonhoeffer was concerned with the problem of faith and community.[10]

Speaking specifically of the relation between Bonhoeffer and Barth, Eberhard Bethge observes that "Bonhoeffer comes much more quickly to the church and to Christology than Barth did." [11] The church, like christology, was formally at the center of Barth's understanding of theology after his development from "dialectical" to "dogmatic" reflection; but in both areas he failed to press on to their full material implications because of his lingering transcendentalism. Bonhoeffer, with his own passion for theological concreteness as well as the advantage of building from the beginning on Barth's years of theological evolution, was able to draw these implications before Barth himself did.

References to the church as an interpersonal entity cohering in the person of Christ abound throughout Bonhoeffer's writings. Bonhoeffer was ordained in November, 1931, and took on, in addition to his lectures at the University of Berlin, a confirmation class in a socially and economically depressed area of Berlin. He gave himself unsparingly to his unruly lot of fifty boys. In a letter of February 26, 1932, to his friend Erwin Sutz, Bonhoeffer stated that "I have developed all my instructions on the idea of the community [*Gemeindegedanken*]." [12] The catechism which Bonhoeffer wrote for his class has been preserved for us, and the reality of the Christian community is indeed at the center of it. He incorporated two quotations from Luther which are especially revealing on the crucial importance of the church and the concrete, interpersonal existence of Christ in the church. In answer to the question, "Who is the Holy Spirit?" Bonhoeffer's catechism replies that the Spirit working uniquely within the church is the fulfillment of the Godhead; "for [quoting Luther] 'if thou didst not have a church, thou wouldest not be God.' " [13] Bonhoeffer desired, as we have seen, to claim the most intimate and material relationship between revelation (Jesus Christ) and the church. The question, "Do I need the church?" receives the answer that in the church, to use Luther's words again, " 'one shall be Christ to the other.' " [14] Here is Bonhoeffer's central affirmation that "the Thou of the other man is the divine Thou."

A striking passage on the theme that each Christian shall be Christ to the other appears in a lecture entitled "The Church Is Dead," which Bonhoeffer delivered in August of 1932 at an ecumenical conference in Gland, Switzerland. He issued an impassioned call for the recognition that it is Christ alone who unifies the church and breaks down individual and national barriers by speaking to each Christian quite concretely in the humanly unfamiliar voice of the Christian brother:

Is it not precisely the significance of these conferences that where someone approaches us appearing so utterly strange and incomprehensible in his concerns and yet demands a hearing of us, we perceive in the voice of our brother the voice of Christ himself, and do not evade this voice, but take it quite seriously and listen and love the other precisely in his strangeness? That brother encounters brother in all openness and truthfulness and need, and claims the attention of others is the sole way in which Christ encounters us at such a conference. . . . Christ encounters us in our brother, the German in the Englishman, the Frenchman in the German.[15]

The ecumenical movement, groping its way along with no common confessional or sacramental basis, knew itself to be the church only in its interpersonal unity in the person of Christ, wherein each Christian was concretely Christ to the other. The cutting off of Christians in Germany from fellow Christians in other lands by the war served to intensify and solidify this awareness. Bonhoeffer's understanding of the given ecclesiological unity amid the great diversity within ecumenical Christianity is still entirely valid, despite the large strides which have been made since 1932.

Bonhoeffer argued for what we might now call a "christopersonal" view of the church on purely exegetical grounds in his book *The Cost of Discipleship,* written in 1937:

The Body of Christ is identical with the new humanity which he [Christ] has taken upon him. It is in fact the Church. Jesus Christ is at once himself and his Church (I Cor. 12:12). Since the first Whit Sunday the Life of Christ has been perpetuated on earth in the form of his Body, the Church. Here is his body, crucified and risen, here is the humanity he took upon him.[16]

In this passage Bonhoeffer strongly asserts a relationship of material identity between Christ and the church. It sounds like (although it is not, as we shall see) the position of classical Catholicism; it actually follows Luther's ecclesiology, which has nevertheless not usually been stated so forcefully by Protestantism, with its emphasis on the transcendence of God and the fallibility of man.

In Bonhoeffer's view, Paul's "in Christ" therefore means to be in the church. But conversely, if we "are in the Church we are verily and bodily in Christ." "Verily and bodily": Bonhoeffer interprets Paul's language in a quite realistic, non-metaphorical way.[17]

In a statement which would have gladdened the hearts of the Anglican Tractarians, Bonhoeffer goes on to assert that "since the ascension, Christ's place on earth has been taken by his Body, the Church. The Church is the real presence of Christ." [18] The revelation of God in Christ is *essentially* historical, spatial-temporal, and therefore after the ascension of the earthly Jesus he continues to reveal himself to the world as the church. In his christology lectures Bonhoeffer asserted that "the Logos of God has extension in space and time in and as the community." [19]

In *The Cost of Discipleship* Bonhoeffer reaffirmed his early personalist understanding of the church on the basis this time of a thoroughgoing exegesis: "We should think of the Church not as an institution, but as a *person,* though of course a person in a unique sense." In what "unique sense" is the church a person?

> The Church is One Man. All who are baptized are "one in Christ" (Gal. 3:28; Rom. 12:5; I Cor. 10:17). The Church is "Man," the "New Man." . . . The "new man" is one, not many. . . .
>
> The new man is both Christ and the Church. Christ is the new humanity in the new man. Christ is the Church.[20]

It seems clear that Bonhoeffer's personalist exegesis of the New Testament teaching on the church was molded in part by his I-Thou philosophical conceptuality. The theological affirmation of Christ as the ontological and prototypical person was the ground and focus of Bonhoeffer's personalism. It was the doctrine of the church, with its human sociality and christological unity, which afforded him the fullest scope for developing his "christopersonal" outlook. Since his ascension, Christ "exists as community": he is present within the church and to the world in the concrete I-Thou existence of the Christian community. The Thou of the Christian is the divine Thou, the Thou of Christ. The many Thous of the Christian community are one, because they are concrete media of the One Thou of Christ. Christ is the recapitulation of the whole race of persons: he is the New Man. Since he now exists on earth as the church, the church is likewise the New Man.[21]

But is not Bonhoeffer's ecclesiology therefore simply a highly personalized (and for that reason more dangerous) version of the old Roman Catholic *societas perfecta,* the simple identification of the church with Christ and the kingdom of God?[22] We must now turn to the other side of Bonhoeffer's doctrine of the church to show that this is not the case. Like Luther, Bonhoeffer saw the church in intensely dialectical terms as *simul justus et peccator.* The intimate and concrete identification of Christ with the church is one half of the dialectic. But this positive assertion of the church stands in tension with what Tillich has called "the Protestant principle": the prophetic insight of Luther and the Reformers that in the New Testament the church is sinful as well as holy; that Christ stands over and even against his church as well as within it, in judgment as well as in sanctification.

Bonhoeffer's short essay "What is the Church?" presents his ecclesiological dialectic dramatically and succinctly, in a series of contrasts. "We can only say what 'is' the church," he begins, "if we say at once both what it is from the human side and what it is from the divine side. The two belong indissolubly together. Its nature consists in this duality."[23] Bonhoeffer then proceeds to elaborate this hypothesis.

The Christian community is first of all both *worldly* and *holy:*

The church is a bit of the world, a lost, godless world, under the curse, a complacent, evil world. And the church is the evil world to the highest degree because, in it, the name of God is misused, because in it God is made a plaything, man's idol. . . . But the church is a bit of the qualified world, qualified by God's revealing, gracious Word. . . . The church is the presence of God in the world. . . . The church is not a consecrated sanctuary, but the world, called by God to God. . . .[24]

Secondly, the church is both a *social institution* and the *judgment of God* on society:

The church is an institution for maintaining Christian piety and morality. . . . It "serves" public life, order, the state. It is not a particularly exemplary organisation, not very influential, not a very imposing institution, always in dire need of improvement. But the church is an office from God, an office for preaching the message of the living God. . . . For the church is the presence of Christ and his judgment.

Thirdly, the church is both a *religious organization* and the *communion of saints:*

The church is a union of religiously inclined, interested men, strangely fond of displaying their religiosity in their form of "church." They belong today mostly to a level of society whose prominent characteristic might be regarded, not as a particularly lively spirituality or a special creative power, but at best as a certain comfort in their own righteousness. . . . But, the church is "community," the communion of saints, those freed by God from loneliness, one hearing the other, giving himself, knowing himself responsible because he is bound by God to him.[25]

Bonhoeffer sums up his discussion of the "two natures" of the church by saying, "The church is always both at the same time; anyone who sees only one of the two does not see the church." He then rejects two frequent misunderstandings of the church's dialectical unity. The first misunderstanding seeks to resolve the tension into a simple matter of *present and future:*

A great deal would have been achieved if one could understand the two expressions of the nature of the church in such a way that the first said what the church is and the second said what the church should be. Then we would have a handle for our church activity. But even that is utterly refused us. The fact that the church is from God in all the ostensible fullness of what has just been said makes the church the church. . . . God makes the church what it is. We do not.[26]

Easing the tension by evacuating the present church of its divine claims and placing them wholly in a vaguely defined future tended to be the approach of the Anglo-American liberal Christianity of the first decades of the twentieth century. Strongly influenced by modern progressivism, it understood the dynamic of the church in terms of the real and the ideal, rather than as *simul justus et peccator.* The divine aspect of the church was a hope, a goal, toward which Christians were continually to strive. It was this concept of the church's duality which Bonhoeffer often encountered during his stay in America and in ecumenical work with Britons and Americans.

A more significant misunderstanding which Bonhoeffer rejected, however, was the resolution of the dialectic by means of the familiar Reformation doctrine of *the visible and the invisible church:*

One might finally avoid this stumbling-block [i.e., that God makes the empirical church what it is] and say that in some way two churches were being spoken of here. But even that misses the key point. The church is one and the same with its visible form and its hidden godliness. Just as there is one and the same Lord, the carpenter's son from Nazareth and the Son of God.[27]

The rejection of the doctrine of the invisible church is a consistent theme throughout Bonhoeffer's writings. In *The Communion of Saints* he explains what he means by "believing in the church":

We do not believe in an invisible church, nor in the kingdom of God existing in the church as *coetus electorum;* but we believe that God has made the actual empirical church, in which the Word and the sacraments are administered, into his community, that it is the Body of Christ, that is, the presence of Christ in the world, and that according to the promise God's Spirit becomes effective in it.[28]

To Bonhoeffer the idea of the invisible church as the "true church," the church of the elect, the divine reality, was unbiblical. It failed to take with complete seriousness the full concreteness and historicity of the Incarnation and the New Testament (especially Pauline) doctrine of the earthly church as the form or body of the incarnate Lord. Furthermore, it led all too easily, in Lutheranism, to the doctrine of "cheap grace," the dissociation of election from concrete obedience.

If we take seriously the visible, bodily existence of the Son of God during his earthly ministry and the New Testament teaching about the relation of Christ to the church, then, maintains Bonhoeffer, we can only understand the church as Christ's visible, bodily life on earth after his ascension. "The body of the exalted Lord is also a visible body in the shape of the Church." [29] Yet just as the Incarnate One was a human being who prayed and referred to God the Father as distinct from himself, who suffered temptation and bodily weakness, who experienced psychological distress; so the church as the continuation of his bodily existence on earth is distinct from God and marked by human frailty. Christ, however, is the perfect unity of God and man, a unity which his church possesses fully as its origin and goal but always dialectically in its life "between the times." The divine-human dialectic which is the church is a real analogy *and* a real continuation of the divine-human paradox of the Incarnation, but it is the analogy and continuation of forgiven sinners with their Lord. The *vere deus vere homo* of the Incarnation takes the form of *simul justus et peccator* in the church.

Clearly, then, Bonhoeffer's ecclesiology is not the simple identification of the church with Christ, which is the historical tendency of Catholicism. Nor is it, however, the ecclesiological "Nestorianism" of Reformed Protestantism, which tends in various ways toward the transcendentalistic and tangential in understanding the relation of divine and human in the church. Bonhoeffer's doctrine of the church takes a middle position, the intimately dialectical interpretation of what might be called "original Lutheranism." Following Luther, he understood the church in vigorously concrete terms as simultaneously the actual, literal presence of Christ on earth and a sinful, broken, compromising religious society.[30]

We have already seen how important also was the contribution of Bonhoeffer's I-Thou personalism to this concept of the church, with his insistence that Christ himself is present and speaks in the physical presence and speech of the sinful Christian. It is likewise important to add that both Lutheran and existentialist influences were subordinate in Bonhoeffer's own mind to what he considered to be the material basis of all theology: the exegesis and exposition of the Scriptures. Hence he wished his ecclesiology, like his christology and all other aspects of his theology, to be judged by its faithfulness to the testimony of the Bible. He could not, of course, escape being influenced by his own religious and intellectual heritage; but he earnestly endeavored to utilize the insights of Luther and personalism primarily because he believed them to be correct insights into the meaning of Scripture.

In Luther's thought the *simul justus et peccator* dialectic is profound and subtle, but for that very reason extremely difficult to hold in proper tension. Precisely the same holds for the dialectic as applied to the divine-human nature of the church. Bonhoeffer, like Luther, saw and affirmed the full dialectical reality of the church as it appears in the New Testament—concretely holy, the bearer

169

of God to the world with God's own authority; and sinful and struggling until God's complete triumph over sin, Satan, and death in the Parousia. That ancient Catholicism should have found this paradoxical duality of the apostolic witnesses impossible to hold in solution is not surprising. The post-apostolic church, faced with heresy and a hostile world, tended to resolve the paradox by identifying the presence of Christ *simpliciter* with ecclesiastical institutions such as the ministry, the sacraments, the creeds, and ecumenical councils. Nor is it surprising that after Luther and Calvin, Protestantism should have resolved the dialectic by emphasizing the utter transcendence of Christ over the church in face of centuries of the Catholic synthesis, a synthesis seen to be biblically insufficient and historically corrupted.

With the same boldness which he showed in Christian ethics, however, Bonhoeffer, like Luther, accepted the full paradox of the divine-human nature of the church and worked out its implications rigorously and thoughtfully. His insistence that with all its frailties the church is nevertheless the actual presence and voice of Christ in the world took, in fact, a chiefly *ethical* form. In the essays "What is the Church?" and "A Theological Basis for the World Alliance?" where Bonhoeffer states that the church is "the presence of God in the world" [31] and "the presence of Christ on earth," [32] he goes on to argue from this premise that the church's *word* to the world must always be a concrete, contemporary word. If the visible, empirical church is really the living Christ in the world, then its voice must assume the responsibility of being his voice—and Jesus never speaks generally or abstractly. The same is obviously true of the church's commission to undertake bold, decisive *action* in and on behalf of the world, embodying the Spirit of the One who risked life itself for the sake of the world he loved. As with the apostle Paul, the indicative of the church's divine reality is for Bonhoeffer the urgent basis for the ethical imperative: "Become what you are!"

Bonhoeffer's concern for concrete words and actions and his rejection of the church's usual general pronouncements and inactivity were a manifestation of his commitment to Luther's *simul justus et peccator* in all its tension and rich profundity. Justification by faith alone meant for Bonhoeffer, as for Luther, liberation for courageous and responsible speaking and acting in the world. So, too, the doctrine that the empirical, erring church is nevertheless, by God's grace, the very presence of

Christ in the world, frees the church to speak and act boldly for the world's sake. The church "in Christ" is the community of forgiven sinners who are empowered by their participation in Christ to transcend the fearful timidity of customary ethics and to "launch out into the deep" as those whom God has wondrously accepted in spite of themselves.

The church lives in and for the sake of the world. For Bonhoeffer, as for Barth, all men have been objectively reconciled to God in Christ. The church is simply that portion of mankind which is subjectively conscious of the glad tidings of forgiveness; that consciousness is the mysterious work of God the Holy Spirit, "the subjective reality of revelation," to use Barth's phrase.[33] The task of the Christian community is to proclaim to the rest of the world, in word and deed, the joyous good news which is true of all mankind. That is the only privilege of the church—not superior sanctity or wisdom, but simply and wonderfully the knowledge of the glory of God in the face of Jesus Christ. The church stands together with the world under the curse of sin and death and the judgment of God; but the church knows that sin and death have been overcome and God's judgment reversed.

Bonhoeffer's essay "Thy Kingdom Come," written at the beginning of the German church struggle (1932), is a passionate assertion of the solidarity of the church with the world. Here his highly concrete ecclesiology fuses with his Nietzschean love of the earth in a dramatic way. "The kingdom of God," Bonhoeffer states,

is not to be found in some other world beyond, but in the midst of this world. . . . God wants us to honor him in our fellow man—and nowhere else. He sinks his kingdom down into the cursed ground.

Even the consummation, the fullness of God's kingdom, is to be understood in terms of this world:

God will create a new heaven and a new earth. But it will really be a new earth. Even then there will be a kingdom of God on earth, on the new earth of the promise, on the old earth of the creation.[34]

It is highly significant that Bonhoeffer refused to "spiritualize" the strongly realistic biblical references to the fullness of God's kingdom, as is commonly done in modern eschatological interpretation. He was

171

a deeply "biblical man" in his almost constitutional inability to imagine eternal life in "other-worldly" terms.

Turning specifically to the church's role in the light of the prayer for the coming of the kingdom, Bonhoeffer insists that "if we are to pray for the coming of the kingdom, we can do so only as those who are wholly on earth." With an eye definitely to the growing crisis in Germany, he went on to say:

The hour in which the church today prays for the kingdom is one that forces the church, for good or ill, to identify itself completely with the children of the earth and of the world. It binds the church by oaths of fealty to the earth, to misery, to hunger, to death. It makes the church stand in full solidarity with evil and with the guilt of the brother.[35]

Such is the negative side of the Christian community's solidarity with the world: sharing fully in the world's weakness and sin and suffering and death. The total picture, positive as well as negative, appears a few pages later, and it is a remarkable passage. The prayer, "thy kingdom come,"

is prayed solely by the congregation of the children of the earth, who refuse to separate themselves from the world and who have no special proposals to offer for its improvement. The people of this community also do not consider themselves superior to the world, but persevere together in the midst of the world, in its depths, in its trivialities and bondages. They persevere because in this kind of existence they now demonstrate their loyalty in their own curious way, and they steadfastly keep their eyes on that strange place in this world where they perceive in utter amazement God's breaking through the curse, his unfathomable "Yes!" to the world. Here at the very center of this dying, disrupted, and desirous world something becomes evident to those who can believe—believe in the resurrection of Jesus Christ. . . . It is just in this occurrence that the old earth is affirmed and that God is hailed as Lord of the earth. . . . God's kingdom is the kingdom of the resurrection on earth.[36]

In Bonhoeffer's words on the church's participation in the world, supremely in the last passage quoted, there are four elements of basic importance for his later "religionless" thought: (1) Bonhoeffer's enthusiastic Christian world affirmation lies at the heart of his pleas in his last years that the church say "Yes!" to the modern secular world, the world which has "come of age," as the earth which God loves, judges, forgives, and reconciles in Jesus. (2) But Bonhoeffer's this-worldliness is no shallow optimism or uncritical acceptance. As a Christian, he affirmed the world with full recognition of its tragedy, its perversity, its suffering, its dying. He knew that it is a fallen world, under the curse. But he knew further that there is "hidden treasure in the cursed ground";[37] that God has both condemned and renewed this world in Jesus Christ. Bonhoeffer reaffirmed this profoundly dialectical, authentically Christian world affirmation in the prison writings. (3) The resurrection of Jesus is not an other-worldly but a this-worldly phenomenon: the affirmation by God of this earthly, bodily existence, and at the same time the re-creation, the making new, of that existence. The "religionless" Bonhoeffer dealt critically with the church's usual interpretation of Christ's resurrection as a "religious" "salvation-myth," the guarantee of another world beyond the grave, and argued for a thoroughly "this-worldly" understanding of this central Christian event. (4) The church's solidarity and identification with the world was radicalized in Bonhoeffer's "Christianity without religion" project. We shall examine his remarks on the church in a secular world later in this chapter.

Another aspect of Bonhoeffer's Lutheran understanding of the church was his appreciation of liturgical worship and private devotion in the life of the Christian community.[38] Nowhere is this better seen than in the little book *Life Together*, written out of Bonhoeffer's experience as director of the Confessing Church seminary at Finkenwalde; here the common life of Christians is centered and grounded in the daily and weekly rhythms of corporate, Scripture-centered worship and private prayer and confession. Bonhoeffer retained his traditional devotional practices in prison side by side with his call for a radically "secularized" Christianity. Even in his "religionless" proposals he envisioned an *Arkandisziplin*, a "secret discipline," for the Christian community in a world "come of age." While he mentions only the theological importance and function of the secret discipline, he almost certainly intended it to include the church's liturgical and devotional life. The new form of the church which emerges in Bonhoeffer's prison reflections is characteristically dialectical, its radical public this-worldliness rooted in a traditional arcane discipline of worship, prayer, and teaching.

The Church in a World "Come of Age"

In his first letter dealing with the subject of "religionless Christianity" Bonhoeffer raises a number of questions which he believes are posed for Christianity by a "non-religious" world. Among the most disturbing of these questions are those which have to do with the existence and life of the church: "If our final judgment must be that the western form of Christianity, too, was only a preliminary stage to a complete absence of religion [*einer völligen Religionslosigkeit*], what kind of situation emerges for us, for the church?" [39] Bonhoeffer goes on to raise questions specifically about such matters as the meaning and place in a "religionless" world of ecclesiastical institutions, Christian community, worship, prayer, preaching, and the Christian way of life.[40] We shall look first at Bonhoeffer's criticisms of the church as it presently exists; then at the dialectical form of the church which he envisages for a mature secular world.

Pietism, Orthodoxy, and the Confessing Church

Three forms of Protestant Christianity existed in Germany during most of Bonhoeffer's adult life. Pietism and orthodoxy represent theological and ecclesiastical *attitudes* within all the evangelical (Lutheran, Reformed, and United) churches of Germany, rather than separate *churches*. Only the Confessing Church, the anti-Nazi Protestant body of which Bonhoeffer was so active a member, can be labeled "church," since it was explicitly organized as a church, with a confession of faith and a list of members, and claimed against the pro-Nazi "German Christians" to be the legal evangelical church of Germany. It transcended Lutheran, Reformed, and to a certain extent intramural, theological divisions, however, in the name of confessional unity and opposition to Hitler, and therefore it can be seen as a "position" as well as a church. Although Bonhoeffer's remarks are confined to these three forms of Protestantism in his own country, similar outlooks can be found within Protestant churches outside Germany.

In his "Outline for a Book" Bonhoeffer describes pietism as "a last attempt to maintain evangelical Christianity as a religion." [41] German pietism, which began in the seventeenth century as part of the great international religious revival which later included Wesleyanism in Britain and the Great Awakening in America, was a radical internalizing of Christianity in protest against the sterile objectivism of Lutheran orthodoxy. The pietist movement, whose leaders were men like Spener, Francke, and Zinzendorff, emphasized definite, dramatic conversion, the power of the Holy Spirit, strict morality and personal holiness of life, and the affective side of religion. Through Schleiermacher pietism became a formative element in the liberal German theology of the nineteenth and twentieth centuries, and its influence can be seen in liberals like Harnack and Herrmann. Hence there are both the older conservative and the newer liberal forms of pietism in Germany.

Pietism has been an incalculable force for good in modern Christianity, witnessing again and again to the importance of personal belief (which Bonhoeffer himself keenly prized) and the reality of life in the Spirit over against a lifeless, official orthodoxy. Yet Bonhoeffer puts his finger directly on the fundamental weakness of pietism when he calls it "a last attempt to maintain evangelical Christianity as a religion." For pietism individual religious experience is everything: Religious experience replaces the church and validates the gospel. It is Protestantism interpreted as pure "religion," with all that that implies of intense inwardness, ascetical tendencies, and visible religiosity. In an increasingly "non-religious" world pietist Christianity makes contact with only a few persons of a certain psychological or temperamental inclination, since it has made psychological manifestations the decisive mark of Christian faith. Bonhoeffer's words about Christian apologetics generally are especially applicable to pietism: "It confuses Christ with one particular stage in man's religiousness." [42] "Come-of-age" man is no longer capable of being "religious." The inwardness and piety which characterize "religion" are alien to him, because they are vestiges of an era in human history which is irrevocably past—an era which he cannot and should not try to recapture.

Bonhoeffer's criticisms of the pietist form of the church recur throughout the prison writings. His own reticence about invoking the holy name of God and his concern over the way Christians speak of God too easily and apply the ultimacy of his name too hastily to penultimate situations are especially applicable to pietism. Bonhoeffer's vigorous criticisms of "religion" for claiming man's "inner life" as the last domain of God apply quite explicitly to pietism. Bonhoeffer himself refers to "pietism and methodism" in his discussion of this "modern" approach to Christian apologetics. His robust plea for bold action by the Christian in the world must be seen as an implied rejection of the quietism and passivity which have been a mark especially of Lutheran pietism.[43] The asceticism of "religion," in which life in the world becomes all cross and no blessing and everything is "spiritualized," is also a theme of Bonhoeffer's which strikes particularly at the pietist form of Christianity.

Orthodoxy, in Bonhoeffer's usage, means traditional, institutional Lutheran confessionalism. He describes it as "the attempt to rescue the Church as an institution for salvation [*Heilsanstalt*]." [44] In his criticisms of fellow theologians, Bonhoeffer seems to consider Paul Althaus a modern representative of the temperament of Lutheran orthodoxy: "Althaus (carrying forward the modern and positive line with a strong confessional emphasis) tried to wring from the world a place for Lutheran teaching (ministry) and Lutheran worship, and otherwise left the world to its own devices." [45] Bonhoeffer's remarks on orthodoxy, though brief, indicate his basic objections: Orthodoxy retreats from real encounter with the world "come of age" behind the church conceived as an institution and its confessional documents interpreted as changeless symbols. The same criticism applies to all forms of orthodoxy, both Protestant and Catholic (Catholicism, of course, would probably have been for Bonhoeffer the apotheosis of orthodoxy), as the following passage from his "Outline for a Book" suggests:

"What *must* I believe?" is the wrong question; antiquated controversies, especially those between the different sects; the Lutheran versus Reformed, and to some extent the Roman Catholic versus Protestant, are now unreal. They may at any time be revived with passion, but they no longer carry conviction. There is no proof of this, and we must simply take it that it is so. All that we can prove is that the faith of the Bible and Christianity does not stand or fall by these issues.[46]

Ecumenical Christian faith transcends institutionalism and confessionalism, taking its stand instead as the I-Thou community of those who believe as a matter of personal faith that the Christ of the Scriptures is the center of life. The church is always at the heart of Bonhoeffer's thought, but he never conceives of its essence in institutional but rather in personalist terms. Institutionalism and confessionalism are an inevitable and integral part of the church's dialectical existence, but precisely because that existence *is* a dialectic of holiness and sinfulness, they must never be elevated into fixed absolutes.[47]

Most of Bonhoeffer's criticisms of the existing forms of the church are directed toward the Confessing Church, and we can see in his special attention the same concern born of close association that we see in his criticisms of Karl Barth. The Confessing Church, born out of the early Christian resistance to Hitler, was at its inception the ecclesiastical expression of a vigorously biblical, christocentric theology inspired overwhelmingly by Barth. The Barmen Declaration of 1934 was the confessional crystallization of this theological basis. Furthermore, the Confessing Church was in the early years an informal, deeply interpersonal brotherhood, created and sustained by a new outpouring of the Spirit in the face of crisis. On both counts it was highly congenial to Bonhoeffer's own theological and ecclesiological outlook.

Bonhoeffer took an active role in the Confessing Church during the 1930's, pressing vigorously for its ecumenical recognition as the true evangelical church of Christ in Germany and directing one of its seminaries. With the outbreak of the war and his own totally secular involvement in the double life of a German Military Intelligence employee and a German Resistance worker, he became largely cut off from the church's life. When he had time to reflect on the state of the Confessing Church while in prison, he was able to speak from the standpoint of a devoted Confessing Christian who for three years had been completely immersed in "the world." From this perspective he leveled two fundamental criticisms at his church.

The first charge was that the Confessing Church had lapsed from being a true community under the Word of God into the institutionalism of orthodoxy: "The Confessing Church has now largely forgotten all about the Barthian approach, and has lapsed from positivism into conservative restoration." [48] The Confessing Church, increasingly on the defensive in a hostile environment, had come to fall away even from the halfway house of Barth's "revelation-positivism" (in which the church's structure is still an open and dynamic affair subordinated to the scriptural word) into a Protestant traditionalism which sought to shore up its institutional form and its confessional orthodoxy as ends in themselves.

In his projected book on "religionless Christianity" Bonhoeffer planned to analyze the failure of the Confessing Church. His "Outline" again directs remarks against the church's ecclesiasticism: "Generally in the Confessing Church: standing up for the Church's 'cause,' but little personal faith in Christ. . . . The decisive factor: the Church on the defensive. No taking risks for others [*Kein Wagnis für andere*]." Bonhoeffer makes two points here which should be noted. The first is his accusation that the Confessing Church represents "little personal faith in Christ." The obverse side is what Bonhoeffer earlier calls "a 'factual' [*"sachliches"*] interest in Christianity": a corrupted Barthian positivism in which the true objectivity of the biblical revelation is fossilized into the false objectivism of the "facts of faith" as enshrined in the Creeds and Confessions. Christianity becomes a fixed world view, a set of propositions, a battle cry, to which the church can point quite externally as its ground and its stance over against the world. Bonhoeffer sought instead to call the Christian and the church to personal sincerity and intellectual integrity of belief. The objectivity of God in his revelation is not the "facts of faith" but the *person* Jesus Christ. Without faith which is not only *assensus* but more essentially *fiducia* in correlation with the objectivity of God in Jesus, we are left with the objectivism which is the confessional dimension of ecclesiasticism or orthodoxy.

The second point to be noted is Bonhoeffer's portrayal of the Confessing Church as unwilling to take "risks for others." Authentic church existence is boldly risking concrete words and actions on behalf of the world. The Christian community is the dialectical reality of forgiven sinners who have been liberated from timidity and defensiveness for full service to humanity. For Bonhoeffer the church is essentially outward-looking, the presence *in the world* of the Man whose very being is being for others.

Bonhoeffer's other basic charge against the Confessing Church was its failure to *interpret* the gospel, to translate it into "non-religious" terms for a world "come of age." In the "Outline" he speaks of the church's "heavy incubus of difficult traditional ideas." [49] And in the letter of June 8, 1944, while recognizing with appreciation that the Confessing Church has maintained "the great concepts of Christian theology," Bonhoeffer argues that these concepts are left heteronomous and unrelated to modern man because "there is no interpretation of them." [50] Such criticism, of course, reflects Bonhoeffer's central object in seeking a "religionless Christianity," a "non-religious interpretation of biblical concepts"—the translation of the gospel into terms which do not require a "religious" precondition. The situation created by the rise and development of secularity demands a radical approach to the hermeneutical task which the church, Bonhoeffer believed, has so far failed to appreciate.

The Renewed Form of the Church

Theologically the church is the very form, the body, of Jesus Christ in the world; yet its present human forms, the imprisoned Bonhoeffer believed, are woefully inadequate to the challenge of a mature world. The "religionless" Bonhoeffer was driven to raise the question whether perhaps the real form of Christ in a secular world does not require a radical overhauling of existing ecclesiastical structures. In the "cover letter" to his "Outline for a Book," Bonhoeffer says to Bethge:

The Church must come out of its stagnation. We must move out again into the open air of intellectual discussion with the world, and risk saying controversial things, if we are to get down to the serious problems of life.[51]

Once again we see Bonhoeffer's call for risk, boldness, action, over against the church's usual defensiveness. The renewed form of the church will take the initiative with the world; it will inaugurate vigorous and sympathetic dialogue with secularity. The renewed church will not fear upsetting people in the name of the Christ who turned the whole world upside down.

In an essay written for his grandnephew and godchild (Bethge's son Dietrich) on the occasion of his baptism, Bonhoeffer portrays the church of the present, adrift and confused in a world which it does not understand, and projects a vision of the mature, "religionless" form of the church of the future.[52] Central to Bonhoeffer's remarks is the contrast between the church's "earlier words" and the "new language" which, like Jesus' own words, will speak directly and liberatingly to "non-religious" men—of the renewed and reborn church of the future. Here again he suggests that the church's "new language" will shock the world: It "will shock people and yet overcome them by its power."

Until the new re-formation of the church, its traditional "religious" language will "lose its force," become ineffective, and must "cease." The church must humbly stop talking for awhile. Its old words are

179

useless; what is more, it has forfeited the right to speak to the world by its defensiveness and inactivity: "Our Church, which has been fighting in these years only for its self-preservation, as though that were an end in itself, is incapable of taking the word of reconciliation and redemption to mankind and the world." The inseparability of word and action, so basic to Bonhoeffer's outlook, appears here in his negative assessment of the church of today: incomprehensible words and self-centered inactivity.

The present church may not and cannot *speak* to a world "come of age." It must be modestly content with silent *action:* "Our being Christians today will be limited to two things: prayer and righteous action among men." "Secret" prayer by the individual Christian and within the church, and active, unassuming concern for the secular neighbor: that is all the church has left. But it is precisely the case that "all Christian thinking, speaking, and organizing must be born anew out of this prayer and action." Out of the quiet, unostentatious, "secret" fellowship of the Christian community and responsible "worldly" existence by individual Christians in their public life the new form of the church will emerge.

This purgatorial time of transition for the church has already begun: "We are not yet out of the melting-pot, and any attempt to help the Church prematurely to a new expansion of its organization will merely delay its conversion and purification." It is very important to observe that Bonhoeffer is opposed to hurrying the renewal of the church in artificial ways. The renewed form of Christ in the world will truly emerge only out of the quiet and thorough inner renewal of the life of today's Christians through prayer and "metanoic" action in the world. Bonhoeffer does not wish to prophesy how long the process will take; but he firmly believes that the church's reshaping must and will become a reality some day.

Interestingly enough, Bonhoeffer incautiously contradicts himself when he does in fact prophesy that by the time his grandnephew (then an infant) is grown up, "the Church's form will have changed greatly." As Alec Vidler has commented of this prediction: "It is consistent with accepting Bonhoeffer as a prophet for our time to acknowledge that, like other prophets, he saw things too much in black and white and also that he foreshortened the realization of what he expected, as when he told his godchild that, *by the time he was grown up,* the form of the church would have changed beyond recognition." [53] Vidler got the exaggerated phrase "beyond recognition" from the original English translation of *Letters and Papers,* a phrase which is unwarranted, as the German text (*"sehr verändert"*) and the revised translation make clear. Bonhoeffer does not prophesy an "unrecognizable" new form of the church, but rather a marked change in its present form, by the time his nephew reaches maturity. Nevertheless, Vidler is correct in interpreting Bonhoeffer's prophecy as a visionary compression of the church's "new reformation" into the space of a few years.

Bonhoeffer's godchild and namesake, Bethge's son Dietrich, is now a grown man. The form of the church looks to many depressingly the same. The failure of the church to shatter and significantly reconstitute itself in twenty years, however, after 1600 years of "Christendom," should surprise nobody living under normal conditions. We can only surmise that Bonhoeffer, himself at the very center of the holocaust which consumed Western civilization in the 1940's, thought that the destruction and chaos would be so great and so final, at least in Germany, that nothing would survive without dramatic alteration. Despite decisive changes wrought by the war, especially in political life throughout the continent of Europe, Bonhoeffer failed to reckon with the tenacious ability of human beings to return as rapidly as possible to "business as usual," to restore the secure symbols of the past and cultural continuity, of which a chief symbol is the church.

Ecumenists of the present day, however, would maintain that Bonhoeffer's prediction was only slightly premature and exaggerated. They would point to the dramatic renewal of the church, both Protestant and Catholic, which has begun to occur during the last twenty years. While the form of the church has not perhaps changed "greatly," it *has changed* in ways which people before the war would not have thought possible. In Germany itself much of the renewal of the church has grown directly out of the Christian rebirth which the Confessing Church (for all its faults) represented,[54] and from the powerful impact of the war on the lives of Christians and the structure of the church. Significantly, too, church renewal is being seen to a large extent in terms of "prayer and righteous action among men." The church has increasingly come in humility to understand itself as the servant of its suffering Lord in the midst and on behalf of the world. Bonhoeffer's own prison thoughts on the church and the mature world have become a basic inspiration for new appreciation by Christians of both the true meaning of the church's mission and the status and integrity of secular existence.

At the same time, we must ask whether Bonhoeffer would have been entirely pleased with certain central aspects of ecumenical renewal today. In the light of his ecclesiology and his radical suggestions for church reform (which we shall examine in the next section), there is a strong likelihood that he might be quite impatient with the interpretation of unity in terms of church mergers which is so prevalent on the Anglo-American scene at the present time. Would Bonhoeffer perhaps have seen in this simply a new form of the old ecclesiasticism, and not an authentically new form of the church? As his participation in the early years of the ecumenical movement shows, he was passionately devoted to the concrete unity of the church; but it was a unity grounded solely in mutual obedience to the truth of the Word of God revealed in Scripture and constituted simply by recognition of Christ in the Christian brother. There is always an informality about ecclesiastical structure per se in Bonhoeffer's thought, a conviction that it is distinctly subordinate to the essential reality of communities of neighbors-in-Christ.

Prayer within and responsible human (not "churchly") action without, secret discipline and public discipleship: these are the dialectical forms of Christian existence out of which the reformation of the church will emerge. Not the "religiousness" of pietism, the ecclesiasticism of orthodoxy, or the neo-ecclesiasticism of the Confessing Church, but simply the hidden community of neighbors in Christ and the responsible this-worldliness of the individual Christian. In the opening letter containing his explicitly "religionless" proposals, Bonhoeffer says: "How this religionless Christianity looks, what form it takes, is something that I am thinking about a great deal." [55] We shall examine the few remarks he was able to make on the new form of the church, first on its outward or public side, and then in its inner or "secret" life.

The Servant Community: The Church Scattered

The church's impact on a mature world will be supremely the leaven of mature Christian lives permeating the life of the world. The public church is the church "scattered" as individual members rather than "gathered" as the worshiping, teaching, praying community.

Bonhoeffer makes specific proposals for the radical reform of public church life in a significant but all-too-brief section of his "Outline for a Book." [56] At the outset we are confronted with Bonhoeffer's central "religionless" concept of "being-there-for-others": "The Church is the Church only when it exists for others." Being one's true self is being conformed to the man Jesus, the one whose whole being is being-there-for-others. Being-there-for-others in a world "come of age" means the most responsible secular existence possible: an existence defined by wholehearted response to the claim of the neighbor in the midst of the world.

The church must make a convincing and quite concrete public demonstration that it exists only for humanity. Bonhoeffer recommends that the Christian community give away all its endowments—a symbol of "Christendom" with its heritage of ecclesiastical privilege—to those in need. Pastors should be supported totally by their congregations; it may even be that they should work during the week at a secular job. Bonhoeffer's remarks on the dispensing of church property and the desirability of congregations being fully responsible for their minister's salary reflect the church situation in Germany, which has a form of establishment in which the churches benefit as property holders from long-standing endowments and are supported in part by a tax on everyone within the parish boundaries who wishes to claim the benefits of the local church. Similar situations exist in other countries which have an established church. Bonhoeffer seems to favor here a definitely and radically "free church" concept, a concept which he had toyed with but rejected earlier in his life.[57] His desire that the church turn its back completely on its traditional privileges and become simply the confessing congregation living wholly in and for the world is a manifestation of his strong conviction that the church must be radically reformed. The form of Jesus Christ in the world is not ecclesiastical or "religious," but simply human. For the church to remain tied to the "religious" and ecclesiastical privileges which a wholly secular society still deferentially allows it, is to perpetuate "Christendom," a historical phenomenon with form but no real content in a secular world. The Christian community must have the courage to live in the world like anyone else, taking its place humbly alongside its secular neighbors who cheerfully make their own way without special assistance.

Bonhoeffer's suggestion that perhaps the clergy should "engage in some secular calling" is more radical still. Interestingly enough, however, it represents simply a return to the practice of Judaism and primitive Christianity, in which every man had a "worldly" trade and in addition might also be a rabbi or a presbyter or deacon. In modern times the Mormons have revived this practice, and Baptist ministers who were part of the westward movement of settlers in the United States worked as farmers as well as pastors. French Roman Catholicism has tried something of the same idea in the worker-priest movement. The practice is not uncommon among sectarian groups with predominantly working-class or rural memberships. Bonhoeffer's willingness to entertain the idea is further evidence of his desire that the church cut itself loose from its established status as an institution for the preservation of "religion" and be renewed by the gospel alone.

Obviously Bonhoeffer's very brief proposals for the structural reshaping of the church raise a host of questions and problems. Nevertheless, they must be taken seriously as reflections of his passionate belief that the present forms of the church are simply not effectively conformed to the Christ who is Lord of the world "come of age." He is joined in his concern by an increasing number of contemporary churchmen.

Bonhoeffer points explicitly to the servant role of the church when he says that it "must share in the secular problems of ordinary human life, not dominating, but helping and serving." The church has presumed to stand over society by a kind of divine right; now it must simply stand within society as servants by divine commission. The church scattered still has a word to speak, but that word is an unpretentious and "non-religious" sharing with others "what it means to live in Christ, to exist for others." It is a word which will be only as strong as the concrete existence-for-others of the one who speaks it.

An exhortation specifically to the German church appears among Bonhoeffer's proposals: "In particular, our own Church will have to take the field against the vices of *hubris,* power-worship, envy, and humbug, as the roots of all evil." The vices which Bonhoeffer lists are of course the basic sins which enabled Hitler to come to power and to mesmerize the German people for twelve tragic years. Notice that they are "spiritual" sins, "demonic" sins which Bonhoeffer elsewhere regarded as the sins of "strength." [58] They must be combated by the

Christian graces of strength: "moderation, purity, trust, loyalty, constancy, patience, discipline, humility, contentment, and modesty."

The decisive aspect of the renewed form of the public life of the church appears in Bonhoeffer's plea that the church "must not underestimate the importance of human example (which has its origin in the humanity of Jesus and is so important in Paul's teaching) ." Here is the very heart and soul of "religionless Christianity" on the side of action. The mature, "non-religious" Christian life is simply the fully human life, conformed to the pattern of the Man whose whole being is being-there-for-others. The difference between the Christian and other secular men is that he believes that the meaning of what it is to be a human being has been given us in the man Jesus. To be a human being according to the Christ pattern is above all to be an I for a Thou, one who is ethically responsible for his neighbor in every area of life.[59] Such responsibility demands persons who, like Christ, live in and for the world; who are integrated within themselves, disciplined, and truly free; who in all things simply put themselves at God's disposal, whether in strength or weakness, joy or suffering, life or death. Word and action were inseparable in Bonhoeffer's life and thought, and decisively characterize his "religionless Christianity" project. In the section of his "Outline" on the reformation of the church's public life, he himself speaks succinctly of the fundamental importance of action—human example—as the embodiment of the church's words: "It is not abstract argument, but example, that gives its word emphasis and power." Too often the traditional Lutheranism of Bonhoeffer's Germany had retreated into the quietism of "cheap grace" and the Neo-Reformation theology of the Confessing Church degenerated into an external, "facts of faith" justification of the gospel. In both cases a one-sided fear of "works righteousness" had caused them not only to depreciate but largely to forget about the integral place of human example—concrete obedience—in authentic biblical faith.[60]

The passage we have been considering concludes with three specific but unexplained suggestions for church renewal: (1) revision of the church's confessions (Bonhoeffer specifies the Apostles' Creed) ; (2) revision of Christian apologetics; and (3) reform of "training for the ministry and the pattern of clerical life." We can only speculate as to what may have been in Bonhoeffer's mind. If he was seriously proposing the revision of the church's ancient and Reformation creeds and confessions, then his frame of mind on the "religionless Christianity" project may have been even more experimental than we might have expected in the light of his own classical belief and conservative Lutheran liturgical and devotional outlook.

In discussing "The Failure of Christian apologetics and Its Secular Counterparts" and "Paul Tillich," I have examined Bonhoeffer's profound dissatisfaction with and even animosity toward traditional apologetics, as well as his rejection of the more contemporary apologetical theology of someone like Tillich. Clearly Bonhoeffer believed that Christian apologetics needed a complete overhauling as part of the "non-religious" renewal of the church. Even his own "non-religious interpretation of biblical concepts" cannot be called "apologetics" in the strict sense. Like Barth, Bonhoeffer believed that theology was dogmatics: the obedient exposition of the biblical revelation. "Religionless Christianity" was simply a radical understanding of the hermeneutical task involved in obedient exposition of the biblical message in a secular world. It is intriguing, therefore, to speculate about what he may have had in mind in even using the word "apologetics" in proposing revisions in church life and thought. Perhaps he was using the word loosely to mean "the way the church presents its message to the world," but we cannot be certain.

Bonhoeffer's proposal for the reform of training for the ministry is highly significant in the light of the way his theological development has come to be understood by some interpreters. The period of his directorship of a Confessing Church seminary (1935-39), during which he called for the retrenchment and inner strengthening of the church in the face of a hostile environment, has been seen as a kind of pietistic or fundamentalist diversion from the main "non-religious" direction of Bonhoeffer's thought. Bonhoeffer fashioned the life of the *Bruderhaus* community at Finkenwalde around his strong conviction that traditional German theological education, which took place entirely within the universities, was utterly lacking when it came to equipping pastors with spiritual discipline for the whole of their lives. In a letter of September 11, 1934, to his friend Erwin Sutz, he wrote:

I no longer have faith in the university. . . . The whole education for the ministry today belongs to the church—monastic-like [*kirchlich-klösterliche*] schools in which pure doctrine, the Sermon on the Mount and the Liturgy are taken seriously. In the university none of these is taken seriously, and it is impossible to do so under present conditions.[61]

The tone of *Life Together,* the literary product of Bonhoeffer's Finkenwalde experience, with its almost monastic attention to strict discipline and detailed organization of the Christian's life, is unpalatable to those who read the prison writings in an *undialectically* this-worldly sense.

What must be said is simply that the Finkenwalde experiment is in no sense a detour from the main course of Bonhoeffer's theological development. I submit rather that it became the basis of his "religionless" proposals for the reform of ministerial training and the inner life of the church. We shall look in the next section at the way Bonhoeffer's view of Christian community in 1935-39 influenced his later thoughts on the need for a "secret discipline." At present we are concerned with his brief mention of the need to reform the training of the church's ministry. This proposal must be seen to belong integrally with his plea for a "free church" existence for the Christian community: "To make a start, it must give away all its property to those in need. The clergy must live solely on the free-will offerings of their congregations, or possibly engage in some secular calling." Earlier in this section I interpreted Bonhoeffer to mean by these remarks the rejection by the church of "Christendom" and all the privileges which that entails. The community of neighbors in Christ must be content to live independently of all favored relations with society; it must be the servant church, living side by side and not "above" its secular neighbors. Although Bonhoeffer merely mentions the reform of the training of pastors, he can only have had in mind essentially the pattern of training which he had developed at Finkenwalde: seminaries run entirely by the church which train men not only in "pure doctrine, the Sermon on the Mount and the Liturgy," but also in rigorous Christian discipline of life. For Bonhoeffer, the mature, "religionless" Christian is liberated and integrated precisely because he is thoroughly self-disciplined. Only the strong, disciplined Christian is up to the task of participating fully and "metanoically" in secular life. There is no evidence to indicate that Bonhoeffer ever changed his mind on the matter of training for the ministry; on the contrary, what little evidence there is points to a reinforcement of his previous outlook. The servant church in a world "come of age" must live solely by the word of God; it must be stronger and more disciplined than ever before in order to be both fully Christian and radically secular.

Bonhoeffer's almost monastic conception of theological education is perhaps the appropriate context in which to make brief mention of his relation to Roman Catholicism. There seems little doubt that especially in the latter part of his life Bonhoeffer found much to admire in Catholicism. Even in his earlier years, during a sojourn in Rome at the age of eighteen, he was deeply impressed by the Roman liturgy. Above all, I think, Bonhoeffer appreciated Catholic discipline. The Finkenwalde experiment was greeted with shock and protest by members of the Confessing Church who thought that Bonhoeffer was secretly engaged in "catholicizing."

Furthermore, Bonhoeffer believed that Catholics by and large had a healthier, more authentically biblical attitude toward suffering than Protestants. Protestants, he felt, were too inclined to see suffering in "spiritual" rather than in bodily terms, which was neither anthropologically nor soteriologically scriptural.[62]

It is not at all without significance that Bonhoeffer did some of the writing on his *Ethics* while he was living at the Roman Catholic monastery at Ettal.[63] As letters to Bethge from Ettal show, Bonhoeffer was taking advantage of the opportunity to read in Catholic ethics and moral theology, and was in conscious dialogue with the Catholic position at certain points.[64] Although he clearly opposed Catholic ethics at fundamental points, his attempt, in the *Ethics,* to reshape the concept of natural law in fully christological terms, with his concepts of the penultimate and especially of the "natural," reflects a deep-seated appreciation of the sphere to which Catholic natural law theory points.[65] In the concrete working out of the categories of natural life, Bonhoeffer showed a large measure of agreement with Catholic ethics on such issues as euthanasia, suicide, and particularly abortion.[66]

Having pointed out Bonhoeffer's appreciation of Catholicism at several points, I must go on to say that he remained to the end a thoroughly evangelical theologian. His admiration for certain aspects of Catholicism was a manifestation of his largeness and ecumenicity of spirit, of his conviction that Catholicism as well as Protestantism (and in some cases better than Protestantism) had preserved vital aspects of a fully biblical Christianity. This is borne out in his decisive transmutation of Catholic emphases into fully evangelical terms, as if to call Protestantism to a deeper and richer scriptural faith. Among these emphases are the Christian's and the church's intimate and concrete union with the living Christ, which we examined in considering Bonhoeffer's ecclesiology and his ethical concept of man's "trans-moral" union with his divine origin through Christ; the place of active obedience in Christian life, which Bonhoeffer spelled out in vigorously evangelical terms in *The Cost of Discipleship;* the central significance of the church's "arcane discipline" of liturgy, prayer, instruction in the faith, and regulated life to authentic Christian witness in the world, which Bonhoeffer inculcated in the Finkenwalde community and articulated in *Life Together;* and the vital relevance of the ethically "penultimate," of attention to the specific problems of the "natural life," which Bonhoeffer sought to give a purely christological and biblical foundation in the *Ethics*.[67]

Arkandisziplin: The Church Gathered

The public church is the servant church, scattered through individual Christians participating fully in the life of the world. But what of the church's inner, corporate existence? "What is the place of worship and prayer in a religionless situation?" Bonhoeffer included an item on "Cultus," the problem of worship and prayer, in his "Outline for a Book," but it was simply listed with the comment: "Details to follow later, in particular on cultus and 'religion.' "[68]

Bonhoeffer made very few remarks in the prison writings on the role of the church "gathered" as the preaching, teaching, worshiping, and praying community. What he did have to say, however, is sufficient to indicate that a vigorous "secret discipline" (*Arkandisziplin*) is an integral element in "Christianity without religion."

The clearest statement which we have on the church's secret discipline appears as part of Bonhoeffer's criticism of Barth's "revelation-positivism." While criticizing Barth for presenting Christian dogma as a "law of faith," Bonhoeffer nevertheless recognized the important need for the preservation and constant renewal of the great historical affirmations of Christianity in the inner life of the church. On the reconstructive side of his critique of Barth, he asserts that "a secret discipline must be restored whereby the *mysteries* of the Christian faith are protected against profanation."[69]

Bonhoeffer's underlining of the word "mysteries" (*Geheimnisse*) reveals his own apprehension of the historical realities of revelation over against what he believes to be Barth's "positivism." The word "mysteries" connotes both the transcendence and the elusiveness to human understanding of encounter with the biblical witness to Christ. In the intimate and "secret" fellowship of the christopersonal community in the world "come of age," as in its very earliest days, the mysterious activity of God for our redemption is appropriated, shared, worshiped, and meditated upon. The church has for its task the perpetual "veneration of these sacred mysteries," the transmission of their meaning from age to age, and the living of its life in their power. This *Arkandisziplin* would exist to preserve the faith of the church from profanation. To understand the beliefs of Christians as a "law of faith" is to open wide the door to profanation, for it sets them before both church and world as an alien thing—"facts of faith"—to be attended to, heard, and rejected in a quite external way. Historically, all forms of positivism lay themselves open to profanation because of their tendency to erect into an absolute standard a particular human formulation. By speaking of revelation in terms of mystery, Bonhoeffer seeks sensitively to recognize "degrees of knowledge and degrees of significance" in the church's and the individual Christian's understanding of their faith and the profoundly *personal* (more precisely, the "christopersonal") character of the self-disclosure of God. These can be preserved best in the I-Thou fellowship of neighbors in Christ, meeting together for worship, prayer, Bible study, and teaching.

Bonhoeffer's statement on the arcane discipline is concerned specifically with the church's *teaching*, with the preservation of "pure doctrine"; but, as in the community of seminarians at Finkenwalde and in the book *Life Together, Arkandisziplin* must definitely be assumed also to embrace the whole internal activity of the church, as I have already suggested. Bonhoeffer seems to be calling for a renewal of the church along the lines of the primitive pattern. That which belongs to the inner fellowship of the church is to be "secret," "hidden in the catacombs," as it were. Bonhoeffer's statement, "our earlier words are . . . bound to lose their force and cease, and our being Christians today will be limited to two things: prayer and righteous action among men," bears out this interpretation. The church's impact upon the world will be largely the leaven of its members' lives, serving their secular neighbors modestly and quietly alongside them. The inner life of the Christian community will be "a silent and hidden affair." The former pattern, wherein the church sought to adorn its Lord by embellishing and displaying publicly its corporate life, must be abandoned in a secular world.

Yet it is precisely in this "catacomb" situation that all the strength and power for renewal lies for Christianity in a secular world. We looked at the cruciality of the inner discipline for the reform of the training of pastors. The same remarks apply to Christians as a whole. Only from rigorous discipline of life—thorough instruction in the Bible and the church's teaching, regular worship together, and constant prayer—will Christians be made mature and fully equipped to live as *Christian* secular persons (rather than simply as secularists) and to serve responsibly and intelligently in a world "come of age." Congregations of Christians must become "cell groups," fellowships of committed disciples grounded solely in the Word of God proclaimed in Jesus Christ according to the Scriptures. Here is where "secular Christianity" is born and nurtured. The idea that in the "religionless Christianity" project Bonhoeffer set the church to one side is simply without foundation. However problematic the church's forms had become, however radical Bonhoeffer's proposals for its renewal, the Christian community remained to the end of his days at the center of his thought. The form, the body, of Christ in the world was still the I-Thou community of forgiven sinners called together in his name. We can see the *Arkandisziplin,* in fact, as the radicalizing or intensification of Bonhoeffer's doctrine of the church.[70]

Classical Theology and Spirituality in the Prison Writings

What appears in this section is little more than a thematic collation of references to classical "churchly" beliefs and practices which occur in *Letters and Papers from Prison.* They are to document that Bonhoeffer's "religionless Christianity" project is not liberal reductionism or secular humanism, but rather the translation of a fully biblical and theological faith into terms which do not require what he called "religion" as a precondition. The material presented is the classical background to Bonhoeffer's experimental proposals, and appears side by side with the "religionless" remarks in the prison writings.

God

Perhaps the most striking thing about the prison writings, in the light of our present concern, is the juxtaposition of the "non-religious interpretation" of God as Jesus' being-there-for-others with graphic statements affirming the "wholly other" transcendence, the sovereignty, and the wrath of God. What is often forgotten about Bonhoeffer's extreme christocentricity is that to confess that all we know of God is to be found in Jesus Christ is to say a great deal. If in Jesus Christ we behold God supremely as the one who suffers beside us and for us, it is nevertheless *God* whom we behold, the One who infinitely transcends us, the Creator of all being, the Lord of all history, the Judge and Redeemer of all men. In a secular, "de-divinized" world, however, it is only by attending first to the sacrificially human, weak, powerless, dying Christ that we are able to "come out on the other side," to see into the *real* (rather than the spuriously "religious") meaning of God's transcendence, creatorship, historical sovereignty, judgment, and redemption.

Of the sovereignty of God over human history Bonhoeffer wrote quite explicitly in one of the brief essays which comprise "After Ten Years." It is entitled "A Few Articles of Faith on the Sovereignty of God in History": "I believe that God can and will bring good out of evil, even out of the greatest evil, . . . that God is no timeless fate, but that he waits for and answers sincere prayers and responsible actions." [71] Of interest in this essay is the importance of human obedience and "responsible actions" in Bonhoeffer's theology of grace, an emphasis which we have seen again and again in his thought. Another essay entitled "Sympathy" reminds the reader that "We are not lords, but instruments in the hand of the Lord of history." [72] And in one of the last of Bonhoeffer's letters which have been preserved (August 14, 1944) he affirms:

God does not give us everything we want, but he does fulfill all his promises, i.e. he remains the Lord of the earth, he preserves his Church, constantly renewing our faith and not laying on us more than we can bear, gladdening us with his nearness and help, hearing our prayers, and leading us along the best and straightest paths to himself. By his faithfulness in doing this, God creates in us praise for himself.[73]

Bonhoeffer's personal experience of the privations and devastations of the war gave him an especially deep sense of the wrath of God, and at the same time of the grace of which even God's wrath is the sign: "Never have we been so plainly conscious of the wrath of God, and that is a sign of his grace." [74] Speaking of the air raids which the prisoners frequently endured, Bonhoeffer wrote: "While the bombs are falling like that all round the building, I cannot help thinking of God, his judgment, his hand stretched out and his anger not turned away (Isa. 5:25 and 9:11–10:4), and of my own unpreparedness." [75]

Even within the explicit context of Bonhoeffer's "non-religious" reflections, it is crucial to remember that in no sense is "religionless Christianity" the substitution of a purely human Jesus for a God who is "dead" or "absent." The sovereign Lord of history is precisely the one who allows himself to be weak and powerless in Christ; he is the one who shatters all "religion"; he is the one who has led man to historical, secular maturity. In a profound sense, the whole process of the world's "coming of age" is the will of God, the fruition of a purpose which began with the calling of Israel and received its full expression in Jesus Christ. That purpose is the raising up of man to the full humanity, the "mature manhood" which is "the measure of the stature of the fullness of Christ" (Eph. 4:13). Hence the disappearance of "religion," with its boundary dependence on the metaphysical "God of the gaps," is the work of God himself in leading man from adolescence into maturity.[76]

The World

We have already seen abundant evidence that from beginning to end Bonhoeffer's world affirmation was strongly dialectical and Christian. Even the "come-of-age" world is both radically fallen and radically redeemed when seen in the light of Jesus Christ. Bonhoeffer was an optimist, but by no means in the progressivist, Enlightenment sense. His sober optimism was grounded solely in faith in the Lord who brings about his purpose in history and calls men into responsible partnership in fulfilling that purpose.

The "coming of age" of the world in no sense raises earthly life to the status of an absolute. Man is still under God; earth is still in an equipoise of struggle with heaven. Speaking of the tensions existing in life, Bonhoeffer remarks: "I have long had a special affection for the season between Easter and Ascension Day. . . . How can people stand earthly tensions if they know nothing of the tension between heaven and earth? " [77] The resurrection of Christ means the transformation of this earthly life; but the risen Lord must return to the Father from whom he was sent forth, the source and goal of all earthly life. The New Creator is also the Judge who reigns from heaven.

One day, after a bombing raid during the previous night, Bonhoeffer reflects on how his own reactions during air raids quite instinctively manifest human sinfulness: "It seems to me absurd how one cannot help hoping, when an air raid is announced, that it will be the turn of other places this time. . . . Such moments make one very conscious of *natura corrupta* and *peccatum originale,* and to that extent they may be quite salutary." [78]

The world's maturity and the world's sinfulness do not cancel each other out as contraries; that can only happen when the church insists on psychologizing the theological affirmation of the objective state of the world as fallen away from God. Man's fallen condition manifests itself psychologically, to be sure. But the full apprehension of original sin is known only by faith, which sees the world in the light of Christ. As we saw in discussing Bonhoeffer's remarks on the failure of Christian apologetics and its "secularized off-shoots," "psychotherapy" and "existentialism," to try to show secular, "nihilist" man that in his "inner life" he is really wretched and helpless and therefore desperately in need of "God," as if original sin and the gospel were thereby vindicated, is nothing but "religion"—the attempt to claim God as the *deus ex machina* who comes to our aid in the private, individual sphere. "Come-of-age" man is really a sinner, a participant in a godless world; but he is not weak, helpless, base, and wretched. As Bonhoeffer remarked on one occasion, "man is certainly a sinner, but is far from being mean or common on that account." [79]

As if anticipating the superficial objections which are sometimes voiced about the concept of a "world come of age"—the charges of overoptimism and an inadequate awareness of the full depths of human sinfulness—Bonhoeffer expressly wrote to Bethge: "When we speak of God in a 'non-religious' way, we must speak of him in such a way that the godlessness of the world is not in some way concealed, but rather revealed, and thus exposed to an unexpected light. The world that has come of age is more godless, and perhaps for that very reason nearer to God, than the world before its coming of age." [80] To be a Pollyanna in a prison cell in the midst of a war one would have to be almost psychotically self-deluded. To acknowledge fully man's radical corruption and at the same time to affirm clearheadedly man's "coming of age," as did Bonhoeffer, is a mark of Christian maturity and insight.

Christ

At the center of "religionless Christianity" is the Christ of the Scriptures and classical theology, a point which was argued in detail in Chapter Six. Here I wish merely to indicate classical christological material which appears in *Letters and Papers from Prison.*

The doctrine of the Incarnation, that in Jesus Christ God the Son has taken our manhood upon himself, is of course the unshakeable foundation of Bonhoeffer's thought. In discussing what he calls the "polyphony" of the mature Christian life, Bonhoeffer sees it as an analogy of the interpretation of the two natures of Christ set forth by the Council of Chalcedon in 451: "Where the *cantus firmus* is clear and plain, the counterpoint can be developed to its limits. The two are 'undivided and yet distinct,' in the words of the Chalcedonian Definition, like Christ in his divine and human natures. May not the attraction and importance of polyphony in music consist in its being a musical reflection of this Christological fact and therefore of our *vita christiana?*" [81]

In the essay "Contempt for Humanity?" Bonhoeffer concluded: "God himself did not despise humanity, but became man for men's sake." [82] The strongly Lutheran character of Bonhoeffer's understanding of the Incarnation comes out in his reflections on the Nativity at Christmas time of 1943, and in the decisive emphasis on the suffering and death of Jesus in his "non-religious" christological interpretation. He wrote to his parents on December 17, 1943, his first Christmas in prison:

That misery, suffering, poverty, loneliness, helplessness, and guilt mean something quite different in the eyes of God from what they mean in the judgment of man, that God will approach where men turn away, that Christ was born in a stable because there was no room for him in the inn— these are things that a prisoner can understand better than other people; for him they really are glad tidings. . . . [83]

And in the following passage, part of Bonhoeffer's "non-religious" reflections, he does not simply say "Jesus," but rather "God," when he speaks of weakness, powerlessness, and the cross: "God lets himself be pushed out of the world on to the cross. He is weak and powerless in the world, and that is precisely the way, the only way, in which he is with us and helps us." [84]

The atonement, as the objective reconciliation of man to God in the cross of Christ, is absolutely integral to the theology of "Christianity without religion." The death of Jesus is God's actual, universal judgment, forgiveness, and liberation of the human race. In the essay on "Sympathy," Bonhoeffer writes: "Christ, so the Scriptures tell us, bore the sufferings of all humanity in his own body as if they were his own —a thought beyond our comprehension—accepting them of his own free will." [85]

In a letter written on the fourth Sunday in Advent, 1943, Bonhoeffer writes briefly but movingly of the Irenaean christological idea of *anakephalaiosis*—recapitulation: "Nothing is lost, . . . everything is taken up in Christ, although it is transformed, made transparent, clear, and free from all selfish desire. Christ restores all this as God originally intended it to be, without the distortion resulting from our sins. The doctrine derived from Eph. 1:10—that of the restoration of all things, *anakephalaiosis, recapitulatio* (Irenaeus) —is a magnificent conception, full of comfort." [86]

We have noted Bonhoeffer's remarks on the lordship of God in human history. In a letter to his parents of June 4, 1943, he wrote likewise of the kingship of Christ in the world as the risen, exalted, and reigning Lord: "Today is Ascension Day, and that means that it is a day of great joy for all who can believe that Christ rules the world and our lives." [87]

One of Bonhoeffer's finest summary statements of his full incarnational faith in Christ as "the Word made flesh" appears in one of his last published letters:

All that we may rightly expect from God, and ask him for, is to be found in Jesus Christ. The God of Jesus Christ has nothing to do with what God, as we imagine him could do and ought to do. If we are to learn what God promises, and what he fulfils, we must persevere in quiet meditation on the life, sayings, deeds, sufferings, and death of Jesus. . . . In Jesus God has said Yes and Amen to it all, and that Yes and Amen is the firm ground on which we stand.[88]

Of particular interest here is Bonhoeffer's call to "persevere in quiet meditation" on the person and work of Christ, another reminder of the "secret discipline" of prayer and Bible study which is to be the foundation of the church's life in a secular world. The *Arkandisziplin*, like every single aspect of Christianity, is to be absorbed wholly in the biblical Christ who is at the same time the present, living Christ *pro me*; for it is by attending to him that the Christian and the church will again and again "learn what God promises, and what he fulfils."

The Holy Spirit, the Church, and the Sacraments

Bonhoeffer had little to say about the Holy Spirit in the prison writings, but it is clear that the reality of the Spirit was a constant source of strength and comfort to him. For him, the Spirit of God was linked indissolubly with the existence and life of the church. In a letter to his parents written on Whitsunday, 1943, he reflects on the Day of Pentecost:

Every hour or so since yesterday evening I have been repeating to my own comfort Paul Gerhardt's Whitsun hymn with the lovely lines "Thou art a Spirit of joy" and "grant us joyfulness and strength," and besides that, the words "If you faint in the day of adversity, your strength is small" (Prov. 24), and "God did not give us a spirit of timidity but a spirit of power and love and self-control" (II Tim. 1). I have also been considering again the strange story of the gift of tongues. That the confusion of tongues at the Tower of Babel, as a result of which people can no longer understand each other, because everyone speaks a different language, should at last be brought to an end and overcome by the language of God, which everyone understands and through which alone people can understand each other again, and that the Church should be the place where that happens—these are great momentous thoughts.[89]

Bonhoeffer practiced a Scripture-centered discipline of meditation and prayer while in prison. Of special interest are the biblical and hymnodical references, all but one of which have to do with strength and discipline. Strength or discipline was crucial to his understanding of mature Christianity.

Bonhoeffer was more keenly aware of the reality of the church than ever before, cut off as he was from the physical contacts of corporate worship and fellowship. When he wrote *Life Together* he was remarkably prophetic of his own later experience as a Christian in prison.

197

There he maintained that the opportunity for Christians to worship, pray, live, and work together was sheer grace, because until the consummation of all things "God's people remain scattered, held together solely in Jesus Christ, having become one in the fact that, dispersed among unbelievers, they remember *Him* in the far countries. So between the death of Christ and the Last Day," he continued,

it is only by a gracious anticipation of the last things that Christians are privileged to live in visible fellowship with other Christians. It is by the grace of God that a congregation is permitted to gather visibly in this world to share God's Word and sacrament. Not all Christians receive this blessing. The imprisoned, the sick, the scattered lonely, the proclaimers of the Gospel in heathen lands stand alone. They know that visible fellowship is a blessing.[90]

Bonhoeffer goes on to say of Christians who are cut off from the community that "what is denied them as an actual experience they seize upon more fervently in faith. Thus the exiled disciple of the Lord, John the Apocalyptist, celebrates in the loneliness of Patmos the heavenly worship with his congregations 'in the Spirit on the Lord's day' (Rev. 1:10)."[91] In the Whitsun letter to his parents he remarked: "When the bells rang this morning, I longed to go to church, but instead I did as John did on the island of Patmos, and had such a splendid service of my own, that I did not feel lonely at all, for you were all with me, every one of you, and so were the congregations in whose company I have kept Whitsuntide."[92]

In *Life Together* Bonhoeffer wrote that "the Christian in exile is comforted by a brief visit of a Christian brother, a prayer together and a brother's blessing; indeed, he is strengthened by a letter written by the hand of a Christian."[93] He came to know the full meaning of this sentence during his imprisonment, when the frequent letters and an occasional visit from his family, his fiancée, and his closest friend Eberhard Bethge meant much to him.

As a prisoner, then, Bonhoeffer was able to affirm quite concretely that the communion of saints is "a Christian fellowship breaking the bounds of time and space."[94] He realized this even with regard to the sacraments, those supremely visible signs of Christianity community. In his first letter to Bethge after being imprisoned (November 18, 1943), Bonhoeffer wrote: "I . . . felt it to be an omission not to have carried out my long-cherished wish to attend the Lord's Supper once again with you . . . , and yet I know that we have shared spiritually, although not physically, in the gift of confession, absolution, and communion, and that we may be quite happy and easy in our minds about it." [95]

Bethge's son Dietrich was baptized while Bonhoeffer was in prison. As godfather to the boy, Bonhoeffer was deeply concerned about the baptism, both as to arrangements for the ceremony and the theological significance of the act. He set forth some of his views on baptism, and they reveal his patient attention to this traditional aspect of the church's life. Bethge had decided to postpone the baptism until he himself could be present, despite the uncertainty of things brought about by the war. Bonhoeffer commented:

We have sometimes urged that children should be baptized as soon as possible (as it is a question of a sacrament), even if the father cannot be present. . . . Yet I am bound to agree that you will do well to wait. . . . The New Testament lays down no law about infant baptism; it is a gift of grace bestowed on the Church, a gift that may be received and used in firm faith, and can thus be a striking testimony of faith for the community; but to force oneself to it without the compulsion of faith is not biblical. . . . So we can quite well wait a little and trust in God's kindly providence, and do later with a stronger faith what we should at the moment feel simply to be burdensome law. . . . what is more important than any purely legal performance is that it should be celebrated in the fullest possible faith.[96]

Bonhoeffer here combines a traditional Lutheran understanding of infant baptism with his own passionate concern for sincerity and personal faith, which for him was grounded solidly in Scripture.

The Kingdom of God

Despite his decisive emphasis on the actual, ontological reconciliation of all things in the Incarnation, Bonhoeffer never compressed the coming of the kingdom of God into an entirely "realized" eschatology as Bultmann has. Perhaps his preoccupation with the ethically penultimate is one of the best evidences of the tension between past, present, and future in Bonhoeffer's theology of the Kingdom. He speaks vividly of the kingdom of God as present and future in a letter written on May 21, 1944, the day of his godson's christening:

There is no place for sentimentality on a day like this. If in the middle of an air raid God sends out the gospel call to his kingdom in baptism, it will be quite clear what that kingdom is and what it means. It is a kingdom stronger than war and danger, a kingdom of power and authority, signifying eternal terror and judgment to some, and eternal joy and righteousness to others, not a kingdom of the heart, but one as wide as the earth, not transitory but eternal, a kingdom that makes a way for itself and summons men to itself to prepare its way, a kingdom for which it is worth while to risk our lives.[97]

These remarks reveal Bonhoeffer's consistent biblical objectivity, his sober realism about the reality of the Kingdom. The infant Dietrich's baptism is no occasion simply for the "sentimentality" of "religion," but much more a time for rejoicing and thankfulness that the mighty God, Lord of heaven and earth, is calling this child by his grace and power into his Kingdom. And that Kingdom is not merely an "inner" reality, "a kingdom of the heart," but a historical, corporate reality "as wide as the earth." At the same time, the kingdom of God is not just temporal but eternal, the transformation of this transitory world into an everlasting place of "joy and righteousness."

Bonhoeffer's Spirituality

Bonhoeffer's own life of prayer, meditation, liturgical observance, and pastoral work while in prison is the most impressive testimony of all to the "secret discipline" which is the inner foundation and sustenance of "religionless Christianity." He even remarks, in the midst of a "non-religious" discussion of the this-worldliness of the Christian: "These theological thoughts are . . . always occupying my mind; but there are times when I am just content to live the life of faith without worrying about its problems. At those times I simply take pleasure in the day's *Losungen*." [98]

He experienced "arid" periods which he mentioned quite frankly, when he was unable to make himself read the Bible, but daily Scripture reading and meditation following the *Losungen* was at the heart of his spiritual discipline. In the letter which initiated his remarks on "religionless Christianity," Bonhoeffer mentions his practice of reading the Bible "every morning and evening." [99] There can be no doubt that his continued practice of grounding his daily life in the Word of

God was an incalculable source of strength to him throughout his imprisonment.

Psalms and hymns were an especially prominent part of Bonhoeffer's devotional life. In a letter to his parents he says, "I read the Psalms every day, as I have done for years." [100] In another letter, describing his daily routine, he tells them, "Before I go to sleep I repeat to myself the verses I have learnt during the day, and at 6 a.m. I like to read psalms and hymns." [101] The hymns of the great Lutheran hymn writer Paul Gerhardt were Bonhoeffer's favorites. (Interestingly enough, Gerhardt's hymns are usually described by commentators as "pietistic"!) In his first letter from prison to his parents, Bonhoeffer remarked: "It is good to read Paul Gerhardt's hymns and learn them by heart, as I am doing now." [102] And in the first letter to Bethge, with whom Bonhoeffer felt he could unburden himself more freely concerning the rigors of his first fortnight in prison, he wrote: "Paul Gerhardt has been an unexpectedly helpful standby, and so have the Psalms and Revelation. During this time I have been preserved from any serious spiritual trial." [103] In one of the last of the prison letters, written almost a year later, Bonhoeffer was still speaking of "Paul Gerhardt's beautiful hymns," to which he is "always glad to go back." [104] The role of hymns as comfort and help in times of danger and stress appears in the context of Bonhoeffer's confession to Bethge that the psychological strain of prison is at times unbearable: "My grim experiences often pursue me into the night and . . . I can shake them off only by reciting one hymn after another, and . . . I am apt to wake up with a sigh rather than with a hymn of praise to God." [105]

Bonhoeffer set apart regular times for prayer each day, and during the course of the day ejaculatory prayers must have been frequently on his lips. Reflecting on the meaning of enforced separation from loved ones in a Christmas Eve (1943) letter to Bethge, he states that "from the moment we wake until we fall asleep we must commend other people wholly and unreservedly to God and leave them in his hands, and transform our anxiety for them into prayers on their behalf." [106]

An interesting devotional habit which Bonhoeffer acquired while in prison is revealed in the following passage:

I have found that following Luther's instruction to "make the sign of the cross" at our morning and evening prayers is in itself helpful. There is something objective about it, and that is what is particularly badly needed here. Don't be alarmed; I shall not come out of here a *homo religiosus!* On the contrary, my fear and distrust of "religiosity" have become greater than ever here.[107]

Significantly, it was precisely the "objectivity" of crossing himself, not its "religiousness," which caused Bonhoeffer to take up the practice.

The hazards and strains of prison life made Bonhoeffer ponder the whole matter of prayer in time of trouble. He believed that biblical faith advocated it quite unashamedly, and yet he could not help feeling ashamed at the psychological fact that it usually took a crisis to force most people to pray at all and to drive Christians to a deeper life of prayer.[108]

In the "cover letter" which he sent to Bethge together with his "Outline for a Book" on "religionless Christianity," Bonhoeffer, having spoken of the church's need to get out of its intellectual stagnation and of the responsibility of the theologian, concludes with a significant remark: "How very useful your help would be! But even if we are prevented from clarifying our minds by talking things over, we can still pray, and *it is only in the spirit of prayer that any such work can be begun and carried through.*" [109] Here is another impressive testimony to the fully dialectical reality of "Christianity without religion": radical, "non-religious" theological reconstruction must always grow out of the ongoing "secret discipline" of the church and the individual Christian.

The deep friendship between Bonhoeffer and Bethge was rooted firmly and continuously in prayer for each other, which obviously meant more than ever when they were separated by Bonhoeffer's imprisonment and Bethge's military service. The poignancy of a tragically fulfilled prophecy as well as the joy of the Christian hope appears in these words of Bonhoeffer to Bethge:

Let us promise to remain faithful in interceding for each other. . . . And if it should be decided that we are not to meet again, let us remember each other to the end in thankfulness and forgiveness, and may God grant us that one day we may stand before his throne praying for each other and joining in praise and thankfulness.[110]

Bethge did manage to see Bonhoeffer on at least two one-day visits, but their eager plans for real reunion after the war were never to be realized.

Bonhoeffer's private discipline was oriented quite consciously around the liturgical Christian year which the Lutheran Church follows. It was both a way of "praying with the church" and a fully christological framework for his meditation and prayer throughout the year. He always dated letters written on or around the great festivals of the Christian year with the name of the particular feast, such as Ascension Day and Pentecost in letters written on those days. On Easter Sunday, 1943, Bonhoeffer wrote with distinct reference to his imprisonment: "Good Friday and Easter free us to think about other things far beyond our own personal fate, about the ultimate meaning of all life, suffering, and events; and we lay hold of a great hope." [111]

Bonhoeffer did all he could to be a Christian example and even a pastor to his fellow prisoners. Survivors of the war who shared his imprisonment testify to the remarkable influence he had on both the prisoners and the warders. With his self-discipline and unflagging Christian hope he must have been a tower of strength to the many who were being hopelessly fragmented by the situation. Fellow prisoner Payne Best, a British officer, writes in *The Venlo Incident* that "Bonhoeffer . . . was all humility and sweetness; he always seemed to me to diffuse an atmosphere of happiness, of joy in every smallest event in life, and of deep gratitude for the mere fact that he was alive. . . . He was one of the very few men that I have ever met to whom God was real and close." [112] A friend and fellow resistance worker, Fabian von Schlabrendorff, occupied the cell next to Bonhoeffer during part of his last months in prison. He relates the following: "Outwardly, he [Bonhoeffer] betrayed no sign of what he had gone through: he was always in good spirits, always pleasant and considerate to everyone— so much so, in fact, that very soon and to my complete amazement even our guards fell under the spell of his personality."

Von Schlabrendorff goes on to tell of Bonhoeffer's unquenchable hopefulness and his selflessness:

As far as our relationship was concerned, he was always the hopeful one. He never tired of pointing out that the fight is lost only when you yourself give up. Often he would smuggle a scrap of paper into my hands on which he had written words of comfort or hope from the Bible. . . .

With sparkling eyes he told me of the letters from his fiancée and parents whose love and care, he felt, surrounded him even in the Gestapo prison. On Wednesdays, when he had received his weekly package containing clean underwear, and usually cigars, apples, and bread as well, he promptly used the first unobserved moment to share his presents with me, full of happiness that even in prison he was still able to give.[113]

An account of Bonhoeffer's "pastoral" concern for those around him is particularly relevant to our present discussion:

To the very end, even in those dark days when the Nazi rule was crumbling, Dietrich Bonhoeffer felt himself the chosen servant of the word of Jesus Christ. By that time the prisons had become so overcrowded that the inmates could no longer be segregated. Bonhoeffer took advantage of this condition by arranging prayer services, consoling those who had lost all hope, and giving them fresh courage. A towering rock of faith, he became a shining example to his fellow prisoners.[114]

The very day on which Bonhoeffer was taken away to Flossenbürg to be executed was a Sunday, and at the prisoners' request Bonhoeffer was conducting a service. Bethge's account of the service reveals Bonhoeffer's deep respect for and sensitivity to the integrity of both non-Protestant Christians and "non-religious" men. [115] Payne Best, who took part in the service, relates that Bonhoeffer "spoke to us in a manner which reached the hearts of all, finding just the right words to express the spirit of our imprisonment and the thoughts and resolutions which it brought." [116]

Bonhoeffer composed prayers for his fellow prisoners. In his first letter to Bethge he wrote that "at the moment I am trying to write some prayers for prisoners; it is surprising that there are none, and perhaps these may be distributed at Christmas." [117] These prayers have been preserved for us among the prison writings.[118] Interestingly, writing to Bethge two months later, he commented:

The desire for confession . . . is infrequent here, because people are not primarily concerned here, either subjectively or objectively, about "sin." You may perhaps have noticed that in the prayers that I sent you the request for forgiveness of sins does not occupy the central place. . . .[119]

We are reminded here of one of Bonhoeffer's remarks concerning modern secular man: "Is even death, which people now hardly fear, and is sin, which they now hardly understand, still a genuine boundary [of human existence, and therefore a 'contact point' for 'God'] today?" [120]

A profound sense of the providence of God was one of the most striking characteristics of Bonhoeffer's faith. It was the "submission" side of a vigorous dialectic of action/submission which typified his own life. He expressed it in the letter of July 28, 1944: "Not only action, but also suffering is a way to freedom. In suffering, the deliverance consists in our being allowed to put the matter out of our own hands into God's hands." [121] In a letter to Bethge of December 22, 1943, Bonhoeffer says: "I must be able to know for certain that I am in God's hands, not in men's. Then everything becomes easy, even the severest privation. It is not now a matter (I think I can say this truthfully) of my being 'understandably impatient,' as people are probably saying, but of my facing everything in faith. . . ." [122]

Bonhoeffer's unswerving faith that God is there even in the midst of the blackest events, so reminiscent of Luther, finds expression in a letter of January 23, 1944. Bonhoeffer tells Bethge that their

life has now been placed wholly in better and stronger hands. . . . Whatever weaknesses, miscalculations, and guilt there is in what precedes the facts, God is in the facts themselves.[123]

Elsewhere he makes the same affirmation even more vividly: "Not everything that happens is simply 'God's will,' and yet in the last resort nothing happens 'without your Father's will' (Matt. 10:29), i.e. through every event, however untoward, there is access to God." [124]

A sure sense that his life, despite the deprivations of war and imprisonment, had been guided at every point by God, sustained Bonhoeffer during his last two years. "I am often surprised," he wrote to Bethge, "how little . . . I grub among my past mistakes and think how different one thing or another would be today if I had acted differently in the past; it does not worry me at all. Everything seems to have taken its natural course, and to be determined necessarily and straightforwardly by a higher providence." [125] Recalling his decision to return to Germany from America in 1939, turning his back on safety and security to face danger and uncertainty, Bonhoeffer commented:

[Never] have I ever regretted my decision in the summer of 1939, for I am firmly convinced—however strange it may seem—that my life has followed a straight and unbroken course, at any rate in its outward conduct. It has been an uninterrupted enrichment of experience, for which I can only be thankful. If I were to end my life here in these conditions, that would have a meaning that I think I could understand.[126]

A month later he wrote to Bethge:

I believe that nothing that happens to me is meaningless, and that it is good for us all that it should be so, even if it runs counter to our own wishes. As I see it, I am here for some purpose, and I only hope I may fulfil it. In the light of the great purpose all our privations and disappointments are trivial.[127]

Excerpts from Bonhoeffer's last two letters to Bethge may fittingly conclude this section. In direct contrast to the outlook of the recent "religionless Christianity"-inspired "death of God" theologies, Bonhoeffer discloses his own intimate and vivid awareness of the near presence of God in his life:

I am so sure of God's guiding hand that I hope I shall always be kept in that certainty. You must never doubt that I am travelling with gratitude and cheerfulness along the road where I am being led. My past life is brimfull of God's goodness, and my sins are covered by the forgiving love of Christ crucified. I am most thankful for the people I have met, and I only hope that they never have to grieve about me, but that they, too, will always be certain of, and thankful for, God's mercy and forgiveness.[128]

It is certain that we may always live close to God and in the light of his presence, and that such living is an entirely new life for us; that nothing is then impossible for us, because all things are possible with God; that no earthly power can touch us without his will, and that danger and distress can only drive us closer to him. It is certain that we can claim nothing for ourselves, and may yet pray for everything; it is certain that our joy is hidden in suffering, and our life in death; it is certain that in all this we are in a fellowship that sustains us.[129]

206

"Religionless Christianity" as Bonhoeffer conceived it is a "radical" interpretation of Christian faith and life into secular terms for a world which has truly "come of age"; but it is an interpretation rooted and grounded in "the faith once delivered to the saints," the church's ancient "secret discipline" of worship, prayer, instruction in the faith, Bible study, and honest Christian fellowship. There is no better concrete example of "Christianity without religion" than Dietrich Bonhoeffer himself.

Chapter Eight

Biblical Hermeneutics

After his early interest in the formal problems of dogmatic theology, evidenced in *The Communion of Saints* and *Act and Being,* Bonhoeffer came increasingly to devote himself simply to the material dogmatic task of interpreting the text of the Holy Scriptures. His theology became a thoroughly dogmatic-exegetical enterprise, rooted solidly in the concrete, living, divine-human drama to which the Bible witnesses. This deepening understanding and appreciation of the biblical material contributed in no small degree to the singular character of the "Christianity without religion" project.

Bonhoeffer's writings after 1932 consist largely of theological exegesis and homiletics. His exegetical principle, of course, was the christological foundation stone of Barthian dogmatics: "The name Jesus Christ . . . stands for the reality of revelation itself." [1] Bonhoeffer's passionate christocentricity appears in such exegetical works as *The Cost of Discipleship, Creation and Fall, Temptation,*[2] "König David," [3] and *Das Gebetbuch der Bibel: Eine Einführung in die Psalmen.*[4]

The strictly biblical approach to theology which Bonhoeffer espoused in the 1930's reveals his driving concern for the concrete and the ethical. Theological exegesis of the Scriptures constantly directed his attention to the humanity of God in his self-disclosure to men. In the 1930's he was especially intent upon bringing the New Testament to life. The vigorously human Jesus and the eternal Christ were powerfully fused in Bonhoeffer's exegeses.[5] This was a pattern which was to be pressed to its outer limits in the final "non-religious interpretation of biblical concepts."

Dogmatic-Theological Exegesis

At a meeting of the Confessing Church of Saxony in 1935, Bonhoeffer gave a lecture on "The Interpretation of the New Testament." [6] It is the most systematic exposition of his attitude toward and use of the Bible which we possess. The lecture reveals Bonhoeffer's fundamentally Barthian understanding of Scripture and dogmatic exegesis.[7]

Bonhoeffer begins by distinguishing two possible ways of understanding the interpretation of the Bible:

Either the biblical message must justify itself in the present age and must therefore show itself capable of interpretation or the present age must justify itself before the biblical message and therefore the message must become real.[8]

In the light of what we have studied of Bonhoeffer's theology thus far, there can be little doubt on which side he comes down:

The intention should be not to justify Christianity in this present age, but *to justify the present age before the Christian message*. Interpretation then means that the present age is brought before the forum of the Christian message, in other words that the question is of the *fact* . . . of the Christian message instead of being of the character of the present age, as in the false concept of relevance. True relevance lies in this question of the fact. It is felt of the *fact itself* that where it is really expressed it is in itself completely and utterly relevant; it therefore needs no other special act of interpretation, because the interpretation is achieved in the fact itself.[9]

Like Barth, Bonhoeffer always conceived of theology as the obedient exposition of the Scriptures. If the dogmatic-exegetical task is done faithfully, there is no need to worry about "relevance," about apologetics or polemics. It is crucial to a proper understanding of the "radical" theological proposals in Bonhoeffer's prison writings to bear in mind that they do not represent a departure from his lifelong exegetical-dogmatic concept of theology. "Religionless Christianity" as Bonhoeffer conceived it is not an attempt to justify Christianity before the present age; it is not apologetics. It is rather a deeply serious attempt to exegete the Scriptures in contemporary language, which is precisely the way Bonhoeffer had always understood the theological task. In the prison writings he criticized Barth, not for his theological theory, but for his failure to carry through with it in practice. Exegesis in a world "come of age," a "religionless" world, is, in Bonhoeffer's phrase, "the non-religious interpretation of biblical concepts." The world must still justify itself before the Christian message; the "religionless" Bonhoeffer called this understanding the world "better than it understands itself," i.e., in the light of the biblical testimony to Christ. Theology remains the faithful exposition of "the fact itself." The crux of the matter lies in the conception of faithful or obedient exposition, not in "the fact itself." And for the Bonhoeffer of the prison writings obedient exposition of the Bible is "non-religious" interpretation.

The false notion that the biblical message must be justified before the present age assumes that the principles and norms of interpretation are in the interpreter himself, in his reason, conscience, or experience. But "the norm for the Word of God in Scripture is the Word of God itself, and what we possess, reason, conscience, experience, are the materials to which this norm seeks to be applied." This Word of God is not some "eternal principle" which we "discover." God always speaks his Word through the temporal, historically conditioned words of man:

> The word of man does not cease to be a temporal, past word by becoming the Word of God; it is the Word of God precisely as such a historical temporal word. . . . Distinction between the eternal and the temporal, the contingent and the necessary, in the Bible, is fundamentally false.[10]

Here is Bonhoeffer's insistence on concreteness as applied to the interpretation of Scripture. We have seen, in the chapter on Bonhoeffer's christology, his rejection of Barth's early tendency to abstract the eternal God from the historical Jesus. In discussing Bonhoeffer's doctrine of the church, we noted his highly dialectical insistence on the wholly concrete union of the divine and the human in the church and his corresponding rejection of the notion of an "invisible" church. His understanding of the inextricability of the Word of God and the word of man in interpreting the Scriptures is all of a piece with his christology and his ecclesiology, and flows, in fact, from the former.

Genuine exegesis does not extract from the full content of Scripture "general truths, general ethical norms, or myths."

> Holy Scripture is rather as a whole the *witness* of God in Christ, and . . . [exegesis] will be concerned to bring out the witnessing character of the

Word in every passage. There are in principle no special places, unless we understand "special" to refer to degree of clarity. *Interpretation is achieved not by the choice of certain texts but by the demonstration of the whole of Holy Scripture as the testimony of the Word of God.*[11]

The "religionless" Bonhoeffer continued this insistence on interpreting the Bible *as a whole* as God's witness to Christ. In the prison writings he criticizes Rudolf Bultmann for making the older liberal mistake of trying to extract the true "essence" of Christianity from the mythological wrapping in which the Bible veils it. Bonhoeffer contends that "the full content, including the 'mythological' concepts, must be kept." [12] This is what Bonhoeffer called "thinking theologically" over against the liberal and Bultmannian approach.[13]

Bonhoeffer, following Barth and the Reformers, saw the Scriptures as a *witness to Christ,* and here is the guiding principle of all his exegesis.

The New Testament is the *witness* of the promise of the Old Testament fulfilled in Christ. It is not a book which contains eternal truths, doctrines, norms or myths, but it is a unique *witness* of the God-man Jesus Christ. In its entirety and in all its parts it is nothing but this witness of Christ, his life, his death and his resurrection. This Christ is witnessed to not as the eternal in the temporal, as the meaning in a world of chance events, as essence in the inessential, but as the absolutely Unique One, who was born, died and rose again, and this uniqueness of Christ in history fills the whole New Testament. Here there is no difference between doctrinal texts (in the Epistles or in the sayings of Jesus) and the historical texts. Both are equally witnesses to the unique Christ.[14]

In this passage Bonhoeffer stresses the wholly concrete character of both Christ and the Scriptures. Jesus is the Word of God become visible, tangible flesh at a particular place and time in human history. The Bible is simply the historic witness to the Incarnation by a large and varied number of persons whose finite words God made his Word of revelation to man. He mentions Scripture "in its entirety and in all its parts" as the witness and he rejects the popular idea that the Bible is a book of "eternal truths" or that the revelation in Christ is "the eternal in the temporal." Of special interest is the phrase "the meaning in a world of chance events," which Bonhoeffer includes among the false

211

interpretations of Christ. In the prison writings he was to argue strongly that Jesus is not "the meaning of life," the "answer" to our questions and problems. In taking this ostensibly "shocking" viewpoint, the "religionless" Bonhoeffer was simply standing where he had always stood christologically: Christ is the prior, the defining, the all-embracing reality; in no sense does he "enter" a world which has been previously and independently defined (e.g., as "finite," "fallen," or "meaningless") , as the "answer" to its needs and problems.[15]

Against Protestant scholasticism and fundamentalism, Bonhoeffer insisted that the significance of a witness is *extrinsic:*

The New Testament bears *witness* in both doctrine *and* history; it is nothing *in* itself, but bears witness of something else; it has no value in itself, but only as a witness to Christ; it does not rest on itself, but reaches beyond itself; its words and statements are not in themselves true and eternal and holy, but only insofar as they bear witness to Christ—i.e. let only Christ himself be true. [16]

Here is the key to the very subtle dialectic of theological exegesis as practiced by Barth and Bonhoeffer. The words of the biblical witnesses are fallible human words; they contain inaccuracies of detail, greater and lesser degrees of significance, and historical and cultural conditioning. Yet insofar as they point to Jesus, the Word of God incarnate, they are also the Word of God. But it is always the Holy Spirit, "the subjective reality of revelation," who brings it about that the words of Scripture speak to us as the Word of God: *"The most essential element of the Christian message and of textual exposition is not a human act of interpretation but is always God himself, it is the Holy Spirit."* [17]

An important paragraph on the *freedom* of the biblical expositor foreshadows a fundamental concern of the "religionless" Bonhoeffer. He states that one of the basic freedoms of the theological exegete is that of translation of the original text into the language of the present day. "Translation," he says, "is the first and necessary legitimate form of presentation." He concludes with the significant statement that "the problem of a right theological and church language is extremely important and has still not as yet been settled." [18] Bonhoeffer's continuing concern for the language into which the gospel is translated became decisive in his "non-religious interpretation of biblical concepts," the fruit of his conviction that the proper language of biblical exposition in our day must be a "non-religious" language insofar as possible. "Religionless Christianity" was the beginning of the contribution which Bonhoeffer hoped to make to this "extremely important," unsettled problem of "a right theological and church language."

Historical Criticism

What was Bonhoeffer's precise attitude toward biblical criticism? Unfortunately, we find in his writings very little basic reflection on specific problems raised by historical-critical study, such as the crucial issue of demythologizing which so greatly exercised Rudolf Bultmann.[19] Bonhoeffer's most explicit remarks on the subject appear in *Christ the Center,* and there in connection with and subordinate to his christological discussion. It is perhaps appropriate, however, that his own use of biblical criticism should be examined in connection with the central theological theme of the doctrine of Christ.

Bonhoeffer contents himself with general remarks on the Bible such as the following: "We have in the first place to do with a book, which we find in the secular sphere. . . . It is meant to be read with all the means of historical and philological criticism." [20] The theologian, he says, is faced with the paradox that faith is bound solely to the word of this historically problematic book as the one Word of God to man. The only final guarantee that faith's foundation is not untenable is the present witness of the risen Lord to himself.

The preacher is faced with difficulties which cannot be avoided, such as "the problematic situation of having to preach about a saying which we know from philological and historical criticism never to have been spoken in its present form by Jesus." Because of the uncertainty which surrounds exegesis, Bonhoeffer insists, as in his lecture on New Testament interpretation, that "we may never stick at one point, but must move over the whole of the Bible, from one place to another."

In *Christ the Center* Bonhoeffer criticizes Protestant scholasticism and fundamentalism from a slightly different position from the one he was to take in the lecture on interpretation. With all the difficulties surrounding the acceptance of historical criticism, he says, it is nevertheless the case that "verbal inspiration is a bad surrogate for the resurrection. It means the denial of the sole presence of the Risen One. It eternalizes history instead of seeing and recognizing history in the light of God's eternity."

Bonhoeffer's positive theological interpretation of historical criticism sees the problematic character of the biblical testimony as a witness to the "hiddenness" or *incognito* of God in human affairs, which for Bonhoeffer means the humiliation of Christ:

We must be ready to admit the concealment in history and thus accept the course of historical criticism. But the Risen One encounters us right through the Bible with all its flaws. We must enter the straits of historical criticism. Its importance is not absolute, but at the same time it is not a matter of indifference. In fact it never leads to a weakening of faith but rather to its strengthening, as concealment in historicity is part of Christ's humiliation.[21]

These words show that Bonhoeffer took an affirmative and constructive attitude toward biblical criticism, and even found in it a christological insight.[22] Beyond these general remarks he does not go.

An example of Bonhoeffer's exegetical position on christological matters, however, is illuminative of a difference in dogmatic use of the Scriptures between Bonhoeffer and Barth which was to have some significance in the later "non-religious interpretation of biblical concepts." Once again, Bonhoeffer's remarks are brief and general, but they are sufficient to indicate his standpoint. The issue is the Virgin Birth of Christ, and it mirrors better than perhaps any other biblical-critical question a basic difference in theological style between Bonhoeffer and Barth. Bonhoeffer regarded the doctrine of the Virgin Birth as problematic from both a historical and a dogmatic point of view. He believed that the doctrine reflected a preoccupation with the "How?" of the Incarnation; and, as we have seen in examining his christology, "How?" questions are to be regarded as dubious, misleading, and futile in the realm of dogmatic theology. "Strictly speaking," Bonhoeffer says.

we should really talk, not about the Incarnation, but only about the Incarnate One. An interest in the incarnation raises the question "How?" The question "How?" thus underlies the hypothesis of the Virgin Birth. It is both historically and dogmatically questionable. The biblical evidence for it is uncertain. If the biblical evidence gave decisive evidence for the real fact, there might be no particular significance in the dogmatic obscurity. The doctrine of the Virgin Birth is meant to express the incarnation of God and not just the fact of the Incarnate One. But does it not miss the decisive point of the incarnation by implying that Jesus has *not* become man wholly as we are? The question remains open, just as and just because it is already open in the Bible.[23]

This is an extremely important statement of Bonhoeffer's combination of high christology and a sensitive and "evangelical" openness about certain biblical questions. Clearly he does not consider the doctrine of the Virgin Birth to be central or even essential to a full biblical-dogmatic christology. In this he is more strictly "biblical" than Barth, because he recognizes more forthrightly, as he puts it in the prison writings, "degrees of knowledge and degrees of significance" in the scriptural witness. Bonhoeffer's sensitivity to the nuances of biblical faith and his unwillingness to discourse at length from modest biblical evidence on the mysteries of God stand over against Barth's tendency to give equal weight, as it were, to a series of classical doctrines extracted from the Bible (such as Virgin Birth, Trinity, divine election, and the origin and nature of evil) as if they were all of a piece and to elaborate them to an extent which is unwarranted by the biblical evidence and the insights of the Reformers.[24]

Significantly, this difference in theological use of the Scriptures was to become a key issue in the "religionless" Bonhoeffer's criticism of Barth's response to a secular world. Bonhoeffer's own "non-religious interpretation of biblical concepts" was made possible at least partly because of his theological appreciation of problematic and peripheral elements in the biblical witness and his reticence about speculating in detail on the revelation contained therein.

In his critical and theological attitude toward the doctrine of the Virgin Birth and in his later criticism of Barth for treating it as a "necessary part of the whole," Bonhoeffer stands closer to Emil Brunner than to Barth. Brunner set forth his own position on the relevance of the dogma to christology in his massive christological work *The Mediator*. After reviewing the highly problematic historical evidence, he deals with the matter from the same theological standpoint as Bonhoeffer. While Brunner does not set up the question in Bonhoeffer's explicit form of "Who?" versus "How?" he clearly has the same sort of distinction in mind:

The question is not: Is the birth of the Person of Christ a divine saving miracle, the miracle of the Incarnation or not? But it is this: Are we obliged to represent to ourselves the divine miracle of the Incarnation of the Son of God as a Virgin Birth or not? [25]

Faith acknowledges with the New Testament that Jesus is the Christ, God and man: This is surely the prior apprehension, and in no way a deduction from the Virgin Birth, as the New Testament itself witnesses. Sounding very much like Bonhoeffer, Brunner states that "the fact itself should be enough for us; the way in which it happened is God's secret." [26] "All depends upon the miracle of the Incarnation of the Son of God, . . . but nothing depends upon the manner in which it took place." [27]

In Part One of *Truth as Encounter* Brunner faults Barth for the change of emphasis which occurred in his shift from "dialectical" to "dogmatic" theology. Brunner believes that the symbol and turning point of this wrong direction was "the adoption of the ancient Catholic doctrine *natus ex Maria Virgine*" in the first volume of the *Church Dogmatics*.[28] Barth's preoccupation with the doctrine of the Virgin Birth witnesses to a subtle shift in his theology from the truly evangelical theology of the Reformers to the traditionalist orthodoxy of Protestant scholasticism and Catholicism. Brunner puts it this way:

The truth that authenticates itself in our conscience has been replaced by a supernatural *fact*, which "must be believed" on the strength of authority. This was the point from which long ago the transformation of the confession of the ancient church took its departure. It was in the direction of this "faith" that the dogma of the church developed as the doctrine of the Triune God and of the two natures in Christ. It was this doctrine, summarized in the Creed, which Karl Barth from 1924 onward expounded in his *Dogmatics* as the subject of belief.[29]

A symptom of Barth's "scholasticism" is the fact that "he found it necessary to draw ever finer distinctions to satisfy the requirements of the intellect, so that the volume of his *Church Dogmatics* continually swelled in bulk, and became a gigantic work comparable in size to one of the medieval *Summae*." [30] Brunner gives as an example of Barth's finely spun "objectivism" his treatment of the doctrine of the Trinity, which I have mentioned in the same connection. Barth, he says, "neglecting the warning of the Reformers, . . . gave hundreds of pages to the mystery of the Trinity."

What lies at the root of Barth's "scholasticism," his elevation of the doctrine of the Virgin Birth to a central place in christology, and his exhaustive speculations into matters of which the Bible speaks with reticence? According to Brunner, it was the detachment of theological reflection from the faith which gave rise to it. "The *objectum fidei,* the 'object of faith,' exercised so great a fascination upon him that he had neither interest in, nor understanding of, the identity of subject and object in faith, which was for the Reformers the very central doctrine of Christian faith." [31] Brunner calls this

an objectivism that was just as far away from the center of the Biblical faith of the Reformers as the subjectivism of the theology of a Schleiermacher, which Barth attacks. While it was precisely the decisive insight of the Reformers that all discourse about God was the discourse of faith, and that therefore a thought about the Trinity and election which bypassed faith, i.e., without a continual bearing in mind that our thought is an exposition of faith, would lead into the *merae tenebrae rationis,* and that consequently only the knowledge about God given us by faith has any importance for us—in Barth this correlation between God and faith is broken.[32]

Barth, who desires to be the obediently biblical dogmatician, has let himself drift away from the truly evangelical insight that in the Scriptures revelation and faith are correlative and equally important—since the former cannot be recognized without the latter—and that theology is reflection on what faith already apprehends as a living, ever new reality. In the faith of the Bible and the Reformers there is a clear recognition of the central and the peripheral, the essential and the nonessential, the certain and the dubious; while in Barth, along with Catholicism and Protestant orthodoxy, essential and nonessential appear as parts of a seamless fabric, "to be swallowed as a whole," the imprisoned Bonhoeffer was to remark, "or not at all." To Brunner it appears that Barth, in his eagerness to embrace the fullness of Christian theological tradition, has abandoned the sensitively biblical outlook of the Reformers for the sake of a position which comes dangerously close to regarding revelation as a *depositum* rather than God himself in dynamic correlation with man's faith.

As early as the first part of the first volume of the *Church Dogmatics,* Barth protested that "to my regret I am continually having it said that my occupation is to put revelation and faith from the believer's stand-

217

point up in the clouds, to teach a *fides quae creditur* 'without considering the *fides qua creditur,* the intimate personal conviction and experience of faith.' " [33] This is precisely Brunner's criticism. Barth denied that it is a just criticism. He always understood the knowledge of God to be by faith alone: "Faith . . . is what takes place in real knowledge of the Word of God and makes this knowledge possible." [34] The science of dogmatic theology can be practiced only by men of faith who stand within the church. Theology has no special access to knowledge of God; it is simply reflection on what faith already knows.

Hence Barth intends that his theology shall always reflect both the object of faith and faith itself, and his method in the *Dogmatics* is to treat the two together within each theological topic, as the objective and the subjective sides of the reality of revelation. Yet clear priority is given to the objective, Godward side, since it is the prior and wholly determining reality: "The possibility of knowing the Word of God lies in the Word of God and nowhere else." [35] Man is totally "without organ or capacity to receive God," [36] and therefore together with his disclosure of himself God graciously produces in man the capacity to receive it, which is faith.

It is just here, on the matter of actual *emphasis,* that Barth may be legitimately criticized as Brunner and (later) Bonhoeffer have criticized him, granting the soundness of his original intentions. The emphasis in Barth's *Church Dogmatics* is unmistakably and overwhelmingly on the objective, Godward side, so much so that in fact the balance between Word of God and faith continually runs the risk of being obscured. It is precisely this "objectivistic" preoccupation which leads Barth into what Bonhoeffer would have called "restorationism": a scrupulous attention to the traditional *depositum fidei* of Catholic and Protestant orthodoxy. Hence his exhaustive speculations on such matters as the Trinity, election, and evil, and his insistence on the necessity of the doctrine of the Virgin Birth to a full christology.

I do not believe that Barth can be faulted as to his basic recognition of the essential dipolarity of God's self-disclosure and the response of faith: It is a foundation stone of his entire conception of theology and its method. But the question must be seriously raised whether he has not, in the actual development of his *Dogmatics,* been so fascinated with the objective side that he has often left the rather modest claims of living biblical and evangelical faith far behind.

218

I have tried to show in previous chapters that Bonhoeffer's dogmatic presuppositions and method were basically those of Barth, and in this important regard he must always be seen as a follower of Barth over against Brunner. The all-sufficiency of christology is of course the central premise on which Bonhoeffer and Barth are at one. But in working with Barthian principles Bonhoeffer was rigorously and yet creatively faithful to Barth's intentions to a degree which surpassed the master himself. Bonhoeffer was always a more modestly "biblical" theologian than Barth, and in this regard he stands nearer to Brunner. There is an intensely concrete, non-speculative attitude toward the Bible in Bonhoeffer's thought, a radically "human" and ethical character, which is lacking in Barth's toweringly brilliant but verbosely "scholastic" systematization of Christian faith. Bonhoeffer was in no sense less "objective" than Barth in his understanding of the complete priority and externality of the revelation of God in Jesus Christ. But he never allowed this Godward preeminence either to dwarf the concrete witness of faith or to lead him beyond what he believed to be warranted by the biblical witness into meticulous theological probings. We may say that Barth tends toward the "scholastic" objectivism of received dogma, while Bonhoeffer more nearly achieves the objectivity of faith which the biblical witnesses affirm. The difference comes dramatically to the surface in Bonhoeffer's criticisms of Barth in the prison letters and his own "non-religious" reconstruction of dogmatic theology. Just as the young Bonhoeffer had found the early "dialectical" Barth too abstract in his understanding of the concrete realities of God and revelation, so the "religionless" Bonhoeffer was to find the mature "dogmatic" Barth too traditionalistic in his reconstructive response to the modern world.

What of Barth's own treatment of the doctrine of the Virgin Birth, in contrast to that of Bonhoeffer and Brunner? The discussion in the second half of the Prolegomena to the *Church Dogmatics* leaves much to be desired as a convincing argument from critical-historical study of the Scriptures. "It certainly cannot be denied," Barth concludes his exegetical section, "that the outward, explicit evidence for the dogma in the statements of Holy Scripture is hedged about by questions. But still less can it be asserted that the questions raised are so hard to answer that one is forced by exegesis to contest the dogma." It is clear that Barth's real defense is theological and not historical:

The final and proper decision [on the dogma] is whether in accordance with the demands of Church dogma this testimony is to be heard, and heard as the emphatic statement of the New Testament message, or whether in defiance of Church dogma it is not to be heard, i.e., only to be heard as a sub-statement of the New Testament message which is not binding. This decision can be supported by answering the literary questions in one sense or the other. But it does not stand or fall with these questions.[37]

Barth carefully delimits the theological significance of the doctrine of the Virgin Birth, subordinating it strictly to the mystery of the Incarnation itself as sign to thing signified: "The doctrine of the Virgin Birth is merely the description and therefore the form by and in which the mystery is spoken of in the New Testament and in the creeds." Barth sees the miraculous fact of the Virgin Birth in direct correspondence with the miraculous fact of the Empty Tomb: Both are signs of the boundless mystery of God's full revelation of himself in Jesus Christ, one marking the beginning and the other the end of Christ's earthly ministry. But for Barth the full affirmation of the mystery cannot take place without affirming the sign as well as the thing signified. He describes the necessity of holding the two together with regard to the Empty Tomb and the Resurrection, which for him serves as an illustration also of the situation with regard to Virgin Birth and Incarnation:

We might say that so far as the New Testament witness to Easter is the account of the empty grave, it merely describes the mystery, or the revelation of the mystery, "Christ is risen." It describes it by pointing to this external fact. No one will dream of claiming that this external fact in itself and as such had the power to unveil for the disciples the veiled fact that "God was in Christ." But was it revealed to them otherwise than by the sign of this external fact? Will there be real faith in the resurrection of the Lord as revealing His mystery, as unveiling His divine glory, where the account of the empty grave is thought to be excisable as the mere form of the content in question, or where it can be left to Christian liberty to confess seriously and decisively the content alone? With this form are we not also bound in fact to lose the specific content of the Easter message for some other truth about the resurrection? . . . This is the question we have to put to ourselves even in regard to the Virgin Birth.[38]

The assertion, made here by the indirection of rhetorical questions, of the necessity of the doctrine of the Virgin Birth, leads to the question as to whether the doctrine is therefore binding on each individual Christian. "We must answer," Barth says, "that there is certainly nothing to prevent anyone, without affirming the doctrine of the Virgin Birth, from recognising the mystery of the person of Jesus Christ or from believing in a perfectly Christian way." It is a different matter, however, for the church as a whole:

> But this does not imply that the Church is at liberty to convert the doctrine of the Virgin Birth into an option for specially strong or for specially weak souls. The Church knew well what it was doing when it posted this doctrine on guard, as it were, at the door of the mystery of Christmas. It can never be in favour of anyone thinking he can hurry past this guard. It will remind him that he is walking along a private road at his own cost and risk. It will warn him against doing so. It will proclaim as a church ordinance that to affirm the doctrine of the Virgin Birth is a part of real Christian faith. It will at least require of its servants, even if there are some who personally cannot understand this ordinance, that they treat their private road as a private road and do not make it an object of their proclamation, that if they personally cannot affirm it and so (unfortunately) withhold it from their congregations, they must at least pay the dogma the respect of keeping silence about it.[39]

Bonhoeffer and Brunner would both agree with Barth that there are fundamental things which the church as a body must say about the Christian faith despite the reservations of its individual members; Bonhoeffer had as lively a concept of "right doctrine" and "heresy" as Barth. But from a truly evangelical, biblically christocentric point of view, the very problematic and peripheral dogma of the Virgin Birth cannot be one of these "fundamental things"—and just here is where Bonhoeffer and Brunner part company with Barth. Barth has attempted to prop up as necessary to a full christology something which is simply not vital to christology at all. He has allowed church tradition to overshadow the demands of an authentically biblical, Reformed, and contemporary evangelical faith.[40]

Bonhoeffer's biblical exegesis, viewed from a strictly historical-critical point of view, came down rather consistently on the conservative side. Yet, as the issue of the Virgin Birth shows, he combined a fully christocentric dogmatic theology with a reverent openness and reticence about matters which the Bible only hints at or leaves to one

221

side. His close attention to the actual words and situations of Scripture and to the priorities—the "degrees of knowledge and degrees of significance"—which biblical faith itself recognizes, gave his interpretation of Christianity modernity, freshness, and life. It is not at all without significance that Bonhoeffer's writings, apart from the early ones, are homiletical and above all ethical in their themes. The expounding of a Christian ethic, a biblical, christological ethic, was the major task of Bonhoeffer's last years. The immediate project of his future years, of course, was to have been the "non-religious interpretation of biblical concepts." In both areas Bonhoeffer was moving decidedly away from system building, from that intense preoccupation with the internal problems of dogmatics which characterized the development of Barth's theology.

"Non-religious Interpretation of Biblical Concepts"

As a theologian for whom theology was entirely biblical in its basis, Bonhoeffer envisioned "religionless Christianity" fundamentally as "the non-religious interpretation of biblical concepts." He considered the basic task of "non-religious" theological reconstruction to be that of "marshalling the biblical evidence." Bonhoeffer was working at this ground-laying enterprise in prison, but he found the situation too distracting and the task too great to get much done. In the letter of July 8, 1944, Bonhoeffer tells his friend Bethge that it is just too hot to think properly about the subject. Working out the biblical basis of "religionless Christianity"

needs more lucidity and concentration than I can command at present. Wait a few more days, till it gets cooler! I have not forgotten, either, that I owe you something about the non-religious interpretation of biblical concepts.[41]

Eight days later he complains, "I am only gradually working my way to the non-religious interpretation of biblical concepts; the job is too big for me to finish just yet." [42]

In an examination of the biblical basis of "religionless Christianity," we must bear in mind both the fundamental importance of the theme in Bonhoeffer's own mind and the fact that he was prevented from developing it to any extent beyond occasional references.

Bonhoeffer's prison writings contain numerous Scripture references, and it might be expected that they would provide us with important clues to the biblical foundations of "religionless Christianity." The varied citations, however, taken both individually and all together, do not of themselves suggest Bonhoeffer's "non-religious interpretation." Only a selective and contextual consideration of biblical references in *Letters and Papers* will provide such insights.

Among Old Testament books, the Psalms were Bonhoeffer's favorite, and he quotes from and refers to them more often than any other part of the Bible.[43] Proverbs is not far behind in frequency of appearance. Isaiah and Jeremiah, among the prophetic books, are the two other chief sources from the Old Testament. Although he cites the book only once, he was "particularly fond of" Job;[44] Ecclesiastes and the Song of Songs also fascinated him. In the New Testament, the Gospel according to St. Matthew is most frequently quoted,[45] followed by the Epistle to the Ephesians; St. John's Gospel and First Corinthians come next.

Many of Bonhoeffer's biblical references in the prison writings do not pertain to a discussion of "religionless Christianity." A great many topics, both personal and intellectual, appear in *Letters and Papers*. Bonhoeffer often cites or quotes at random a verse of Scripture appropriate to the topic or the occasion. He quotes or refers to passages dealing with such matters as friendship, the steadfastness of God amid tribulation, and a baptism and a wedding which he was prevented from attending.

Actually, very few of Bonhoeffer's explicit references to the Bible remain to be classed as pertinent to his thoughts on "Christianity without religion," but those that remain are extremely important.

The Old Testament

The Old Testament came to dominate Bonhoeffer's theological reflections during his years in prison, and must be seen as a central element in his "religionless" interpretation of Christianity. In the letter of the second Sunday of Advent, 1943, he declares:

My thoughts and feelings seem to be getting more and more like those of the Old Testament, and in recent months I have been reading the Old Testament much more than the New. . . . In my opinion it is not Christian to want to take our thoughts and feelings too quickly and too directly from

223

the New Testament. . . . One cannot and must not speak the last word before the last but one.[46]

This preoccupation with the Old Testament was an important form which Bonhoeffer's lively concern with the "penultimate" took in his last years.[47] It was entirely natural that his keen interest in the penultimate issue of a world "come of age" should have found its biblical counterpart in a new attention to the Old Testament. Perhaps, he seems to be saying, a Christianity for a penultimately "non-religious" world requires a fresh look at the penultimate within Christianity: the Old Testament.

The Old Testament provides the key to "non-religious" interpretation of the Scriptures above all because of its *this-worldliness (Diesseitigkeit)*. What is this-worldliness? First of all, it is commitment to *historical existence* rather than preoccupation with deliverance beyond death.[48]

"Religion" is inwardness, piety. One of the marks of inwardness is an interest in the salvation of one's soul from death. "Religion" is also metaphysics, which includes the exaltation of the eternal, by speculative or imaginative means, over against the temporal. Both these characteristics of "religion" are virtually absent from the faith of the Old Testament, in contrast to the "redemption-myth" religions of Egypt, Babylonia, and the Greek Orphic mystery religions.[49] So likewise is secularity a full commitment to the redemption of historical existence, with virtually no interest in salvation beyond death or in metaphysics.

Bonhoeffer goes on to argue that the traditional interpretation of Christianity as a "salvation myth" is mistaken. He replies that this interpretation divorces Christ from the Old Testament and thereby misses the essence of the resurrection hope: "The difference between the Christian hope of resurrection and the mythological hope is that the former sends a man back to his life on earth in a wholly new way which is even more sharply defined than it is in the Old Testament." [50] Here is an important example of the beginnings of Bonhoeffer's fragmentary thoughts on "non-religious" exegesis. Viewed solidly against its Old Testament background, the gospel is not release from the body and from death (as the Gnostics tried to make it) but new life in the here and now of historical existence. "The Christian," continues Bonhoeffer, "unlike the devotees of redemption myths, has no last line of escape available from earthly tasks and difficulties into the eternal. . . . This world must not be prematurely written off; in this the Old and New Testaments are at one." [51]

It is easy to criticize Bonhoeffer for a one-sided exegesis of the New Testament material on Christ's resurrection and ours. There is clearly a deeply "otherworldly" strain in the New Testament which is a direct result of the tension in which the primitive church believed itself to be between the raising of Jesus from the dead and the dissolution of the present world order by his return in glory. The recovery of the profoundly eschatological dimension both in Jesus' teaching and action and in the early church's hope and mission by Johannes Weiss, Albert Schweitzer, and others, prevents us from totally "immanentalizing" the time/eternity motif into *nothing more* than "eternal life in the midst of time."

Yet it must be pointed out, first of all, that in the above quotation Bonhoeffer is concerned with "the *decisive* factor" of Christianity. The Christian belief in the continuation of life beyond death is not per se distinctive; virtually every religion holds such a belief in one form or another. It is the belief, which Christianity took over directly from its Old Testament roots, that *history itself* is redeemed by the action of God which is the *distinctive* feature of Christianity in its resurrection faith and hope.

Secondly, the "religionless" Bonhoeffer has reaffirmed a vital element of Christian proclamation which is so often neglected: the doctrine that Jesus' resurrection, as the firstfruits of God's transformation of the entire universe, creates the possibility of new life in the midst of history and everyday existence, and not just beyond the grave. If Bonhoeffer's exegesis here seems one-sided, we must remember that he was deeply concerned to combat the one-sidedly otherworldly interpretation which has tended to predominate in the church. His full doctrine of Christian this-worldliness, as we might expect, is vigorously dialectical and eschatological.

In another letter Bonhoeffer examines the truly historical commitment of the Old Testament explicitly within the context of the contemporary problem of "religion." [52] Metaphysics and inwardness, the two hallmarks of "religion," are irrelevant, nonessential, to the faith of the Bible. Bonhoeffer never says that the Scriptures do not contain "religion," but the key to his whole "non-religious interpretation" of Christianity is the assumption, pioneered by Barth, that the biblical faith is not *essentially* "religious." By linking together "the Bible message" and "the man of today" as non-metaphysical and non-individualistic, Bonhoeffer indicates his conviction that the Scriptures and the world "come of age" both transcend "religion." Here is the real "point of contact" between Christianity and the secular world, and the task of exegesis is to interpret the Bible so as to bring out its fundamentally "non-religious" character.

The secular man of a world "come of age" is not particularly introspective, according to Bonhoeffer. The church, the "existentialists," and the "psychotherapists" have tried to make modern man focus on his "inner life," but they have largely failed with ordinary, healthy-minded people. Bonhoeffer suggests that secular man is not particularly concerned with his personal salvation, and rightly feels that there are more important matters to worry about. Significantly, Bonhoeffer adds that perhaps other matters are not really more important than salvation itself, but they are certainly more important than *bothering about* salvation. As a Christian, he did believe that the ultimate destiny of the individual was a matter of the highest importance; but as a Christian who viewed all things in the perspective of the objective reconciliation of all things in Christ and not out of his own subjectivity, he was liberated from *worrying* about personal salvation as if it depended upon himself.

The Scriptures come into the picture when Bonhoeffer, having remarked on the unimportance and the virtual nonexistence of concern for personal "soul-saving" in the modern world, goes on to say:

I know it sounds pretty monstrous to say that. But, fundamentally, is it not actually biblical? Does the question about saving one's soul appear in the Old Testament at all? Are not righteousness and the Kingdom of God on earth the focus of everything, and is it not true that Rom. 3:24 ff. is not an individualistic doctrine of salvation, but the culmination of the view that God alone is righteous? *It is not with the beyond that we are concerned, but with this world as created and preserved, subjected to laws, reconciled, and restored.* What is above this world is, in the gospel, intended to exist *for* this world; I mean that, not in the anthropocentric sense of liberal, mystic pietistic, ethical theology, but in the biblical sense of the creation and of the incarnation, crucifixion, and resurrection of Jesus Christ.[53]

Salvation in the Bible means "the Kingdom of God on earth," in contrast to the saving of one's individual soul. Bonhoeffer took with utter seriousness the New Testament references to the coming of the Kingdom as the transformation by God of this present universe, the "making new" of the "old creation." [54] The bodily resurrection of Jesus is the "first installment" of this universal renewal of the created order. Salvation is corporate, not simply individual; more than that, it is cosmic, a reality in which in an ineffable way all created things participate, and not just man. The kingdom of God is not release from bodily, historical existence and death, but affirmation of this world and triumph over death by the God who created all things good and caused the light to shine out of darkness. The Creator and the Redeemer are indissolubly one in Bonhoeffer's thought. Any devaluation of this world or "spiritualization" of salvation as escape from the fetters of worldly existence is a Christian heresy, a form of Marcionism. It is because the one God both creates and renews in the Old and New Testaments that Christianity can be authentically this-worldly.

In the last sentence of the passage under consideration Bonhoeffer distinguishes what he means by biblical this-worldliness from the this-worldliness of theological liberalism. The sentence reminds us of his Barthian orientation—what he called "thinking theologically." It is important to keep in mind that Bonhoeffer affirms his classical biblical theology within the context of a plea for a "religionless Christianity," and explicitly rejects the older liberalism's use of the Bible. For all its "radicality," "religionless Christianity" as Bonhoeffer conceived it is in no sense a return to liberalism of the traditional sort. It is rather the pressing of a rigorously biblical-dogmatic theology to a particular conclusion on the basis of the new hermeneutical situation created by modern secularity.

Another "religionless" contribution of the Old Testament, and one which is a central aspect of its this-worldliness, is its affirmation that God is *at the center of life*. God as "the center of life" (*die Mitte des Lebens*) is one of Bonhoeffer's characteristic phrases, not only in the prison writings but throughout the development of his thought.

In Chapter One we discussed Bonhoeffer's interpretation of biblical anthropology as *a holistic view of man*. Biblical anthropology, especially that of the Old Testament, must be seen as another scriptural foundation of Bonhoeffer's "Christianity without religion." The Old

227

Testament does not compartmentalize man into a temporal body and an eternal soul, or even into "outer" and "inner," as do Platonism, the mystery religions, and modern philosophical and religious outlooks such as idealism. There is simply the human being, who in his psycho-physical wholeness obeys or rejects God. Any sort of transhistorical salvation (to which the Old Testament came very late) must be in some mysterious way a bodily as well as a "spiritual" existence; hence, in the Bible, the "resurrection of the body" rather than the "immortality of the soul." [55]

One of the most interesting and significant elements of Old Testament faith to the "religionless" Bonhoeffer was the Jews' reverent refusal to speak *the name of God*. In a letter of November 21, 1943, while discussing his own "fear and distrust of 'religiosity,' " he says, "The fact that the Israelites *never* uttered the name of God always makes me think, and I can understand it better as I go on." [56] And two weeks later he remarks that "it is only when one knows the unutterability of the name of God that one can utter the name of Jesus Christ." [57] The following April, in the letter which was the introduction of Bonhoeffer's "non-religious" reflections, he raises the question, "How do we speak (or perhaps we cannot now even 'speak' as we used to) in a 'secular' way about 'God'?" [58] He goes on to make the personal observation that he is frequently drawn to the "religionless" rather than to the "religious" person. He illustrates this experience with the name of God. "Religious people," Bonhoeffer says, "speak of God when human knowledge (perhaps simply because they are too lazy to think) has come to an end, or when human resources fail." [59] They talk about God on the borders of life, in the boundary situations —as an intellectual stopgap in their knowledge or as a desperate hope in the face of emergency, guilt, suffering, and death. In short, "religion" speaks of God as the *deus ex machina*.

What is more, "religion" profanes the name of God by chattering about it *ad nauseam*. The holy name "God" becomes a mere word which "religious" people all too hastily drop into human situations as a kind of magic invocation, as if all that human needs and problems require for their solution is "God." His name further becomes a stick with which to beat the "non-religious" on the head. Hence it is only when the Christian, like the Jew, apprehends with awe and reverence the unutterability of God's name, with all that his name stands for of power, holiness, majesty, mystery, and love, that he transcends "religion." It is only when he hardly dares speak the name of God that he begins to know with all his being what it means to speak the name "Jesus Christ." And Jesus Christ is not "religion," but God as man. "Religion" leaps too quickly to the ultimate: It goes around applying God's name unthinkingly and tiresomely to every human situation instead of dealing with the situation in its own right. "Religionless Christianity" perceives that the ultimacy of God's name and the integrity of the penultimate direct the Christian to grapple concretely with penultimate problems instead of superficially and irresponsibly dragging in "God" as the magic cure.

We are fortunate in having Bonhoeffer's exposition of "The First Table of the Ten Commandments," which he wrote while in prison and to which we alluded in discussing modern "nihilism." In commenting on the second commandment ("You shall not take the name of the Lord your God in vain; for the Lord will not hold him guiltless who takes his name in vain"), Bonhoeffer elucidates in detail his theological reflections on the sacredness of the name of God.

He begins by distinguishing the Judeo-Christian from other meanings of "God" as the difference between a *name* and a *word:*

> "God" for us is not a general concept with which we designate the highest, holiest, and mightiest that can be conceived. On the contrary, "God" is a name. . . . For us, God is our God, the Lord, the Living One. "God" is a name, and this name is the greatest sanctuary that we possess, because we have in it not at all something that we have conceived, but God himself in his whole essence, in his revelation. God in inconceivable grace has given himself to be known by us, and it is solely for this reason that we may say "God." . . . The word "God" is nothing at all; the name "God" is everything.[60]

Bonhoeffer's insistence that "God" is always a name and never merely a word is precisely the Jewish recognition that God has various designations (*Elohim, Adonai*) but only one name, the name he vouchsafed to Moses: *Yahweh.* The name of God, the tetragrammaton (YHWH), became so sacred to the Jews that they ceased to pronounce it and substituted the generic word *Adonai* or various circumlocutions when reading from the Old Testament.[61] Bonhoeffer, like Judaism and what he would consider to be biblical Christianity, always understood God as a Thou who encounters us in living, historical, personal, and social relationship. Whoever encounters us as a Thou has a name, and therefore "God" is a name and not a word or a concept.

Because Christians know God in I-Thou encounter—because they know his name—they can commit the sin of misusing his name: "Whoever knows the name of God and misuses it dishonors and violates the sanctity of God." To misuse God's name is to use it as a mere word: "We who know the name of God misuse it when we utter it as if it were only a word, as if God himself did not always speak to us in this name." [62]

There is a misuse with evil intentions, such as invoking God's blessing on an evil cause. But there is a well-intentioned misuse of God's name, and this is even more dangerous because it is harder to spot. This is the "religious" misuse:

It occurs when we Christians constantly utter the name of God so self-evidently, so glibly, and so intimately that we detract from the sanctity and the miracle of his revelation. It is misuse when, for every question and affliction, we are on hand precipitately with the word "God" or with a Bible quotation, as if it were the most self-evident thing in the world that God answers all human questions and is always prepared to help in every difficulty. It is misuse when we make God into a stopgap for our embarrassments. It is misuse when we want to put a stop to genuinely scientific or artistic endeavors simply with the word "God." . . . It is misuse when we speak about God without being aware of his living presence in his name. It is misuse when we talk of God as if we had him at all times at our disposal, and as if we had sat in his council. In all these ways we misuse the name of God, because we make it into an empty human word and impotent idle chatter, and in this way we desecrate it more than the blasphemers can desecrate it.[63]

Here Bonhoeffer compresses the elements which he mentions in his letters in connection with the "religious" misuse of the name of God: glibness, and invoking God at the intellectual and existential boundaries of life.

Bonhoeffer concludes his discussion of the misuse of the name "God" with a highly significant statement: *It is certainly better not to pronounce the name of God than to degrade it to a mere human word.* He adds: "Yet we have the sacred commission and the high privilege to bear witness to God before one another and before the world. That happens when we utter the name of God only in such a way that in it the word of the living, present, righteous, and gracious God himself is attested." [64] Although he raised the question whether it is even possible to speak of God in a secular world, it is clear from the above passage that Bonhoeffer called for a deeply chastened but continued use of the name of God by Christians. The significance of his statement that it is better not to pronounce the name of God at all than to use it "religiously" lies in what a recent theological trend has made of the idea. The American "New Theologians," Paul M. van Buren, William Hamilton, and Thomas J. J. Altizer, have attempted to draw out Bonhoeffer's ideas to their wholly secular conclusion. They maintain that in a world "come of age" it is no longer possible even for Christians to speak of God at all. Van Buren has developed this notion the most fully in his book *The Secular Meaning of the Gospel.*

Whether reverence for the name of God in a "religionless" world takes the moderate form of an extreme reticence about using his name or the radical form of not using his name at all, it is certain that the Old Testament apprehension of the name of God and the reverent silence of the Jews influenced Bonhoeffer in a way which has profound implications for modern Christianity.

Among the specific books of the Old Testament which figure in Bonhoeffer's "non-religious interpretation," four favorites of his should be grouped together: Ecclesiastes, Proverbs, Job, and Song of Songs. Significantly, perhaps, three out of the four represent Jewish Wisdom literature. The Wisdom tradition was characterized by practical sense, a kind of "bourgeois" moderation, a healthy-minded worldliness, a sense of "everything in its place" in the universe, and a humble frankness about the mystery of life.[65]

Behind the ostensible cynicism of Ecclesiastes Bonhoeffer appreciated the Preacher's recognition that "for everything there is a season, and a time for every matter under heaven" (3:1). The author of this strange book affirmed that life itself, the daily business of eating and drinking and toiling (3:13), is a proper regard of man under God. God "has put eternity into man's mind" (3:11), but "there is nothing better . . . than to be happy and enjoy themselves as long as they live; . . . it is God's gift to man that every one should eat and drink and take pleasure in his toil" (3:12-13). There is a time for thinking about eternity, life beyond death, and the paradise of the blessed, but there is equally a time for accepting and living to the full the very earthly joys of this life.[66]

Bonhoeffer thinks the Preacher's thoughts after him in the following passage:

I believe that we ought so to love and trust God in our *lives,* and in all the good things that he sends us, that when the time comes (but not before!) we may go to him with love, trust, and joy. But, to put it plainly, for a man in his wife's arms to be hankering after the other world is, in mild terms, a piece of bad taste, and not God's will. We ought to find and love God in what he actually gives us; if it pleases him to allow us to enjoy some overwhelming earthly happiness, we must not try to be more pious than God himself and allow our happiness to be corrupted by presumption and arrogance, and by unbridled religious fantasy which is never satisfied with what God gives. God will see to it that the man who finds him in his earthly happiness and thanks him for it does not lack reminder that earthly things are transient, that it is good for him to attune his heart to what is eternal. . . . But everything has its time, and the main thing is that we keep step with God, and do not keep pressing on a few steps ahead—nor keep dawdling a step behind. It is presumptuous to want to have everything at once—matrimonial bliss, the cross, and the heavenly Jerusalem.[67]

The first thing to be noted in Bonhoeffer's interpretation of Qoheleth is criticism of "religion." One sign of "religion" is being ascetical and self-denying, even Manichaean, about earthly things. "Religious" piety tends to see everything earthly in terms of cross, not of blessing. It feels ashamed and guilty (even if only unconsciously) when it turns its attention away from contemplation of heavenly things. Such an attitude springs from the "inwardness" of religion: The "religious" sphere, the place where God is at work, is the "inner man," who tends to be set over against the "outer man" and the externalities of life in the world as "soul" over against (and in constant warfare with) "body." Bonhoeffer counters this with the *Menschlichkeit* of the Old Testament, of Luther, and supremely of the incarnate Lord: the acceptance as a whole person of both blessing and cross in the midst of earthly life as gifts of God. This brings us to the second aspect of the passage quoted above, its relation to the positive interpretation of Christianity in "non-religious" terms. Bonhoeffer's use of Ecclesiastes underlies his description of the "religionless" Christian:

By [Christian] this-worldliness I mean living unreservedly in life's duties, problems, successes and failures, experiences and perplexities. In so doing we throw ourselves completely into the arms of God, taking seriously, not our own sufferings, but those of God in the world—watching with Christ in Gethsemane. That, I think, is faith, that is *metanoia;* and that is how one becomes a man and a Christian.[68]

The mature Christian in the modern world does not turn his back on the life God has given him, but accepts it fully and responsibly from God's hand. The writer of Ecclesiastes, Bonhoeffer believes, witnessed to such a life, a life in which God "has made everything beautiful in its time" (3:11). To Qoheleth and the "secular" Christian there is a time for everything in this earthly life, for all the times are in God's hands.

The Proverbs express a similar '"worldly wisdom" in a more workaday and unselfconscious manner. They are full of ageless folk common sense transmuted by the biblical faith. They concern themselves with the qualities of good husbands and wives, fathers and children, and friends; with the temptations to which human flesh is ordinarily prone—money, power, intemperance, sensuality, untruthfulness and dishonesty, slander and gossip. A certain hard-headed, "bourgeois" life acceptance pervades Proverbs. The book is a practical attempt to apply faith to concrete, everyday situations.[69] There is much here that would appeal to Bonhoeffer's "religionless" thinking. His psychological interpretation of the topography of the section of Germany in which he was raised could equally well characterize the psychology (though not necessarily the topography!) of an Old Testament Jew brought up on the teaching of Proverbs: "Perhaps 'my' central hills are 'bourgeois' in the sense of what is natural, not too high, modest and self-sufficient (?), unphilosophical, satisfied with concrete realities, and above all 'not-given-to-self-advertisement.'"[70] Naturalness, modesty, and contentment with concrete realities are hallmarks of Bonhoeffer's own character; so also are truthfulness, honesty, integrity, and self-discipline. His attack on "existentialism," "psychoanalysis," and some forms of Christian apologetic for preying on man at the extremities of his life, coupled with his profound appreciation of the large numbers of people who somehow cope successfully with everyday life, reflects an attitude which would find Proverbs congenial.

Bonhoeffer never discusses the Book of Job, but it speaks eloquently to a theme which exercised his "religionless" thoughts, the "religious" theme of God as the metaphysical *deux ex machina*. For "religion" God is the answer to life's problems, the *deux ex machina* who resolves them into a happy ending. The "religionless" Bonhoeffer objects strenuously to this "stopgap" apprehension of God: "It is simply not true to say that only Christianity has the answers. . . . As to the idea of 'solving' problems, it may be that the Christian answers are just as unconvincing—or convincing—as any others. . . . Christ. . . . is the centre of life, and he certainly did not 'come' to answer our unsolved problems." [71] The Book of Job poses an age-old "religious" problem: Why do the just suffer and evildoers prosper? The "answer" in Job is no answer at all (chap. 38–41); Job is simply confronted by the mystery of God's lordship and his own utter dependence upon such a God.[72] His "problem" is not "answered." He encounters the living God and the result is not intellectual or "religious" satisfaction but *metanoia:* "Therefore I despise myself, and repent in dust and ashes (42:6)." The mystery and inscrutability of God viewed as the "religious" answer to human problems appears also in Ecclesiastes, although much less dramatically (3:11, 21; 11:5). The God of Israel, the God incarnate in the man Jesus, is living and active in the midst of life. The Christian in an adult or "come-of-age" world simply participates in the blessing and suffering of such a God; that is *metanoia,* and it has nothing to do with "answers" to "problems."

The Song of Songs fascinated Bonhoeffer because of its earthiness, naturalness, and unblushing but nonprurient sensuality. Even more than Ecclesiastes, its inclusion in the Old Testament canon is a riddle. But Bonhoeffer sees real significance in its inclusion:

> Even in the Bible we have the Song of Songs; and really one can imagine no more ardent, passionate, sensual love than is portrayed there (see 7:6). It is a good thing that that book is in the Bible, in face of all those who believe that the restraint of passion is Christian (where is there such restraint in the Old Testament?).[73]

Here again is the critique of "religion" which we saw in discussing Ecclesiastes, with only slight variation. The "religious" Christian considers the life of faith a burdensome but necessary suppression of natural vitality and life affirmation. This is the result of the "religious" mistake of viewing life in terms of two spheres—the sacred and the profane, the inner and the outer, the spiritual and the carnal. It is that unhealthy asceticism which Bonhoeffer believed to be so foreign to the Bible. True to the long-standing ascetical tendencies of Christianity, the classical interpretation of Song of Songs is to treat it as an allegory of Christ and the church. Bonhoeffer rejects this "spiritualized" treatment in favor of a literal and natural one: "I should prefer to read it as an ordinary love song, and that is probably the best 'Christological' exposition." [74] It is precisely by reading the Song of Songs as a poem about the joys and beauties of earthly love between a man and woman that we read it christologically. For Christ is the man at the center of life, the man who exists for others in all the concrete encounters and activities of daily life. Although Bonhoeffer does not himself say it, perhaps we are to read the Song of Songs together with the account of Jesus' participation in and enhancement of the marriage feast at Cana (John 2:1-11).

Bonhoeffer might have made extensive use of the prophetic books as biblical basis for a "non-religious" approach to Christianity. The prophets pioneered the "critique of religion," calling Israel back from a purely cultic piety divorced from life to ethical obedience to Yahweh-God in the totality of national existence (Amos 5:21-24; Hos. 6:6; 8:13; Isa. 1:11-17; Jer. 6:19-20). Caught up by the God who acts at the center of life as its present Lord, they spoke to such "secular" issues as social injustice (Amos 8:4-6), corruption among civil officials (Hos. 7:3-7), and disastrous foreign policies (Jer. 2:18). Here was a vision of life in which the boundary between "sacred" and "secular" had no place. The whole spectrum of concrete, mundane human affairs was the stage in which the living God encountered and summoned men.[75]

The prophets testified to the God who reveals himself as the divine Thou through the confrontation of concrete human Thous in the midst of life. The Holy One of Israel effects his purpose in political and military engagements, civil justice, and the policies of rulers. As Bonhoeffer puts it, the "beyond" of the God of Israel "is the beyond in the midst of life." The Old Testament, and supremely the prophetic faith, know nothing of metaphysical or epistemological transcendence. Transcendence is always concrete, social, and ethical.

These "religionless" emphases in the prophets were doubtless congenial to Bonhoeffer, and are to be thought of as part of the general biblical fabric which undergirds "religionless Christianity." The only prophets explicitly mentioned in the prison writings, however, are Isaiah and Jeremiah, and nothing of a particularly "non-religious" nature can be gleaned from the references cited, since most of them appear in contexts other than the "Christianity without religion" discussion. Isaiah 53, the great "Suffering Servant" chapter, is mentioned in connection with Bonhoeffer's "non-religious" interpretation of *metanoia*. *Metanoia*, repentance, is participation in the sufferings of Jesus, who as the man for others was servant of all.[76]

The New Testament

Bonhoeffer employs the New Testament more explicitly in his "non-religious" reconstruction of Christianity. "The Pauline question," he states, "whether *peritomé* [circumcision] is a condition of justification seems to me in present-day terms to be whether religion is a condition of salvation. Freedom from *peritomé* is also freedom from religion." [77] Here is a specific example of "non-religious" exegesis, one of the few instances in the prison writings of the application of Bonhoeffer's "non-religious interpretation of biblical concepts." None of the Pauline references to the circumcision issue in the early church (Rom. 2:25-29 and 4:1-12; I Cor. 7:18-19; Gal. 5:2-6 and 6:12-15; Phil. 3:2-3; and Col. 2:11) are specifically cited by Bonhoeffer, but he clearly has them in mind when he speaks of "the Pauline question whether circumcision is a condition of justification." Perhaps Bonhoeffer would have considered Gal. 6:15 the most "religionless" expression of the issue: "For neither circumcision counts for anything, nor uncircumcision, but a new creation."

John 1:14, the classic statement of the Incarnation: *ho Logos sarx egeneto,* also figures in an explicitly "religionless" context in *Letters and Papers*. Again, Bonhoeffer is concerned with the problem of "non-religious" exegesis: "I am thinking about how we can reinterpret in a 'worldly' sense—in the sense of the Old Testament and of John 1:14— the concepts of repentance, faith, justification, rebirth, and sanctification." [78] In this passage we encounter Bonhoeffer's conviction that the Old Testament interprets the realities of God and faith in a thoroughly this-worldly sense. He exegetes John 1:14 in this Old Testament manner. The Word has truly become flesh—"in the world," *diesseits*, "secular"—and the enfleshed Word is the only God we know or need to know. Therefore interpretation of the event of Christ is per se worldly, i.e., "non-religious," interpretation. We have already explored the christological expression which emerges from this framework, in Chapter Six.

A New Testament text which appears twice in a "non-religious" connection is Mark 15:34, Jesus' cry of dereliction from the cross: "My God, my God, why hast thou forsaken me?" Bonhoeffer first uses it in the letter in which he contrasts the historical, this-worldly redemption of the Old Testament with the salvation beyond the grave which the religions offer. He believes that redemption in the New Testament is also primarily "this side of death." Bonhoeffer goes on to describe the mature Christian and Christ himself in this light:

> The Christian, unlike the devotees of the redemption myths, has no last line of escape available from earthly tasks and difficulties into the eternal, but, like Christ himself ('My God, why hast thou forsaken me?'), he must drink the earthly cup to the lees, and only in his doing so is the crucified and risen Lord with him, and he crucified and risen with Christ. This world must not be prematurely written off; in this the Old and New Testaments are at one.[79]

The cry of dereliction expresses Jesus' complete involvement in the God-forsakenness, the "secularity," the "worldliness," of the world. The cry of dereliction reveals that Christ had no "ace in the hole," no Gnostic "inside track" on salvation which enabled him to stand aloof from the world and to contemplate it with serenity and even with a certain contempt. Christ exists wholly for the world, and therefore he fully shares the world's condition, shouldering its burdens and rejoicing in its blessings as a whole man. Indeed, the radical God-forsakenness of the world "come of age" is itself the work of God:

> We cannot be honest unless we recognize that we have to live in the world *etsi deus non daretur*. And this is just what we do recognize—before God! God himself compels us to recognize it. So our coming of age leads us to a true recognition of our situation before God. God would have us know that we must live as men who manage our lives without him. The God who is with us is the God who forsakes us (Mark 15:34). The God who lets us live in the world without the working hypothesis of God is the God before whom we stand continually. Before God and with God we live without God. God lets himself be pushed out of the world on to the cross. He is

237

weak and powerless in the world, and that is precisely the way, the only way, in which he is with us and helps us. Matt. 8:17 makes it quite clear that Christ helps us, not by virtue of his omnipotence, but by virtue of his weakness and suffering.[80]

Jesus' cry of dereliction is paradoxically the cry of God himself, who in Jesus reveals himself and redeems the world through powerlessness, weakness, and suffering. God in Christ chooses to empty himself, to live "without God" in the world, for the sake of a God-forsaken world. Now that this world has "come of age," God is teaching us to live without "religion" and its metaphysical and emotional comforts.

The prison writings reveal Bonhoeffer's fascination with human example in the Bible, specifically with the human example of Jesus and of those whose lives were touched by his, as recorded in the Gospels and Acts. During the 1930's, he developed profound appreciation of and insight into the dynamic, personal-social character of the biblical drama. His early and continuing I-Thou understanding of revelation as concretely human and social gave force to this biblical personalism, which found its culmination in the "non-religious" concentration solely on human example.

In the prison writings Bonhoeffer was preoccupied with the New Testament concept of *metanoia* as a key term in the "non-religious" understanding of Christianity. As a basic aspect of the style of life of the mature Christian of the modern world, *metanoia* is discussed in a section of its own in the next chapter.

Chapter Nine

The Development of a Christological Ethics Under the Third Reich

Bonhoeffer considered the writing of a Christian ethics to be the most important task of his lifetime. Because of his untimely death the task was realized only in a disconnected and unfinished form in the notes and essays which make up the posthumously edited and published *Ethics*.[1]

Of necessity we have already been examining Bonhoeffer's ethics in previous chapters, for his ethical concerns permeate and inform every aspect of his theology.

Orders of Preservation

It remains in this chapter to round out our discussion of the place of ethics in Bonhoeffer's theology by examining other major ethical themes in his writings. Christian ethics was thrown into disrepute during the 1930's by the "German Christian" apologists for Nazism, who found in the ethics of Lutheran pietism, in the ethical deliverances of the German liberal Christian tradition, and in contemporary attempts at constructing Protestant ethical systems, grist for their mill. The strong tradition of Lutheran pietism in Germany espoused an ethical dualism, a distorted version of Luther's "two kingdoms" doctrine.[2] The kingdom of God reigns in the sphere of the inner man, the proper concern of the gospel; the kingdom of the state rules in the outer sphere, the realm of law.[3] Outward conformity to the Third Reich could be justified as a matter simply of giving Caesar his due. Even contemporary Neo-Reformation theologians like Emil Brunner effected another sort of ethical dualism with their separation of "orders of creation" (*Schöpfungsordnungen*) from the revelation in Christ.[4] By perverting such dualistic ideas the "German Christians" were able to justify devotion to blood, race, and soil as "orders of creation" to be obeyed until the world's consummation.[5]

Early in the 1930's Bonhoeffer joined in the ethical quest for a workable Protestant theology of creation, a lively topic among German-speaking Christians of the day. He countered Brunner's *Schöpfungsord-nungen* with a doctrine of *Erhaltungsordnungen* ("orders of preservation"). Bonhoeffer was aiming in the same direction as Brunner, Paul Althaus, Friedrich Gogarten, and other "non-German Christians" who were seeking to establish "orders of creation"; but he considered their efforts insufficiently christological and eschatological. Furthermore, he was one of the first in German theological circles to see how the Nazi-sympathizing Christians were perverting this breaking apart of Christ and creation. His notion of "orders of preservation" was evolved to avoid the misunderstandings which laid the "orders of creation" idea open to perversion by government religious propagandists. By emphasizing preservation rather than creation, Bonhoeffer brought into sharper focus the foundation of Christian ethics wholly and exclusively in Christ's first and second comings. The world redeemed in Christ is preserved by God in concrete ways until its consummation. By beginning with creation, theological ethicists like Brunner ran the risk of getting behind Christ to certain realities which are to be regarded as independent of him, thus opening the door to elements foreign to the gospel.

In his paper, "A Theological Basis for the World Alliance," which was written in 1932, Bonhoeffer set forth his criticisms of the "German Christian" use of "orders of creation" and developed his own doctrine of "orders of preservation." He asks the question, "Whence does the church know God's commandment for the moment?" and lists some alternative answers which were being put forward at the time. One answer was the pro-Nazi version of "orders of creation":

Because certain orders are evident in creation, one should not rebel against them, but simply accept them. One can then argue: Because the nations have been created different, each one is obliged to preserve and develop its characteristics. That is obedience towards the Creator. And if this obedience leads one to struggles and to war, these too must be regarded as belonging to the order of creation. . . . The commandment of God is thought of as something which has been given once and for all, in definite ordinances which permit of discovery.

Such was the "German Christian" *Schöpfungsordnungen* argument. What was wrong with it?

The danger of the argument lies in the fact that just about everything can be defended by it. One need only hold out something to be God-willed and God-created for it to be vindicated for ever, the division of man into nations, national struggles, war, class struggle, the exploitation of the weak by the strong, the cut-throat competition of economics.[6]

The fatal flaw in the argument, which enables it to sanction whatever exists just because it is part of the "created order," is a wholly inadequate recognition of the fallenness of creation:

It is not realised in all seriousness that the world is fallen and that now sin prevails and that creation and sin are so bound up together that no human eye can any longer separate the one from the other, that each human order is an order of the fallen world and not an order of creation. There is no longer any possibility of regarding any features *per se* as orders of creation and of perceiving the will of God *directly* in them. The so-called orders of creation are no longer *per se* revelations of the divine commandment, they are concealed and invisible.

The only possible basis for regarding the commandments of God is Jesus Christ.

The commandment cannot stem from anywhere but the origin of promise and fulfilment, from Christ. From Christ alone must we know what we should do, . . . from him as the one who gives us life and forgiveness, as the one who has fulfilled the commandment of God in our place, as the one who brings and promises the new world. We can only perceive the commandment where the law is fulfilled, where the new world of the new order of God is established. Thus we are completely directed towards Christ.[7]

In the light of the new creation which Jesus has brought we can understand the old creation for the first time:

> Now with this we also understand the whole world order of fallen creation as directed solely towards Christ, towards the new creation. . . . We know that *all* the orders of the world only exist in that they are directed towards Christ; they *all* stand under the preservation of God as long as they are still open for Christ, they are *orders of preservation*, not orders of creation. They obtain their value wholly from outside themselves, from Christ, from the new creation. . . . They . . . only exist as long as they are open for the revelation in Christ. Preservation is God's act with the fallen world, through which he guarantees the possibility of the new creation. *Orders of preservation are forms of working against sin in the direction of the Gospel.*[8]

Bonhoeffer concludes by saying that *"any order*—however ancient and sacred it may be—*can be dissolved,* and must be dissolved when it closes itself up in itself, grows rigid and no longer permits the proclamation of revelation. From this standpoint the church of Christ has to pass its verdict on the orders of the world." [9] Such talk was clearly anathema to the Nazis. Bonhoeffer's doctrine of orders of preservation was one form of the Confessing Church's fundamental theological protest against the Third Reich. That protest was embodied in Article Two of the Barmen Declaration of 1934:

> Just as Jesus Christ is the pledge of the forgiveness of sins, just so—and with the same earnestness—is he also God's mighty claim on our whole life; in him we encounter a joyous liberation from the godless claims of this world to free and thankful service to his creatures.
> We repudiate the false teaching that there are areas of our life in which we do not belong to Jesus Christ but another lord, areas in which we do not need justification and sanctification through him.[10]

The Recall to Ultimacy

But just as others were taking up the term *Erhaltungsordnungen,* Bonhoeffer dropped it. After 1933 he became silent about the whole discussion. Bonhoeffer agreed that the problem was a crucial one which had not been treated satisfactorily; but he believed that the decisive moment for dealing with it had passed. As the demonic proportions of the Nazi state became increasingly apparent, he abandoned the search for any sort of "penultimate" ethics, realizing the use to which the "German Christians" were putting it.

In a more exclusively Barthian direction, Bonhoeffer came in the latter part of the prewar years to espouse a radically eschatological ethics, an ethics of the purely "ultimate" for a church which was living as if in the crisis of the End. This is the ethics we see in *The Cost of Discipleship*. Here Bonhoeffer spells out quite literally and concretely the demands of radical obedience to the gospel. He treats the Sermon on the Mount, not as the vague set of ideals it is often considered to be in the life of the church or of the individual Christian, but as hard, specific demands of the crucified and risen Lord upon the disciple.[11] He berates the church for fostering the idea of easy or "cheap" grace, for severing faith from obedience, for talking in glittering generalities. *The Cost of Discipleship* is a trumpet call to the church in the midst of the Last Days. "The Church," Bonhoeffer states,

has never forgotten Christ's promise of his imminent return, and she has always believed that this promise is true. The exact manner of its fulfilment remains obscure, but that is not a problem for us to solve. This much is clear and all-important for us to-day that the return of Jesus will take place suddenly. That fact is more certain than that we shall be able to finish our work in his service, more certain than our own death. This assurance that in their suffering they will be as their master is the greatest consolation the messengers of Jesus have.[12]

More than one commentator on Bonhoeffer's theology has noted that the tone of the ethics in *The Cost of Discipleship* borders on sectarianism. Bethge describes the period of Bonhoeffer's life and thought in which it was written under the heading "The Narrow Pass for Christianity." [13] During this period (the late 1930's) Bonhoeffer's ethical writing and activity called the church to look inward, to restore and strengthen itself at its roots, to stand over against the world sharply. These years saw the Finkenwalde experiment, when Bonhoeffer directed an illegal seminary of the Confessing Church. He organized the Finkenwalde community along semi-monastic lines, inculcating a daily and weekly discipline of prayer and worship. The seminary and Bonhoeffer were accused of "catholicizing." For him, however, it was simply a vigorously biblical answer to the German church's desperate need to get theological education out of the arid atmosphere of the universities, where it had often succumbed weakly to the blandishments of Nazism, and into living workshops of Christian community and discipleship. It was more of his conviction that the church had to retrench behind the fortifications of the gospel in the face of a largely hostile environment.

Bonhoeffer's ethical attitude during the late 1930's is quite understandable in the light of the difficult position in which Christians found themselves with regard to the Third Reich.[14] His "sectarianism" was consonant with the whole approach of the Confessing Church of which he was an active leader. Barth himself certainly took a "Let the church be the church!" approach. His quite favorable remarks on *The Cost of Discipleship* in the *Church Dogmatics*, written twenty years later, are instructive in this regard. The Barmen Declaration and the other documents of the Confessing Church emphatically represented a "retrenchment," a biblical and theological judgment on the society which was denying its true Lord and erecting an idolatrous one named Adolf Hitler.[15] As in previous times of persecution, any attempt by the church to "lose itself" in the world, to meet the world halfway, to extol the realm of "penultimate" values or "natural" ethics, meant selling out to the powers of darkness. At this time Bonhoeffer set forth the seemingly intolerable statement that "whoever knowingly separates himself from the Confessing Church in Germany separates himself from salvation." [16] In the midst of the German *Kirchenkampf* that statement was not without reason and meaning.

A Second Look at the Penultimate

Germany's declaration of war against Europe in 1939 and Bonhoeffer's subsequent participation in the German Resistance movement turned his ethical thought away from the radically eschatological approach he had taken previously. Close association with nonbelievers who were willing to risk their lives simply for the freedom and dignity of man joined forces with his love of the earth to produce renewed thinking on the penultimate problems of Christian ethics. What place was there in a completely ultimate ethics for the ethics of the *bonus vir*, the good pagan who was suffering and dying alongside the Christian in defense of truth, justice, and humanity? What was the church to say to the pressing problems of reconstructing German society and government after the devastation of war? These and other questions exercised Bonhoeffer's imagination and turned his ethical thought once again in a penultimate direction.

In the writings which make up the *Ethics* we find Bonhoeffer experimenting with new ethical ideas at various stages in terms of christology, anthropology, and concrete social and personal issues. In the *Ethics* Bonhoeffer was explicitly developing a positive evaluation of the secular. His starting point was Barth's: All creation has already been reconciled to God in the man Jesus Christ. But Bonhoeffer carried this idea forward to concrete fulfillment in the *Ethics* and in *Letters and Papers*. He raised the ethical questions and analyzed the demands implied in encountering the world not as a separate, "profane" sphere, but as the world-reconciled-to-God-in-Christ. Likewise every man, whether Christian or nonbeliever, was not to be thought of as "man" in isolation, but as the man-reconciled-in-Christ.[17]

The most important and original notion in the *Ethics* is Bonhoeffer's return from a purely eschatological ethics to an ethics of the ultimate *and* the penultimate. There are still the "Last Things" (*die letzten Dinge*); but between Christ's first and second comings the "Things Before the Last" (*die vorletzten Dinge*) assume great importance.[18]

In the idea of the penultimate Bonhoeffer reintroduced in slightly altered form his early doctrine of "orders of preservation." He thus continued to avoid what he regarded as the principal error in the introduction of a "natural" ethics or an ethics of "creation": the error of looking at a part of reality apart from Christ. If in Christ "we can henceforward no longer see God without the world or the world without God," [19] then there can be no place in Christian ethics for anything outside the pale of christology. Penultimate ethics is Christian ethics for the concrete situations of here and now in a world which has been reconciled in Christ but which must exist until the fulfillment of all things.

The ultimate is the justification of sinful man by God. This word of grace is a reality which has invaded the fallen creation in Jesus Christ, but which will not be the fullness of reality until God is "all in all." The "final word" is thus past (in the Incarnation), present (in the daily justification of the sinner), and future (in the Eschaton). Because Christians live "between the times," in the tension and conflict of the inaugurated but not fulfilled new creation with the fallen old creation, they must reckon seriously with the penultimate.[20] The penultimate is recognized as penultimate only on the basis of the ultimate. The value of the penultimate is not inherent but extrinsic; it is determined by and subordinate to the ultimate: "When we speak of the things before the last, we must not speak of them as having any value of their own, but we must bring to light their relation to the ultimate. It is for the sake of the ultimate that we must . . . speak of the penultimate." [21]

Bonhoeffer gives an example of the relation of penultimacy to ultimacy in his understanding of man:

It is only on the basis of the ultimate [i.e., the Word of God in the manhood of Christ] that we can know what it is to be man. . . . And yet the relationship is such that manhood precedes justification, and that from the standpoint of the ultimate it is necessary that it should precede it. The penultimate does not therefore rob the ultimate of its freedom; but it is the freedom of the ultimate that validates the penultimate. And so, with all necessary reservations, it is now possible to speak of manhood, for example, as a penultimate to justification by faith. Only man can be justified, precisely because only he who is justified becomes "man." [22]

This highly dialectical anthropology is thoroughly christocentric; yet at the same time it enables the church to concern itself with man in his existence apart from his conscious espousal of the word of grace. The penultimate side of Bonhoeffer's anthropological dialectic became extremely important in the "religionless Christianity" project, above all in a profound sensitivity to and affirmation of man simply as man. Recognition of the penultimate freed Bonhoeffer to love the earth and its people as realities with an integrity and life of their own.

The purpose of the things before the last is "preparing the way for the word." [23]

Christ comes indeed, and opens up His own way, no matter whether man is ready beforehand or not. No one can hinder His coming, but we can resist His coming in mercy. There are conditions of the heart, of life and of the world which impede the reception of grace in a special way, namely, by rendering faith infinitely difficult.[24]

Grace is sovereign and alone efficacious, but it works within the concrete human situation, which involves countless factors which can impede it:

Grace must in the end itself prepare and make level its own way and grace alone must ever anew render possible the impossible. But all this does not release us from our obligation to prepare the way for the coming of grace, and to remove whatever obstructs it and makes it difficult. The state in which grace finds us is not a matter of indifference, even though it is always by grace alone that grace comes to us.[25]

Bonhoeffer's recognition of the important role of actual human obedience and disobedience even within a theology of *sola gratia* is characteristic of his lifelong sensitivity to the relation of the gospel to living human beings amid the complexities of their historical, psychological, and sociological situation. It is a recognition which the early Barth neglected in his concern to protest against the prevailing anthropocentric theology of liberalism. Some of Barth's early statements leave the impression of a monistic exaltation of God and the corollary annihilation of man.[26] Among Neo-Reformation theologians other than Bonhoeffer, it was Emil Brunner who preserved most faithfully the role of human obedience in the biblical understanding of the relation of God to man.[27]

Bonhoeffer goes on in his *Ethics* to give practical illustrations of the importance of the penultimate in preparing or impeding the way of the ultimate word of grace:

The hungry man needs bread and the homeless man needs a roof; the dispossessed need justice and the lonely need fellowship; the undisciplined need order and the slave needs freedom. To allow the hungry man [for example] to remain hungry would be blasphemy against God and one's neighbor, for what is nearest to God is precisely the need of one's neighbor.[28]

"Man does not live by bread alone, but by every word which proceeds out of the mouth of God." "Nevertheless," someone has wisely recognized, "man *does live* by bread." Hunger, homelessness, injustice, loneliness, bondage of one kind or another, all these can prevent persons from hearing the ultimate word of grace. For the sake of the ultimate, for the sake of Christ who has forgiven and reconciled all men, the penultimate tasks of feeding the hungry, pleading the cause of the victims of injustice, befriending the lonely, and freeing the enslaved, are vitally important tasks of the Christian and the church. The Christ who not only proclaimed the Good News but also healed the bodily and mental diseases of specific persons embraces the penultimate within the ultimacy of his own person and calls his followers to prepare his way in the same manner.

Bonhoeffer's own involvement in the church struggle and in political resistance to Hitler manifested a deep-seated commitment to the Christian significance of the things before the last. Some members of the Confessing Church protested at great risk against the sadistic injustices perpetrated against the Jews in Germany. Bonhoeffer himself stated that "only he who cries out for the Jews may also sing Gregorian [chant]." [29] In the opposition movement in Germany during the war, which sought to unseat Hitler and overthrow the Nazi regime, Bonhoeffer saw a decisive claim on himself as a Christian.[30] Germany could be saved for a future of justice and freedom only by being defeated in war. "It is quite certain," he wrote in his *Ethics,* "that the preparation of the way is a matter of concrete interventions in the visible world." Carefully preserving Christian priorities, however, he added, "yet everything depends on this activity being a spiritual reality, precisely because ultimately it is not indeed a question of the reform of earthly conditions, but it is a question of the coming of Christ." [31]

Bonhoeffer approached the reality of the penultimate from a more closely reasoned and concretely illustrated angle in his concept of the *natural.* What he says about the penultimate under the heading of the natural is virtually identical with what he had said in the early 1930's about the orders of preservation:

> The natural is that which, after the Fall, is directed towards the coming of Christ. The unnatural is that which, after the Fall, closes its doors against the coming of Christ. . . . The natural does not compel the coming of Christ, and the unnatural does not render it impossible. In both cases the real coming is an event of grace. And it is only through the coming of Christ that the natural is confirmed in its character as a penultimate, and that the unnatural is exposed once and for all as destruction of the penultimate.[32]

Another passage makes the link between the natural or penultimate and orders of preservation even more explicit: "The natural is the form of life preserved by God for the fallen world and directed towards justification, redemption and renewal through Christ." [33] Like the orders of preservation, the natural or penultimate is wholly subordinate to, and to be understood only in the light of, the Incarnation:

> Natural life must not be understood simply as a preliminary to life with Christ. It is only from Christ Himself that it receives its validation. Christ Himself entered into the natural life, and it is only through the incarnation of Christ that the natural life becomes the penultimate which is directed towards the ultimate. Only through the incarnation of Christ do we have the right to call others to the natural life and to live the natural life ourselves.[34]

Bonhoeffer went on, under the heading of the natural, to discuss particular ethical issues such as individual freedom, the right to bodily life, suicide, reproduction, the rights of the mind, and truth-telling, interpreting them both ultimately and penultimately in the light of the reconciliation achieved in Christ's cross and resurrection.[35]

In the prison writings the notion of the penultimate continued to fascinate Bonhoeffer, as in his discussion of the name of God.[36] In previous chapters we have already seen, under other headings, how at the end of his life Bonhoeffer was developing the concept of the penultimate in striking ways. Two penultimate topics became extremely important to the "religionless" Bonhoeffer. One was the necessity for Christians to affirm earthly life honestly and unreservedly: "It is only when one loves life and the earth so much that without them everything seems to be over that one can believe in the resurrection and a new world." Here is a lifelong theme of Bonhoeffer's which found radical expression in the prison writings. We studied his early insistence on the intimate relation between the old creation and the new in his essay "Thy Kingdom Come." In the prison writings Bonhoeffer afirmed even more decisively the importance of living in the penultimate, of loving this earth in all its brokenness. His positive evaluation of secularity must be seen in large part as a manifestation of this appreciation of the penultimate, the natural. In the letter which opens his train of reflections specifically on a "Christianity without religion," Bonhoeffer raises a number of questions posed for the existence of the Christian and the church by secularization. Significantly, he concludes his questions by asking, "Does the secret discipline, or alternatively the difference . . . between penultimate and ultimate take on a new importance here?" [37]

It is highly important to note here Bonhoeffer's linking of the ultimate-penultimate distinction with his concept of the "secret discipline." His remarks, brief as they are, reinforce what I have argued from the beginning: that Bonhoeffer saw "religionless Christianity" as an intensely *dialectical* reality. The dialectic of ultimacy/penultimacy corresponds to the ecclesiological dialectic between the church gathered (the secret discipline) and the church scattered (secular existence). The ultimate, which is the gospel, is proclaimed, studied, meditated upon, and appropriated ever anew within the "secret" fellowship of the Christian community. Here is provided the perspective out of which the Christian thinks and acts, the ultimate will of God and condition of man. The penultimate comprises to a large degree the sphere of the Christian's secular existence in and for the world. Here the Christian must grapple seriously with the relativities and novelties of an ongoing historical situation in the light of the ultimacy of Christ.

In another letter Bonhoeffer reflects on the mature, "secular" Christian of a world "come of age," describing him as "not a *homo religiosus,* but simply a man, as Jesus was a man." In the same letter in which this description appears, Bonhoeffer recalls a conversation he had had while in the United States in 1930-31 with the noted Christian pacifist Jean Lasserre.[38] Discussing what they hoped to do with their lives, Lasserre had aspired to become a saint, while Bonhoeffer had said he wanted to learn to have faith. He realizes thirteen years later that he had not realized at the time how profound was the difference between the two aspirations. He had written *The Cost of Discipleship,* he remarks, under the assumption that one could attain faith by striving for a kind of holiness.

In *The Cost of Discipleship* Bonhoeffer had turned from penultimate to purely ultimate ethical concerns. The renewal and intensification of his concern for the penultimate during the war years took the form of preoccupation with the nature of secularity and the search for a penultimate, "secular" interpretation of the gospel and the Christian life. Concern purely for the ultimate tends to be concern for "eschatological existence," holiness, or, in the case of the French pastor, sanctity. Involvement with the penultimate means instead coming to grips with the problem of existing as a Christian who is at the same time, in the modern world, a "non-religious," secular person.

The other important theme touched on in the material from *Letters and Papers* is Bonhoeffer's increasing love of the Old Testament during his last years. The Old Testament, of course, is the "penultimate" Word of God for Christians.

A final ethical topic which exercised Bonhoeffer in the last years was what he called "conformation," the concrete molding of personal and social life to the reality and pattern of the incarnate Lord. We shall discuss this important motif below when we attempt to reconstruct Bonhoeffer's theological portrait of the mature or "religionless" Christian of a world come of age. At the center of "religionless Christianity" is *reconciliation,* the foundation of Bonhoeffer's later ethics. Jesus is "the man for others," in whose reconciling activity among men we know all we can know of God and divine transcendence. Since all we know of God is seen in the reconciling humanity of Jesus, Christian ethics involves concretely following the pattern of manhood proclaimed in his words and actions, chiefly his sufferings in and for the world. Jesus the man who reconciles also continued to be the foundation of Bonhoeffer's highly perceptive analysis of secularity. The world is still the world-reconciled-in-Christ; more than that, it is the world liberated from the adolescence of "religion" for full maturity and humanity by this very Christ who is not *homo religiosus* but simply man. It is clear that actual, "inaugurated" reconciliation stands behind Bonhoeffer's remarks about secularity and his general world affirmation in the prison writings.

Stemming from the fact of reconciliation in the midst of the world, concern for the penultimate naturally became urgently important to Bonhoeffer in the light of his hypothesis that "religion" was dying in the modern world. The death of "religion" meant the death of human preoccupation with the ultimate—guilt, death, eternal life, the transcendent, etc. What is extraordinary about Bonhoeffer's prison reflections, as Gerhard Ebeling notes, is precisely his unselfconscious zeal to grapple with radically this-worldly problems such as the decay of "religion" and the triumph of secularity.[39] We should perhaps expect a Christian awaiting the real eventuality of death to be supremely exercised in the contemplation of the "Last Things" rather than the "Things before the Last." It is an eloquent testimony to Bonhoeffer's utter personal and intellectual involvement in the world for which Christ died that to the end he was caught up in the penultimate questions.

We have seen that Bonhoeffer chided Barth for contenting himself with general theological and ethical principles. Significantly, in the later volumes of the *Church Dogmatics,* in which Barth discusses ethical problems in greater detail, he refers frequently to Bonhoeffer and by and large considers the latter's ethical insights to be the profoundest in contemporary theology.[40] Barth took over Bonhoeffer's expression "cheap grace," and his tremendous admiration for the ethics of *The Cost of Discipleship* appears in the following statement in the *Dogmatics:* "[In *The Cost of Discipleship*] the matter is handled with such depth and precision that I am almost tempted simply to reproduce them in an extended quotation. For I cannot hope to say anything better on the subject than what is said here by a man who, having written on discipleship, was ready to achieve it in his own life, and did in his own way achieve it even to the point of death." [41] Only slightly more restrained is Barth's approval of Bonhoeffer's *Ethics.* Yet it is significant that Barth embraces the purely eschatological ethics of *The Cost of Discipleship* enthusiastically and unreservedly. It is vital to keep in mind that Bonhoeffer moved back from a purely "ultimate" ethics to a more comprehensive view, from an ethics of the kingdom of God to an ethics grounded in the appearance in history of the word of grace in Jesus Christ. It is not unfair to Barth, I think, to contend that he has held fast to an ethical position which Bonhoeffer came to find inadequate.[42] Nevertheless, in recent years Barth came closer to Bonhoeffer's willingness to grapple with concrete issues. It is probably much less true of the later Barth that he fails "to give any concrete guidance in either ethics or dogmatics."

The "Religionless" Christian

Among the questions which Bonhoeffer raises in his initial letter concerning the "Christianity without religion" project are the following: "Are there religionless Christians? . . . In what way are we 'religionless-secular' Christians, . . . not regarding ourselves from a religious point of view as specially favoured, but rather as belonging wholly to the world?" [43]

Bonhoeffer's portrait of the "religionless" Christian, the one who at the same time serves Christ and affirms a world "come of age," is equally as important to his "religionless Christianity" project as his "non-religious interpretation" of the central themes of Christian theology. Word and action were inseparable for Bonhoeffer. It is basic to a right understanding of his "religionless" project to realize that the radical translation of Christian *language* into secular terms comprises only half of the church's task in the modern world. The other, and decidedly the more difficult, half is the raising up of Christians who witness to their Lord in the midst of the world through an appropriate *style of life.* In the essay "Bonhoeffer the Man," which introduces the two shorter writings of Bonhoeffer in *Preface to Bonhoeffer,* John Godsey puts the matter in the German theologian's own perspective:

> The whole question of man's language and its ability to express meaning —the hermeneutical question—has been raised in a decisive way, and for the church it has become acute with respect to the translation of the meaning of the biblical language into the language of the twentieth century. Many consider this an altogether academic problem, but not Bonhoeffer. For him it was not merely the question of finding the proper language, although obviously it is important when one wants to express himself non-religiously, that is, without making religion the precondition of faith. The more basic question for Bonhoeffer was whether our lives authenticate or belie our words.[44]

Speech and action, words and life, theology and obedience, these are correlates which belong intrinsically together for Bonhoeffer. Language articulates and evokes action; action embodies and gives concrete reality to language.

As the integrated man that he was, Bonhoeffer pioneered "religionless Christianity" in deed as well as in word. His full secular involvement in the German Resistance during the war is the supreme example, but throughout his life he was a vigorously world-affirming Christian. His description of the mature or "religionless" Christian admirably fits himself. Perhaps unselfconsciously, Bonhoeffer painted a portrait of the kind of Christian he was striving to become, and had in fact become to a high degree.

Piecing together Bonhoeffer's picture of the "religionless" Christian is like putting together a jigsaw puzzle. His remarks on the mature Christian of a secular world are scattered in brief fragments throughout *Letters and Papers.* Nowhere does he attempt to set forth a comprehensive statement on the matter. Hence the characteristics into which this discussion is divided have been distilled from the conglomerate of Bonhoeffer's incidental remarks. On the basis of careful analysis of both the prison letters and Bonhoeffer's thought as a whole, I believe that they embody his main emphases.

Conformation

The theological basis of Bonhoeffer's remarks on the "religionless" Christian is his concept of *conformation (Gleichgestaltung)*. It is in his *Ethics* that he sets forth the idea, and there he advances it as the key to a genuinely christological ethics: "Ethics as formation . . . means the bold endeavour to speak about the way in which the form of Jesus Christ takes form in our world, in a manner which is neither abstract nor casuistic, neither programmatic nor purely speculative. . . . Here there are concrete commandments and instructions for which obedience is demanded." [45] The "way in which the form of Jesus Christ takes form in our world" is the concrete, obedient con-formation of men to the form of the biblical Christ, the man whose existence for others even to the point of death and beyond is the world's true reality:

The Holy Scriptures speak of formation in a sense which is at first entirely unfamiliar to us. Their primary concern is not with the forming of a world by means of plans and programmes. Whenever they speak of forming they are concerned only with the one form which has overcome the world, the form of Jesus Christ. . . . Formation comes only by being drawn in into the form of Jesus Christ. It comes only as formation in His likeness, as *conformation* with the unique form of Him who was made man, was crucified, and rose again.

Is conformation with Christ "becoming like Jesus," in the pietist-modernist sense? No, replies Bonhoeffer: "Just as we misunderstand the form of Christ if we take Him to be essentially the teacher of a pious and good life, so, too, we should misunderstand the formation of man if we were to regard it as instruction in the way in which a pious and good life is to be attained." Our pattern is not the "historical Jesus" of modern pious and liberal imagination, but the biblical Christ, God as man, who sovereignly conforms us, each in his own way, to his image as "the Incarnate, Crucified and Risen One." [46]

The form of Christ, then, is not a "religious" pattern to which we are to conform; it is rather the pattern of true manhood. Jesus the man for others is what it means to be a human being in the fullest sense:

> To be conformed with the Incarnate—that is to be a real man. It is man's right and duty that he should be man. The quest for the superman, the endeavour to outgrow the man within the man, the pursuit of the heroic, the cult of the demigod, all this is not the proper concern of man, for it is untrue. The real man is not an object either for contempt or for deification, but an object of the love of God. The rich and manifold variety of God's creation suffers no violence here from false uniformity or from the forcing of men into the pattern of an ideal or a type or a definite picture of the human character. The real man is at liberty to be his Creator's creature. *To be conformed with the Incarnate is to have the right to be the man one really is.* Now there is no more pretence, no more hypocrisy or self-violence, no more compulsion to be something other, better and more ideal than what one is. God loves the real man. God became a real man.[47]

Here is a concept of the Incarnation and Christian obedience which is by no means new with Bonhoeffer, but which, in his prison writings, becomes the basis of a radically secular interpretation of what it means to be a Christian. If Jesus is "simply a man," and not merely "religious" or heroic man, then to be conformed to him is not essentially a "religious" but a human phenomenon. Conformation to the Man for others, according to the above passage, involves freedom, honesty, modesty, and, running through them all as a theme with variations, this-worldliness. The man conformed to Christ, says Bonhoeffer, "lives in the world like any other man. Often there is little to distinguish him from the rest. Nor does he attach importance to distinguishing himself, but only to distinguishing Christ for the sake of his brethren." [48]

In the light of Bonhoeffer's central theological concerns, we might expect his notion of Christian life as conformation to the form of Christ to be linked intimately to the *church,* and such is the case in the *Ethics:*

> "Formation" . . . means in the first place Jesus' taking form in His Church. What takes form here is the form of Jesus Christ Himself. The New Testament states the case profoundly and clearly when it calls the Church the Body of Christ. The body is the form. So the Church is not a religious community of worshippers of Christ but is Christ Himself who has taken

255

form among men. . . . The Church . . . bears the form which is in truth the proper form of all humanity. . . . The Church is nothing but a section of humanity in which Christ has really taken form.[49]

To Bonhoeffer, the church, as the form of Christ among men, is simply those human beings who are conscious of their true humanity, and not essentially a "religious" community. He states the matter even more strongly a few lines later:

The Church is the man in Christ, incarnate, sentenced and awakened to new life. In the first instance, therefore, she has essentially nothing whatever to do with the so-called religious functions of man, but with the whole man in his existence in the world with all its implications. What matters in the Church is not religion but the form of Christ, and its taking form amidst a band of men.[50]

We have seen how, in the prison writings, the present shape of the church became highly problematic to Bonhoeffer as the appropriate form of Christ in the world, and what were his suggestions concerning a renewed form of the church which would authentically transcend "religion" in the direction of humanity. Here we are concerned with the individual Christian as a "religionless" person; but obviously the Christian and the church are inseparable for Bonhoeffer, and the attributes of the latter are those of the former "writ large." I have introduced the church at this juncture primarily, however, because it is integrally bound up with the concept of conformation which is the theological basis of the come-of-age Christian.

This-worldliness

The form which Christ takes among men in the world "come of age" is essentially *this-worldly.* Bonhoeffer reflects quite explicitly on this basic theme of the Christian style of life, relating it directly to its christological foundation:

During the last year or so I have come to know and understand more and more the profound this-worldliness of Christianity. The Christian is not a *homo religiosus,* but simply a man, as Jesus was a man—in contrast, shall we say, to John the Baptist. I don't mean the shallow and banal this-worldliness of the enlightened, the busy, the comfortable, or the lascivious, but the profound this-worldliness, characterized by discipline and the constant knowledge of death and resurrection. I think Luther lived a this-worldly life in this sense.[51]

These words are important, because they clearly distinguish between a *Christian* humanism or secularity and several superficial forms of secularity which, to use Tillich's phrase, lack the "dimension of depth." Bonhoeffer's this-worldliness is rooted in the biblical-dogmatic proclamation that real life, authentic existence, is the new life which accepts the dark forces within reality and triumphs over them in the power of Christ's cross and resurrection. The new life which is Christian this-worldliness is "characterized by discipline." A tough-minded, disciplined affirmation of the world grounded in the reality of Jesus' death and victory—this is part of the "beyond" in Christian this-worldliness, which sets it apart from the hedonistic positivism which "this-worldliness" usually connotes. We shall examine this "beyond" in the lifestyle of the "religionless" Christian in more detail under the heading of *metanoia*.

Bonhoeffer goes on to define further what he means by Christian this-worldliness.[52] "Living unreservedly in life's duties, problems, successes and failures, experiences and perplexities" is basic to Bonhoeffer's understanding of the "religionless" Christian, and he spells it out in terms of *metanoia*, polyphony, strength, freedom, and the dialectic of action and submission. Of particular interest is his statement that one must abandon the attempt, not only to become a "religious" man, but even "a righteous man or an unrighteous one." Here is a reaffirmation of Bonhoeffer's early insight into the "trans-moral" standing point of the Christian. We shall look again briefly at this position "beyond good and evil" in "non-religious" terms under the rubric of the *freedom* of the "religionless" Christian.

The theme of "living completely in this world," without trying to be "religious," also appears in explicitly theological terms in the following passage, where Bonhoeffer says that the Christian

must . . . really live in the godless world, without attempting to gloss over or explain its ungodliness in some religious way or other. He must live a "secular" life, and thereby share in God's sufferings. He *may* live a "secular" life (as one who has been freed from false religious obligations and inhibitions) . To be a Christian does not mean to be religious in a particular way, to make something of oneself (a sinner, a penitent, or a saint) on the basis of some method or other, but to be a man—not a type of man, but the man that Christ creates in us. It is not the religious act that makes the Christian, but participation in the sufferings of God in the secular life.[53]

From a theological standpoint, the world come of age is still a *godless* world and should be accepted and affirmed as such. To live a this-worldly life in a godless world is to "share in God's sufferings" in the world, i.e., to be conformed to the Christ whose being-for-others supremely took the form of suffering and dying at the hands of the godless for whom he lived. Participation in the suffering of God in the world is central to Bonhoeffer's concept of *metanoia*.

In his "non-religious interpretation of biblical concepts" Bonhoeffer sets the fundamental this-worldliness of biblical faith over against the other-worldliness of "religion." He also expresses this difference in terms of the biblical versus the "religious" apprehension of divine transcendence. For the Scriptures God is the "beyond" at the center of life, while "religion" looks for him at the boundaries, where human strength fails.

The message of Ecclesiastes, that "there is a time for everything," was a significant biblical influence on the "religionless" Bonhoeffer— enjoying and being truly grateful for earthly blessings when God grants them and reflecting on death and eternity when the time comes, but without mixing them together and casting a "religious," ascetical pall over earthly joys and the fullness of life.

Metanoia

The discussion of Bonhoeffer's "non-religious" interpretation of christology in Chapter Six brought into focus two affirmations about divine transcendence which seem to be contradictory. There appears to be an incongruity between interpreting God as the "beyond" in our strength and prosperity and at the same time as the "beyond" of reconciliation revealed in suffering and weakness. Bonhoeffer seems to have been aware of this tension in his understanding of the "otherness" of God, but nowhere does he spell out its resolution as clearly as we might wish. However, he does say certain things which indicate that the two ideas are dialectical and not contradictory. The clearest discussion of the issue is to be found in a letter of July 28, 1944. Here Bonhoeffer seeks to understand blessing and suffering, not as mutually exclusive, but as contained within each other.

He begins by replying to Bethge's statement that "the Bible has not much to say about health, fortune, vigour, etc." Bonhoeffer protests that this is not at all true of the Old Testament, and not as true of the New as is often assumed. In the Bible there is a term which mediates between God and human fortune, and that is the category of *blessing:* "In the Old Testament—e.g. among the patriarchs—there is a concern not for fortune [*Glück*], but for God's blessing [*Segen*], which includes in itself all earthly good. In that blessing the whole of the earthly life is claimed for God, and it includes all his promises." [54] In other words, in the Old Testament those things which apart from God are called "good fortune"—joy, health, prosperity—are seen in the light of God's creatorship and lordship as divine blessings.

Bonhoeffer goes on to say that the natural interpretation of the New Testament is to "spiritualize" the Old Testament idea of blessing and to set in its place only a cross. He resists this interpretation, however, citing in support of his view the association of physical sickness and death with the misuse of the Lord's Supper in I Cor. 11:30, Jesus' role as healer of men's bodies as well as their spirits, and the statement in the Gospels that while the disciples were with him they "lacked nothing." Bonhoeffer illuminates this "worldly" interpretation of the New Testament in the letter of June 30, 1944. "Never," he says, "did he [Jesus] question a man's health, vigour, or happiness, regarded in themselves, or regard them as evil fruits; else why should he heal the sick and restore strength to the weak? Jesus claims for himself and the Kingdom of God the whole of human life in all its manifestations." [55]

In the light of such an interpretation of the New Testament, Bonhoeffer asks, "is it right to set the Old Testament blessing against the cross?" He mentions that Kierkegaard did this, but criticizes the tendency because it "makes the cross, or at least suffering, an abstract principle." The sundering of cross and blessing generates "an unhealthy methodism" which is foreign to the Bible. Above all—and this is central—it "deprives suffering of its element of contingency on a divine ordinance." [56] Suffering is never an absolute; it is not an end in itself or even a higher state of godliness than blessing. Both suffering and blessing are fruits of setting ourselves entirely at God's disposal. Being at God's disposal means acknowledging him as creator and reconciler of earthly life. Being at God's disposal means being free from self in order to exist for others. Being at God's disposal is participation in his transcendence. Thus it is that in being at God's disposal we may experience transcendence in both suffering and blessing. For this reason suffering and good fortune, cross and blessing, are truly contingent upon a divine ordinance.[57] Bonhoeffer points out that in the Old Testament the one who receives a blessing has to endure suffering as part of the bargain—he mentions Abraham, Isaac, Jacob, and Joseph —"but this never leads to the idea that fortune and suffering, blessing and cross are mutually exclusive and contradictory—nor does it in the New Testament."

Bonhoeffer concludes his discussion of blessing and suffering by drawing an epigrammatic parallel between the two Testaments: "Indeed, the only difference between the Old and New Testaments in this respect is that in the Old the blessing includes the cross, and in the New the cross includes the blessing." [58] The only distinction, then, is a matter of emphasis. Participation in the transcendence of God is participation in both blessing—man's health and prosperity—and suffering—man's weakness and powerlessness.

While neither blessing nor suffering is an end in itself but rather contingent upon God's ordinances, we find in Bonhoeffer a definite priority given to suffering. This priority, however, is not the superiority of self-denial over life in the world, which is "religious" asceticism. The priority of suffering is simply a recognition of the fallenness of the world. In a world which is turned in upon itself the deepest and most significant participation in divine transcendence is participation in the suffering of God. For Bonhoeffer transcendence is the reconciliation manifested in the man Jesus, which in him is freedom to be for others. The resistance offered to this existence-for-others by a world which has its being in existence-for-self often results in suffering. The strength and power of existence-for-self in the world also frequently reveal existence-for-others to be weak and powerless. Hence those situations in which participation in the "beyond" of God involves suffering, powerlessness, or weakness, are peculiarly luminous to the fullness of divine transcendence. In such situations is revealed most decisively the stark contrast between the light of God and the darkness of the world. Nevertheless, since there is for us no "God" and no "world," but only God-in-the-world, God is most truly known in suffering, powerlessness, and weakness in the midst of life. Thus it is that Christ *crucified* is "the power of God, and the wisdom of God" (I Cor. 1:24) . The cross is the chief focal point for the "otherness" of

God, because it is in this act that we behold the full cost of reconciliation between God and world. In the suffering unto death of the one whose whole being was his being-for-others, the full dimensions of the world's being-for-self are revealed.

In line with what we may now call the "objective" and "worldly" (rather than "subjective" and "religious") priority of suffering as the revelation of divine transcendence, Bonhoeffer discusses the meaning of *metanoia* (repentance) as man's participation in this suffering. Characteristically, he rejects a "religious" definition of *metanoia:* "That is *metanoia:* not in the first place thinking about one's own needs, problems, sins, and fears, but allowing oneself to be caught up in the way of Jesus Christ, into the messianic event." Christ as the messianic event is the Suffering Servant who fulfills Isaiah 53. Hence for Bonhoeffer *metanoia* is not simply "repentance" in the usual sense. He lists examples of persons in the New Testament who were caught up in Jesus' messianic suffering without any specific confession of sin and "repentance" in the constricted sense in which Christians often use it. The list is designed to show the rich varieties of *metanoia* in the Bible, providing examples of what Bonhoeffer elsewhere calls the "degrees of knowledge and degrees of significance" in biblical faith: the call to discipleship (Matt. 4:18-22; Mark 1:16-20; Luke 5:1-11); Jesus' table fellowship with sinners (Matt. 9:10-13; Mark 2:15-17; Luke 5:29-32); the conversion of Zacchaeus the publican (Luke 19: 1-10); the woman who anointed Jesus' feet (Matt. 26:6-13; Mark 14: 3-9; Luke 7:36-50; John 12:1-8); Jesus' healing of the sick (Matt. 8:16-17; Mark 1:32-34; Luke 4:40-41); the shepherds and the wise men who were present at Jesus' birth (Matt. 2:1-12; Luke 2:8-20); the centurion of Capernaum (Matt. 8:5-13; Luke 7:1-10); the rich young ruler (Matt. 19:16-20; Mark 10:17-31; Luke 18:18-30); the eunuch whom Philip baptized (Acts 8:26-39); Cornelius and his household (Acts 10); Nathanael (John 1:47); Joseph of Arimathea and the women at the tomb (Matt. 27:57-60; 28:5-8; Mark 14:42-46; 16:5-8; Luke 23:50-54; 24:3-8a; John 19:38-42). [59]

In collecting this diverse array of persons and situations from the New Testament and calling them all instances of *metanoia*, Bonhoeffer cuts through the church's traditional formulaic descriptions of the necessary ingredients in repentance and conversion. Too often the baffling variety of persons in the Gospels whose lives Jesus transformed is either neglected or else squeezed artificially into a preconceived mold which emphasizes certain specified, subjective aspects to which conversion should conform in order to be genuine. It is another manifestation of the church's "religious" error: the psychologizing of that which is properly theological. By making the objective event of the revelation of God in the man Jesus wholly determinative, Bonhoeffer frees those New Testament figures from a retrospective subjectivism which they did not possess. He allows each of them to be simply a human being rather than a *homo religiosus:* a human being, living in the world like other men and women, who has been graciously caught up in Jesus' messianic suffering. In short, Bonhoeffer allows the New Testament cast of characters to be "religionless," as he believes a number of them genuinely are: "The only thing that is common to all these is their sharing in the suffering of God in Christ. That is their 'faith.' " [60] Some of these central themes we have encountered before: faith and new life as participation in Jesus' freedom to be for others, which is in the final analysis participation in his weakness and suffering. Faith and new life, which are acts of *metanoia,* are to be understood objectively, as being caught up in God's suffering in the world. Bonhoeffer speaks explicitly of the this-worldly life of the Christian in these terms:

> We throw ourselves completely into the arms of God, taking seriously, not our own sufferings, but those of God in the world—watching with Christ in Gethsemane. That, I think, is faith, that is *metanoia;* and that is how one becomes a man and a Christian (cf. Jer. 45!). How can success make us arrogant, or failure lead us astray, when we share in God's sufferings through a life of this kind? [61]

The *objective* priority of divine suffering over human *metanoia* is important to a "non-religious" understanding of transcendence, as well as to the seeming contradiction between the "beyond" of God in strength and in weakness. It is *"religion,"* in its *subjectivity,* which makes sin, suffering, and repentance things apart from the rest of life. It is only when in *faith* we view life as a whole, created and reconciled by God in Christ, that we do not divorce suffering from blessing, and repentance from healthy-mindedness. For "religion," God himself is divorced from the rest of life: He is a *deus ex machina.* For faith, God is not revealed apart from the world and the world is not understood apart from God. This is the objectivity of the "religionless" Christian: He understands life as a unity. He refuses to relegate God to a small corner of life, to the "inner" or "personal" sphere. He refuses to make God a stopgap in our knowledge or a panacea for our weaknesses. Such reductions of God and his transcendence belong to "religion," says Bonhoeffer; Christianity is about life as a whole. That is why the terms *faith* and *new life* replace *religion* and *piety* in a "religionless Christianity." [62]

Both cross and blessing are participation in the transcendence of God. That is because neither is a subjective, "religious" state separate from the other or from the rest of life. Both are contingent upon the divine ordinances embodied in creation and reconciliation. Both are experienced in the midst of life, and in both the "beyond" of God is revealed. Suffering has a certain priority as a revelation of transcendence, but this is because of the objective state of the world and not because of a "religious," ascetical judgment as to the intrinsic godliness of self-denial. Both blessing and suffering are to be accepted as part of the pattern of all life by him who in faith has put himself at God's disposal.

Therefore Bonhoeffer insists repeatedly that we must confront people with the gospel in their strength and prosperity, and not merely in their weakness and poverty. To try to convince the strong and joyous and good that they are really miserable wretches, tactics denounced by Bonhoeffer as those of "existentialists," "psychotherapists," and many Christian apologists, is an unworthy attempt to convince a mature world that it is adolescent. It is to perpetuate the "religious" error: the divorcing of God from life. "Religionless Christianity" does not suffer from this schizophrenia, argues Bonhoeffer. If the "beyond" of God is reconciliation in the midst of life, then weakness and strength, suffering and blessing, are not opposites but are rather contained within each other.

In the world as it is, the strong and the good are often those who suffer and are weak. Bonhoeffer was experiencing in his own persecution and in the persecution of others who witnessed to human freedom and dignity in Nazi Germany that the God who is at the center of life is the "beyond" in both our strength and our suffering. It is precisely the strong and the good who experience at its deepest level the frustration of high ideals, the pain of weakness and suffering. God encounters man in his health and prosperity, says Bonhoeffer; and suffering and weakness then become, not ascetical self-denial, but the extension of strong human action into the possibility of a transfigured freedom.[63] The fundamental reality of the life of faith is simply placing oneself at God's disposal. Both blessing and suffering, all actions and experiences in life, are contingent upon that reality.

Bonhoeffer's radical concern for intellectual honesty and personal sincerity of belief, which is integral to the "Christianity without religion" project, is to be seen theologically within the context of *metanoia*. Intellectual honesty demands that Christians see the world as "come of age," as a world which is able to function *etsi deus non daretur*. Bonhoeffer explicitly identifies such honesty as a form of *metanoia* in his discussion of the world's "coming of age." [64]

Closely linked with intellectual honesty is personal sincerity of belief. Although Bonhoeffer does not link personal sincerity explicitly with *metanoia*, as he does intellectual honesty, it is clear that they are for him two aspects of the same reality. Intellectual honesty may be seen as the critical, and integrity of personal conviction as the confessional, stance of the "religionless" Christian. Both are manifestations of placing oneself simply and wholly at the disposal of the God who is Jesus Christ, the God who as the prior, objective reality liberates the man of faith from idolatrous dependence upon either the "religious world view" or the "faith of the church." To be free from, to turn one's back on, these collective securities is part of repentance and faith, part of *metanoia*.

Bonhoeffer's remarks on personal conviction occur entirely and significantly within the context of his criticisms of the church. The following passage, from his "Outline for a Book," also welds personal belief intimately together with intellectual honesty:

What do we really believe? I mean, believe in such a way that we stake our lives on it? . . . Karl Barth and the Confessing Church have encouraged us to entrench ourselves persistently behind the "faith of the Church," and evade the honest question as to what we ourselves really believe. . . . There may be a place for all these considerations, but they do not absolve us from the duty of being honest with ourselves.[65]

We have examined Bonhoeffer's criticisms of his own Confessing Church, but it is important also to see these criticisms within the framework of the "religionless" Christian. Here is a new plea for individual (not at all to be confused with "individualistic") rather than purely "churchly" confession of faith. Authentic personal faith, over against collective confessionalism, demands searching intellectual honesty and radical trust in Jesus Christ alone; and that is *metanoia,* liberation from false securities by placing ourselves unreservedly at God's disposal.

Polyphony

The "religionless" Christian lives an integrated existence, in which the many and conflicting experiences of his life are held together by a unifying theme rather than fragmented into disjointed compartments. Bonhoeffer, a keen music lover, discusses this characteristic of the mature man of faith in terms of the musical analogy of *polyphony.* In a letter of May 20, 1944, he speaks of "polyphony" to his friend Eberhard Bethge in the context of the painfulness of long and enforced separation from those one loves:

> God wants us to love him eternally with our whole hearts—not in such a way as to injure or weaken our earthly love, but to provide a kind of *cantus firmus* to which the other melodies of life provide the counterpoint. . . . Where the *cantus firmus* is clear and plain, the counterpoint can be developed to its limits. The two are "undivided and yet distinct," in the words of the Chalcedonian Definition, like Christ in his divine and human natures. . . . Only a polyphony of this kind can give life a wholeness and at the same time assure us that nothing calamitous can happen as long as the *cantus firmus* is kept going.[66]

The Christian's love of God and his love of the things of earth, such as friendship, are not mutually exclusive. Rather, the love of God undergirds all earthly affections as the basic melody of, say, a fugue that sets the pattern for and finds infinitely varied expression in the contrapuntal themes which are developed from it. It is both together, *cantus firmus* and counterpoint, which mingle architectonically to form the whole fugue. So life is not complete without the harmonious expression of the love of God in the love of the earth. Here is a further articulation of Bonhoeffer's lifelong theme of the inseparability and mutual relationship of the two parts of the summary of the law: love of God and love of neighbor.

The varied forms of love of the earth are at the same time autonomous. They have a life of their own, just as the contrapuntal themes of a fugue are in no sense merely a repetition of the *cantus firmus*. Such a plea for the rights and integrity of earthly concerns takes its place within the framework of Bonhoeffer's affirmation of the autonomy, the adulthood, of the modern world. "Where the *cantus firmus* is clear and plain"—where the "beyond" at the center of life is surely grasped—"the counterpoint can be developed *to its limits*." [67]

It is of course entirely predictable that Bonhoeffer should find the source and focus of the idea of polyphony in Jesus Christ who in classical terms is the perfect unity of God and man, of *cantus firmus* and counterpoint, and who in "non-religious" terms is the completely integrated man, who is utterly free to be for others. We can see here the intimate link in Bonhoeffer's thought between christology and the Christian life, the central theme of conformation: "May not the attraction and importance of polyphony in music consist in its being a musical reflection of this Christological fact and therefore of our *vita christiana?*"

It is worthwhile to note in passing Bonhoeffer's remarks on the Bible, and particularly on the Old Testament book Song of Songs. They provide a kind of brief exegetical commentary on the theme of polyphony. Of significance is Bonhoeffer's rejection of the common notion that "the restraint of passion is Christian." The mature Christian, on the contrary, is full of passion and zest for earthly life, for the whole fascinating contrapuntal reality which unfolds before him. The key is not restraint, which is a form of asceticism and therefore of "religion," but a "clear and plain" *cantus firmus,* an underlying unity which gives meaning and direction to the diversity of full-blooded participation in earthly existence. This is simply another way of expressing the idea of *metanoia. Metanoia* is not "religious" world denial, but placing oneself at God's disposal in all of life. Being at God's disposal throughout a sensitive and affirmative participation in the midst of life is the unity of *cantus firmus* and counterpoint.

The negative counterpart to the polyphony, the integration, of the mature Christian is the cacophony (a musical term which Bonhoeffer himself does not use, but which seems analogically appropriate) or fragmentation of many people. Bonhoeffer sees examples of this fragmentation among his warders and fellow prisoners, especially in times of emergency.[68] The fragmented, cacophonous person has no unity, no focus, to bring to the multifarious and often violently conflicting experiences of life. Each separate experience is a whirlpool bearing him inexorably and helplessly into its vortex like a piece of flotsam, and then spewing him out again to be caught by an eddy and carried into yet another whirlpool. In Bonhoeffer's musically analogical terms, there is no *cantus firmus* from which to develop and into which to resolve richly varied contrapuntal themes; there is only the noise of disconnected melodies vying with one another to be heard.

The person who is entirely at the mercy of the emotion of the moment, in this fragmented way, lacks *strength:* He is helpless, weak, unable either to perceive or to respond in a way which transcends immediacy. The "religionless" Christian, by contrast, possesses strength of insight and action through his unity with the "beyond" in the midst of all emotions and experiences. Bonhoeffer expresses the "polyphonic" idea that God and the world belong together in the fully integrated approach to reality: "We make room in ourselves, to some extent, for God and the whole world." He then goes on to spell out this polyphony concretely from his prison experience under emergency conditions.

Bonhoeffer's remark within this context that the ability to *think* is an important liberating and stabilizing aspect of mutli-dimensionality provides a bridge between the Christian and the secular person of liberal culture. Like the mature Christian, the man of liberal education has been trained to be multi-dimensional and therefore strong.[69] Linking "the Christian and the 'cultured' man" together quite explicitly, Bonhoeffer says that neither the one nor the other can

split up his life or dismember it, and the common denominator must be sought both in thought and in a personal and integrated attitude to life. . . . Here we have the *anthropos teleios* (*teleiōs* originally means "whole" in the sense of "complete" or "perfect"); "You, therefore, must be perfect (*teleios*), as your heavenly Father is perfect" (Matt. 5:48)—in contrast to the *anēr dipsychos* ("a double-minded man") of James 1:8. . . . We can never achieve this "wholeness" simply by ourselves, but only together with others. . . .[70]

Bonhoeffer appeals to Scripture for an anthropology of the "whole man." This is the biblical basis of the characteristic of polyphony. We have examined the importance of the biblical doctrine of the *an-*

thrōpos teleios to Bonhoeffer's "non-religious interpretation" of Christianity. The last sentence of the above quotation is a manifestation of Bonhoeffer's intense I-Thou personalism. My existence is defined ethically and ultimately theologically by God who encounters me only in this responsible meeting with my neighbor: "We can never achieve this 'wholeness' simply by ourselves, but only together with others." Polyphony is always forged out of living interdependence with my neighbor.

The "good man without God," the secularist of integrity and decency, for whom Bonhoeffer had such profound understanding and sympathy, is capable of polyphonous existence apart from conscious belief in God. (He may indeed possess "unconscious faith" or *fides directa*, as Bonhoeffer suggested.) The epitome of the secular "good man" is the man of liberal culture, who has been brought up from his early years on the highest human values and aspirations. He is the secular counterpart of the "religionless" Christian, and his spiritual brother in suffering for the sake of human freedom and dignity.

Strength

Polyphony or wholeness demands *strength*. An important key to understanding Bonhoeffer's own life is the fact that he was himself a person with enormous strength of character. His personal strength manifested itself in a high degree of self-discipline, the freedom to risk bold thoughts and actions, the ability to endure privation and suffering, a wholeness which enabled him to transcend his immediate experiences, and complete personal integrity and honesty. It was natural that Bonhoeffer should have regarded spiritual strength as one of the basic elements in the life of the mature Christian.

Bonhoeffer speaks of strength mainly in terms of *self-discipline*. In a passage which points out the intimate connection between strength and polyphony, he says:

Is it not characteristic of a man, in contrast to an immature person, that his centre of gravity is always where he actually is, and that the longing for the fulfilment of his wishes cannot prevent him from being his whole self, wherever he happens to be? . . . There is a wholeness about the fully grown man which enables him to face an existing situation squarely. He may have his longings, but he keeps them out of sight, and somehow masters them. . . .[71]

It is the *mature* person, typified by "the fully grown man," who possesses the discipline to discern and act in an integrated manner. The
"immature person" is fragmented by immediate experience. Large
numbers of non-Christian, "non-religious" men and women have
learned to cope in a disciplined and realistic manner with life's problems; they are the secular "good people" whom the Christian meets in
strength rather than weakness. Such a world demands mature disciplined Christians to serve it and witness to it. The efforts of "modern"
pastors and their "secularized offshoots," the "existentialists" and "psychotherapists," to prey upon the vestigial weaknesses of the mature
world are unworthy attempts to turn people back into children, helplessly fragmented by life and in need of deliverance.

Significantly, "Discipline" appears as the first of Bonhoeffer's "Stations on the Road to Freedom," a poem which was one of his last writings to be smuggled out of prison. It is a poignant expression of his own
pilgrimage to Christian martyrdom. The following is the stanza entitled "Discipline":

> If you set out to seek freedom, then learn above all things
> to govern your soul and your senses, for fear that your passions
> and longings may lead you away from the path you should follow.
> Chaste be your mind and your body, and both in subjection,
> obediently, steadfastly seeking the aim set before them;
> only through discipline may a man learn to be free.[72]

Here discipline is affirmed to be the secret of real freedom, another
mark of the "religionless" Christian. Like multi-dimensionality, freedom can be achieved only out of strength, the strength which enables
a person to transcend his immediacy in vision and action. Unlike the
false freedom of libertinistic weakness, true freedom lies on the farther
side of rigorous self-discipline.

The disciplined strength of the mature Christian enables him to
participate fully in life, accepting its joys sensitively and expansively
and enduring its suffering manfully. In this his secular counterpart,
the "good man without God," especially the man of liberal culture,
shares to a remarkable extent. "To renounce a full life and its real
joys in order to avoid pain," says Bonhoeffer, "is neither Christian nor
human." [73]

Another sign of strength in the "religionless" Christian is a healthy-

269

minded self-respect. In a letter to Bethge written from Klein-Krossin on October 9, 1940, Bonhoeffer coined the expression "self-less self-love" (*"selbstlose Selbstliebe"*). He remarked that unfortunately this vital ethical concept had no place in the "official evangelical ethic," with its Augustinian horror of human pride and self-assertiveness.[74] Bonhoeffer uses the expression again in a prison letter to Bethge, written on May 6, 1944:

I shall be writing next time about Christians' "egoism" ("selfless self-love"). I think we agree about it. Too much altruism is oppressive and exacting [*anspruchsvoll*]; "egoism" can be less selfish and less demanding [*anspruchsloser*].[75]

Unfortunately, Bonhoeffer did not follow through with his proposal to discuss "Christians' egoism," so all we have is this brief passage on the subject. It is not difficult, however, to see what Bonhoeffer is seeking to express in the idea of "selfless self-love." Strength of character involves realistic self-acceptance. It is a psychological axiom that only the person who genuinely respects himself can freely respect others. Certain kinds of Christian altruism spring from an often unconscious self-disparagement which in turn arises out of a wrong understanding of human sinfulness and Christian humility. This sort of altruism is rooted in insecurity; it is not love freely given out of strength and wholeness. It is done as compensation or expiation; hence it never believes it has done enough, and nervously smothers the other person with solicitude. Self-disparaging altruism is not free, and therefore it does not let the object of its love be free. Its solicitous attentions are so many subtle claims on the recipient, since he is in a certain sense an instrument in the altruist's efforts to expiate his sins—and an instrument is expected to do what the user wants it to do. Hence self-disparagement is selfish, while genuine self-love is selfless. The mature Christian loves his neighbor freely as himself, allowing him to exist as a human being in his own right.

The theme of "selfless self-love" is to be linked closely with Bonhoeffer's abiding concern for a healthy reserve among persons for the sake of mutual freedom in Christ. A healthy self-respect is a basic element in the recognition of the neighbor's right to integrity and privacy. The modest reserve which characterizes authentic I-Thou relationships springs, not from prudery or indifference, but precisely from a passionate zeal for human freedom grounded in the liberating word of Christ. Humanly speaking, such zeal finds one of its poles in the insight gained through mature self-love, which is a manifestation of strength.

The obverse side of the strength of the "religionless" Christian is Bonhoeffer's conviction that the sins worthy of real concern are precisely the sins of strength, not the sins of weakness.[76] Here is an important theme in Bonhoeffer's thought. It is completely wrong of Christianity and its "secular counterparts" to prey upon men's weaknesses, to "spy out" the secrets of their inner life in order to expose their wretchedness. That is unbiblical: The Bible is concerned with the whole man in the fullness of his life. In biblical faith the root sin of man arises, not from his weakness, but from his strength: The lofty creature created in the image of God himself desires to "be like a god." The "big" sins are therefore the sins of strength, the "spiritual" (rather than "carnal") sins: pride, the hunger for power, the overstepping of the limits of creaturely existence. It is these "satanic" sins which are the vigorous negative counterpart to the "pneumatic" graces of the mature Christian: both are characterized by strength. Part of encountering "come-of-age" man in his strength rather than in his weakness is being willing to call him from strength to strength, not to demand his spiritual emasculation.

Bonhoeffer regards the sins of weakness as frequently more destructive to our humanity:

We are often told in the New Testament to "be strong" (I Cor. 16:13; Eph. 6:10; II Tim. 2:1; I John 2:14). Is not people's weakness (stupidity, lack of independence, forgetfulness, cowardice, vanity, corruptibility, temptability, etc.) a greater danger than evil? Christ not only makes people "good"; he makes them strong, too. The sins of weakness are the really human sins, whereas the wilful sins are diabolical (and no doubt "strong," too!).[77]

There are hints in the prison writings that Bonhoeffer tended to be impatient with weakness: "There is a kind of weakness that Christianity does not hold with, but which people insist on claiming as Christian, and then sling mud at it."[78] A man's weaknesses are what drag him down and prevent him from attaining to his full humanity;

271

they are his childish and adolescent features which linger on and arrest the development of his maturity. Weakness is worse than the sins of pride and power, because it prevents or erodes strength, while they are manifestations of strength, however diabolical. "It is weakness rather than wickedness that perverts a man and drags him down," Bonhoeffer says, "and it needs profound sympathy to put up with that." [79] Bonhoeffer's reaction to the weakness and fragmentation of some of his fellow prisoners, which came to light dramatically during bombing raids, was not at all approval of the way they talked so freely of their fear after the "all clear" had sounded. Fear is a human weakness, he maintained, and should be included theologically under the *pudenda*, the things a person should be ashamed of, keep to himself, and try to overcome. Bonhoeffer would probably have classed human weaknesses generally under the theological category of *shame:* They are the aspects of our fallen condition which the strong person will overcome within himself through self-discipline, for the sake of the neighbor whom he is called to serve.

Freedom

In his words and in his deeds, Bonhoeffer affirmed again and again that freedom is one of the central hallmarks of the Christian. In the Incarnation man has been liberated to be a full human being by being returned to his "transmoral" union with God through forgiveness and justification. As one empowered by God himself, beyond the relativities of human good and evil, the Christian is freed for creative, spontaneous, responsible action in the world. As a sinner who knows that in Jesus Christ he has been both condemned and forgiven, the Christian receives the freedom to "sin boldly," to risk bold, decisive words and deeds on behalf of his neighbor.

Among the *Letters and Papers* is an essay entitled "Civil Courage?" in which Bonhoeffer speaks of the responsibility of the citizen in terms of Luther's *pecca fortiter:*

Civil courage . . . can grow only out of the free responsibility of free men. Only now are the Germans beginning to discover the meaning of free responsibility. It depends on a God who demands responsible action in a bold venture of faith, and who promises forgiveness and consolation to the man who becomes a sinner in that venture.[80]

272

Another essay entitled "Sympathy" speaks of the Christian as one who, like his Master and empowered by his Master's ministry and cross, does not stand back in passive sympathy when others suffer but takes the risk of acting here and now on behalf of sufferers:

> We are not Christ, but if we want to be Christians, we must have some share in Christ's large-heartedness by acting with responsibility and in freedom when the hour of danger comes, and by showing a real sympathy that springs, not from fear, but from the liberating and redeeming love of Christ for all who suffer.[81]

Bonhoeffer's *Menschlichkeit* shines through his thoughts on freedom in the prison writings, as when he contrasts the true liberation of the mature Christian and the "moralism" of the purely ethical.[82] The Christian should be precisely the person who can affirm the fullness and spontaneity of life, the importance of art, play, real education (i.e., learning and wisdom), and friendship. Ordinary human happiness, says Bonhoeffer, is a legitimate sphere of Christian interest and involvement; in fact, it should find its foundation and rationale in a true understanding of the church. "Come-of-age" man is not alone in his genuine affirmation of these activities as authentic and vital human concerns; he is joined by the "religionless" Christian, who stands beside him on the basis of the liberation and reconciliation of all reality in the man Jesus.

Action/Submission

The German title of Bonhoeffer's prison writings is *Widerstand und Ergebung,* "resistance and submission." This title expresses the dialectic of his own existence as a prisoner, a dialectic which found theological expression in his letters and papers written in prison. A dialectical existence which knows when to act and when to endure emerges as an integral part of Bonhoeffer's portrait of the "religionless" Christian. He describes the whole matter succinctly in a letter of February 21, 1944:

> We must confront fate . . . as resolutely as we submit to it at the right time. . . . It is therefore impossible to define the boundary between resistance and submission on abstract principles; but both of them must exist, and both must be practised. Faith demands this elasticity of behaviour.[83]

This passage contains familiar elements which we have encountered previously. It is the freedom of the Christian which enables him to deal with each situation concretely, on its own terms: he possesses "elasticity of behaviour." As the justified sinner, he risks bold, specific action in the world for the sake of others. As one who participates in the messianic sufferings of Christ, he also knows how to submit to the inevitable when the time comes.

Bonhoeffer felt that Christians too often interpret Christianity entirely on the side of passivity and submission: "There is such a thing as a false composure which is quite unchristian. As Christians, we need not be at all ashamed of some impatience, longing, opposition to what is unnatural, and our full share of desire for freedom, earthly happiness, and opportunity for effective work." [84] He saw this quietistic attitude in abundance in the Christianity of his fellow German Lutherans, with their tradition of a radical separation between gospel and law, spiritual and political, internal and external. Elsewhere he speaks of a "false, premature, pious submission" [85] which is not fully Christian.

In his poem "Stations on the Road to Freedom," Bonhoeffer gives lyrical expression to his belief in strong action on the part of the Christian:

> Daring to do what is right, not what fancy may tell you,
> valiantly grasping occasions, not cravenly doubting—
> freedom comes only through deeds, not through thoughts taking wing.
> Faint not nor fear, but go out to the storm and the action,
> trusting in God whose commandment you faithfully follow;
> freedom, exultant, will welcome your spirit with joy.[86]

The mature Christian, then, does not prematurely give in to "fate" or the force of circumstances. He leaps into the historical fray and tries to alter events in the name and the freedom of the Lord of history, Jesus Christ. He even chafes under many forms of inactivity, and tries to break out of them rather than "piously submitting."

Yet there are times when the Christian is bound and constrained by events bigger than himself, by "fate" or "necessity." In these circumstances the mature Christian possesses the faith, the strength, and the "polyphony" of self-possession, to endure patiently. If he is lucky he may be granted the insight to see that his "fate" is the providence of

God; but he is called immediately simply to endure in the name of his suffering Lord and perhaps for the sake of others. Addressing his remarks to his friend Bethge in the latter's own dangerous situation, Bonhoeffer articulates the relation between action and submission: "We ought first of all to do everything we can to change those facts while there is still time; and then, if we have tried everything, even though it has been in vain, they will be much easier to bear." [87]

Bonhoeffer distinguished between submission—what he was experiencing as a prisoner—and real suffering.[88] Submission is simply a general resignation to events beyond one's control. Suffering is something far more serious. Bonhoeffer's remarks reveal his personal unselfconsciousness and modesty. He was subjected to intense, exhausting ill-treatment when he was first arrested, and underwent long, grueling interrogations throughout his incarceration. He was cut off almost completely from his family and friends and suffered deep loneliness. He had little freedom of movement, and had to take exercise by walking around his cell. He experienced a number of bombing raids in which fellow prisoners were killed. After the first year he knew that his chances of release were increasingly hopeless. With the failure of the plot of July 20, 1944, to assassinate Hitler, he realized that his own death was simply a matter of time, since he was implicated deeply in the Resistance movement and Hitler was bent on an orgy of revenge. Yet Bonhoeffer shrank from applying the word "suffering" to himself.

A second thing to note in this connection is Bonhoeffer's belief "that physical sufferings, actual pain and so on, are certainly to be classed as 'suffering,' " with the corresponding observation that "we so like to stress spiritual suffering." Here is Bonhoeffer's biblical anthropology, his utter seriousness about the whole man, "body" and "soul," as the experiencing subject and the object of God's reconciling love in Christ. Protestantism, Bonhoeffer contends, talks too much about purely "spiritual" suffering. That is a manifestation of inwardness, of the isolation of the "inner life" of the soul from bodily, external existence which is one of the marks of "religion." In real suffering the whole person suffers.

Yet suffering must at the same time be seen as an intense form of submission, as a profounder "station" on the "road to freedom" which is the Christian's pilgrimage:

Not only action, but also suffering is a way to freedom. In suffering, the deliverance consists in our being allowed to put the matter out of our own hands into God's hands. In this sense death is the crowning of human freedom. Whether the human deed is a matter of faith or not depends on whether we understand our suffering as an extension of our action and a completion of freedom.[89]

This passage, already quoted in the discussion of *metanoia,* is central to an understanding of Bonhoeffer's dialectic of action and submission: both are "contingent upon a divine ordinance." Neither action nor submission is a "religious" end in itself; both are simply ways of putting ourselves entirely at the disposal of the God who is Jesus Christ in differing concrete situations in the midst of life.

Of significance is Bonhoeffer's suggestion that suffering is "an extension of . . . action and a completion of freedom." Some light is shed on his meaning by a passage from the essay on "Sympathy" which serves to ground the idea christologically: "Christ kept himself from suffering till his hour had come, but when it did come he met it as a free man, seized it, and mastered it." [90] Christ-like suffering, like Christ-like submission generally, is the act of free persons who out of their existence for others willingly undergo frustration, impotence, weakness, pain, and even death. Freedom exercised to its farthest extremity in a fallen world is paradoxically freedom constrained and suffering. Freedom consummated by fire is freedom perfected by God into something more glorious than anything previous which we call freedom. Bonhoeffer gives voice to this theme again in "Stations on the Road to Freedom," where "Suffering" appears as the next-to-the-last station:

A change has come indeed. Your hands, so strong and active,
are bound; in helplessness now you see your action
is ended; you sigh in relief, your cause committing
to stronger hands; so now you may rest contented.
Only for one blissful moment could you draw near to touch freedom;
then, that it might be perfected in glory, you gave it to God.[91]

Here again we find the suggestion that the submission and suffering which are the result and the extension of free, responsible action in the world are in some sense a relief. In situations of constraint and suffering, the mature Christian knows that things are out of his hands, and with grateful resignation he gives his cause over wholly into the hands of God, to do with as he will.

The very title of Bonhoeffer's poem, "Stations on the Road to Freedom," indicates that discipline, action, and suffering are progressive stages in the bringing of Christian freedom to perfection. The final, consummating stage is the human inevitability which suffering may hasten—death. In an essay entitled "Insecurity and Death," Bonhoeffer describes the kind of death which is an act of freedom: "It is we ourselves, and not outward circumstances, who make death what it can be, a death freely and voluntarily accepted." [92]

But in the final stanza of "Stations" Bonhoeffer speaks of death in terms of the wider freedom which lies on its far side:

> Come now, thou greatest of feasts on the journey to freedom
> eternal;
> death, cast aside all the burdensome chains, and demolish
> the walls of our temporal body, the walls of our souls that
> are blinded,
> so that at last we may see that which here remains hidden.
> Freedom, how long we have sought thee in discipline, action,
> and suffering;
> dying, we now may behold thee revealed in the Lord.[93]

Death is the gateway to the "glorious liberty of the children of God" (Rom. 8:21), that perfect freedom of complete fellowship with the God "whose service is perfect freedom," of which the earthly freedom even of the mature Christian is only a dim foretaste. This stanza, written just after news of the failure of the 20th-of-July Plot which meant Bonhoeffer's own almost certain execution, is also a moving personal testimony. The last words Bonhoeffer spoke just before he was taken away to be hanged on April 8, 1945, recorded by fellow prisoner Payne Best in his book *The Venlo Incident,* expressed precisely and tersely the same unshakeable belief: "This is the end. For me the beginning of life." [94]

It may seem odd that a discussion of the "religionless" Christian should end on a note of "other-worldliness." The answer is quite simply that Bonhoeffer himself and the mature, "worldly" Christian believe unashamedly in the resurrection hope of eternal life—but not in an "other-worldly" sense. Life beyond death is the rich *fulfillment* of the fullness of life on this earth, not its negation. In previous chapters we noted Bonhoeffer's highly realistic understanding of the Christian hope beyond death as the transformation of the entire created order, both "bodily" and "spiritual." His conviction that death is the final stage in man's pilgrimage to freedom and the entrance to the perfection of earthly freedom is part of this vivid sense of eternal life as the real fulfillment, the perfecting, of earthly life.

Furthermore, following Qoheleth, Bonhoeffer affirmed that

we ought so to love and trust God in our *lives,* and in all the good things that he sends us, that when the time comes (but not before!) we may go to him with love, trust, and joy. . . . God will see to it that the man who finds him in his earthly happiness and thanks him for it does not lack reminder that earthly things are transient, that it is good for him to attune his heart to what is eternal. . . .[95]

Like the dialectic of action/submission, the dialectic of earth/heaven is to be lived by taking life as it comes, facing each situation simply as a responsible person living wholly for others here in the midst of the world. The "religionless" Christian lives in the light of eternity most faithfully simply by living as a human being for the sake of his neighbor. He best proclaims the coming redemption of all creation by participating in the renewal of this present world which was initiated by the resurrection of Jesus. When the Christian is called to endure, to suffer, and to die, then the time will have come to contemplate eternal life; but he will never prematurely write off this earthly life out of a false piety which is ascetical and world-despairing.

Chapter Ten
Paths in Bonhoeffer Interpretation

Divergence or Dialectic?

All major interpreters of Bonhoeffer recognize an underlying unity throughout the twists and turns of his life and intellectual development. Within this broad area of agreement, however, there are those on the one hand who are impressed by the irreconcilabilities, the detours, the loose ends, and the dramatic changes in Bonhoeffer's outlook; while on the other hand there are those who are chiefly struck by the "polyphonic" character of his whole development, who see it as the "contrapuntal" unfolding of the various poles of an essential dialectical unity in response to rapidly changing historical situations.

The preceding chapters have both reflected and attempted to substantiate the "polyphonic" interpretation of Bonhoeffer's theological development. By no means does this imply, in my case or in the case of those other students of Bonhoeffer who tend to take the "unitary" approach, a lack of awareness of the intellectual shifts, the stresses and strains, and the loose ends, in his arrested career. But it seems to me that his theological development is most accurately and illuminatingly understood as the serial unfolding of a remarkable dialectical unity.

This fundamental difference of emphasis in interpreting Bonhoeffer's development as a whole manifests itself in differences of opinion over specific issues in his thought. Are there, for example, as John

Phillips suggests, two incompatible approaches to christology (which we might call "churchly" and "worldly") in Bonhoeffer's theological pilgrimage which he tried somewhat unsuccessfully to bring together in *The Cost of Discipleship* and *Ethics* but left largely unreconciled in the prison writings? Or do we have instead a unitary christological development, as Eberhard Bethge and John Godsey tend to see it, in which the dimensions of both church and world are constantly present in dialectical tension in Bonhoeffer's christology but are singly emphasized in the light of his perception of the demand posed by the historical "moment"? Clearly, I have found myself in agreement with the latter view.

I am loath to criticize Phillips' study of Bonhoeffer, because it is an extremely careful, thorough, subtle piece of work. In his main thesis, however, the struggle between two opposing christologies in Bonhoeffer's theological development, Phillips seems to have transformed a valuable recognition into an untenable theory.

Initially he states his thesis as follows:

Bonhoeffer struggled, throughout his life, to give adequate expression to his conviction that the revelation of God in Jesus Christ was visible, tangible, concrete, apprehensible by all men. Almost to the end of his life, he demonstrated this concretion by pointing to the church as the Body of Christ, where Christ was present. In his last years he explored the possibility of pointing to this reality and "participating" in it within secular, worldly life, without undue concern for the ecclesiological implications of his discoveries. . . . His theology issued from the tension, we shall argue, between unreconciled elements in its Christological centre. Thus, in 1940, he found that his ecclesiology could no longer serve as the conceptual partner of his Christology, and he set aside the former to concentrate on the development of the latter.[1]

Phillips goes on later to suggest that in Bonhoeffer's theological concerns during the period 1931-33 we can see "an emerging Christology of the person and work of Christ, separate from and in some opposition to his 'Christ existing as the church.' "[2] The key writing which exemplifies this new christological departure is the 1933 christology lectures, *Christ the Center*. The exigencies of the German church struggle which followed, however, preoccupied Bonhoeffer once again in an intensely ecclesiological direction. Phillips describes the rest of Bonhoeffer's christological development:

As long as the issues of the church struggle remained clear, an uneasy balance between these two Christologies was possible. But in 1939, removed almost entirely from church life and work by government decree and surrounded by men of affairs of widely different creeds and political persuasions, all working for the future of Germany, Bonhoeffer once more broke free from his intractable ecclesiological theory. The *Ethics* represents his attempts to set these two Christologies together without the sectarian overtones of *The Cost of Discipleship* and *Life Together*. These experiments proved fruitful but not wholly successful and, in the prison letters, Bonhoeffer set his ecclesiology to one side altogether, in order to meditate on the problems he had been skirting, without regard for the consequences of these meditations. In a final, brief vision he eventually united his two Christologies.[3]

That there is a somewhat different christological starting point in the 1933 christology lectures from the one taken in *The Communion of Saints* and *Act and Being* is undeniable. But there is far more congruence among the three than Phillips will allow, and his theory of "two christologies" builds on too slight a foundation.

I have shown with illustrations from *Christ the Center* as well as from *The Communion of Saints* and *Act and Being* the common underlying personalism which undergirded and united Bonhoeffer's doctrines of Christ and the Christian community. I have cited a number of references to the church which appear in the christology lectures and show the same understanding of the relation between Christ and his church which we find in the earlier "ecclesiological" writings as well as in the later *Cost of Discipleship* and *Life Together,* and in the ecumenical writings. Phillips curiously neglects these references.

The shift which we find in *Christ the Center* is best to be explained, it seems to me, as an important "moment" in which Bonhoeffer has the chance to explore in more detail that side of the New Testament christological dialectic in which Christ is understood as Lord over the world as well as over the church. He does this by exploring further the implications of his personalist understanding of Christ. But this "worldly" side of Bonhoeffer's christology is there in the earlier "ecclesiological" writings; only there, the fundamental focus is the "churchly" side of Christ's lordship, the side which in the New Testament itself is clearly identified with his being and revelatory presence to the world. Both poles in Bonhoeffer's christological dialectic remain in fruitful relationship and tension throughout all his writings; he grows into the emphasis which emerges now on the one side, now on the other, and develops it in light of the historical situation. But this growth and development are clearly dialectical and not oppositional in nature.

I see no evidence in *Ethics* and *Letters and Papers* that the Christian community is understood in a fundamentally different way from that in *The Communion of Saints* and *Act and Being*. In the light of Bonhoeffer's large shift of attention to what he called the "secular sector" at the end of his life, we certainly find ample criticism of the church and a profound appreciation of the work of Christ in the world. But of criticism of the church, despite its lofty (but always dialectical!) identification with Christ and revelation, Bonhoeffer's earlier writings are full. The criticisms assume a different form during the *Kirchenkampf* and during the war; but they are united by some similar and continuing concerns, exemplified in such concepts as the "secret discipline" and discipleship as active obedience in the world. Phillips further underplays the quantity and significance of material on the church which we find in the prison writings. In a criticism of Godsey's treatment of Bonhoeffer, he writes:

Godsey is probably [!] correct in saying that Bonhoeffer did not envisage a total disappearance of the church in favour of "worldliness." But he misses the significance of the fact that the letters discuss the implications of Bonhoeffer's discoveries for the church *only as a side issue* and in a very sketchy fashion. As in much of the *Ethics,* the church is set off to one side. The discoveries themselves are not ecclesiological. No reader of the prison letters can fail to miss the polemical nature of the thoughts on "religionless Christianity" and the fact that this polemic is directed towards the church and her traditional apologetic. Up to the beginning of the *Ethics* in 1940 the church was the central theme in his thinking. But there follows an unmistakable break with this pattern.[4]

I have indicated in detail how ecclesiological considerations of a positive nature constitute an integral part of the very warp and woof of "Christianity without religion." We must describe Bonhoeffer's remarks on the church in the prison writings as "sketchy"; but so indeed must we describe *all* his remarks on "religionless Christianity." That the church is "only a side issue" in the prison letters is simply not the case. That it is unrelated to the christology of the "non-religious interpretation" is also an unjustified conclusion. What is not sufficiently emphasized is that Bonhoeffer is speaking throughout of "religionless *Christianity*": He issues a radical call for renewal of individual and corporate Christian existence by pushing toward a more adequate vision of Christ and the form his lordship takes in a world which has "come of age."

To expand the "churchly" and "worldly" christological *emphases* in Bonhoeffer's doctoral and inaugural dissertations and in his christology lectures into two *different christologies* whose struggle dominated Bonhoeffer's later thought is to force his doctrine of Christ out of its natural shape into an unnatural division. The mistake stems, I think, from an inadequate appreciation of the intense dialectic in Bonhoeffer's theology which is there from the very beginning and works itself out in new and varied ways throughout his career.

Perhaps another seeming incongruity in Bonhoeffer's early thought which does not trouble his interpreters will provide a parallel case. The "ultra-ecclesiological" *Communion of Saints* was submitted for the degree in 1927 and published in 1930; *Act and Being*, with its continued resolution of the problem of revelation in the concept of the church, appeared in 1931. In 1929, during Bonhoeffer's pastorate in Barcelona, he gave the address entitled "What is a Christian Ethic?" It is robustly this-worldly (Nietzsche and Antaeus appear prominently) and "individualistic," and contains few references to the Christian community. Are we to conclude that this essay, written between *The Communion of Saints* and *Act and Being*, represents a "new departure," an opposing and irreconcilable direction? I think not. It is far more natural, in light of all the other evidence we have in Bonhoeffer's writings, to see it as one pole in a basic dialectic between church and world. The same consideration should apply in the case of the somewhat altered christological starting point in *Christ the Center*.

In regard to Bonhoeffer's christology, it seems to me that John Godsey and Eberhard Bethge have offered a sounder interpretation. From beginning to end, writes Godsey of Bonhoeffer, "theology was essentially Christology, but because Christ is not without his body, Chris-

283

tology includes ecclesiology within itself." [5] He points out that the varied christological emphases in Bonhoeffer's development "are to be found in some degree in each period" of his career: "One of the aspects was dominant in each period, and . . . each succeeding period represents an expansion of Bonhoeffer's christological understanding." "From this perspective," Godsey concludes, "we are able to view the striking contrast between his original emphasis on the church and his final emphasis on the world, not as a break in his theology, but as the two poles of a development." [6]

In Bethge's highly perceptive essay on "Bonhoeffer's Christology and his 'Religionless Christianity,'" his thesis is that "In the theology of Dietrich Bonhoeffer there exists an intimate connection between Christology and a non-religious expression of the witness for Christ, although the specific formulation—non-religious interpretation—did not originate until near the end of his life. . . . His mind had been occupied with the issue for many years." [7] "It can be shown today," Bethge goes on to say, "that the theme of 'non-religious interpretation' is present and working in the many different approaches he took in his writings, no matter how conservative or 'religious' those writings may now appear." [8] According to Bethge, for Bonhoeffer " 'non-religious interpretation' is first and last 'christological' interpretation," and Bonhoeffer's "Christology always tried to present itself in the form of non-religious interpretation." [9] Dealing specifically with the relation of ecclesiology to christology in Bonhoeffer's thought with reference to "non-religious interpretation," Bethge states that his friend's

antispeculative quest had led Bonhoeffer to begin his theologizing with the *church* as the given fact of Christ's presence and to continue with his fight for the visible church and its realm in Nazi Germany. For that reason he nearly equated Christology with ecclesiology . . . . But at the same time it was his Christology which empowered him for his bitter criticisms of the actual church, to such a degree that near the end, in 1944, nearly all ecclesiology seems to be absorbed by Christology . . . . But . . . Bonhoeffer is quite aware that there must be an ecclesiology if there is to be a Christology, that there are always persons, visibly gathered and drawn into the fate of the Christ-person. Christology without ecclesiology is endangered by abstracts.[10]

Both Godsey and Bethge, it seems to me, recognize more adequately than does Phillips that Bonhoeffer's christological development is dialectical and not divergent. There is no doubt that Bonhoeffer moved from an absorbing preoccupation with the Christian community at the beginning of his career to an intense preoccupation with the world in which the church finds itself at the end of his life. But the world is there from the beginning, just as the church is there at the end. Bonhoeffer's christological development represents the deepening and unfolding of a basic dialectical affirmation that the Christ who is present to man in the form of the Christian community of persons is at the same time the Person in whom the whole of reality is to be understood and affirmed. Such a development does not require the hypothesis of two competing christologies—a hypothesis which seems to me to move too far beyond the textual evidence—but only the recognition of the essentially dialectical character and movement of Bonhoeffer's christology from first to last.

Another closely related issue of basic and continuing importance in Bonhoeffer interpretation is his doctrine of the church. Is Bonhoeffer's "ultra-ecclesiological" outlook, especially during the latter half of the 1930's, merely a detour from the central thrust of his thought which culminates in the "religionless Christianity" project, or perhaps an unsatisfactory beginning which Bonhoeffer transmutes into secular terms, as Hanfried Müller and other "radical" interpreters have suggested? Or is it an integral dialectical "moment" which is developed, to be sure, but at the same time taken up squarely into Bonhoeffer's last theological reflections, as Regin Prenter (along with Godsey and Bethge) insists? I regard the latter as the more adequate interpretation of the relation of ecclesiology to "non-religious interpretation."

In his original and provocative *Von der Kirche zur Welt*, Müller praises the first part of Bonhoeffer's *Cost of Discipleship* for its interpretation of discipleship as active obedience to the crucified Lord and the church as existing simply wherever this active obedience is manifested. According to Müller, we have here an important early expression of Bonhoeffer's emerging rejection of the institutional church as represented by Western Christendom and his return to the early-Reformation rediscovery that the gospel brings into being a radically human and not merely an institutional and cultural reality. It was not, however, until *Ethics* and supremely *Letters and Papers* that Bonhoeffer began to see with startling clarity some of the implications of this de-clericalization and de-culturization. Müller maintains that

285

in the prison writings Bonhoeffer moved, at least in terms of the function of his thought, in the direction of replacing *Gemeinschaft* by *Gesellschaft,* the Christian community by secular society. Active obedience becomes simply human conformation to the messianic sufferings of Christ as a full participant in the creation of a positive secular order of existence in which man is truly enabled to "come of age" (which Müller, of course, sees best epitomized in Marxist socialism).

Müller interprets Bonhoeffer's suggestions concerning the relation of the church to a world "come of age" in terms of a complete dualism. The Christian community and the world in which the individual Christian participates are to be entirely separate from each other—a new "two kingdoms" idea. The church is to be totally "invisible," with no influence *qua* church on the secular world. Müller interprets the *Arkandisziplin* in precisely this way: It functions by way of "ending the public nature of Christian religiosity." [11] Only in this way will Western Christendom be fully and radically put behind us and both the gospel and the mature secular world freed for their proper existence.

But while Müller can appreciate that part of *The Cost of Discipleship* which dwells much more on active obedience in the world than on the inner life of the Christian community, as an inchoate beginning for Bonhoeffer's full affirmation of the "religionless Christian" as a "man, pure and simple," he regards *Life Together,* published a short time later, as a "detour" from this central development. Significantly, of course, *Life Together* is devoted to a study of the inner life of the Christian community, based upon Bonhoeffer's experiences at Finkenwalde. Like some of Bonhoeffer's Confessing Church colleagues, Müller sees this work as expressive of a "catholicizing tendency" and an ecclesiastical escapism which Bonhoeffer later rejected. Hence Müller can find no real place for the ecclesiology expressed in *Life Together* in the development of Bonhoeffer's theology which culminated in the "Christianity without religion" ideas.

I have argued, in contrast, that the disciplined fellowship of worship, instruction, prayer, and mutual help which we see described in *Life Together* and practiced in the *Bruderhaus* experiment became the basic model for the "secret discipline" of "religionless Christianity." Bonhoeffer's life and thought as a whole during his incarceration was thoroughly oriented toward the Christian community. "Religionless

Christianity" was for Bonhoeffer a far more intensely dialectical reality than Müller will allow; the "internal" concerns expressed in *Life Together,* far from being a detour, became an integral part of this dialectical existence of the Christian in the modern world. The strong, disciplined Christian who is capable of fully affirming both Christ and the secular world is for Bonhoeffer rooted profoundly in the disciplined "life together" of the community of neighbors in Christ; without such roots "secular Christianity" simply withers away and is replaced with undialectical secularity.

To be sure, the imprisoned Bonhoeffer made radical proposals about the public life of the church. He insisted that the Christian community must decisively free itself from Western Christendom and take its place alongside its secular neighbors as the quiet, humble, servant community of those who take their orientation to the secular world from faith in Christ. Bonhoeffer also saw the real impact of the church in the "come-of-age" world as the leaven of the lives of its individual members. To this extent Müller seems to me to be on the right track. But he makes far too much of this "invisibility" and continually threatens to collapse Bonhoeffer's dialectic with the substitution of a radical dualism. However quiet, however unostentatious, the renewed christopersonal community remains for Bonhoeffer a fundamental and integral dimension of Christian existence, the roots out of which that whole existence springs. Bonhoeffer's radical demands that the church detach itself from "Christendom" and become revivified in a new "catacomb" style of life is entirely to the point, and still remains to be taken with sufficient seriousness by the church. But with equal radicalness he offers us a picture of the internal life of a "come-of-age" church which must be (and has not been) taken just as seriously: a community of people who have put religiosity behind them, who come together for disciplined worship, instruction in the faith, prayer, and mutual strengthening. "Invisibility" *qua* church does not mean passivity vis-à-vis the secular world or unimportance. For Bonhoeffer, both sides of this ecclesiological dialectic were of supreme importance; there could be no mature or "religionless Christianity" without both sides. It seems to me that Müller has failed to recognize this, and therefore he cannot, or does not, wish to make sense out of a writing like *Life Together.*

I add "does not" advisedly. Hanfried Müller is a Christian who

287

wishes to affirm not merely secularity but Marxist secularity. As such, his book on Bonhoeffer stands as a landmark in the rise of the Christian-Marxist dialogue in recent years and as a continual reminder to the West that there are Christians behind the Iron Curtain who genuinely (and rightly) believe that they have a positive, and not merely negative, vocation as a Christian in the society in which they find themselves. The eagerness with which Müller embraces Marxist categories, however, distorts both his interpretation of Bonhoeffer's ecclesiology and his interpretation of the "Christianity without religion" project as a whole. This eagerness, and the particular form it takes, cause Müller to underplay what he considers the "traditional" elements (such as the continued centering of Christian existence in the Christian community) in Bonhoeffer's "non-religious" interpretation. A full appreciation of Bonhoeffer's affirmation of secularity does not require such a disproportionate de-emphasizing of his classical Christianity; the reason is to be found instead in the exigencies of Marxist ideology.

Müller forever reminds us that "the right way to follow Bonhoeffer is to take up his development, his path, his intention and the tendency of his work: to follow him rather than stifle his vigour and vitality with a system." [12] In this way it is always possible to excuse Müller on the grounds that he is not simply "repeating" but "developing" Bonhoeffer, not simply systematizing his thought but drawing out its intentions and implications in terms of another framework of ideas. But it is clear from Müller's treatment of Bonhoeffer that he does in fact end up presenting Bonhoeffer himself as pointing in the direction Müller delineates. Furthermore, and most disturbingly, by taking the approach he does, Müller forces Bonhoeffer's theology, above all the "religionless Christianity" ideas, into an aprioristic framework, i.e., the Marxist ideology and conceptuality. In this way Müller succeeds at times in constructing a highly strained, artificial picture of Bonhoeffer's ideas rather than letting the ideas speak for themselves. In terms of an accurate analysis of Bonhoeffer, we would be better off with the perhaps more pedestrian attempts of other interpreters simply to find out first of all what Bonhoeffer himself indeed thought and saw as its implications. *Then* if we wish to move in a Marxist or "death of God" or some other direction on the basis of Bonhoeffer, we shall at least have begun with a clear idea of both the similarities and the differences between what Bonhoeffer said and what we are saying by way of extension therefrom.

On this matter it may be that we have been too accepting of Müller's limitations because of our appreciation of his achievement. The ideological Marxist jargon in Müller's presentation, and the way he employs it, can only be called dogmatic (it is also repetitiously tedious, as so much Marxist literature is). In good Marxist fashion, Müller forces the complexities of Western history into oversimplified explanations using the familiar pat terminology such as "bourgeois," "revolutionary," "reactionary," "imperialism," "Fascism," etc. Everywhere this sort of historical-cultural analysis strikes the person trained in empirical Western historiography as aprioristic and forced in the extreme. When Müller forces Bonhoeffer's prison statements about past, present, and future into this dogmatic conceptual framework the result is egregious distortion. Bearing all this in mind about Müller's treatment of Bonhoeffer, we should not be surprised at what an injustice he does to the full dialectic of his ecclesiology.

One of the most adequate and balanced appreciations of the full dialectic of Bonhoeffer's doctrine of the church and its continuity through the prison thoughts is to be found in the writings of Regin Prenter on Bonhoeffer. Prenter agrees with Müller (albeit non-ideologically) that "the world has finally outgrown all earlier attempts at christianization and has come of age in its relationship to the church. The church which respects and affirms the fact that the world has now come of age is solely the church under the cross. Since the church no longer wishes to rule the world, it lives for the world in the crucified one." But Prenter goes on to recognize the dialectical continuity and fundamental rooting of Bonhoeffer's "religionless" Christian community in his previous ecclesiological outlook:

In Bonhoeffer's ideas concerning the non-religious interpretation of the gospel in the world come of age, nothing is retracted from what he said in *The Cost of Discipleship* about the need for Christians to break with immediacies and about their salvation as separation from the world, or about their frontal attack on the world, or about the visibility of the church. Nor is anything retracted of what he said in *Life Together* about "Christian brotherhood." All this is an indispensable presupposition of the non-religious interpretation.[13]

289

In his perceptive and importantly definitive essay on the relationship between Bonhoeffer and Barth, "Dietrich Bonhoeffer and Karl Barth's Positivism of Revelation," Prenter warns against the general "radical" tendency to evacuate the churchly side of Bonhoeffer's "religionless" vision in favor of straightforward, undialectical secularity: "It would be completely erroneous to conclude from Bonhoeffer's 'religionless' concept of faith, that he had in mind a kind of secularization of the life of the church and that the religionless interpretation of faith would lead to a *substitution* for her worship in sermon and sacrament of merciful action in the world." [14] Of Bonhoeffer's call for silence and chastened speech on the part of the church in the "come-of-age" world, Prenter writes:

> It is not the intention of Bonhoeffer that henceforth the church should no longer speak of God, Christ, reconciliation, baptism, communion, etc., but only of the world come of age. What he does want to say is that if the church today is unable to speak of God, Christ, reconciliation, baptism, communion, etc., *in such a way* that their meaning is immediately plain to the world, and to show that here is a witness to God's being for the world and not a call to man's salvation out of the world into a religious inwardness, then the church may be forced, for the sake of the Gospel, to be *silent* and witness to God's being for the world "by example only." [15]

With his firm recognition of Bonhoeffer's relationship to Barth, Prenter seems to me to have a more sensitive grasp of the entire dialectical subtlety of Bonhoeffer's "religionless" ecclesiology than does Müller.

Conservative, Radical, or Liberal?

The other significant lineup in Bonhoeffer interpretation is among conservative, liberal, and radical assessments of his revolutionary influence. In terms of widespread and even popular impressions of Bonhoeffer, the differences among these varied "paths" seem more significant and far-reaching than the seemingly "academic" issues raised in the debate we have been considering (although they are by no means unrelated). It is largely through the claiming of the Bonhoeffer of *Letters and Papers* as the radical precursor of "death of God" theology (as in the writings of William Hamilton and Paul van Buren), or as the liberal ally of Tillich and Bultmann (as in Bishop Robinson's *Honest to God*), that he has been transmitted to the church at large, and even to numbers of scholars in the field of religion. Less frequently in the United States (but more in Germany), Bonhoeffer the conservative has been presented as the "true" Bonhoeffer: the loyal Barthian and Lutheran of the *Kirchenkampf* whose prison writings were penned under enormous physical and psychological strain and therefore must be taken with a large grain of salt.

The first sort of misunderstanding comes from a *conservative* standpoint. Within this general outlook I would distinguish two perspectives: traditionalism (what Bonhoeffer characterized as "orthodoxy") and Barthianism. The traditionalist view finds extreme expression in the sincere but amazingly misguided words of a German pastor: "One may still hope that at the very end Bonhoeffer regained his faith." [16] Traditional orthodoxy tends to find the "religionless" reflections either puzzlingly irrelevant or downright wrongheaded and destructive of faith. Bonhoeffer's "non-religious interpretation of biblical concepts" is misunderstood as humanism or liberalism and his concept of a world "come of age" as a dangerously unrealistic optimism about a godless world.

The Barthian misunderstanding, unlike the traditionalist, has a full grasp of Bonhoeffer's theological background even in the prison writings, but there precisely the misunderstanding begins. Barth himself regarded Bonhoeffer's criticisms of his own position as mistaken and the "non-religious" reflections as a puzzling detour from the real business of theology. As Godsey says, Barth was "inclined to stress the enigmatic character of the thoughts from prison, pointing out that Bonhoeffer tended to be an impulsive, visionary thinker, who would suddenly become consumed by an idea (in this case an idea grounded in a particular philosophy of history!), only later to stop at some penultimate thesis and turn to another." [17] Barth, and those theologians who would generally be styled "Barthians," tend to regard the prison writings as the moving but quite momentary and private musings of an essentially classical theologian cast up in an unusual and abnormal situation. That Bonhoeffer was an essentially classical Christian and theologian must be an indisputable conclusion; that the "religionless" thoughts are a "side issue" or a vagary, however, simply cannot be supported on the basis either of the prison writings themselves or of the direction of Bonhoeffer's thought as a whole, as I have tried to show throughout this study.

A leading Barth-inspired theologian, Thomas F. Torrance, gave the Barthian conservative view of Bonhoeffer expression in a review of the English translation of Bonhoeffer's christology lectures.[18] Professor Torrance attempts to bring Bonhoeffer squarely under the aegis of Barth. He regards *Christ the Center* as showing Barth's direct influence on "even the language in page after page." He is so sure that Bonhoeffer's christology was heavily indebted to Barth that he makes the serious accusation that the editor of the lectures (Bethge) has "deliberately suppressed" all mention of Barth in the lectures. Since Bonhoeffer himself was impeccably honest and would naturally have referred to Barth whenever he used his ideas, Torrance can only conclude that those responsible for the publication of the lectures are in some sinister way "anti-Barth" and have systematically expunged his name. Not only does the internal evidence of Bonhoeffer's writings as a whole, which refer to Barth remarkably seldom by name and then often critically, fail to substantiate such a charge; Bethge himself directly refuted Torrance's accusation, and we may assume that Bethge knows better than anyone else whether the manuscripts from which *Christ the Center* was compiled do in fact mention Barth.[19]

It is possible fully to agree with Torrance that Bonhoeffer must be understood within the general tradition of classical theology and the particular tradition of Barth's theological conception and methodology without having to go to the unnecessary lengths of making Bonhoeffer display his indebtedness at every point. Bonhoeffer was an original and independent "Barthian" who came to a full material grasp of several of the later, "dogmatic" Barth's central themes before Barth himself did, including the key area of christology. Furthermore, as his modest, nonspeculative attitude to Scripture reveals, Bonhoeffer understood the truly evangelical limitations of Barth's biblicism better than Barth did.

Professor Torrance is quite anxious to counter what he believes to be the growing "Bonhoeffer myth," the claiming of his "Christianity without religion" project for all sorts of theological viewpoints which Bonhoeffer himself would have rejected, above all, various forms of "neoliberalism" and Bultmann-inspired existentialism. I fully share this concern, as the whole rationale and development of my study have tried to indicate. But in his anxiety Torrance has gone to the opposite extreme of a conservative "domestication" of Bonhoeffer which is as great a misunderstanding as existentialist "liberalization" or death-of-God "radicalization." Bonhoeffer is not Bultmann; but he is not Barth either. He is a Barth-inspired but independent and original theologian who stands alongside but not "behind" Bultmann and Barth as an important theological figure of our time.

It is extremely important to add, too, that Bonhoeffer stands there *not in spite of but because of the "religionless Christianity" project.* The tragedy is that this last development of his thought was so prematurely nipped in the bud. It is precisely the fact that Bonhoeffer's theological reflections from prison, on which, after all, he was working in a preliminary way in the *Ethics* before his arrest, are a "mainstream" development of his theology which the Barthians are unwilling to acknowledge. Torrance dismisses Bonhoeffer's "non-religious interpretation" far more peremptorily and superficially than does Barth, by means of what I would call psychological innuendo, a familiar conservative way of lightly dismissing the prison writings. He describes Bonhoeffer's prison reflections as "stray sentences of an exaggerated kind penned under the stress of Nazi oppression in Buchenwald."[20] A traditionalist (rather than Barthian) conservative theologian, Eric Mascall, echoes Torrance when he writes: "It would be perhaps unfair to Bonhoeffer to take *au pied de la lettre* words written from a Nazi prison camp under conditions of grave physical and emotional distress."[21]

Severe hardships and privations were Bonhoeffer's lot as a prisoner; but there is absolutely no evidence in the prison writings or in the accounts of Eberhard Bethge and of fellow prisoners to show that the "non-religious" reflections are in any way the ecstatic product of excessive psychological strain. On the contrary: The "religionless Christianity" project is an intrinsically reasonable development of Bonhoeffer's whole theology at which he was explicitly hinting in letters and other writings (notably, of course, the *Ethics*) at least two or three years before he was arrested. His serious intention to write a book on the subject, for which we have his preliminary outline, can hardly be called the random musings of a man living in extreme crisis. Furthermore, one of the most remarkable things about the prison writings is precisely Bonhoeffer's amazing self-control and inner discipline, his sanity of outlook and clarity of vision, his ability to read widely and to write creatively, amid the rigors of his situation. Fellow prisoners of

Bonhoeffer's testified to his courage, self-discipline, cheerfulness, rationality, and "existence for others." What emerges from the prison writings is a picture of enormous strength, not of psychological fixation or disintegration. To be sure, Bonhoeffer also recorded his loneliness, his despair, the contrast between his inner insecurities and his outward confidence; but he clearly assimilated these normal experiences of imprisonment into his unwavering faith and strength of mind. To dismiss the "Christianity without religion" project by psychological innuendo is not only somewhat irresponsibly facile; it is also an unfair and inaccurate portrayal of Bonhoeffer himself.

The *radical* outlook on Bonhoeffer's religionless Christianity, at the other pole, is not so much a misunderstanding as an independent development based squarely, however, on suggestions in the prison writings. Radical Bonhoeffer-inspired theologians, above all two exponents of the American "death of God" school of theology, Paul van Buren and William Hamilton,[22] explicitly recognize that their version of "Christianity without religion" is not necessarily the same as Bonhoeffer's; they would simply regard him as the theologian whose seminal thoughts have provided the basic inspiration for their own theological reconstruction.

At the same time, however, the radical perspective on Bonhoeffer may be regarded as a misunderstanding, insofar as it is precisely the radical theologians through whose eyes Bonhoeffer is commonly seen (as Torrance rightly recognizes). In the semi-popular literature on the subject Bonhoeffer suffers a kind of "guilt by association." In this sense the radical point of view may be called a misunderstanding. Eric Mascall's brief comments on Bonhoeffer in the work cited are a case in point. He seems to see Bonhoeffer entirely through the eyes of van Buren (and of J. A. T. Robinson, whose presentation in *Honest to God* I regard, however, as "liberal," not "radical").

It is in terms of the intensely dialectical character of Bonhoeffer's theology that I believe the "death of God" theology is to be seen. Bonhoeffer's christology is collapsed into a one-dimensional "Jesusology," as in van Buren's abandonment, on linguistic-empirical grounds, of any meaning to the concept "God" and his humanistic interpretation of Jesus as the supremely free man.[23] In van Buren's theology the supreme dialectic, that the reality of Jesus is the reality of God, is collapsed or reduced from full christocentricity into "Jesu-centricity."

For van Buren, "God" is no longer an operative concept; Jesus' transcendence is reduced to purely human and ethical terms such as "contagious freedom." While Bonhoeffer *translated* the deity of Christ insofar as he could into humanly understandable ethical terms, he never *reduced* Christ simply to a human reality; that would have been "liberalism" and therefore untheological and unbiblical. In the "death of God" theologians, theological dialectic is flattened into humanist ethic.[24] Ecclesiologically, the empirical church, which Bonhoeffer biblically affirms in spite of everything as "the presence of Christ on earth," is simply abandoned by Hamilton in favor of a fully secular existence.[25] Bonhoeffer's analysis of the disappearance of the metaphysical "God" of "religion" as the work of the God who in Christ is vividly near is collapsed into the "absence" or "death" of God per se, or into our inability even to use the word. As van Buren himself seems clearly to recognize, what we have here is simple reductionism: the compressing of Bonhoeffer's ideas into purely "historical and ethical dimensions." [26] The keynote of the "death of God" theology is a radical version of Bonhoeffer's affirmation of modern secularity. It must be said of van Buren and Hamilton, however, that their secularity is optimistic but not unrealistic; like their non-Christian counterpart, Bonhoeffer's "come-of-age," nihilist man, they do not blink before the realities of evil and suffering. They simply no longer find the "answers" of "religion," including organized Christianity in any form, "any more compelling than any others."

In between the conservative and the radical approaches to Bonhoeffer's "Christianity without religion" project is what I would call the *liberal* outlook. Like conservatism and radicalism, it is open to misunderstandings and misrepresentations of Bonhoeffer. The liberal viewpoint is adopted principally by theologians who attempt, in varying degrees, to synthesize the insights of Bonhoeffer with those of Bultmann and of Tillich.

The "Bultmannian synthesis" is probably the most popular current attempt to utilize Bonhoeffer's thought in the ongoing work of theology. We see it primarily in the writings of Gerhard Ebeling[27] and Ronald Gregor Smith.[28] Central to the Bultmann-inspired outlook on Bonhoeffer is the twofold assumption that Bultmann has from the beginning fully and explicitly shared Bonhoeffer's intense concern for the communication of the gospel to modern secular man, and furthermore that Bonhoeffer's "dereligionizing" of biblical concepts and Bultmann's "demythologizing" of the New Testament are much closer together, both in intention and in execution, than Bonhoeffer imagined.

I would not wish to deny the actual similarity between Bonhoeffer and Bultmann in these two areas. But there remain actual and quite fundamental differences in terms of *presuppositions* and *methodology* which are too quickly glossed over by Bultmann interpreters. Significantly, Barth's influence on Bonhoeffer tends to be minimized, which softens some rather hard contrasts between Bonhoeffer and Bultmann.[29]

The basic difference between Bonhoeffer and Bultmann is christological. From beginning to end Bonhoeffer, like Barth, focused on the concrete objectivity of the historical figure of Jesus Christ, the man proclaimed by the New Testament as "God with us." All reflection on the subjective response of faith was wholly correlative to this reality. Bultmann and his students, on the other hand, have been primarily concerned to translate theology into anthropology, to interpret the gospel in terms of human self-understanding. For Bultmann himself, and especially for his "left-wing" followers like Fritz Buri and Schubert Ogden, the flesh-and-blood Jesus of the Gospels becomes simply the occasion of our faith; in himself he remains historically unapproachable and in the last analysis theologically nonessential. Significantly, Bonhoeffer's New Testament exegesis was correlatively conservative; Bultmann's is extremely skeptical. For Bonhoeffer, as for Barth, the historical reality of Jesus Christ is the sole basis of all ontological statements about God, man, and the world. In the Bultmannian scheme, theology must begin with an independent ontological inquiry into the structures of human existence (of which Martin Heidegger's is regarded as the most satisfactory) and then interpret the New Testament revelation in this light. Since Bonhoeffer's "Barthian" christology lies peculiarly at the very foundation of his "religionless Christianity" project, more serious thought will have to be given to this basic christological divergence from Bultmann than has so far been forthcoming. It is a divergence which affects our whole utilization of the prison reflections.

Closely linked with the Bultmannian existentialist preunderstanding is the second difference to which I would call attention: Bonhoeffer's conception of the world as "come of age." Despite the fact that

Bultmannian theologians are presently in the vanguard of theological world affirmation, I cannot but believe that their existentialist *Weltanschauung*, which emerged out of the pessimistic, individualistic, introspective view of man which characterized European thought between the two World Wars, prevents them from fully appreciating what Bonhoeffer meant by his conception of modern "nihilist" man. "Nihilism" in Christian existentialist parlance is basically a negative term which evokes the image of despair and meaninglessness. However, "nihilism" as applied to "come-of-age" man by Bonhoeffer has nothing to do with despair or meaninglessness; it means rather the inability to worship anything at all, which may exist alongside healthy-minded life affirmation. In Bonhoeffer's scheme "nihilism" is part of a basically optimistic view of secularized man. One of the most striking features of the prison writings is his excoriation of "existentialism" for refusing to recognize the adulthood of the world. It must be said that from Bonhoeffer's point of view existentialist world affirmation lags behind that of "religionless Christianity."

There is the further related point that existentialist theology sees "practicing" secularity as an *ideological* phenomenon. R. G. Smith, for example, describes "modern secularism" (which he distinguishes from authentic or "radical secularism") as "a congeries of competing ideologies, . . . a creeping nihilism which takes various ideological or utopian forms." [30] He goes on to describe this "modern secularism," which he believes to be the predominant form today, in classical existentialist terms which could equally well have been used in the 1930's and 1940's. He speaks of depersonalization, mass manipulation, *ersatz* religion, collectivism, and Orwell's *1984*. What is singular about Bonhoeffer's idea of a world "come of age," however, is precisely the conviction that "ideological man" in all his forms is dying out. The "new man" can no longer really be ideological; in terms of the current interpretations of Bonhoeffer's concept, he is functional, pragmatic, technocratic in outlook. Obviously the ideological *Götterdämmerung* is still very much with us: Marxism and nationalism are perhaps the hardiest of the dying gods. Large numbers of people are still prey both to the appeal and to the oppression of ideologies. What strikes some of today's observers, however, is the declining hold of ideologies in all areas. An increasing number of people, they argue, are suspicious of all promises of salvation, both religious and political; they are more interested in day-to-day realities such as work, food, justice, and individual freedom. Governments, whether democratic or Marxist, are required more and more to answer to the same basic needs and demands of human beings: sound economics, simple justice, responsible participation, and creative opportunity. Ideologies find themselves increasingly subordinated to the stubbornly empirical outlook brought about by the scientific-technological revolution of the West.

I have already spoken critically of J. A. T. Robinson's admittedly somewhat informal synthesis of the "religionless" Bonhoeffer and Paul Tillich. I suggested that perhaps the chasm between the two was too great. There is much better ground for a "Bultmannian" than for a "Tillichian" synthesis. The glaring contradiction between Bonhoeffer and Tillich, of course, is that the former believed "ultimate concern" to be a dying phenomenon, while the latter believed that secularity (as well as every other facet of human existence) was shot through with it. Bonhoeffer was christocentric, biblicistic, and non-metaphysical; Tillich was a mystic and religious ontologist.

Two recent comments on the possibility of synthesizing Bonhoeffer's "religionless Christianity" and the thought of Tillich seem to me to voice a dramatically negative view. The first is by Lesslie Newbigin in his book *Honest Religion for Secular Man*. He speaks of the relatively unrewarding attempt of the Bishop of Woolwich "to squeeze his [Bonhoeffer's] thought into a mould of the thought of Paul Tillich who is really saying the precise opposite of Bonhoeffer." [31] The second comment is the conclusion to a brief but damning criticism of Tillich by Alan Richardson in *Religion in Contemporary Debate*. Although Richardson's attack seems to me to be unnecessarily merciless and unchivalrous in its sweeping generalizations, there is an element of truth in his final statement as applied to Bonhoeffer's project: "Nothing could better illustrate the confusion of some of those who seek to meet the needs of a religionless age than their admiration for one who has so diligently sought to translate secular philosophical theory into religious language." [32] Despite their basic incompatibility of outlook, however, some of Tillich's profound cultural insights and terminological distinctions can be used, I believe, to shed light on Bonhoeffer's project.

The difficulties in the "liberal" uses of Bonhoeffer revolve about the two focuses of theological presuppositions and method on the one hand

and the true character of the modern world on the other. Here as elsewhere, my concern is with Bonhoeffer's thoughts and their differences from those of other theologians. The "uses of Bonhoeffer" can only properly begin from an accurate knowledge of his own position and proceed by explicitly indicating the similarities, differences, and problems involved in adapting his thinking to another frame of reference.

The most serious distortions and confusions of Bonhoeffer have come out of this conservative-radical-liberal array of interpretations—a matter of some concern, since it is writings produced with these interests which have largely created the "Bonhoeffer image." That is why comprehensive studies of the carefulness and thoroughness of Phillips, Kuhns, and Bethge are so vitally necessary in keeping before us an accurate picture of the precise extent of Bonhoeffer's indebtedness to and departure from Barth, his relationship to Bultmann and Tillich, the intense dialectic between his classical faith and radically positive affirmation of secularity, and above all his own fresh originality throughout.

There is an interesting, although by no means neat, relationship between the conservative-radical-liberal lineup of approaches and the "polyphony-divergence" differences discussed earlier, a relationship which makes the latter not as purely "academic" as it might appear. For obviously it is to the advantage of the liberal or radical interpreter of the later Bonhoeffer if he can find real hiatuses or irreconcilable shifts in his theological development; while the conservative seemingly has support for his approach if the consistent unity of Bonhoeffer's thought from beginning to end can be demonstrated.

In view of the fact that I have already come down on the side of those who see Bonhoeffer's theological development "polyphonically," it might be hastily assumed that I agree with those who take what I have called a conservative outlook. If "conservative" is understood in the sense in which I have used it in attempting to categorize the streams of Bonhoeffer interpretation, however, then the answer is that I definitely do not. To subsume Bonhoeffer's theology neatly under Karl Barth, as Professor Torrance, for example, would have it, or under Lutheran orthodoxy, as some of Bonhoeffer's fellow German Protestants have almost desperately wished, is to do fundamental violence both to the actual influence of Barth and Lutheranism on Bonhoeffer and to his own independence and originality. On the other hand, the liberal assimilation of Bonhoeffer with Bultmann, and even with Tillich, does equal violence from the other side, since his theological presuppositions and method, if not his material conclusions, remained closest to Barth. And certainly the radical, reductionist-humanist filter through which Bonhoeffer has been passed in recent years distorts him seriously by collapsing the extreme dialectical tension between faith and worldliness in the prison writings.

I cannot accept, therefore, any of the general pigeonholes into which the "religionless" Bonhoeffer's thought is often inserted. However, since I understand his theological development as essentially "polyphonic," I definitely consider the theologian even of the prison writings as *classical*, which I take to bear a broader sense than the "conservatism" either of the later Barth or of Lutheran orthodoxy. Bonhoeffer was classical in his use of the Bible, his full acceptance of the ancient christological and trinitarian formulations, his doctrine of the church, and his overall theological method. Bonhoeffer, however, was also classical in the "evangelical" sense of the young Luther: fully committed to the "whole Christ" witnessed in Scripture and properly interpreted by the Councils, but critical and open precisely on the basis of the principle of *sola Scriptura* and the priorities which that principle itself demands. It was Bonhoeffer's complaint against the "dogmatic" Barth and, to a larger degree, of Lutheran orthodoxy and Bonhoeffer's own anti-Nazi Confessing Church, that they had become "conservative" in the bad sense, devoted to systematization and institutionalization and no longer sensitive to the living dynamic of biblical faith as recovered by the early Reformers and revived and carried forward by the neo-orthodox movement.

Bonhoeffer the classical Christian never departed from a historically "conservative" and always theological hermeneutical approach to the Bible; he never departed from an all-embracing christology of which he regarded Chalcedon as a proper framework of interpretation, if not the last word; while very critical of the church in his last days, it remained for him the unique community of God described so loftily in the New Testament. To be classical in his faith and theology did not mean, however, to be uncritical. In prison he wrestled, more intensely than ever before, with the real priorities which he believed the Scriptures themselves dictate as the normative witness to Christ; he sought with keen liberality and self-criticism for what the Bible itself considered central and sat with new lightness on what it deemed peripheral. But none of this freshness, this originality, this liberality of spirit, makes the later Bonhoeffer a "liberal" whom we can without further ado join with Bultmann; it certainly does not make him a "radical" in the reductionistic sense which that word has come to have. Bonhoeffer was to the end a classical evangelical Christian who was marked by a rare degree of boldness and originality in interpreting by word and deed the faith and the modern world.

I have tried to show throughout this entire study that perhaps the fundamental key to Bonhoeffer's theological outlook and development is a rigorous *dialectic.* A dialectical methodology obviously derived from Barth but worked out in a unique, boldly concrete direction is the principal element, I believe, in understanding the range of Bonhoeffer's reflections, including christology, ecclesiology, biblical interpretation, and ethics. It is the almost unbearable intensity with which Bonhoeffer held together in fruitful tension a whole complex of theological polarities that to a large degree has produced what I consider to be the chief misunderstandings of his thought. The interpreter, for example, who views Bonhoeffer's development as marked by basic irreconcilabilities, does not sufficiently appreciate this stringent dialectical unity out of which various elements sift in the course of Bonhoeffer's career in response to the demands of the historical "now." The conservative does not, among other things, fathom how the writer of the *Ethics* and the prison letters can talk like Barth one minute and like Harnack the next. The liberal does not want to believe that a classically understood and largely "un-demythologized" christomonism lies side by side with all the talk about transcendence as Jesus' "being-there-for-others." The radical would like very much to appropriate the imprisoned Bonhoeffer's severe criticism of the church and his call for Christian worldliness, and to forget about or underplay the "secret discipline."

Perhaps Bonhoeffer's all-embracing dialectic, so expressive of his totally theological mind, is simply too intense even for *Christian* man "come of age." But it was the way Bonhoeffer himself approached all issues, and therefore in order to understand *him* we must recognize it and highlight it in its fullness, not in some truncated form. Furthermore, there is the possibility that only by such an exhaustive sort of

301

dialectic could Bonhoeffer, or anyone else, hold together a fully classical Christian faith and a full-blooded affirmation of the modern world. The fact that it is so difficult to retain the former without retreating from the latter, as conservatives tend to do; or to embrace the latter authentically without reducing the former, as liberals and radicals have felt themselves compelled to do—these opposite sides of the dialectical fence upon which most of us fall should help us to enter sympathetically into the difficulty and the achievement of Bonhoeffer's dialectic. Nowhere is this more urgently true than in the attempt to understand his "non-religious interpretation."

Notes

Chapter One: Liberal Culture and Secularity

1. On the lasting impact of liberal theology on Bonhoeffer, see Eberhard Bethge, "The Challenge of Dietrich Bonhoeffer's Life and Theology," The Alden-Tuthill Lectures for 1961, *Chicago Theological Seminary Register,* vol. LI, no. 2, Feb. 1961, p. 5 (reprinted in Ronald Gregor Smith, ed., *World Come of Age* [Philadelphia: Fortress Press, 1967], pp. 22-88; page references throughout the present study are from the original publication in the *Chicago Theological Seminary Register*); Jaroslav Pelikan, "Bonhoeffer's *Christologie* of 1933," in Martin Marty, ed., *The Place of Bonhoeffer* (New York: Association Press, 1962), pp. 145-64, and Marty's Introduction, p. 12. See also Gerhard Ebeling, *Word and Faith,* translated by James W. Leitch (Philadelphia: Fortress Press, 1963), pp. 103-6.
2. For an excellent critical study of Bonhoeffer's use of sociology in *The Communion of Saints,* see Peter Berger, "Sociology and Ecclesiology," in Marty, ed., *The Place of Bonhoeffer,* pp. 53-79. Jürgen Moltmann also deals at some length with Bonhoeffer's early use of sociology in "The Lordship of Christ and Human Society," translated by Reginald H. and Ilse Fuller and published in Fuller, ed., *Two Studies in the Theology of Bonhoeffer* (New York: Charles Scribner's Sons, 1967); see esp. pp. 23-47. See also the critical account by John A. Phillips, *Christ for Us in the Theology of Dietrich Bonhoeffer,* pp. 35-39, 48-56.
3. Delivered on June 15, 1930. Printed in NRS, p. 30.
4. Pelikan in Marty, ed., *The Place of Bonhoeffer,* p. 146.
5. E, p. 34.
6. LPP, p. 126.
7. LPP, p. 60.
8. LPP, p. 79.
9. LPP, p. 135.
10. Bonhoeffer's "aristocratic" outlook on society can be seen in what might be called (from a nineteenth-century standpoint) the "classical liberalism" or (from a twentieth-century perspective) "enlightened conservatism" of his attitudes in social ethics and politics. See E, pp. 239-44 and 297-317. "The sense of quality," which is in fact the title of one of the brief essays which Bonhoeffer wrote shortly before he was put in prison (LPP, pp. 35-36), permeates the prison writings throughout, emerging into clearer focus than in any of his previous writings. Of particular interest, along with the essay mentioned above, is his "Thoughts on the Baptism of D. W. R." (LPP, pp. 165-72.)
11. LPP, p. 123.

12. See in Chapter Nine, "The Development of a Christological Ethics Under the Third Reich," the discussion of "The 'Religionless' Christian."

13. In his *Essays in Liberality* (London: SCM Press, 1957), pp. 9-28.

14. Pp. 21-22.

15. LPP, p. 208. Interestingly, Bonhoeffer goes on to prophesy that "there will not be many of the younger men in whom these two trends are combined." In this pessimistic forecast Bonhoeffer would rejoice to know that he has been proved wrong by the postwar trend of continental theology, a trend which his own posthumous influence helped to create. Current Protestant theology, both in Europe and in the United States, can be aptly characterized as an attempt, on various fronts, to synthesize the best insights of the older liberalism and neo-orthodoxy.

16. LPP, p. 180.

17. LPP, p. 182.

18. It must be added, however, that Bonhoeffer considered even the most "liberal" of the other Neo-Reformation theologians to have failed to come to grips either with the all-sufficiency of Christ or with the radical secularity of the world come of age. In a diary entry for June 22, 1939, written during Bonhoeffer's brief second visit to America, he records that he has been reading Reinhold Niebuhr's *Interpretation of Christian Ethics*. He criticizes Niebuhr for describing the biblical faith simply as "myth" and for his extremely free-wheeling use of the biblical material. By failing to subject himself quite concretely to the objective reality of revelation in Jesus Christ and the actual text of the Scriptures which witness to him, Niebuhr has not genuinely transcended liberalism (GS I, 305, 307). The Bonhoeffer of the prison writings would furthermore have found Niebuhr's pessimism about modern secular outlooks to be unwarranted, along with his tendency to present Christian faith as the most adequate "answer" to human problems. In the case of Rudolf Bultmann and Paul Tillich, Bonhoeffer likewise faulted their inability to take seriously the radical character of modern "nonreligiousness," and would certainly have taken exception to the inadequately christocentric persuppositions and methods which inform their theologies.

19. See Bonhoeffer's own early awareness of the difference between Barth and his disciples in his correspondence with Erwin Sutz from Bonn in 1931: "They have a sharp scent for thoroughbreds here. No negro passes 'for white'; they even examine his finger-nails and the soles of his feet. Up till now they still haven't shown me hospitality as the unknown stranger. Now with Karl Barth himself, of course, everything is completely different. One breathes in an orderly way, one is no longer afraid of dying of suffocation in the thin air." (NRS, p. 120.)

During the Second World War, the period of Bonhoeffer's "non-religious" reflections on the gospel, he came to accuse the anti-Nazi Confessing Church itself, of which he had been so vigorous a member and which had been theologically molded by Barth (the chief symbol of which was the Barmen Declaration of 1934), of being "Barthian" in a reactionary ecclesiastical way.

20. See his *Die Protestantische Theologie im 19. Jahrhundert* (Zürich: 1952). Eleven chapters were trans. into English by Brian Cozens under the title *From Rousseau to Ritschl* (London: SCM Press, 1959).

21. For a clear recognition of Bonhoeffer's contribution to the contemporary discussion, see Gerhard Ebeling, *Word and Faith*, pp. 98-161.

22. Torrance, *Karl Barth: An Introduction to His Early Theology, 1910-1931* (London: SCM Press, 1962), pp. 23-25.

23. Bethge, "The Challenge . . . ," in *Chicago Theol. Sem. Register*, LI (February 1961), 24-25; and Busing, "Reminiscences of Finkenwalde," *The Christian Century*, LXXVIII (September 20, 1961), 1108-11.

24. GS II, 278. See also CS, pp. 194-98.

25. John Godsey, *The Theology of Dietrich Bonhoeffer* (Philadelphia: Westminster Press, 1960), p. 88.

26. I have enclosed "existentialism" and "psychoanalysis" in quotation marks whenever these words indicate the phenomena which Bonhoeffer castigates so bitterly in the prison writings. I do so to warn the reader that these general terms which cover a broad and intensely varied spectrum of ideas are being used by Bonhoeffer in a partial and somewhat obscure way. The existentialist elements in his own thought, which we shall examine in the next chapter, are sufficient to admonish us against taking Bonhoeffer's unguarded assaults on "existentialism" as a blanket condemnation. His attacks seem to be directed at tendencies or popularized expressions of a certain sort, rather than at these movements in their entirety.

    I have done the same with the word "religion" throughout the present study, to warn the reader that what is meant is *Bonhoeffer's interpretation* of religion. Since his definition of religion, especially in the prison writings, seems to many readers unjustifiably partial and negative, and to others simply baffling in light of what they have always understood as religion, I have thought it best, even at the risk of tediousness, to indicate with quotation marks where I am dealing only with Bonhoeffer's understanding of religion.

27. See Berger, "Camus, Bonhoeffer and the World Come of Age," *The Christian Century*, LXXVI (April 8, 1959), 417-18, and (April 15, 1959), 450-52; and Hamilton, *The New Essence of Christianity* (New York: Association Press, 1961), pp. 30, 55-58.

28. One can pick up any volume of Camus's writings and discover his twofold *joie de vivre* and serious probing of the problems of justice and suffering. See in particular his novel *The Plague* and his mature philosophical statement *The Rebel*.

29. LPP, p. 178.

30. LPP, pp. 195-96.

31. Carl F. von Weizsäcker, *The World View of Physics*, trans. by Marjorie Greene (London: Routledge & Kegan Paul, 1952).

32. LPP, p. 174.

33. *The World View of Physics*, p. 155.

34. *Ibid.*, p. 177.

35. *Ibid.*, pp. 156-57. Laplace, of course, is famous for his "non-religious" reply to Napoleon's question as to where God fitted into his scientific theory of the world. "Sir," replied Laplace, "I have no need of that hypothesis."

36. *Ibid.*, p. 180. Weizsäcker's own positive statement on the relation of Christianity to the modern world is very similar to Karl Heim's. See pp. 177-81.

37. LPP, pp. 195-96.

38. LPP, p. 196.

39. LPP, p. 178.

40. LPP, p. 209.

41. LPP, pp. 208-9.

42. Daniel Jenkins, in his book *Beyond Religion* (Philadelphia: Westminster Press, 1962), seeks to make this point in the context of discussing Bonhoeffer and other contemporary theologians on the phenomenon of religion; see p. 35.

43. See Barth, *Church Dogmatics*, 1/2, trans. by G. T. Thomson and Harold Knight (Edinburgh: T & T. Clark, 1956), p. 323, where he says of the atheist critique of religion: "The result of this critical turning against religion is simply the founding of a new religion"; and Bonhoeffer, E, pp. 38-39; "Western godlessness . . . is itself a religion, a religion of hostility to God. . . . Its god is the New Man, no matter whether he bears the trademark of Bolshevism or of Christianity." Note both the similarities in the two positions and Bonhoeffer's own attitude just a few years before the prison writings.

44. LPP, p. 185. Italics mine.

45. "The First Table of the Ten Commandments," trans. by John D. Godsey from an unpublished manuscript and printed in Godsey, ed., *Preface to Bonhoeffer: The Man and Two of His Shorter Writings* (Philadelphia: Fortress Press, 1965). The Lutheran Church, following the Roman Catholic tradition, includes the prohibition

of images in the first commandment, while the rest of Protestantism considers it a second commandment. Hence the Lutheran "First Table" contains three commandments, while the Reformed and other Protestant First Table contains four. Bonhoeffer is a bit confusing in the passage quoted from his letter, since there he follows the Reformed tradition and refers to the prohibition of images as commandment "No. 2." However, in his exposition of the First Table he includes it, Lutheran-style, in the first commandment.

46. *Ibid.*, p. 57.

47. "We *are moving* towards a completely religionless time *(wir gehen einer völlig religionslosen Zeit entgegen)*." LPP, p. 152. Italics mine.

48. A good example of this phenomenon is a book such as Julian Huxley's *Religion Without Revelation* (new ed.; New York: New American Library, 1959).

49. LPP, p. 200. Eberhard Bethge ably and succinctly counters the "naïve optimism" charge against Bonhoeffer's concept of the secularized world as in the process of "coming of age": "Bonhoeffer never pointed to an optimistic analysis of man as becoming better and better . . . . The main notion for Bonhoeffer is 'responsibility,' the unreversible capability and duty of adults individually to answer the questions of life in their own particular fields and within their own autonomous structures. This includes, to be sure, the joy which follows when human beings grow into their own manhood, but it also includes the integration of historical determinations, guilts, failures, even when they turn childish, immature, or tyrannical." ("Bonhoeffer's Christology and his 'Religionless Christianity,'" in Peter Vorkink, ed., *Bonhoeffer in a World Come of Age* [Philadelphia: Fortress Press, 1968].)

50. LPP, p. 196.

51. E, p. 184.

52. E, p. 183. In the prison writings Bonhoeffer explores the relation of "good people" to Christ in terms of the New Testament concept of *metanoia* (repentance), which we shall discuss in Chapter Nine.

53. E, p. 182.

54. E, pp. 182-83.

55. LPP, pp. 204-5.

56. E, p. 178. Italics mine. By "taking refuge with Christ" Bonhoeffer in no sense means a "return to religion," a flocking back to the churches of their "wayward children." It is precisely the churches, as purveyors of an often-dubious and, in a mature world, highly problematic activity called "religion," which have lost the power to capture the hearts and minds of many "good people." It is the name of Jesus Christ alone which still has the strange power to shield and protect the diverse forces of truth and goodness. See E, p. 179.

57. E, p. 175. Note Bonhoeffer's resolute grounding of all thought about reality in the biblical revelation centering in Christ.

58. Perhaps the best sustained argument for a universal "unconscious faith" is that of John Baillie in *Our Knowledge of God* (New York: Charles Scribner's Sons, 1959) and *The Sense of the Presence of God* (New York: Charles Scribner's Sons, 1962). Despite certain important differences in presuppositions and method, Baillie's development of the idea could be of value in illuminating what Bonhoeffer was trying to express.

59. LPP, p. 179.

60. LPP, p. 178.

61. LPP, p. 178-79.

62. LPP, p. 179.

63. LPP, p. 188.

64. LPP, p. 179.

65. LPP, p. 196.

66. LPP, p. 179.

67. LPP, pp. 190-91.

68. LPP, p. 191.
69. LPP, p. 107. See also Bonhoeffer's poem "Who Am I?" (LPP, pp. 197-98), in which he analyzes a psychological split within himself and poignantly asks which is his true identity. The poem ends, "Whoever I am, thou knowest, O God, I am thine."
70. We shall examine his outlook on subjectivity in terms of his concepts of will and conscience in Chapter Three, "The Impact of Luther." It must be added that there was almost certainly a temperamental as well as a theological aspect to Bonhoeffer's suspicion of psychological introspection and his frequent remarks about the importance of what he called a "healthy reserve" among people. Maria von Wedemeyer-Weller, who was his fiancée at the time of his death, has written that in prison "Dietrich often mentioned his reluctance to express his feelings. He pondered the differences between our two families and his own feelings of propriety and privacy." She goes on to quote from one of his prison letters to her: " 'It happens to be the case that certain things remain unsaid in my family, while they are expressed in yours.' " ("The Other Letters from Prison," in Vorkink, ed, *Bonhoeffer in a World Come of Age*, p. 106.)
71. See Chapter Two, "The Personalist-Existentialist Revolution in Philosophy."
72. LPP, p. 179.
73. LPP, p. 191.
74. LPP, p. 192.
75. E, p. 59.
76. LPP, pp. 192-93.
77. LPP, p. 99.
78. LPP, pp. 99-100.
79. LPP, pp. 104-5.
80. *Creation and Fall*, trans. by John C. Fletcher from the German *Schöpfung und Fall* (München: Kaiser Verlag, 1955. New York: Macmillan, and London: SCM Press, 1959), pp. 78-81.
81. E, pp. 145, 148.
82. See, e.g., his *Modern Man in Search of a Soul* (despite the title!) (London: Routledge & Kegan Paul, 1936).
83. See, e.g., an article entitled "Past and Future: The Transformation of Dietrich Bonhoeffer's View of History" in the East Berlin newspaper *Neue Zeit* (December 3 and 12, 1957); portions of it are quoted by Eberhard Bethge in his article "The Editing and Publishing of the Bonhoeffer Papers," *Andover Newton Bulletin*, LII (December 1959), 6-7. See also, and most importantly, Hanfried Müller, *Von der Kirche zur Welt* (Leipzig: Koehler & Amelang, 1961), a thoroughgoing Marxist interpretation of Bonhoeffer's "religionless Christianity" proposal.
84. LPP, p. 196. Italics mine.

Chapter Two: The Personalist-Existentialist Revolution in Philosophy

1. I-Thou or existentialist personalism, largely German in origin, is to be distinguished from the earlier British and American schools of idealist personalism.
2. NRS, p. 31.
3. *God Transcendent: Foundation for a Christian Metaphysic*, trans. by Edgar P. Dickie from the 3rd German ed. of *Glaube und Denken: Philosophische Grundlegung einer christlichen Lebensanschauung* ([Berlin: 1934] London: Nisbet, 1935).
4. Martin Buber, *I and Thou*, trans. by Ronald Gregor Smith from the 2nd German ed. (New York: Charles Scribner's Sons, 1958).
5. Martin Heidegger, *Being and Time*, trans. by John MacQuarrie and Edward Robinson from the 8th German ed. (New York: Harper & Row, 1962).
6. Eberhard Grisebach, *Gegenwart: Eine Kritische Ethik* (Halle: M. Niemeyer, 1928).
7. For a Barthian recognition of this similarity, see Roger Mehl, *The Condition of the*

Christian Philosopher, trans. by Eva Kushner (Philadelphia: Fortress Press, 1964), p. 305. Mehl recognizes, as Bonhoeffer must have, that existentialism is itself the product of a "Christian mental outlook," and can be classed in a number of its manifestations as "unconscious Christianity" or *fides directa* in the sphere of intellectual inquiry. Of course, the explicitly Christian roots of existentialism in the thought of Kierkegaard are fundamental to an understanding of the Christian fabric of the movement.

8. See CC, p. 33: "The ontological question has . . . been put as the question of the being of a person, the person Jesus Christ."

9. According to Barth and Bonhoeffer, to speak of God as a person is not analogical. God himself in his revelation discloses that what he is is "person," and that human "personhood" is a finite and sinful reflection of the person of God. Revelation itself defines the meaning of person; we do not bring the concept to the interpretation of revelation.

10. AB, p. 63.

11. AB, p. 65. See Heidegger, *Being and Time,* p. 251: "Only because Being is 'in the consciousness' that is to say, only because it is understandable in Dasein—can Dasein also understand and conceptualize such characteristics of Being as independence, the 'in-itself,' and Reality in general. Only because of this are 'independent' entities, as encountered within the world, acessible to circumspection."

12. AB, pp. 65-66. Italics mine. The last sentence stands in direct contradiction to the whole method of Rudolf Bultmann's theology, which interprets the gospel in terms of Heidegger's existentialist analysis. See Bultmann's programmatic essay on existentialist interpretation of the New Testament, "New Testament and Mythology," in Hans W. Bartsch, ed., *Kerygma and Myth,* trans. by R. H. Fuller (2nd ed., New York: Harper & Row, 1964), pp. 1-44. For Bultmann's use of Heidegger, see esp. pp. 24-33. An analysis of similarities and differences between Bultmann's "existentialist" interpretation and Bonhoeffer's "religionless" interpretation of Christianity appears in Chapter Five of the present work.

13. "Man in Contemporary Philosophy and Theology," delivered July 31, 1930, and published in NRS, pp. 50-69. The above quotation is from p. 57.

14. NRS, p. 59. Grisebach's use of the word *Gegenwart* as the title of his definitive work intends to convey two meanings of "present," the "over-against-ness" of the neighbor's Thou and the pure "now-ness" of existence.

15. AB, p. 88.

16. NRS, p. 59.

17. NRS, pp. 59-60.

18. AB, p. 88. Italics mine.

19. See NRS, p. 63; and AB, pp. 86-87. See also Gogarten, *Ich glaube an den Dreieinigen Gott* (Jena: E. Diederichs, 1926).

20. "Zu Karl Heims: Glaube und Denken," *Christentum und Wissenschaft,* viii (December, 1932); trans. and reprinted in NRS, pp. 347-59. Italics mine.

21. See Bonhoeffer's article "Concerning the Christian Idea of God," *The Journal of Religion,* xii (April 1932), 177-85: "As long as theology does not see its essential difference from all philosophical thinking, it does not begin with a statement concerning God's reality but tries rather to build a support for such a statement." (P. 177.)

22. Heim, *God Transcendent,* 3rd ed., p. 236. Italics mine.

23. *Ibid.,* p. 195. See also pp. 203-4: "We cannot form any concept of Him"; and p. 213: "We are by nature God-blind."

24. See *ibid.,* p. 202.

25. *Ibid.,* p. 45.

26. See a letter of Feb. 4, 1933, from Barth to Bonhoeffer, in which Barth acknowledges Bonhoeffer's review of Heim's book: "Many thanks . . . for sending me your Heim

article, and not least for your having taken up my cause so boldly and skilfully in it." (NRS, p. 205.)

27. Barth rightly calls this work "a theological miracle." Bonhoeffer submitted it for the degree in 1927, at the age of twenty-one. One of the few Bonhoeffer interpreters to emphasize his early theological personalism and its fundamental importance for his thought as a whole is Jürgen Moltmann, "The Lordship of Christ and Human Society," in Fuller, ed., *Two Studies in the Theology of Bonhoeffer*, pp. 29-35. Moltmann's discussion is an analysis of *The Communion of Saints,* in which, he says, "Bonhoeffer develops a theological personalism exhibiting undeniable affinities with the personalistic thought emerging in the early twentieth century in such philosophers as Dilthey, Buber, Grisebach, Gogarten, Rosenstock-Huessy, and others, though with a distinctive slant of his own." (Pp. 29-37.)

28. CS, pp. 22-37.

29. CS, p. 31. The phrase, of course, is Kierkegaard's and Barth's.

30. CS, p. 31.

31. The term "boundary" (*Grenze*) is one-half of a crucial dialectic in Bonhoeffer's thought; the other half is the word "center" (*Mitte*). God in Christ is the limit or boundary of man's existence, but he reveals himself as the boundary in the center of that existence. It is in the midst of human life that the true limit of our life encounters us. Hence the paradox that the real boundary is at the center. We shall see, in discussing Bonhoeffer's christology (Chapter Six), that a fundamental element in his interpretation of Christ is that he is the "center of life." In the prison writings Bonhoeffer strenuously resisted the common "religious" assumption that God meets us simply at the "boundaries" of life (i.e., in sin, emergency, suffering, and death); God in Christ meets us at the center, in the midst of life's fullness as well as in its crosses. Here, of course, Bonhoeffer uses "boundary" to mean the purely "horizontal" extremities of human life, not the confrontation with the "vertical" extremity (boundary) of God.

32. CS, p. 32.

33. CS, p. 33. Italics mine. See also p. 36: "On the epistemological and metaphysical path one never reaches the reality of the other. Reality cannot be derived, it is simply given, to be acknowledged, to be rejected, but never to be established by proofs, and it is given only to the moral person as a whole."

34. CC, p. 30. Phillips, commenting on *Christ the Center,* explains Bonhoeffer's personalist concept of transcendence in this way: "Personality is created only in confrontation with others, which involves both 'being-for' and 'being-free-from' the other person. Transcendence would thus seem to signify that quality which a person possesses by virtue of the fact that he *is* person, of simultaneously being-for and being-free-from the other." (*Christ for Us,* p. 78.)

35. CC, p. 31.

36. CS, p. 36.

36ª. CS, p. 37.

37. CS, pp. 33-34.

38. See NRS, p. 351; and Heim, *God Transcendent*, pp. 236-39. See also Bonhoeffer's "Concerning the Christian Idea of God": "For Christian thought, personality is the last limit of thinking and the ultimate reality. Only personality can limit me, because the other personality has its own demands and claims, its own law and will, which are different from me and which I cannot overcome as such. Personality is free and does not enter the general laws of my thinking." (*The Journal of Religion,* XII [April, 1932], p. 180.)

39. LT, p. 23.

40. LT, pp. 35-36.

41. LT, pp. 32-33.

42. LT, p. 34.

43. LT, p. 35.

44. LT, p. 36. Bonhoeffer's contrast between "pious, human fervour" and "the clear Word of God," is a manifestation of his distinction between "religion" and the Gospel which took on a radical form in the "Christianity without religion" project.

45. LT, p. 37.

46. LT, p. 101.

47. LT, p. 105.

48. LPP, p. 35. William Hamilton, in " 'The Letters are a particular Thorn' " (in Smith, ed., *World Come of Age*, pp. 131-60), speaks of Bonhoeffer's "deep respect for the inviolability of the inner life of another man." (P. 141.)

49. E, p. 188.

50. E, p. 192.

51. E, p. 197. See also LT, p. 70: "The 'it'-world is only an instrument in the hand of God for the purification of Christians from all self-centeredness and self-seeking. The work of the world can be done only where a person forgets himself, where he loses himself in a cause, in reality, the task, the 'it' . . . . But this can happen only where the Christian breaks through the 'it' to the 'Thou,' which is God, who bids him work and makes that work a means of liberation from himself." It is significant, however, that Bonhoeffer never allows the "I-Thou" world to be detached from the "It" world. In one of the essays which make up his *Ethics*, he criticizes a false kind of personalism, exemplified by Otto Dilschneider's book *Die Evangelische Tat* (Gütersloh: Bertelsmann, 1940), which severs the realm of persons from the realm of things and maintains that Christianity is concerned exclusively with persons in isolation from things. "The isolation of the person from the world of things," says Bonhoeffer, "is idealistic and not Christian. Christ does not detach the person from the world of things but from the world of sin; there is a great difference. There are no things which, on principle, stand outside the realm of persons and therefore outside the range of the divine commandments." (Pp. 291-92.) On this point existentialism and authentic biblical thought, both of which are prominent in Bonhoeffer's theology, are at one. For phenomenological thinkers such as Buber, Heidegger, and Heim, the "It" world is given together with the "Thou" world, and can never be separated from it. At the same time, the world of things is subordinate and instrumental to the world of persons. See Heim, *God Transcendent*, pp. 46-49.

52. E, p. 198.

53. See Moltmann, in *Two Studies in the Theology of Bonhoeffer*, p. 33: "The high point of Bonhoeffer's personalism is to be found in the community of Christ, in the church." We shall examine Bonhoeffer's ecclesiology in Chapter Seven.

54. CD, p. 117.

55. LPP, pp. 212-13.

56. LPP, p. 32. These essays, with the general title "After Ten Years," were not written in prison. Bonhoeffer wrote them around Christmas of 1942 and sent them to a few friends as a Christmas gift.

For an assessment of the continuing centrality of Bonhoeffer's early theological personalism in the "Christian humanism" of his last writings which parallels my own, see Moltmann, in *Two Studies in the Theology of Bonhoeffer*, p. 32: "As I see it, Bonhoeffer's last visions of the 'profound this-sidedness of Christianity' and of 'a world come of age' can be fully understood only when viewed against the background of his early personalism and the doctrine of sociological transcendence in the I-Thou relationship developed here. We encounter the Thou of God in the concrete Thou of social life." See also Ronald Gregor Smith's Introduction to *World Come of Age*, p. 21; "It is a humanism, certainly, of which he [Bonhoeffer] is speaking, the humanism of a liberated humanity in a world which has its own way to go in self-responsibility. But it is at the same time a humanism which is human only in the relation with others, a relation whose reality is both released and confirmed in the being of God for the world in his suffering in Christ."

57. See William Kuhns, *In Pursuit of Dietrich Bonhoeffer* (Dayton, Ohio: Pflaum Press, 1967), p. 8, where Kuhns writes that during his teen and university years Bonhoeffer "read the works of men like Dilthey and Simmel, Dostoevski and Soloviev; but Nietzsche was the most important." See Paul Tillich, *The Religious Situation*, trans. by H. Richard Niebuhr (New York: Holt, Rinehart & Winston, 1932), pp. 97-101. The whole book is an excellent picture of the revolution in European life which was taking place between 1900 and 1930. See also A. S. Duncan-Jones, *The Struggle for Religious Freedom in Germany* (London: Gollancz, 1938), pp. 61-62. This account of the youth movements notes the role of the church in directing these aspirations. It was Hitler, of course, who succeeded to a high degree in channeling the romanticism of the youth movement.

58. NRS, p. 44. Naturally Nietzsche's own writings should be consulted. His short work *The Antichrist* is particularly instructive in considering Bonhoeffer's world-affirmative Christianity. It is a violent criticism of the prevailing Christianity of Nietzsche's time as a destroyer of life, truth, and dignity. The difference between Bonhoeffer's interpretation of Nietzsche and what the Nazis made of him is worth recalling.

59. See E, p. 198.

60. E, pp. 142-43.

61. E, pp. 158-59.

62. In Godsey, ed., *Preface to Bonhoeffer*, p. 29. The whole essay is a robust assertion of the church's "this worldliness."

63. NRS, p. 47.

64. *The Place of Bonhoeffer*, pp. 14-15.

65. In Godsey, ed., *Preface to Bonhoeffer*, p. 34. The church fathers utilized Prometheus as a mythical type of Christ (Prometheus as the savior of mankind), but not as a type even of reconciled Christian man. It is interesting that Prometheus is a patron "saint and martyr" of that most dogmatic form of humanism, Marxism, precisely because he bravely defies the gods on behalf of the autonomy of man. See Hans-Gerhard Koch, *The Abolition of God: Materialistic Atheism and Christian Religion*, trans. by Robert W. Fenn (London: SCM Press, 1963), pp. 23-24.

Chapter Three: The Impact of Luther

1. See "Man in Contemporary Philosophy and Theology," NRS, pp. 61-62.

2. Holl's Luther studies comprise his *Gesammelte Aufsätze zur Kirchengeschichte*, Vol. I: *Luther* (Tübingen: Mohr, 1932). For his interpretation of Luther as "the religion of conscience," see the essay "Was verstand Luther unter Religion?" pp. 1-110. Rather remarkably, this detailed and exhaustive essay scarcely ever mentions the name, much less the role, of Christ in Luther's thinking.

3. Reinhold Seeberg, *Christliche Dogmatik* (Leipzig: A. Deichert, 1925).

4. *Text-book of the History of Doctrines*, trans. by Charles E. Hay (Grand Rapids: Baker Book House, 1958).

5. See some of their early correspondence in NRS, pp. 34-37.

6. AB, p. 105. See Seeberg, *The Fundamental Truths of the Christian Religion*, trans. by George E. Thomson and Clara Wallentin, ed. by W. D. Morrison (London: Crown, 1908), p. 324: "One who knows what he wills and wills what he knows is a moral character. The ideal of his life is his firm possession, and he himself has become a conscious organ of this ideal. One who consciously experiences and wills to experience the sovereignty of God, and who consciously subjects and wills to subject himself to it in faith and love is a Christian character. The Christian character is the highest form of a moral personality."

7. AB, pp. 106-7. See also LT, where Bonhoeffer makes the same point within the

context of the contrast between authentically Christian community and purely human communities: "The basis of all spiritual reality is the clear, manifest Word of God in Jesus Christ. The basis of all human reality is the dark, turbid urges and desires of the human mind. The essence of human community of spirit is darkness, 'for from within, out of the heart of men, proceed evil thoughts' (Mark 7:21). It is deep night that hovers over the sources of all human action, even over all noble and devout impulses." (P. 31.) Bonhoeffer's criticism of Seeberg is of course another manifestation of his suspicion of psychological introspection and "psychotherapy" and his personalist understanding of the impenetrability of the Thou.

8. In *Reformation Writings of Martin Luther*, trans. by Bertram Lee Woolf, I (London: Lutterworth, 1952), 356-79.

9. *Lectures on Romans*, trans. and ed. by Wilhelm Pauck, in *Library of Christian Classics*, Vol. XV (Philadelphia: Westminster Press, 1961).

10. Luther, *The Freedom of a Christian*, p. 373. Compare Bonhoeffer, LT, p. 22: "The death and the life of the Christian is not determined by his own resources; rather he finds both only in the Word that comes to him from the outside, in God's Word to him. The Reformers expressed it this way: Our righteousness is an 'alien righteousness,' a righteousness that comes from outside of us (*extra nos*). They were saying that the Christian is dependent on the Word of God spoken to him. . . . The Christian lives wholly by the truth of God's Word in Jesus Christ. If somebody asks him, Where is your salvation, your righteousness? he can never point to himself. He points to the Word of God in Jesus Christ, which assures him salvation and righteousness. . . . It can come only from the outside. In himself he is destitute and dead."

11. From Luther's "Introduction to the Commentary on the Epistle to the Romans," in J. Theodore Mueller's abridged translation of Luther's *Commentary on the Epistle to the Romans* (Grand Rapids: Zondervan Publishing House, 1954), p. xxii.

12. *Lectures on Romans*, pp. 12-13.

13. *Ibid.*, pp. 53-54.

14. E, p. 148.

15. E, p. 149.

16. E, p. 5.

17. E, p. 159. Phillips, *Christ for Us*, describes Luther's and Bonhoeffer's position on conscience in terms of the distinction between law and gospel: "The relationship of conscience to revelation is . . . that of Law to Gospel. Rather than a sphere reserved for the encounter of God with man, it is the place where man confronts only his prideful self." (P. 63.)

18. Luther, *Lectures on Romans*, p. 87.

19. *Ibid.*, p. 127.

20. *Ibid.*, p. 208.

21. CD, p. 35.

22. CD, p. 40. See Regin Prenter, "Bonhoeffer and the Young Luther" (originally published in the four-vol. collection of essays on Bonhoeffer, *Die Mündige Welt*, Vol. IV [Munich: Kaiser Verlag, 1955-63], trans. by R. Gregor Smith *et al.*, and included among the essays in Smith, *World Come of Age*, pp. 161-81), p. 180: "For Luther . . . faith is a real bodily participation in the living Christ which engages the believer in a real struggle with the enemies of Christ. . . . Faith *is* discipleship."

23. CD, p. 43.

24. GS I, 117. Trans. mine. Cf. NRS, p. 139.

25. GS I, 145. Trans. mine. The publ. English trans. in NRS omits part of the German text: see p. 162.

26. GS I, 146. Trans. mine. Cf. NRS, p. 162.

27. GS I, 146. Trans. mine. Cf. NRS, p. 163.

28. NRS, pp. 163-64. Italics mine. See also a letter of Bonhoeffer to his friend Helmut Rössler on December 25, 1932, in GS I, 63. Here Bonhoeffer describes the church's

authority as utterly unique *(eine ganz andere Autorität)*, because it is an authority which takes the risk of speaking "concrete commands" solely "in faith in the forgiveness of sins." See also in this connection "Acht Thesen zum Vortrag in Cernohorske Kupele," in GS I, an ecumenical document which Bonhoeffer wrote in July of 1932. "Every one of the church's commandments," he declares, "is grounded solely in the faith of the church in the forgiveness of sins." (P. 160.)

29. See LPP, p. 29: ". . . free responsibility . . . depends on a God who demands responsible action in a bold venture of faith, and who promises forgiveness and consolation to the man who becomes a sinner in that venture."

30. See Ebeling, *Word and Faith*, p. 107.

31. LPP, p. 208.

32. In Smith, ed., *World Come of Age*, pp. 161-81. The quotation is from p. 161.

33. *Ibid.*, p. 168.

34. Phillips, *Christ for Us in the Theology of Dietrich Bonhoeffer*, pp. 39-44, 62-63.

35. See *ibid.*, esp. pp. 170-72.

36. *Ibid.*, pp. 95-105.

37. Kuhns, *In Pursuit of Dietrich Bonhoeffer*, p. 23. He adds later that "wherever Bonhoeffer consciously moved from Luther's theology, he would insist that Luther would have done the same" (p. 88). Bonhoeffer remarks in a letter to his parents from prison, written on Reformation Sunday of 1943: "As long as a hundred years ago Kierkegaard said that today Luther would say the opposite of what he said then. I think he was right—with some reservations." (LPP, p. 71.)

38. Of Kierkegaard's explicit influence on Bonhoeffer we have very little knowledge. Like all the Neo-Reformation theologians, Bonhoeffer knew and read Kierkegaard's writings. But beyond brief and occasional references which merely assure us that Bonhoeffer did indeed probably know Kierkegaard's thought well, we have nothing to go on. He mentions Kierkegaard in following his criticism of philosophical idealism (AB, p. 25), his concept of our contemporaneousness with the biblical Christ (CC, p. 74), and his idea of the divine incognito in Christ (CC, p. 113) —Kierkegaardian themes which all the Neo-Reformation theologians shared. As we might expect from his overarching concern for sociality and the Christian community, Bonhoeffer criticized Kierkegaard for his individualism and consequent neglect of interpersonal relationships and the church (CS, p. 212) —an inadequacy which Bonhoeffer found repeated by the early dialectical theologians and which others have familiarly observed in more recent evaluations of Kierkegaard.

Of Bonhoeffer's few references to Kierkegaard in *Letters and Papers* the most important appears in a discussion of whether the category of "blessing" (health, good fortune, worldly happiness, etc.) in the Old Testament is replaced in the New only by the cross and accordingly "spiritualized" (LPP, pp. 205-6). Bonhoeffer claims that Kierkegaard interpreted the New Testament in this way, and criticizes him for his unhealthily ascetical tendencies at that point. The divorcing of cross and blessing, with the focus only on the former as the lot of the Christian, is unbiblical and "religious," because it subjectivizes Christian existence and isolates it from the wholeness of life. Bonhoeffer counters this "methodism," as he calls it, with his concept of Christian existence as *metanoia*: simply placing oneself with thanksgiving at God's disposal in the midst of life, in both blessing and suffering. We shall discuss *metanoia* as Bonhoeffer works it out in the prison writings in the section of Chapter Nine entitled "The 'Religionless' Christian." Bonhoeffer's criticism of Kierkegaard's "asceticism" is not entirely just, as the present discussion attempts to show.

39. Bonhoeffer remarks in the prison writings that "As long as a hundred years ago Kierkegaard said that today Luther would say the opposite of what he said then. I think he was right—with some reservations." (LPP, p. 70) The discussion preceding this statement, which appears in a letter written on Reformation Day of 1943, makes it fairly clear that Bonhoeffer means that if Luther could have returned in the nine-

teenth or the twentieth century and seen what had happened to his central ideas, he would have had to switch his emphasis to those facets of his interpretation of the totality of Christian existence which had precisely required *de*-emphasis in the sixteenth century. Both Kierkegaard and Bonhoeffer sought to do just that.

40. *The Attack upon "Christendom,"* trans. by Walter Lowrie (Boston: Beacon Press, 1960), p. 27.

41. The same mistake has been made with the Bonhoeffer of the prison writings, but in the opposite direction: i.e., to regard him as "this-worldly" in an undialectical sense, by divorcing his robust life affirmation from his remarks about the Christian's disciplined participation in the sufferings of Christ in the world. See the sections on "The Church in a World 'Come of Age'" and "Bonhoeffer's Spirituality" in Chapter Seven; and the section on "The 'Religionless' Christian" in Chapter Nine.

42. Bonhoeffer, like many other interpreters of Kierkegaard, did not adequately appreciate the "worldly," humanistic side of the dialectic of Kierkegaard's thought and life. For two revealing vignettes from Kierkegaard's life, see Robert Bretall, ed., *A Kierkegaard Anthology* (New York: Modern Library, 1959), pp. 173-74. Kierkegaard's "ascetical" tendencies are largely to be accounted for biographically, in the melancholy side of his personality and in his intense belief in his unique "calling" which under the pressure of events became for him a martyrdom.

43. *Training in Christianity,* trans. by Walter Lowrie (Princeton: Princeton University Press, 1960), p. 71.

44. *Fear and Trembling,* trans. by Walter Lowrie (Garden City, N.Y.: Doubleday & Co., 1954), pp. 49-51.

45. See n. 38 above, and the discussion of Bonhoeffer's idea of *metanoia* in Chapter Nine. It seems to me that Kierkegaard was closer to Bonhoeffer at this point than Bonhoeffer thought, fully granting the unmistakable tendency of Kierkegaard's dialectic of Christian existence to break apart in his later years on the side of cross and suffering.

46. See LPP, p. 162, and the discussion of the "polyphony" of the "religionless" Christian in Chapter Nine.

47. *Works of Love,* trans. by Howard and Edna Hong (London: Collins, 1962), p. 269. See also *Concluding Unscientific Postscript,* trans. by David Swenson, completed and ed. by Walter Lowrie (Princeton: Princeton University Press, 1941), p. 437: "Every human being is gloriously constituted, but what ruins so many is, among other things, . . . this wretched tittle-tattle between man and man about that which should be suffered and matured in silence, this confession before men instead of before God, this hearty communication between this man and that about what ought to be secret and exist only before God in secrecy, this impatient craving for intermediary consolation."

48. *Works of Love,* p. 35. A very stimulating recent article which argues cogently that Kierkegaard, contrary to the usual interpretation, possessed a very positive concept of interpersonal relationships, is Stanley Moore's "Religion as the True Humanism: Reflections on Kierkegaard's Social Philosophy" (*Journal of the American Academy of Religion,* XXXVII, 1, March 1969, pp. 15-25). Moore's article reveals close parallels between the way Kierkegaard and Bonhoeffer grounded human I-Thou relationships in the mediation of Christ.

Chapter Four: Karl Barth and the Nature of Theology

1. Chiefly in the areas of christology and ecclesiology, which we shall examine in Chapters Six and Seven. The "religionless" Bonhoeffer came to see an even more fundamental deficiency in Barth's theology: his failure to carry through the theological revolution he had begun, by interpreting it in contemporary terms. On this, see Chapter Five, "Revelation and Religion."

2. NRS, p. 120.

3. NRS, p. 27. See also Kuhns, *In Pursuit of Dietrich Bonhoeffer*, p. 40: "It is questionable whether Bonhoeffer ever felt a kinship with any man more profoundly than that which he felt with Barth."

4. NRS, p. 121.

5. NRS, p 204.
   Clark, 1936), 30-33, 176-77.

6. See Barth, *Church Dogmatics*, I/1, trans. by G. T. Thomson (Edinburgh: T & T.

7. Letter of October 24, 1933, in NRS, p. 234.

8. Letter of November 20, 1933, NRS, p. 240.

9. NRS, p. 239.

10. As we shall see when we come to discuss Bonhoeffer's interpretation of Christian ethics in Chapter Nine, Barth has paid high tribute to Bonhoeffer's treatment of this important theme.

11. See some of Bonhoeffer's extensive correspondence with Dr. Bell in NRS, pp. 254-60, 265-78. Bell labored unsparingly on behalf of both the German Church and the German Resistance prior to and throughout the war; he last saw Bonhoeffer in Stockholm in 1942. For an account of Dr. Bell's work, see his *The Church and Humanity, 1939-1946* (London: Longmans, 1946).

12. *Anselm: Fides Quaerens Intellectum*, trans. by Ian W. Robertson (London: SCM Press, 1960). Bonhoeffer mentions reading it in a letter of December 25, 1931, to his friend Erwin Sutz: "Barth's book about Anselm is a great delight to me; you must read it when you have time. He shows the countless academic cripples, once and for all, that he really does know how to interpret and still remain sovereign." (NRS, pp. 140-41.)

13. In one of the prison letters Bonhoeffer asks Eberhard Bethge if he can send him Vol. II of the *Dogmatics*. In a footnote Bethge says, "*Church Dogmatics*, Vol. II, Parts 1 and 2, sent from Switzerland without title and cover, as they were banned in Germany." (LPP, p. 114.)

14. See, e.g., "The Theology of Crisis," NRS, pp. 361-72; "Concerning the Christian Idea of God," *The Journal of Religion*, XII (April, 1932); and Bonhoeffer's review of Heim's *God Transcendent*, NRS, pp. 347-59. Kuhns, *In Pursuit of Dietrich Bonhoeffer*, remarks: "Bonhoeffer later was to make a not inconsiderable number of reservations about Barth's dogmatic interpretation of Scripture. Yet he remained faithful to the major Barthian themes: the centrality of Christ, the entirely *given* character of revelation, and expecially man's responsibility to listen to the true God, and not to fashion his own version of God." (Pp. 13-14.)

15. See, e.g., "Man in Contemporary Philosophy and Theology," NRS, pp. 50-69; AB; and of course the important criticisms of Barth in LPP.

16. Prime examples are Bonhoeffer's christology, his ecclesiology, his ethics, his critique of religion, and his conception of theological reconstruction, all of which will be discussed in succeeding chapters.

17. Eberhard Bethge describes it this way in "The Challenge of Dietrich Bonhoeffer's Life and Theology" in *Chicago Theol. Sem. Register*, LI (February 1961), 7: "Usually the one was just busy with a topic which the other had left behind or had not yet arrived at. Bonhoeffer, being much younger, did not get his answers from Barth when he asked for them and did not get the praise he might have liked in time."

18. It goes without saying, of course, that these contrasts are not mutually exclusive; they represent dominant tendencies in the thought of the two men.

19. Karl Barth, *Church Dogmatics*, I/2, 766.

20. *Ibid.*, I/2, 772.

21. *Ibid.*, I/1, 11.

22. *Ibid.*, I/1, 304.

23. *Ibid.*, I/1, 3.

24. *Ibid.*, I/2, 872.

25. *Ibid.*, I/1, 7.

26. *Ibid.,* I/1, 18.
27. *Ibid.,* I/2, 823.
28. *Ibid.,* I/1, 18.
29. *Ibid.,* I/1, 45.
30. *Ibid.,* I/1, 46-47.
31. *Ibid.,* I/1, 304.
32. *Ibid.,* I/1, 330.
33. *Ibid.,* I/2, 816.
34. *Ibid.,* I/2, 816-17.
35. *Ibid.,* I/2, 821.
36. *Ibid.,* I/2, 822.
37. *Ibid.,* I/1, 30.
38. *Ibid.,* I/1, 31.
39. *Ibid.,* I/1, 39.
40. *Ibid.,* I/1, 41.
41. *Ibid.,* I/1, 321.
42. *Ibid.,* I/1, 322.
43. *Ibid.,* I/1, 31.
44. *Ibid.,* I/1, 33.
45. *Ibid.,* I/2, 123.

Chapter Five: Revelation and Religion

1. LPP, p. 152.
2. LPP, p. 153.
3. LPP, pp. 153-54.
4. See Seeberg's concept of the religious a priori in his *Die christliche Dogmatik,* I, 104: "The *a priori* is simply the intrinsic capacity . . . for becoming aware of the being and activity of the supramundane God, and accordingly for the receiving of the content of his revelation, as divine, into the soul." Under a variety of forms, early twentieth-century liberal theology was dominated by the idea of a religious a priori, the existence of which would put the whole religious enterprise on as firm a footing as Kant had put the epistemological and ethical spheres with his analysis of their a priori dimension. The classic work on the subject is Rudolf Otto's *The Idea of the Holy,* trans. by John W. Harvey (New York: Oxford University Press, 1950), esp., pp. 112-42, 175-78. See also Max Scheler, *On the Eternal in Man,* trans. by Bernard Noble, (London: SCM Press, 1960), esp. pp. 161-331.
5. LPP, p. 156. Bethge, "The Challenge . . . ," in *Chicago Theol. Sem. Register,* LI (February, 1961), sees *four* elements in Bonhoeffer's conception of "religion": (1) individualistic, (2) metaphysical, (3) divorced from the rest of life, and (4) having a *deus ex machina* apprehension of God. However (3) and (4) are readily subsumed under (1) and (2) respectively in Bonhoeffer's total analysis of "religion," and will be treated in this way in our discussion. I am borne out in this interpretation by Mr. Clifford Green in a perceptive article entitled "Bonhoeffer's Concept of Religion," *Union Seminary Quarterly Review* (November 1963), 17.
6. The title of an essay in *Essays in Liberality,* pp. 171-76.
7. NRS, p. 88.
8. NRS, p. 117.
9. WF, p. 230.
10. WF, pp. 230-31.
11. GS II, 420. Bethge's trans. in "The Challenge of Dietrich Bonhoeffer's Life and Theology," p. 29.
12. LPP, p. 156. By "thinking theologically" Bonhoeffer seems to mean (following Barth) letting one's thoughts be determined by the biblical witness as a whole and exclusively, not bringing to the scriptural data any sort of a priori notion of what

its "essence" really is (as with the liberals and Bultmann), but letting it speak for itself on the matter. The liberal abridgment of the gospel in terms of ethicism and Bultmann's existentialist reduction both "jump the gun," as it were, and therefore fall short of genuinely theological thinking.

13. LPP, p. 156.

14. LPP, pp. 181-82.

15. Godsey, *The Theology of Dietrich Bonhoeffer,* pp. 278-79.

16. Ebeling, *Word and Faith,* p. 103; see also pp. 139-41.

17. Bultmann, "New Testament and Mythology," in *Kerygma and Myth,* p. 16. Italics mine.

18. Bultmann, *Jesus Christ and Mythology* (New York: Charles Scribner's Sons, 1958), p. 18.

19. "New Testament and Mythology," in *Kerygma and Myth,* p. 10. Italics mine.

20. *Ibid.,* p. 10.

21. *Theology of the New Testament,* 2 vols., trans. by Kendrick Grobel (New York: Charles Scribner's Sons, 1951, 1955).

22. See *Jesus Christ and Mythology,* Chapter V, "The Meaning of God as Acting," pp. 60-85.

23. See Ebeling, *Word and Faith,* pp. 139-40. See Bultmann, "The Idea of God and Modern Man," in Smith, ed., *World Come of Age,* p. 265: *"The transcendent* is to be sought and can be found not above or beyond the world, but *in the midst of this world."* Whether Bultmann's understanding of the nature of faith remains focused on this idea, however, is quite another question. See n. 24 below.

24. See Paul M. van Buren, *The Secular Meaning of the Gospel* (New York: The Macmillan Co., 1963), pp. 57-79, for a criticism of the retention of a concept of transcendence by Bultmann and his students which remains "religious" and therefore meaningless to secular man. While van Buren has developed Bonhoeffer's suggestions in a manner different from Bonhoeffer's own, it is likely that Bonhoeffer would have agreed with his remarks about Bultmann.

Bultmann genuinely intends to understand the "eschatological existence" of the Christian in concrete ethical terms. But his language and conceptual scheme constantly suggest a fundamentally "other-worldly" orientation which is absent in Bonhoeffer's tenacious attention to the man Jesus. The following remarks from Bultmann's programmatic essay are typical: "The authentic life . . . would be a life based on unseen, intangible realities. . . . This is what the New Testament means by 'life after the Spirit' or 'life in faith.'" (P. 19.) "Such a life spells deliverance from all worldly, tangible objects, leading to complete detachment from the world and thus to freedom. . . . This detachment from the world is something quite different from asceticism. It means preserving a distance from the world and dealing with it in a spirit of 'as if not.' . . . Everything in the world has become indifferent and unimportant." (P. 20.) Taken as a whole, Bultmann's perspective expresses decisive features even of "secular" Christian existence which are present in Bonhoeffer, e.g., the notion of faith freeing a person for interpersonal responsibilities. But Bonhoeffer would have been very uncomfortable with Bultmann's language, especially talk about "detachment from" and "indifference to" the world. Bonhoeffer's whole understanding of Christ's utter involvement in the world and the Christian life patterned after that involvement went about describing the phenomenon of faith quite differently. Both theologians understand the Christian life as a dialectic of faith and worldliness, but Bonhoeffer succeeds better in preserving the intimate relationship between the two than does Bultmann.

25. See Ebeling, *Word and Faith,* p. 139.

26. See Ronald Gregor Smith, *The New Man: Christianity and Man's Coming of Age* (London: SCM Press, 1956), esp. pp. 85-112; and Ebeling, *Word and Faith,* 139-40. See also Gerhard Krause, "Dietrich Bonhoeffer und Rudolf Bultmann," in *Zeit und Geshichte,* ed. by Erich Dinkler (Tübingen: Mohr [Siebeck], 1964), pp. 439-

60; and Götz Harbsmaier, "Die 'nicht-religiöse Interpretation biblischer Begriffe' bei Bonhoeffer und die Entmythologisierung," in *Die mündige Welt*, II, 74-91.

27. Bonhoeffer in a letter of March 25, 1942: "Now as to Bultmann, I am one of those who welcomed his essay ['New Testament and Mythology']; not because I agreed with it, I regret the twofold point of departure in it (the argument from John 1:14 and from the radio ought not to be confused, though I consider the second too to be an argument—it's just that the separation must be clearer). To this extent I have perhaps remained a pupil of Harnack's. To put it crudely, Bultmann has let the cat out of the bag, not only for himself, but for very many (the Liberal cat out of the Confessing Church bag), and this is what pleases me. He has dared to say what many repress in themselves (I include myself), without having overcome it. In this way he has done intellectual purity and integrity a service. The pharisaism of faith which on the other hand is being offered by many of the brothers strikes me as unfortunate. Now we have to speak and to answer. I should be glad to speak with Bultmann about it, and expose myself to the draught which blows from his direction. But then the window will have to be shut again. Otherwise the susceptible will too easily catch cold." (Quoted by Ronald Gregor Smith in the Introduction to *World Come of Age*, p. 11.) Bonhoeffer's appreciation of Bultmann here is significant, but not as significant as "liberal" interpreters like Smith and Phillips would like to make it. In the first place, Bonhoeffer's remarks about Bultmann must be seen together with the remarks in the prison letters, and in the light of his whole theological outlook. Secondly, the statements in this letter of 1942 are surely ambiguous and bear more than one interpretation. It was a lifelong characteristic of Bonhoeffer's to admire "intellectual purity and integrity," and his mention of Harnack is doubly significant for that reason. But Bonhoeffer's admiration for Bultmann's honesty and the way he had laid bare some fundamental issues about the meaning of the New Testament in the modern world, concerns with which Bonhoeffer himself was increasingly preoccupied in 1942 and thereafter, by no means committed him to Bultmann's presuppositions and method for dealing with them. Nothing in the letter suggests that it did.

28. Bultmann's approval of Smith's exploration of "religionless Christianity" as in line with his own analyses was first made known to me by Prof. Smith in a conversation in Dec. 1962.

29. See Ogden, *Christ Without Myth* (New York: Harper & Row, 1961); and Buri, "Entmythologisierung oder Entkerygmatisierung der Theologie," in *Kergyma und Mythos*, Vol. II, ed. by Hans Bartsch (Hamburg-Volksdorf: Herbert Reich, 1952).

30. LPP, p. 180.

31. See, e.g., Tillich, *The Religious Situation*, p. xxiii: "There is nothing that is not in some way the expression of the religious situation."

32. Italics mine.

33. LPP, p. 182. Italics mine.

34. Tillich, *Systematic Theology*, 3 vols. (Chicago: University of Chicago Press, 1951-63), I, 6.

35. LPP, p. 175. See Phillips, *Christ for Us*, p. 207: "Bonhoeffer is certain that such a methodology [as Tillich represents] puts revelation in the position of being an 'answer' presupposed by the question asked by 'man,' out of his supposedly universal situation of existential estrangement and apart from revelation. . . .

"To picture man as the questioning and questionable creature, Bonhoeffer is saying, is to picture him as essentially *religious*. . . ."

36. See Tillich, *The Courage to Be* (New Haven: Yale, University Press, 1952), pp. 182-90; and *The New Being* (New York: Charles Scribner's Sons, 1955), pp. 15-24.

37. *Honest to God* (Philadelphia: Westminster Press, 1963).

38. *Ibid.*, p. 47.

39. *Ibid.*, p. 56.

40. *Ibid.*, p. 76.

41. LPP, p. 180.
42. See Heim, *God Transcendent*, esp. pp. xvii-xix, 3-27, 209-26; and *Christian Faith and Natural Science* (New York: Harper & Row, 1953), pp. 174-249.
43. LPP, p. 180. See also Bonhoeffer's early review of Heim's *God Transcendent*, in which the young theologian severely criticized Heim's use of the concept of despair from a Barthian perspective (NRS, pp. 353-56). The following is an example, taken from *God Transcendent*, of Heim's delineation of the either/or in terms of "despair or Jesus": "The emergence of the question about God must result *either* in despair, when in the place which is now our supreme concern we see nothing but a yawning void into which we are precipitated; *or* in fervent thanksgiving because, falling into the abyss, we find ourselves in the arms of a Power which wraps us round." (P. 218.)
44. *Christian Faith and Natural Science*, p. 34.
45. *Ibid.*, pp. 38, 217. Heim's appeal to the New Testament for this doctrine of the inner ego stands in direct contrast to Bonhoeffer's holistic interpretation of the biblical anthropology: "For the New Testament . . . the ego is . . . something other than this human body, and this makes possible what would have been inconceivable for primitive man, namely the reincarnation of the ego in a new body." (P. 120.)
46. *Ibid.*, p. 219.
47. A more recent essay of Heim's with the pertinent and revealing title "Christian Faith and the Growing Power of Secularism" (in Walter Leibrecht, ed., *Religion and Culture: Essays in Honor of Paul Tillich* [New York: Harper & Row, 1959], pp. 181-95), manifests both his intellectual either/or and his traditional pietist-evangelical call to oppose the secular as the power of darkness: "Man must choose one of two possibilities: the autonomy of the world or the absoluteness of God." (P. 187.) "All the demonic enemies of Christianity are now forming a solid front. A tremendous battle is being prepared between the demonic powers and the message of the Cross. A great hour has come. Perhaps it is the last hour." (P. 195.)
48. LPP, p. 180.
49. Barth, *Epistle to the Romans*, trans. by Edwyn C. Hoskyns from the 6th German ed. (New York: Oxford University Press, 1933), p. 10.
50. *Ibid.*, pp. 37, 47, 53.
51. *Ibid.*, p. 242.
52. *Ibid.*, 236.
53. *Ibid.*, p. 40.
54. *Ibid.*, p. 78.
55. *Ibid.*, p. 185.
56. *Ibid.*, p. 113.
57. *Ibid.*, p. 236.
58. *Church Dogmatics*, I/2, 315-25.
59. *Romans*, p. 231.
60. *Ibid.*, p. 268.
61. *Ibid.*, p. 184.
62. *Ibid.*, p. 129.
63. *Ibid.*, p. 183.
64. *Church Dogmatics*, I/2, 280-361.
65. CS, p. 94.
66. AB, p. 176.
67. LPP, p. 181.
68. LPP, p. 157. Phillips, *Christ for Us*, observes: "If 'Positivism of revelation' means nothing else, it is at least a judgment of any theology which refuses to give more than a passing glance to man in his secular condition and to the question of relating the revelation which entered history in the culture, thought forms, and language of the Middle East in the first century to this man. Unless this problem is confronted, Christianity can scarcely free itself of ideological overtones, imperialism, possessiveness,

and ultimate trust in theological expressions rather than in the God to whom they direct us." (P. 170.)

Undoubtedly, however, the most learned and comprehensive analysis of Bonhoeffer's concept of "positivism of revelation" and its relation to Barth's theology is Regin Prenter's "Dietrich Bonhoeffer and Karl Barth's Positivism of Revelation," in Smith, ed., *World Come of Age*, pp. 93-130. Prenter's ably reasoned affirmation of the close relation between the theologies of Barth and Bonhoeffer is one with which I am almost wholly in sympathy as the proper perspective on the latter's thought. Prenter rightly states: "Nowhere in his correspondence with Eberhard Bethge does Bonhoeffer criticize Barth's positivism of revelation without first of all praising him in glowing terms as the only one who has made a radical break with the 'religionizing' of the gospel and thereby has uncompromisingly rejected the secularization of the revelation of God in liberal theology." (P. 96.)

According to Prenter, "Bonhoeffer uses the word positivism in order to show the unrelatedness of the statements of faith. Because they are unrelated, they are reduced to mere data (*posita*) and are to be accepted without any further elucidation." (P. 95.) Bonhoeffer saw as the source of this positivism a tendency in Barth to regard "God *vis-à-vis* the world, constituted by him as creator and redeemer, . . . as a negation of the world. . . . The consequence then must be a positivism of revelation. Then all the truths of revelation confront the whole worldly life of men without meaning. This unrelatedness of revelation to the world makes all individual features of revelation appear on the same level, whether it is the virgin birth, the trinity or something else.

"The religionless interpretation of theological concepts, which Bonhoeffer misses in Barth, would, on the contrary, regard the encounter of God with the world not as negation, but as Lordship. And the Lordship of God thoroughly excludes any unrelatedness between revelation and the world." (P. 98.) Prenter goes on to argue that, while negation is only one side, and definitely the "overcome" side, of Barth's dialectic, the development of his theology upon the presuppositions of actualism, analogism, and universalism places his affirmation of man and the world on a different plane from Bonhoeffer's, a plane which the latter believed inadequate as an understanding of the gospel and its relation to modern man (see pp. 105-30).

69. Tillich, *Systematic Theology*, I, 7.

70. Barth, *The Humanity of God*, trans. by John Newton Thomas and Thomas Wieser (Richmond, Va.: John Knox Press, 1960), pp. 58-59.

71. *Ibid.*, p. 59.

72. *Ibid.*, p. 59. Contrast this statement, however, with one similar in language but diametrically opposed in intent, from the early, "religionless" *Epistle to the Romans:* "A wide reading of contemporary secular literature—especially of newspapers!—is . . . recommended to any one desirous of understanding the Epistle to the Romans." (P. 425.)

In the famous Letter to Landessuperintendent P. W. Herrenbrück of December 21, 1952, discussing Bonhoeffer's prison writings, Barth expresses himself in a more puzzled and chastened manner concerning the charge of "revelation-positivism": ". . . I have certainly been disturbed by the question of when and where I have asked anyone to 'take' or 'leave' the virgin birth . . . . But I am somewhat embarrassed by the thought that so sensible and well-meaning a man as Bonhoeffer somehow remembered my books . . . in terms of this enigmatic expression. The hope remains that in heaven at least he has not reported about me to *all* the angels (including the church fathers, etc.) with just this expression. But perhaps I have indeed on occasion behaved and expressed myself 'positivistically,' and if this is so then Bonhoeffer's recollections have brought it to light." (In Smith, ed., *World Come of Age*, p. 90.) The discussion of differences in Barth's and Bonhoeffer's approaches to Scripture in Chapter Eight will attempt to clarify to some extent "the question of when and where" Barth has tended to ask us "to 'take' or 'leave' the virgin birth."

73. *Church Dogmatics*, I/1, 30.

74. *Ibid.*, I/1, 33.
75. E, p. 192.

Chapter Six: The Humanity of God in Christ

1. Bonhoeffer, "Concerning the Christian Idea of God," in *The Journal of Religion*, XII (April 1932), p. 104.
2. *Creation and Fall*, p. 43.
3. E, p. 192.
4. LPP, p. 209.
5. Ebeling, *Word and Faith*, p. 106. Phillips, *Christ for Us*, rightly points out that "practically all" of Bonhoeffer's interpreters have recognized that christology is the central feature of his thought (p. 27). He goes on to claim it as the guiding principle of his own study of Bonhoeffer: "A liberated and many-sided but always *concrete* Christology therefore becomes our guide to the development of Bonhoeffer's theology." (P. 28.)
6. *Word and Faith*, p. 106.
7. Despite lingering traces of the early dialecticism, which we shall note below.
8. But that was sufficient to indicate to Bonhoeffer where Barth was heading theologically, and to evoke corresponding criticism in *Letters and Papers*. Bonhoeffer criticized the early, "dialectical" Barth for an inadequate christology; the later, "dogmatic" Barth for what Bonhoeffer called "revelation-positivism."
9. AB, p. 20.
10. AB, p. 22. See also the succinct discussion of Barth's Kantianism in Bonhoeffer's lecture "The Theology of Crisis," NRS, pp. 367-72.
11. AB, pp. 43-44. See also pp. 80-86, 90-91, 101-3, and 135-37, for Bonhoeffer's full critique of Barth's formalism.
12. Godsey, *The Theology of Dietrich Bonhoeffer*, p. 64. See Barth's *Epistle to the Romans* for the most thoroughgoing and rigorous presentation of his actualism.
13. Bethge, "The Challenge . . . ," in *Chicago Theol. Sem. Register*, LI (February 1961), p. 9. See also Regin Prenter, "Bonhoeffer and Barth's Positivism of Revelation," in Smith, ed., *World Come of Age*, p. 106: "Actualism in relation to revelation means that God is in the world of man only in each specific act of his self-revelation. In an actualistic concept of revelation there is no room for a *being* of the revealed or the revealer in the world." And elsewhere: ". . . God's word cannot have an extension in time, a history as such. It can only touch the world of sinful man in the form of a *futurum aeternum*, which breaks into man's existence each time anew, in the act of God's self-revelation." (P. 109.) Prenter argues that this was and remained Barth's epistemological approach to revelation.
14. *Church Dogmatics*, I/1, 44. See also p. 3: "the essence of the Church . . . is Jesus Christ."
15. *Ibid.*, I/1, 371.
16. See Barth's statement that "there is no Word of God without a physical event. . . . We are reminded of that finally and most highly of all by the corporeality of the man Jesus Christ." (*Ibid.*, I/1, 151.)
17. *Ibid.*, I/1, 369. See Phillips, *Christ for Us*, p. 165: "Barth constructs his Christology in such a way that the direction *always* remains that of above to below, divine to human. . . ."
18. *Church Dogmatics*, I/1, 132.
19. NRS, p. 33. We shall later examine Bonhoeffer's own understanding of the historicity of Jesus later in this chapter.
20. "Act and Being," in Marty, ed., *The Place of Bonhoeffer*, p. 90. The clear *intention* of the "dogmatic" Barth, as we saw in Chapter Four, was to reject decisively all talk about "divine possibilities" and to concentrate wholly upon the actualities of what God has in fact done in Christ. He tended, however, in the material develop-

ment of his approach, to fail to take this principle with utter seriousness. See Herbert Hartwell, *The Theology of Karl Barth: An Introduction* (Philadelphia: Westminster Press, 1964), pp. 25-26.

21. See *Church Dogmatics*, II/2, trans. by G. W. Bromiley *et al.* (Edinburgh: T. & T. Clark, 1957), 60-67, 110-11.

22. AB, pp. 90-91. Already in this early writing Bonhoeffer states that God in Christ "is there" *(ist da)*, foreshadowing the decisive Christological formula of *Letters and Papers*, in which he affirms that Christ "is there for others" ("für andere da ist").

23. Bethge, "The Challenge . . . ," in *Chicago Theol. Sem. Register*, LI (February 1961), p. 9. See also Phillips, *Christ for Us*, p. 172: "The Lutheran Christology of condescension, the conviction that after all has been said, *finitium capax infiniti*, remained the central strand of Bonhoeffer's theology throughout his lifetime." Apropos of our discussion in Chapter Five, Phillips adds that "Bonhoeffer accepted the Lutheran [christological] tradition with all its risks, certain that the alternative cannot but lead to 'positivism of revelation.' "

24. Bethge, "The Challenge . . . ," p. 10. See Phillips, *Christ for Us*, pp. 68-69.

25. Barth, *Church Dogmatics*, I/1, 252.

26. *Ibid.*, I/1, 466.

27. Bethge, "The Challenge . . . ," p. 7.

28. *Ibid.*, p. 8.

29. Barth, *The Epistle to the Romans*, p. 35.

30. CC, p. 28.

31. CC, p. 30.

32. In terms of the Barthian theological method which Bonhoeffer in a profound sense employed more rigorously than Barth himself, we might also say that "How?" questions deal with *possibilities*, which is theologically illegitimate. "Who?" questions are genuinely theological, since they deal with *actualities*, with the historical witness to God's self-disclosure in Christ.

33. CC, p. 32.

34. CC, p. 46.

35. CC, pp. 47-48.

36. See LPP, p. 209, where Bonhoeffer calls Jesus' " 'being there for others' . . . the experience of transcendence." Happily, the new revised English edition of *Letters and Papers from Prison* translates Bonhoeffer's phrase *"für andere da sein"* literally. The original and long-used translation rendered the phrase "concern for others," which was quite misleading. It suggested that Bonhoeffer was speaking in "purely ethical" terms, whereas his language is theological and ontological. He was quite clearly thinking in terms of "being" and not just of ethical attitude. A clause which appears a few sentences later leaves the reader in no doubt that Bonhoeffer's orientation is more than "ethical": " . . . our relation to God is a new life in 'existence for others,' through participation in the being of Jesus" [*unser Verhältnis zu Gott ist ein neues Leben im "Dasein-für-andere," in der Teilnahme am Sein Jesu*]. (LPP, p. 210.) Bonhoeffer is saying here that the very being *(Sein)* of Jesus is "being-there" or "being-available" to others, not simply that Jesus is "concerned for others." A man might be concerned for others and also be many other things. We have here an ethical interpretation of Jesus which is more profound than a "purely" ethical interpretation, because for Bonhoeffer the ethical is always at bottom the theological or (in philosophical language) the ontological (see the whole of his *Ethics*). Just as the Christ of *Christ the Center* is not merely ontically but ontologically *pro me*, so likewise the Christ of *Letters and Papers* is not "ethically" but essentially the one who exists entirely for others, i.e., for man.

See also Phillips, *Christ for Us*, p. 197: "The 'haveability' of Christ, his being *'pro-me,'* his 'taking form in the world'—all of Bonhoeffer's previous Christological formulations which stressed the real presence and availability of Christ to faith—. . . culminated in the formula: Christ, the man for others." Bethge, in "Bonhoeffer's

Christology and His 'Religionless Christianity'" (in Vorkink, ed., *Bonhoeffer in a World Come of Age*, pp. 46-72), writes that while "'Jesus, the man for others' is in fact a new christological title for Bonhoeffer. . . . It is faithful to the tradition, non-speculative, relational, and central for all being and reality." (P. 69.)

37. CC, p. 62.

38. CC, p. 71. In a footnote to the English translation of Bonhoeffer's christology lectures, the translator remarks that "Bonhoeffer does not seem to distinguish the two German adjectives for 'historical'—*historisch* and *geschichtlich*—as precisely as some other German theologians, e.g. Bultmann. Sometimes . . . he even uses them interchangeably." (P. 40.) When Bonhoeffer does distinguish the two words, his meaning is usually clear from the context, as in the above passage.

39. CC, p. 71.

40. CC, p. 72. A "religion of Jesus, in which only the Father plays a role," is a popular, although not wholly accurate description of Harnack's own reconstruction of the "historical Jesus"; see the latter's *What Is Christianity?* trans. by Thomas Bailey Saunders (New York: Harper & Row, 1947), esp. pp. 142-46. This classic of Christian liberalism is a far more profound and subtle treatment of the Gospels and Christianity than the caricatures of liberalism based upon it would suggest.

41. CC, p. 73.

42. CC, p. 74.

43. CC, pp. 74-75.

44. CC, p. 75.

45. CC, p. 64.

46. CC, p. 108.

47. LPP, p. 196.

48. CC, p. 108.

49. While Bonhoeffer always remained closer to Barth as to basic theological method, he was in the actual working out of that method closer in some ways to Brunner, as for example in this issue of an "evangelical" willingness to recognize what he (Bonhoeffer) was later to call "degrees of knowledge and degrees of significance" in the biblical witness to Christ. Bonhoeffer also shared with Brunner a more modest biblicism which, unlike Barth's voluminous meditations on Scripture, felt no compulsion to speculate at length on the mysteries enshrined in the biblical testimonies. There is virtually nothing in Bonhoeffer's writings, e.g., on the doctrine of the Trinity, the origin of evil, the Virgin Birth, and other matters on which Barth has expounded at great length; and in Brunner's writings these matters are always dealt with critically and with a clear reminder of priorities. Bonhoeffer and Brunner alike were more concerned simply with historical biblical realities and with ethical problems. On the theological use of Scripture by Bonhoeffer, Brunner, and Barth with regard to the doctrine of the Virgin Birth of Christ, see Chapter Eight.

50. See LPP, pp. 209-10.

51. LPP, pp. 154-55.

52. LPP, p. 155. Italics mine.

53. LPP, p. 188.

54. In fairness to Kant, it must be recognized, of course, that while on the one hand his thought tended to relegate God "to a realm beyond the world of experience," and thus to allow the thinker to ignore him altogether; on the other hand, precisely by understanding God as a fundamentally *ethical* reality, inseparable from the moral demand, it was Kant who helped to open up the "non-metaphysical," personal-social concept of transcendence which is so characteristic of modern theology, and not least, as we have seen in Chapter Two, of Bonhoeffer's thought. Here as in other areas Kant has been the father of polarities in modern thought. The writings of the eminent Scottish theologian John Baillie should be consulted for an appreciation of Kant's positive contribution to twentieth-century theology, and in particular of his link with ethical-personal approaches to transcendence. See esp. Baillie, *The Interpretation*

of Religion (Apex Books; Nashville: Abingdon Press [1928]), *Our Knowledge of God*, and *The Sense of the Presence of God*.

55. LPP, p. 175.
56. E, p. 192.
57. E, p. 65.
58. LPP, p. 209.
59. LPP, p. 210. See Hanfried Müller, "The Problem of the Reception and Interpretation of Dietrich Bonhoeffer" (in Smith, ed., *World Come of Age*, pp. 182-214), where Müller speaks of the God "who does not hold himself aloof but who himself becomes . . . a man in our secular existence, so that we in our world and our secularity may be with him." (P. 212.)
60. LPP, p. 196.
61. LPP, p. 197. Prenter, in "Bonhoeffer and the Young Luther" (in Smith, ed., *World Come of Age*, pp. 161-81), expresses Bonhoeffer's position eloquently when he writes: "The true God . . . has indeed become flesh: he hangs on the cross, the tree of life, which stands in the centre of the world, and he does not turn up, like the god of the stop-gaps, only in the so-called boundary situations." (P. 169.)
62. E, pp. 180-81.
63. LPP, p. 207.
64. LPP, p. 175.
65. LPP, p. 210. See Bethge, "Bonhoeffer's Christology and His 'Religionless Christianity'" (in Vorkink, ed., *Bonhoeffer in a World Come of Age*), p. 63: "It is not in a 'metaphysical' realm but in the person of Christ that man is faced with real and afflicting transcendence."

Chapter Seven: The Dialectical Reality of the Church

1. Barth, *Church Dogmatics*, I/1, 299.
2. CS, pp. 36-37.
3. AB, p. 126. This passage is awkward in English, because the German expression *es gibt* is usually translated "there is," and thereby fails to make sense in the philosophical context of the quotation above. *Es gibt* here conveys the sense of "givenness," the idea of an entity, a metaphysical object. Bonhoeffer is saying that "there is no God who is an (ontological) object given to our cognition." God is instead a person, known only through persons. See also Bonhoeffer's early article, "Concerning the Christian Idea of God," in *The Journal of Religion*, XII (April 1932), p. 180: The reality of God, he says, "which is said to be transcendent to all thinking, is now to be defined more exactly as 'personality.' The transcendence of God does not mean anything else than that God is personality, provided there is an adequate understanding of the concept of personality."
4. Franklin Sherman in Marty, ed., *The Place of Bonhoeffer*, p. 92.
5. LPP, p. 155.
6. CC, pp. 47-48. Italics mine.
7. The key phrase of CS; see pp. 85, 138, 146. It appears also in AB, p. 121; and in CC, p. 60. See also CC, p. 59: "Christ is the community by virtue of his being *pro me*." See also Bethge, "The Challenge . . . ," in *Chicago Theol. Sem. Register*, LI February 1961), p. 17: "Bonhoeffer always added to the two classical notions of the church in the Lutheran confessions—Word and Sacrament—a third, the fellowship of men." John Godsey, in his essay "Reading Bonhoeffer in English Translation" (Vorkink, ed., *Bonhoeffer in a World Come of Age*, pp. 114-31), writes of the key phrase *"Christus als Gemeinde existierend"*: "It is important to remember that he [Bonhoeffer] does not mean the church as institution, but as a communion of persons." (P. 123.)
8. AB, p. 123. Italics mine. See also CS, p. 89: "The reality of the church is a reality of revelation." Bonhoeffer makes the same point in CC, p. 60: "The community is

. . . not only the receiver of the Word of revelation [i.e., Jesus Christ]; it is itself revelation and Word of God. . . . The Word is *in* the community in so far as the community is a recipient of revelation. But the Word is also itself community in so far as the community is itself revelation and the Word wills to have the form of a created body." William Kuhns, *In Pursuit of Dietrich Bonhoeffer*, calls "the nature of the Church . . . Bonhoeffer's invariable theological theme." (P. 17.) Kuhns, like John Godsey in *The Theology of Dietrich Bonhoeffer*, is an interpreter who views Bonhoeffer's preoccupation with the Christian community as a fundamental clue to the whole of his thought.

9. CS, p. 145.
10. *The Theology of Dietrich Bonhoeffer*, p. 15. See also Phillips, *Christ for Us*, p. 67: "Bonhoeffer was disturbed by the characterization of the church in Barth's *Epistle to the Romans*, the latter's only major work until 1927, as an institution in which 'human indifference, misunderstanding and opposition attain their most sublime and their most naïve form.' Dialectical theology possessed strong individualistic tendencies. . . . What was necessary, to Bonhoeffer's mind, was an unequivocal affirmation of *both* sides of the dialectic; directing the sinner towards a community which was, however sinful, the chosen instrument of God's redeeming grace." Phillips calls attention to the *intensely concrete* character of Bonhoeffer's dialectical method in theology.
11. Bethge, "The Challenge . . . ," in *Chicago Theol. Sem. Register*, LI (February 1961), p. 10.
12. NRS, p. 150.
13. NRS, p. 147.
14. NRS, p. 148. See also LT, p. 111: "Our brother stands in Christ's stead. . . . Christ became our Brother in order to help us. Through him our brother has become Christ for us."
15. NRS, p. 185.
16. CD, p. 216.
17. CD, p. 216. See also CC, p. 60: "The community is the body of Christ. Body here is not just a metaphor. The community *is* the body of Christ, it does not *represent* the body of Christ."
18. CD, p. 216. See again CC, pp. 59-60: Christ's "form, indeed his only form, is the community between the ascension and the second coming."
19. CC, p. 60.
20. CD, p. 217. See also CC, p. 61: "Christ is not only the head of the community but also the community itself. (Cf. I Cor. 12 and the Epistle to the Ephesians.) Christ is head and every member."
21. See LT, p. 24: "When God's Son took on flesh, he truly and bodily took on, out of pure grace, our being, our nature, ourselves. . . . Now we are in him. Where he is, there we are too, in the incarnation, on the Cross, and in his resurrection. We belong to him because we are in him. That is why the Scriptures call us the Body of Christ."
22. I emphasize that this is the "old" or "classical" Roman Catholic teaching about the church. Vatican II and its aftermath have altered this outlook to some degree in the light of the renewal of Catholic biblical studies. See the Constitution on the Church in Walter Abbott, ed., *Documents of Vatican II* (New York: The America Press, 1966), pp. 9-96.
23. NRS, p. 153.
24. NRS, pp. 153-54. Note Bonhoeffer's "worldly" concept of the church in the statement, "The church is not a consecrated sanctuary, but the world, called by God to God."
25. NRS, p. 154. Notice here Bonhoeffer's rather negative recognition, in this essay of 1932, of the "religiousness" of the church as one side of its divine-human dialectic.
26. NRS, p. 155. See also CS, p. 197: "We believe in the church not as an unattainable ideal, or one which has still to be attained, but as a present reality."
27. NRS, p. 155.

28. CS, p. 197. Note the characteristic phrase "the presence of Christ in the world" to describe the church.
29. CD, p. 224.
30. A succinct discussion of the full-bloodedly dialectical character of the church appears in Bonhoeffer's "Zwei Diskussionsbeiträge zum Konfessionsproblem," GS I, 179-81. Here he maintains, against the "romantic" (liberal) conception of the church, that "the concept of the *Una Sancta* is conceivable only in . . . paradoxical form [*paradoxer Gestalt*]." (P. 180.)
31. NRS, p. 154.
32. NRS, p. 161.
33. See Barth, *Church Dogmatics*, I/2, 203-42.
34. Godsey, ed., *Preface to Bonhoeffer*, p. 45. Note the recurrent theme that the Thou of the neighbor is the bearer of the divine Thou: "God . . . wants us to honor him in our fellowman—and nowhere else."
35. *Ibid.*, p. 35.
36. *Ibid.*, pp. 36-37.
37. *Ibid.*, pp. 32-33.
38. See Reginald H. Fuller, "Liturgy and Devotion," in Marty, ed., *The Place of Bonhoeffer*, pp. 169-94, for a thorough treatment of Bonhoeffer's liturgical views and practices.
39. LPP, p. 153.
40. LPP, pp. 153-54. In contrast to Phillips' thesis that, while "Bonhoeffer has not swept the church aside" in the prison writings, he "has set ecclesiology to one side in order to clear his mind of pressing preliminary questions" (*Christ for Us*, p. 25), William Kuhns argues that references from the writings of the war years "suggest that the force behind Bonhoeffer's most creative thinking was precisely this: the changing shape of the Church in the coming age." (*In Pursuit of Dietrich Bonhoeffer*, p. 139.)
41. LPP, p. 209.
42. LPP, p. 179.
43. See also Bonhoeffer's essay "Optimism," in which he observes that "some Christians think it impious for anyone to hope and prepare for a better earthly future. They think that the meaning of present events is chaos, disorder, and catastrophe; and in resignation or pious escapism they surrender all responsibility for reconstruction and for future generations." (LPP, p. 39.)
44. LPP, p. 209.
45. LPP, p. 180. See Althaus, *Communio Sanctorum: Die Gemeinde im lutherischen Kirchengedanken* (Munich: Kaiser Verlag, 1929). It is interesting to note that Althaus published his study of the church after the submission for the degree but before the publication of Bonhoeffer's thesis *Sanctorum Communio*. The difference in the arrangement of the Latin expression for "communion of saints" arose from a conclusion of Bonhoeffer's made on the basis of historical usage; see CS, p. 220, n. 1.
46. LPP, p. 210.
47. Bonhoeffer's reconstructive remarks on the church in the prison writings, which we shall examine throughout the rest of this chapter, suggest a view of the church similar in some respects to that of Emil Brunner in his *The Misunderstanding of the Church*, trans. by H. Knight (Philadelphia: Westminster Press, 1953).
48. LPP, p. 181.
49. LPP, p. 209.
50. LPP, p. 181.
51. LPP, p. 208.
52. LPP, p. 172.
53. "Religion and the National Church," in A. R. Vidler, ed., *Soundings: Essays concerning Christian Understanding* (New York: Cambridge, University Press 1962), p. 253.
54. See, e.g., E. H. Robertson, *Christians against Hitler* (London: SCM Press, 1962);

Stewart Herman, *The Rebirth of the German Church* (London: SCM Press, 1946); and Franklin H. Littell, *The German Phoenix* (Garden City, N.Y.: Doubleday & Co., 1960).

55. LPP, p. 155.
56. LPP, p. 211.
57. See CS, pp. 151-52, 187-90; and NRS, pp. 230-34, 282-84. For Bonhoeffer, the church was always *essentially* the gathered congregation; but prior to and during the church struggle of the 1930's he also sought to affirm the value of a national church both theologically and pragmatically.

The use of the adverb "radically" before "free church" above is quite deliberate. The tenor of Bonhoeffer's proposals suggests a more radical break with dependence upon the "grace and favor" of secular culture than our highly touted "free church" situation in the United States represents. For a provocative, Bonhoeffer-informed analysis of the subtle forms of "religious establishment" in America, see Peter Berger, *The Noise of Solemn Assemblies* (Garden City, N.Y.: Doubleday & Co., 1961).

58. See in Chapter Nine the discussion of "The Religionless Christian," esp. pp. 271-72.
59. Some of Paul's teaching on human example, including its origin in the example of Christ, the apostle's commending of his own example, and love of the neighbor as the whole of the law, is contained in the following passages: Rom. 13:8-10; 15:1-3; II Cor. 4:10-11; 8:9; Gal. 5:14; Eph. 5:2; Phil. 2:5-9; 3:17; Col. 1:24; II Thess, 3:7-9. See also Paul Lehmann, "Faith and Worldliness in Bonhoeffer's Thought" (in Vorkink, ed., *Bonhoeffer in a World Come of Age*, pp. 25-45): "The difference which being a Christian makes is simply faithfulness to the life of God in the world as this life takes shape in Jesus Christ and in human life." (P. 29.)
60. Bonhoeffer goes on to tell Bethge, "I hope to take up later this subject of 'example' and its place in the New Testament." Either he was prevented from doing so, or his exposition appeared in letters which were lost or destroyed. The theme of concrete obedience, of the unity of word and action, was by no means a new one in Bonhoeffer's thought, as we can see from his ecumenical writings and above all in *The Cost of Discipleship*. The idea is simply expanded and radicalized in the prison writings.
61. GS I, 42; trans. by Bethge in "The Challenge of Dietrich Bonhoeffer's Life and Theology." For accounts of the structure and life of the community and seminary at Finkenwalde, consisting of correspondence and reports by Bonhoeffer, see WF, pp. 29-71.
62. LPP, p. 140.
63. See GS II, 373-427.
64. GS II, esp. pp. 394-95, 403-6.
65. E, pp. 101-41.
66. E, pp. 116-21, 122, 128, 130-31. On the other hand, Bonhoeffer disagreed with Catholicism quite explicitly on issues such as the nature of marriage (pp. 129-30), contraception (pp. 131-35), and sterilization (pp. 135-37).
67. For an assessment of Bonhoeffer's relation to Roman Catholicism by a Roman Catholic, see William Kuhns, *In Pursuit of Dietrich Bonhoeffer*, esp. Chapter 16, "A Catholic Looks at Bonhoeffer," but also scattered references throughout the book.
68. LPP, p. 210.
69. LPP, p. 157.
70. One of the most unusual and arresting interpretations of Bonhoeffer's "Christianity without religion" project is that of Martin Thornton in *The Rock and the River: An Encounter Between Traditional Spirituality and Modern Thought* (London: Hodder & Stoughton, 1965). Thornton, an Anglican priest and authority on ascetical and pastoral theology, is concerned to try to spell out, in terms of the Catholic tradition, the practical implications of Bonhoeffer's thoughts on the church for everyday Christian discipline of life.

Thornton distinguishes the "mature" or "religionless" Christian from the "immature" or "beginning" Christian, the church in a world "come of age" from the infant church of ancient and medieval civilization, by means of the ascetical distinction between "habitual recollection" and "actual recollection." (It should be added parenthetically that Thornton regards the classical meaning of "ascetical," i.e., simply "disciplined" or "regulated," to be fully consistent with Bonhoeffer's portrait of mature Christianity, and rejects Bonhoeffer's own negative characterization of asceticism as an attack only on false or perverted asceticism.)

Actual recollection is the immature, affective, "psychological" apprehension of God, "the equivalent to Bonhoeffer's 'religion,' it is 'looking for God in the gaps,' pietism" (p. 70). The faith of the new or immature Christian and the presecular church tends to depend on self-conscious "religious experiences," i.e., emotional states, miracles, mystery, drama, etc. In habitual recollection, on the other hand, "faith settles down to a recollected and stable routine. . . . The affective excitements and shallow desolations of spiritual adolescence give way to a deeper love of God expressed in obedience more than emotion. . . . Corporate worship leads into a continuity of Christian living, and becomes integrated into the whole life, without reference to 'edification' and 'uplift.' In all the ordinary aspects of Christian living . . . the 'actual' gives way to, and fuses into, the 'habitual.' " (Pp. 60-61.) "Habitual recollection," Thornton concludes, ". . . explains the only way in which a Christian can be both fully committed to Jesus Christ, fully dedicated to God, and at the same time wholeheartedly immersed in the secular affairs and problems of the world, and its whole basis is the *regula* of orthodoxy." (P. 68.)

The Rock and the River is not a careful study of Bonhoeffer. Thornton makes some egregious errors in interpreting "religionless Christianity." Nevertheless, his work points the way forward to the importance of doing more serious work along this line, and his own analogy of "habitual" and "actual recollection" contains very useful insights. For Thornton, an Anglican, the frameword and foundation of the "religionless" Christian's *regula* for "habitual recollection" is the Eucharist and the daily Offices. Other traditions (as *Life Together* itself shows) would have varying patterns of "secret discipline." Yet the reality is the same, a reality which is an essential and formative element in the dialectical existence of the Christian and the church as conceived by Bonhoeffer.

71. LPP, p. 34.
72. LPP, p. 37.
73. LPP, p. 213. Note the phrase "he preserves his Church." See also p. 212: " . . . God still reigns in heaven."
74. LPP, p. 100.
75. LPP, p. 122.
76. LPP, p. 196.
77. LPP, p. 148.
78. LPP, p. 144.
79. LPP, p. 192.
80. LPP, p. 200.
81. LPP, p. 162.
82. LPP, p. 32.
83. LPP, p. 76.
84. LPP, p. 196. See Ronald Gregor Smith, *Secular Christianity* (New York: Harper & Row, 1966), pp. 190-91: "Everything that Bonhoeffer says brings us clearly before the message concerning Jesus; but equally, it brings us before the possibility of a relation to God."
85. LPP, p. 37.
86. LPP, p. 112.
87. LPP, p. 54.
88. LPP, pp. 213-14.
89. LPP, pp. 55-56.
90. LT, p. 18.

91. LT, p. 19.
92. LPP, p. 55.
93. LT, p. 21.
94. LPP, p. 76.
95. LPP, p. 88.
96. LPP, pp. 142-43.
97. LPP, p. 163.
98. LPP, p. 201. The *Losungen* are the daily portions or "lots" from Scripture that the Moravians have published annually since 1731 under the title *Die täglichen Losungen und Lehrtexte der Brüdergemeinde.*
99. LPP, p. 152.
100. LPP, p. 46.
101. LPP, p. 43.
102. LPP, p. 41.
103. LPP, p. 87.
104. LPP, p. 201.
105. LPP, pp. 106-7.
106. LPP, p. 117.
107. LPP, p. 97.
108. LPP, p. 122.
109. LPP, p. 208. Italics mine.
110. LPP, p. 89.
111. LPP, p. 42. The recurrent theme is Bonhoeffer's *objectivity*, his orientation and grounding *extra se,* in the reality of Christ. See also Maria von Wedemeyer-Weller, "The Other Letters from Prison," in Vorkink, ed., *Bonhoeffer in a World Come of Age,* p. 109, where Bonhoeffer's fiancée recalls that in prison Bonhoeffer "lived by church holidays and by seasons, rather than by the calendar month."
112. Quoted in Bethge's Preface to LPP, p. 24.
113. Fabian von Schlabrendorff, *The Secret War against Hitler,* trans. by H. Simon (London: Hodder & Stoughton, 1966) , p. 323.
114. *Ibid.,* p. 324.
115. LPP, p. 232.
116. LPP, p. 24.
117. LPP, p. 89.
118. LPP, pp. 90-95.
119. LPP, p. 132.
120. LPP, pp. 154-55.
121. LPP, p. 206.
122. LPP, p. 115.
123. LPP, pp. 118-19.
124. LPP, p. 109.
125. LPP, p. 150.
126. LPP, p. 149.
127. LPP, p. 159.
128. LPP, p. 215.
129. LPP, pp. 213-14.

Chapter Eight: Biblical Hermeneutics

1. Barth, *Church Dogmatics,* I/2, 11.
2. Trans. by Kathleen Downham from the German *Versuchung,* rev. and ed. by E. Bethge ([München: Kaiser Verlag, 1953], New York: The Macmillan Co., 1955) .
3. In *Junge Kirche,* IV (1936) , no. 2, 64-69; no. 4, 157-61; no. 5, 197-203.
4. (Salzuflen: Verlag der Mädchen-Bibelkreise [MBK], 5th ed., 1956) .

5. See, e.g., CD and *Temptation*. I have discussed Bonhoeffer's understanding of the "historical Christ" in Chapter Six.

6. In NRS, pp. 308-25.

7. For Barth's exegetical position, see *Church Dogmatics*, I/1, 98-140; and I/2, 457-740. At the same time, as noted in a previous chapter, there are differences between Bonhoeffer and Barth in terms of the more consistently "evangelical" approach of the former to what he considered to be nonessential or peripheral biblical material. We shall examine this issue in the context of Bonhoeffer's exegesis of biblical christology in the second section of this chapter.

8. NRS, p. 308.

9. NRS, pp. 310-11. Bonhoeffer articulated this position even more vigorously in LT, pp. 53-54: "It is not that God is the spectator and sharer of our present life, howsoever important that is; but rather that we are the reverent listeners and participants in God's action in the sacred story, the history of the Christ on earth. And only in so far as we are *there*, is God with us today also.

"A complete reversal occurs. It is not in our life that God's help and presence must still be proved, but rather God's presence and help have been demonstrated for us in the life of Jesus Christ. *It is in fact more important for us to know what God did to Israel, to His Son Jesus Christ, than to seek what God intends for us today.*" (Italics mine.)

We find here again the fundamental *objectivity* of Bonhoeffer's theological outlook which he shared with Barth over against the existentialist approach of thinkers such as Bultmann and Tillich. While the Bonhoeffer of the prison writings would almost certainly not have used the kind of language he uses in "The Interpretation of the New Testament" and in LT, this highly objective approach to Scripture and theological reflection very definitely remains as the key to understanding the "non-religious interpretation of biblical concepts."

10. NRS, p. 314.

11. NRS, p. 315. See also LT, pp. 50-51: "Holy Scripture does not consist of individual passages; it is a unit and is intended to be used as such. As a whole the Scriptures are God's revealing Word."

12. LPP, p. 181.

13. LPP, p. 156

14. NRS, p. 317.

15. It is important to add that Bonhoeffer of course does not mean that Christ does not in fact meet human needs. His point is that, contrary to the biblical witness, the church by and large attempts to justify Christ before the present age by presenting him as the "answer" to all its conscious and unconscious problems and questions, thus making him a tool of "religion" against a secular world. Bonhoeffer regarded such tactics as false to the reality of both Christ and the modern world. Christ is the "answer," but not by being presented as such; he is the "answer" because he is the reality in which all men stand.

16. NRS, p. 318.

17. NRS, p. 311. In Bonhoeffer's christology, the "present Christ," the risen and reigning Lord, alone guarantees to us that he is none other than the "historical Christ" of the New Testament. The contemporary Christ *pro me* attests this through his Holy Spirit.

18. NRS, p. 322.

19. It is true that in the prison writings Bonhoeffer makes some important remarks about Bultmann's project, countering "demythologizing" with "dereligionizing" and arguing for "non-religious interpretation" over against Bultmann's "existentialist interpretation." Bonhoeffer's remarks are provocative and important; but they bear only the most general character, and their extremely paradoxical and enigmatic form cries out for detailed exposition which Bonhoeffer was prevented from carrying out. His favorable words about Bultmann's programmatic essay in a letter of 1942 (see

Chapter Five, n. 27) are possessed of an even greater vagueness as to just what his "approval" consists in.

20. CC, p. 75.

21. CC, p. 76.

22. Bonhoeffer regarded the conclusions of the "eschatological," the "history of religions," and the form-critical schools of New Testament interpretation as historical-critical supports for a dogmatic christology (see Chapter Six).

23. CC, p. 109.

24. On the Virgin Birth, see Barth, Church Dogmatics, I/2, 172-202; the Trinity, ibid., I/1, 339-560; election, ibid., II/2, 3-506 and evil, ibid., III/3, 289-368.

25. Emil Brunner, The Mediator, trans. by Olive Wyon (Philadelphia: Westminster Press, 1965), p. 324.

26. Ibid., p. 325.

27. Ibid., p. 326. See also Brunner's The Christian Doctrine of Creation and Redemption, trans. by Olive Wyon (Philadelphia: Westminster Press, 1952), pp. 352-56.

28. Brunner, Truth as Encounter, trans. of new part and rev. of first English ed. by David Cairns (Philadelphia: Westminster Press, 1964), p. 42.

29. Ibid., pp. 42-43.

30. Ibid., p. 43.

31. Ibid., p. 44.

32. Ibid., pp. 44-45.

33. Barth, Church Dogmatics, I/1, 239. The inner quotation is from a critical statement of Wobbermin's, made in 1929.

34. Ibid., I/1, 261.

35. Ibid., I/1, 255.

36. Ibid., I/1, 192.

37. Ibid., I/2, 176.

38. Ibid., I/2, 179. On this point I would maintain that the historical evidence for the empty tomb is less problematic than that for the virgin birth. This is appropriate, since the New Testament is centered overwhelmingly on Jesus' resurrection and not on his birth. I agree with Barth that without affirming the fact of the empty tomb we run the risk of diluting or even evaporating the fullness of all that the resurrection is supposed to mean to Christian faith. Unlike him, however, I am compelled by historical evidence rather than by theological deduction. The centrality of Christ's resurrection overshadows everything else in the New Testament; the historical evidence for its "sign," the empty tomb, seems to me reasonably good. This puts it on an entirely different level from the virgin birth and the narratives in which it is related; and only a purely theological and deductive need for logic and balance will insist on considering this doctrine and its historical evidence as on a level with the Easter proclamation. It is just this theological compulsion in the direction of thoroughness and tidiness—which can be exquisitely beautiful, by the way—which is the constant danger of Catholicism and Protestant scholasticism.

39. Ibid., I/2, 181. We may rightly raise the question whether Barth's advice to the preacher who cannot affirm a certain church dogma to "keep silence about it" is not an invitation to dishonesty which Bonhoeffer, with his passion for personal integrity and intellectual honesty, would have rejected.

40. Not that church tradition was not very important to both Bonhoeffer and Brunner; but for neither was it allowed to dominate the theological exegesis of Scripture into artificial positions the way it tended to do for Barth.

41. LPP, p. 190.

42. LPP, p. 195.

43. See LPP, p. 46: "I read the Psalms every day, as I have done for years; I know them and love them more than any other book."

44. LPP, p. 46.

45. Bonhoeffer probably had a special familiarity with and fondness for St. Matthew's

Gospel, because of his constant preoccupation, during the 1930's, with the Sermon on the Mount. *The Cost of Discipleship* is largely an exposition of Matt. 5-7 and 9-10.

46. LPP, pp. 103-4.

47. Cf. below, Chapter Nine.

48. LPP, pp. 185-86. Bonhoeffer's characterization of death in the original German text is "boundary" (*Todesgrenze*); "religion" is preoccupied with life's "boundary" situations, in particular death.

49. For a good study of the basic differences between the Old Testament and the "redemption religions," see A. Th. van Leeuwen, *Christianity in World History* (New York: Charles Scribner's Sons, 1966), pp. 46-104. Esp. pertinent is the following passage: "The Lord sent man forth from the garden of Eden ([Gen.] 3:23): away from the mythical bliss which, out of his fear of death, man has projected beyond death's frontier. It is from a mythical 'eternity,' from a timeless bliss, that man is driven out. In his inexorable mercy God compels man to enter upon the road of history. To the true eternal life which God gives there is no way back, but only a way ahead." (P. 72.) This absorption in historical existence was the "way ahead" to the secularity of the modern world.

50. LPP, pp. 185-86.

51. LPP, p. 186.

52. LPP, p. 156.

53. LPP, p. 156. Italics mine, except for the word *for*.

54. See, e.g., Rom. 8:19-21: "For the creation waits with eager longing for the revealing of the sons of God; for the creation was subjected to futility, not of its own will but by the will of him who subjected it in hope; because the creation itself will be set free from its bondage to decay and obtain the glorious liberty of the children of God."

55. See Th. C. Vriezen, *An Outline of Old Testament Theology* (Oxford: Blackwell, 1958), pp. 201-4; and Edmond Jacob, *Old Testament Theology* (New York: Harper & Row, 1958), pp. 157-72. Both are concise descriptions of Old Testament anthropology. For a discussion specifically of the issue of resurrection versus immortality in the New Testament, see Oscar Cullmann, *Immortality of the Soul or Resurrection of the Dead?* (London: Epworth Press, 1948).

56. LPP, p. 97.

57. LPP, p. 103.

58. LPP, p. 153.

59. LPP, p. 154.

60. Godsey, ed., *Preface to Bonhoeffer*, p. 60.

61. On the Old Testament use of the name of God, see Vriezen, *An Outline of Old Testament Theology*, pp. 194-98; and Jacob, *Old Testament Theology*, pp. 48-55. Bound up with the importance of God's name in the Old Testament, of course, was the ancient notion that a name was a bearer of reality and power; so that the speaking of a name could have forceful consequences for good or for evil. Bonhoeffer (along with Barth) retains this idea when he says that in God's name we possess "God himself in his whole essence, in his revelation."

62. Godsey, ed., *Preface to Bonhoeffer*, p. 61.

63. *Ibid.*, p. 62.

64. *Ibid.*, p. 63. Italics mine.

65. See Edgar Jones, *Proverbs and Ecclesiastes: Introduction and Commentary* (Torch Bible Commentaries; London: SCM Press, 1961): "The maxims and insights of the Wisdom teachers . . . represent the accumulated experience of the ordinary man rather than the profounder insights of the spiritual genius." (P. 45.)

66. See Jones, *Proverbs and Ecclesiastes*: For Ecclesiastes "there is a relative happiness to be found in part of human experience if not in the whole. There is a relative good, fragmentary but real, not illusory. It may be found in the enjoyment of food and drink, human companionship and one's labour. These are to be enjoyed as

gifts from God ([chap. 2,] vss. 24-25)." (P. 269.) "Qoheleth is life-affirming rather than life-denying. Life has to be lived; there are jobs to be done and happiness to be found, although the ultimate questions remain unanswered. His 'Carpe diem' . . . philosophy is not mere pleasure-seeking, but a resolute acceptance of a life that he does not understand. He says 'Yes' to life." (P. 277.)

67. LPP, p. 111.
68. LPP, p. 202.
69. See Jones, *Proverbs and Ecclesiastes:* "Proverbs is an example primarily of the practical strand found in the meaning of Wisdom. The book seeks to perform the urgent task of laying the foundation for living the good life and is directed towards young people." (P. 31.) "The humanism and individualism of this book is born of a growing sense of the reality and presence of God to ordinary men and women." (P. 45.) "Proverbs brings the passion and vision of the prophets to the humdrum and immediate concerns of everyday life." (P. 47.) "The virtues praised include self-control, especially in the exercise of restraint in speech (16:32; 19:11; 21:23); and parallel to this is the prominence given to truthfulness, particularly in bearing honest witness in the court of law (12:22; 14:25; 19:28). Humility is exalted with the deprecation of any overweening pride (11:2; 16:5, 18; 21:4). Industry and hard work are strongly urged (10:5, 26; 19:24; 20:4, 13; 22:13), as is honesty in commerical transactions (11:1; 16:11; 20:10). Humanity and compassion stem from religious faith (14:31; 19:17; 21:13)." (Pp. 48-49.)
70. LPP, p. 131.
71. LPP, p. 175.
72. See Samuel Terrien, "The Book of Job: Introduction and Exegesis," *The Interpreter's Bible*, III (Nashville: Abingdon Press, 1954), 877-1198. According to Terrien, the intention of the author of Job "is to show the divinity of God, the humanity of man, and the specific nature of the relation between a God who is truly God and a man who is truly man—namely, one of grace alone apprehended by faith." (P. 898.)
73. LPP, p. 162.
74. LPP, p. 176. For a survey of the various traditional and modern interpretations of the Song of Songs, see Theophile J. Meek, "The Song of Songs: Introduction and Exegesis," *The Interpreter's Bible*, V (Nashville: Abingdon, 1956), 92-96.
75. Three books which explore the prophets in these terms are E. W. Heaton, *The Old Testament Prophets* (London: Penguin Books, 1961), esp. pp. 55-163; C. F. Whitley, *The Prophetic Achievement* (London: Mowbray, 1963), esp. pp. 45-92, 129-51; and R. B. Y. Scott, *The Relevance of the Prophets* (New York: The Macmillan Co. 1968), esp. pp. 114-238.
76. See LPP, p. 199. We shall examine Bonhoeffer's use of the concept of *metanoia* in Chapter Nine.
77. LPP, p. 154.
78. LPP, p. 157.
79. LPP, p. 186.
80. LPP, p. 196.

Chapter Nine: The Development of a Christological Ethics Under the Third Reich

1. See LPP, p. 107: "I sometimes feel as if my life were more or less over, and as if all I had to do now were to finish my *Ethics*." See also Godsey, *The Theology of Dietrich Bonhoeffer*, p. 196. The supremacy of the ethical in Bonhoeffer's thought is apparent from the beginning to the end of his writings. See e.g., CS, pp. 29-34, 164-65; "What is a Christian Ethic?" in NRS, pp. 39-48; and CD.

In one of the prison letters Bonhoeffer writes to Bethge: "I have reproached myself for not having finished my *Ethics* . . . , and it was some consolation to me that I had told you the essentials, that even if you had forgotten it, it would probably emerge again indirectly somehow. Besides, my ideas were still incomplete." (LPP, p. 88.) Bethge, of course, is responsible for having pieced together and published what Bonhoeffer had written of his *Ethics*.

2. See E, pp. 31-33, 62-67.

3. In the prison writings Bonhoeffer was to launch his biting attack on "inwardness," the separation of inner and outer man, soul and body, as one of the defining characteristics of "religion," which he rejected in the name of the holistic anthropology of Scripture.

4. See Emil Brunner, *The Divine Imperative*, trans. by Olive Wyon (Philadelphia: Westminster Press, 1947). Specifically relevant to our discussion is Chapter XXI: "The Natural Orders and the Kingdom of God," pp. 208-19.

5. See, e.g., Brunner's ethical proposition which opens chap. XXI of *The Divine Imperative:* "As Creator, God requires us to recognize and adjust ourselves to the orders He has created, as our first duty; as Redeemer, as our second duty, He bids us ignore the existing orders, and inaugurate a new line of action in view of the coming Kingdom of God." (P. 208.) A fair and objective reading of *The Divine Imperative* makes it clear that Brunner subsumes the "natural orders" under the redemption in Christ, and allows for protest against an evil state in the name of the kingdom of God. His conservative language, however, and above all his seeming separation of creation and redemption, were the sort of opening wedge on which the "German Christians" capitalized ideologically.

6. NRS, p. 165.

7. NRS, p. 166.

8. NRS, pp. 166-67. Italicizing of the last sentence is mine.

9. NRS, p. 167.

10. Printed in Robertson, *Christians against Hitler*, p. 50.

11. The Sermon on the Mount was Bonhoeffer's fundamental ethical preoccupation during the 1930's, as he turned from penultimate to purely ultimate considerations. In addition to CD, which is primarily a detailed theological exegesis of the Sermon on the Mount, see, e.g., letters to Sutz of April 28 and September 11, 1934, in GS I, 40–43. Bonhoeffer was always profoundly dissatisfied with the usual ways in which the church and Christian ethics manage to sidestep or explain away the Sermon on the Mount. He did not believe that one could be entirely serious about Christian ethics until one had come squarely to grips with the hard, concrete demands of Matt. 5–7.

12. CD, pp. 192-93.

13. Bethge, "The Challenge . . . ," *Chicago Theol. Sem. Register*, LI (February 1961), pp. 17-19.

14. See Robertson, *Christians Against Hitler*, for an account of the witness of the Confessing Church during the 1930's.

15. For a detailed study of the history and theology of the Barmen Declaration, see Arthur C. Cochrane, *The Church's Confession Under Hitler* (Philadelphia: Westminster Press, 1962).

16. The statement appeared in an essay entitled "Zur Frage nach der Kirchengemeinschaft," which was published in the journal *Evangelische Theologie*, III (1936), 214-33; reprinted in GS II, 217-41; trans. and reprinted in WF, pp. 75-96.

17. See E, pp. 191-92.

18. E, pp. 84-91 and the entire 4th chap., "The Last Things and the Things Before the Last." It is significant that in a letter to Bethge of November 27, 1940, from Ettal, where Bonhoeffer was working on his *Ethics*, he mentions "a possible title for my book: 'Preparing the Way and Entering' ["*Wegbereitung und Einzug*"]." (GS II, 384.) He states explicitly that this title expresses "the bifurcation of the book (the before-the-last and the last things)." It seems fairly clear that he intended the whole book to revolve about the two poles of ultimate and penultimate.

19. E, p. 8.
20. E, p. 91.
21. E, p. 84.
22. E, p. 92.
23. E, p. 93.
24. E, p. 93.
25. E, p. 94.
26. See, e.g., Barth's famous debate with Brunner over man's capacity for revelation in *Natural Theology*, trans. by Peter Fraenkel (London, 1946); also *Church Dogmatics* I/1, 213-83.
27. See, e.g., his *Truth as Encounter*, pp. 86-110.
28. E, p. 95. Note the consistent theme of Bonhoeffer's personalism, that God and the neighbor are inextricably bound up together.
29. Quoted in Heinz Zahrnt, "Der Gefangene von Tegel," *Sonntagsblatt*, April 10, 1955, no. 15, p. 1.
30. In his Resistance work Bonhoeffer was able concretely to save a few Jews from extermination. He was employed by the *Abwehr* (Military Counter-Intelligence), which served as a front for Resistance activities. An interesting incident concerning Bonhoeffer's role in helping seven Jews is recounted by fellow conspirator Fabian von Schlabrendorff, *The Secret War Against Hitler*, pp. 168-72.
31. E, p. 96.
32. E, p. 102.
33. E, p. 103.
34. E, pp. 102-3.
35. E, pp. 101-41, 326-34.
36. LPP, pp. 103-4. Italics mine.
37. LPP, p. 154.
38. LPP, p. 201.
39. Ebeling, *Word and Faith*, p. 102.
40. See Barth, *Church Dogmatics*, III/4, 4, 21-22, 404, 406; IV/2, 505, 533-34, 540-42, 553, 599, 641.
41. *Church Dogmatics*, IV/2, 533-34.
42. See the contrast of Barth's ethics with Bonhoeffer's as developed by George W. Forell, "Realized Faith, the Ethics of Dietrich Bonhoeffer," in Marty, ed., *The Place of Bonhoeffer*, pp. 204-8. The following is Forell's conclusion: "In Bonhoeffer's terms Barth's Christocratic ethics operates too hastily with the ultimate in order to make it supply the criteria for ethical action." (P. 208.)
43. LPP, p. 153.
44. Godsey, ed., *Preface to Bonhoeffer*, p. 21.
45. E, p. 25.
46. E, p. 18.
47. E, pp. 18-19. Italics mine.
48. E, pp. 19-20. There are interesting parallels between some of Bonhoeffer's remarks about the "religionless" Christian and Kierkegaard's portrait of the "knight of faith" in *Fear and Trembling* (Garden City, N.Y.: Doubleday & Co., 1954), pp. 49-51.
49. E, pp. 20-21.
50. E, p. 21.
51. LPP, p. 201.
52. LPP, pp. 201-2. Italics mine.
53. LPP, p. 198.
54. LPP, p. 205.
55. LPP, p. 189.
56. LPP, p. 205.

57. The point is that the revelation of God's will in creation and redemption is the prior and fundamental reality, and both blessing and suffering are subjective conditions which are contingent upon this objective ordering of the world.
58. LPP, pp. 205-6.
59. LPP, p. 199.
60. LPP, pp. 199-200.
61. LPP, p. 202.
62. Bonhoeffer's discussion makes it clear that along with Barth and the other "neo-orthodox" theologians he distinguished "faith" from "religion." Scripture speaks everywhere of faith, but almost never of religion. Faith describes man's authentic response to God's self-disclosure in Christ, a response characterized by wholeness; religion, by contrast, describes various psychological attitudes and characteristic practices which are marked by being partial, apart from the rest of life.

Where Bonhoeffer moves beyond Barth's epistemological preoccupation in the understanding of faith is in describing it in terms of a whole style of life rooted not in subjectivity but in the objective reality of Christ. This is a persistent theme, appearing in CD under the rubric of "concrete obedience," in E as "conformation," and in LPP as "*metanoia*."
63. LPP, p. 206.
64. LPP, p. 196.
65. LPP, pp. 210-11.
66. LPP, pp. 162-63.
67. Italics mine.
68. LPP, pp. 173-74.
69. LPP, p. 121.
70. LPP, pp. 123-24.
71. LPP, p. 141.
72. LPP, p. 202.
73. LPP, p. 119.
74. GS II, 375-76.
75. LPP, pp. 157-58.
76. LPP, p. 192.
77. LPP, pp. 214-15.
78. LPP, p. 127.
79. LPP, p. 212.
80. LPP, p. 29.
81. LPP, p. 37. See also the following: "It is infinitely easier to suffer in obedience to a human command than in the freedom of one's own responsibility. . . . Christ suffered as a free man. . . ." (P. 37.)
82. LPP, p. 120. Bonhoeffer developed the concept of the "four divine mandates" of marriage, labor, state, and church in the *Ethics* (pp. 73-78, 252-67).
83. LPP, pp. 133-34.
84. LPP, pp. 89-90.
85. LPP, p. 119.
86. LPP, p. 203.
87. LPP, p. 109.
88. LPP, p. 140.
89. LPP, p. 206.
90. LPP, p. 37.
91. LPP, p. 203.
92. LPP, pp. 39-40.
93. LPP, p. 203.
94. Quoted by Bethge in the Editor's Preface to LPP, p. 24.
95. LPP, p. 111.

Chapter Ten: Paths in Bonhoeffer Interpretation

1. John Phillips, *Christ for Us*, p. 28.
2. *Ibid.*, p. 74.
3. *Ibid.*, pp. 74-75.
4. *Ibid.*, pp. 24-25.
5. Godsey, *The Theology of Dietrich Bonhoeffer*, p. 264.
6. *Ibid.*, p. 266.
7. Bethge in Vorkink, ed., *Bonhoeffer in a World Come of Age*, p. 46.
8. *Ibid.*, pp. 46-47.
9. *Ibid.*, p. 47.
10. *Ibid.*, pp. 64-65.
11. Hanfried Müller, *Von der Kirche zur Welt*, p. 400.
12. Müller, "The Problem of the Reception and Interpretation of Dietrich Bonhoeffer," in Smith, ed., *World Come of Age*, p. 183.
13. Prenter, "Bonhoeffer and the Young Luther," in Smith, ed., *World Come of Age*, p. 175.
14. In Smith, ed., *World Come of Age*, p. 100.
15. *Ibid.*, p. 101.
16. *Die Mündige Welt* I, 19; quoted in Godsey, *The Theology of Dietrich Bonhoeffer*, p. 263.
17. Godsey, *The Theology of Dietrich Bonhoeffer*, p. 263.
18. Thomas F. Torrance, in *The Scotsman*, May 28, 1966, p. 3.
19. Bethge, Letter to *The Scotsman*, June 10, 1966. See also Torrance's reply to Bethge, *ibid.*, June 17, 1966. Prof. Torrance kindly replied to my own criticisms of the review with a long letter to me, which, however, indicated to me all the more clearly his misunderstanding of certain fundamental areas in Bonhoeffer's theological development and his accompanying insistence on "domesticating" Bonhoeffer in terms of Barth.
20. Actually, the correspondence and other writings which make up *Letters and Papers from Prison* were written while Bonhoeffer was in Tegel Prison. He was not removed to Buchenwald until early in 1945, by which time he was forbidden all contact with the outside world.
21. *The Secularisation of Christianity* (London: Darton, Longman & Todd, 1965), p. 41. Mascall, who is a very able defender of Catholic orthodoxy from an Anglican perspective, nevertheless goes on in commenting on the remarks centering in Bonhoeffer's statement, "Before God and with him we live without God," to set forth one of the most remarkably mistaken interpretations of Bonhoeffer's words which have come to my attention. First he suggests that Bonhoeffer's talk about "living without God" is perhaps Bonhoeffer's "spiritual experience of feeling forsaken by God" (p. 41). Bonhoeffer did not feel God-forsaken even in prison; in any case, the context shows clearly that he was speaking theologically and not confessionally. Of Bonhoeffer's assertion that "the God who makes us live in this world without using him as a working hypothesis is the God before whom we are ever standing," Mascall says that it "certainly seems to imply that we must plan our whole lives without any reference to God" (p. 42). Obviously Mascall thinks that by rejecting God as "a working hypothesis" Bonhoeffer means to reject any usable understanding of God at all. Yet the point of all Bonhoeffer's remarks about "living without God," as we have seen, is that in a world which has grown out of false dependencies we must live without the support of the metaphysical "God" of religion, the *deus ex machina*, the "working hypothesis," *in order to* recognize and to live with the true God who comes to us in Jesus Christ. Clearly Mascall does not know what Bonhoeffer means by the phrase "God as a working hypothesis." His misreading is an excellent recent example of the sort of thing which still goes on in Bonhoeffer interpretation: the lifting of phrases and

sentences out of context without knowledge of the context, and presuming to say what they mean.

I agree with Mascall that it is unfair to Bonhoeffer to take his prison reflections as his definitive word on "religionless Christianity," but not because they were written under stress. Bonhoeffer's thoughts on the subject were formative and therefore tentative; above all, they were unfinished.

22. Van Buren's book *The Secular Meaning of the Gospel* is not precisely to be described as belonging to the explicit "death of God" theology of Hamilton and Altizer. For obvious reasons, however, he is usually considered together with them, and I have chosen to do so. I am also aware that van Buren has moved beyond his position in *The Secular Meaning of the Gospel* to an even more "emancipated" pragmatic-empirical outlook; but I am here concerned only with his position in that book.

23. *The Secular Meaning of the Gospel*, pp. 82-105, 121-23.

24. R. G. Smith has rightly analyzed the difference between van Buren and Bonhoeffer in terms of the dialectic of faith; see *Secular Christianity*, pp. 186-93.

25. See, e.g., "Thursday's Child: The Theologian Today and Tomorrow," *Theology Today*, XX (January 1694), 487-95.

26. *The Secular Meaning of the Gospel*, pp. 197 ff.

27. See, e.g., *Word and Faith*, esp. pp. 98-161, 282-87, 333-53.

28. See, e.g., *The New Man;* "A Theological Perspective of the Secular," *The Christian Scholar*, XLIII (March 1960), 11-24; and *Secular Christianity*.

29. To my knowledge, R. G. Smith mentions the influence of Barth on Bonhoeffer only once, and there with regard only to Bonhoeffer's critique of religion (an influence which Bonhoeffer himself explicitly acknowledged in *Letters and Papers*); see *Secular Christianity*, p. 177. Ebeling is considerably more careful at this point, but he fails to give Barth's influence proper weight in an overall assessment of Bonhoeffer; see *Word and Faith*, pp. 100, 106, 134-35.

30. *Secular Christianity*, p. 172.

31. Lesslie Newbigin, *Honest Religion for Secular Man* (Philadelphia: Westminster Press, 1966), p. 98.

32. Alan Richardson, *Religion in Contemporary Debate* (Philadelphia: Westminster Press, 1966), p. 52.

Index